D1527790

DAVID GLENN HUNT
MEMORIAL LIBRARY
GALVESTON COLLEGE

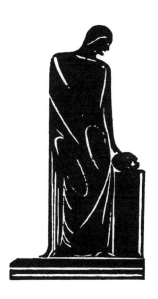

NEW ESSAYS ON *HAMLET*

The Hamlet Collection: No. 1

ISSN

General Editor: John Manning

Other titles in the series under preparation:

Hamlet in Japan, a collection of essays by Japanese scholars ed. Yoshi-ko Uéno;

Hamlet and Film, a monograph by John Worthen;

Critical Responses to Hamlet 1600-1900, ed. David Farley-Hills and Johanna Procter;

Hamlet and the Visual Arts, a volume of essays edited by Alan R. Young

THE HAMLET COLLECTION

NEW ESSAYS ON HAMLET

edited by

MARK THORNTON BURNETT
and
JOHN MANNING

AMS PRESS
New York

DAVID GLENN HUNT
MEMORIAL LIBRARY
GALVESTON COLLEGE

Library of Congress Cataloging-in-Publication Data

New essays on Hamlet/edited by Mark Thornton Burnett and John Manning.
   (The Hamlet Collection, no. 1)
    Includes bibliographical references (p.) and index.
    ISBN 0-404-62311-5
   1. Shakespeare, William, 1564-1616. Hamlet. I. Burnett, Mark Thornton.
   II. Manning, John III. Series.
PR2807.N47 1994
822.3'3—dc20

                                                         93-4052
                                                            CIP

All AMS books are printed on acid-free paper that meets the guidelines for performance and durability of the Committee on Production Guidelines for Book Longevity of the Council on Library Resources.

COPYRIGHT © 1994 BY AMS PRESS, INC.
All rights reserved

AMS PRESS
56 East 13th Street
New York, N.Y. 10003, U.S.A.

Contents

Renaissance Feminisms

Histories and Appropriations

Nation and Culture

Preface

For four hundred years *Hamlet* has continued to exercise a fascination for scholars, theatre-goers and readers, and to exercise an influence on the imagination of writers and artists. It is a seminal text of post-Medieval Europe. *The Hamlet Collection* aims to investigate this phenomenon in all its facets. It will include reprints of seminal studies and sources, as well as collections of new essays and commissioned monograph studies of the literary, textual, and interpretative problems that the play itself presents.

I wish to thank all those who have contributed to the success of the present volume, and for the interest shown in its progress.

For their vision in undertaking this project, the Editor wishes to thank the publishers, AMS Press.

INTRODUCTION

MARK THORNTON BURNETT

In diverse interpretations from a range of cultures and historical periods, *Hamlet* has been read or staged as a text about which gather apparently ir- resolvable mysteries. It is seen as a work which poses stubborn questions, centred upon Hamlet's delay, motivations, isolation and introspective ruminations. Uncertainty still surrounds the exact theatrical and dramatic contexts which gave shape to the play's imaginative production, despite pages of critical endeavour. The ur-*Hamlet*, the key which would sup- posedly unlock Shakespeare's *Hamlet*, is lost, irretrievable. Confronting these issues directly, many of the contributors in this inaugural volume of newly commissioned essays take as a starting-point the enigma of *Ham- let*, the unknowable, unspeakable conflicts which it represents, and its charged place in critical debate.

The essays assembled, which employ a variety of critical methodologies and take up sometimes opposing ideological positions, engage with the vexed status of *Hamlet* in an intersecting fashion. Almost all of the contributors ac- knowledge the endless play of indeterminate meanings that *Hamlet* prolif- erates, but address the problem from competing standpoints. For Bill Read- ings, that which is secret in the play can be traced to the difficulties characters experience in attempting to communicate inexpressible truths; in comparison, Lisa Hopkins finds in *Hamlet* a characteristic rhetorical pattern of verbal in- stability that prohibits the foregrounding of unitary interpretations. An alter- native reading is forwarded by Elizabeth Oakes; in her account, an elemental design lies behind the typological situations that the play anatomizes. Martin Wiggins also identifies the play's interest in processes of mystification and revelation, although the focus of his essay lies mainly with those modes of thinking that have encouraged particular conceptions of Hamlet as character and subject.

The subjectivity of Hamlet is returned to repeatedly in the ensuing discus- sions, invariably to problematize an essentialist or liberal humanist under- standing of how characterization ideally operates. A concern with privacy and

interiority is contextualized by Mark Thornton Burnett in his contribution, but
Hamlet as an authentic subject is perceived to be in thrall to the larger issues
of historical determinacy which the play raises. The Romantic emphasis on a
seamless self is dealt with by Andrew Mousley: he presents Hamlet as site of
struggle, a terrain ravaged by dissonant energies, and he goes on to relate these
contradictions to emergent notions of individualism. Most forceful in this
connection are Christina Britzolakis's and Heiner O. Zimmermann's explor-
ations, which reject the view that *Hamlet* is the repository of timeless or
universal values and query easy biographical speculations; instead, the play
is approached as a key text which was reproduced at times of doubt and crisis,
and invested with a renewed but specific cultural importance.

What these essays share, therefore, is an urge to contextualize *Hamlet* in
terms of the plurality of discourses characteristic of the English Renaissance,
and contemporary changes in critical practice that have overtaken literary and
cultural studies. Interdisciplinary developments in recent years and, in particular, the impact of New Historicism, Feminism, Psychoanalysis and Post-
Structuralist theoretical frameworks, have transformed the ways in which
early-modern texts are expounded. *New Essays on 'Hamlet'* suggests that the
play intervenes in these ongoing advancements and is itself constituted by the
effects they have generated. For instance, that *Hamlet* demonstrates a marked
consideration of honour is a commonplace, but contributors such as Alastair
Fowler and Andrew Mousley push forward this received wisdom and investigate the place of reputation by surveying sixteenth- and seventeenth-century
attitudes towards name, identity and personal combat. Contextualization as a
critical tool and procedure is understood in its broadest possible sense, and
Hamlet emerges as a text that looks backwards to its dramatic antecedents and
forwards to the discontinuities that mark the postmodern moment. Alastair
Fowler and John Manning illuminate a number of crucial textual cruxes in
Hamlet in their analyses of continental emblematic devices, rhetorical methods and echoes of association from earlier dramas. Other contributors situate
their arguments by drawing upon psychoanalytic and materialist models:
Elizabeth Oakes's concern is with Jungian archetypes and sacrificial themes;
Joanna Montgomery Byles employs the concept of the superego to gauge
Hamlet's effects; Alison Findlay relates Ophelia to early seventeenth-century
writings about mental disturbance; and Martin Wiggins initiates a dialogue
between the play and eighteenth-century dramatic theorists.

This technique of using non-Shakespearean discourses as a grid against which *Hamlet* might be understood is instrumental in taking attention away from familiar readings. In particular, the rehearsal of English and European Renaissance contexts points to fresh approaches and allows the subversions of *Hamlet* to be fully recognized. And here several additional points of contact between the essays can be noticed. Inquiry is often directed to the mechanisms whereby *Hamlet* restlessly questions Elizabethan notions of gender and class from a radical perspective. While Andrew Mousley is interested in the transgressive properties of popular entertainment, Robert Barrie builds upon the argument and writes about the desacralizing laughter that animates *Hamlet* in a review of the figures of the Fool and the Vice, and the fortunes of Will Kempe and the Lord Chamberlain's Company. The parent's exploitation of the child is mapped by Joanna Montgomery Byles, and her essay throws new light on the play's undermining of paternalistic discipline. Alison Findlay explains early-modern constructions of madness, the interplay of language and difference, and the challenges the play poses to dominant patriarchal and hegemonic structures. Similarly, in a critique of the language of whoredom that informs *Hamlet*, Kay Stanton reflects upon constricted opportunities for women and the binarisms that police sexuality. Sexuality is linked to Renaissance discourses of secrecy by Mark Thornton Burnett, and Kate Chedgzoy unravels the complex interweaving of masculinity and femininity in Hamlet and post-*Hamlet* versions of the character. The strategies enlisted are divergent; nevertheless, the contributors as a whole are keen to worry over the play's privileged position and to take up opportunities to revise long-held assumptions. In so doing, they highlight the dissident tendencies of *Hamlet* and its dismantling treatment of established early-modern institutions.

At its most immediate level, authority is destabilized in the play by references to writing, scripts and texts. Metatextual questions are fiercely argued over in the contributions, reflecting current debates about the inherent arbitrariness of language and the fragility of all linguistic utterances. In some of the following studies, textual issues are broached through a consideration of the multiple early printed productions of the play, from the quarto to the folio editions. Thus Robert Barrie is able to pinpoint moments of contestatory comedy in his unpicking of lines from the so-called 'Bad Quarto' of 1603. With reference to Hamlet's letters and tables, several contributors (such as Bill Readings and Alison Findlay) angle their arguments more widely and maintain that Hamlet writes to exercise control, to maintain order, to establish claims to a stable identity, and to stave off an inevitable descent into madness and linguistic confusions. Valeria Wagner develops a reading with a particularly self-conscious intertextual slant, using Lacan's seminar as a means whereby *Hamlet*'s relationship to critical commentary can be reformulated. The attention that *Hamlet* draws to its status as a text is urgently detailed, and its interest in problems of theatrical representation is vividly communicated. Links between text and image, the place of writing in the symbolic economy of the play, and the authority of the earliest *Hamlet* publications — the essays wrestle with these and other questions in mutually complementary ways.

Considered broadly, the essays chart a movement from a consideration of the contexts of the play to a confrontation with its current reputation and ideological uses, its non-Shakespearean incarnations and existences. In itself this is a point of interest. The contemporary concern seems to be as much with rewritings of the play as with its linguisitic and textual complications, although these are also matters investigated in the collection. But it is certainly the case that the essays gathered in the latter half of the volume have the phenomenon of 'Hamleticism' as their focus. In a critique of Eliot and Joyce, Christina Britzolakis recovers echoes of *Hamlet* in Modernist texts, showing the appeal of the figure of the alienated intellectual for the twentieth-century literary project. A comparable account is elaborated by Kate Chedgzoy: taking Shakespeare's status as an author as her point of intervention, she questions concepts of native genius, theorizes memorializations and rememberings of *Hamlet*, and establishes the play's imbrication in currents of anxiety concerning paternity. The novels of Angela Carter are cited by Chedgzoy as exemplary instances of this debate about the father's symbolic powers. For Heiner O. Zimmermann, too, *Hamlet* is a play that returns to haunt the modern consciousness; the history of German expropriations of *Hamlet* that he provides powerfully captures the vicissitudes that plague the canonized text, and its transformations in the face of developments in audience taste and shifts in political allegiances.

Indeed, the political ramifications of the rewriting of *Hamlet* trouble the majority of those contributors who tackle the play's appropriations. Michal Kobialka reveals that Jan Kott's arguments about *Hamlet* in *Shakespeare Our Contemporary* are themselves indebted to the theories of Polish playwright, painter and designer, Stanisław Wyspiański, whose essay on the play was a formative influence on those Shakespearean directors staging revolutionary critiques of nationalist policies. Celebrations of the Nietzschean superman and fears of political inertia lie beneath the surface of the German productions of *Hamlet* that Heiner O. Zimmermann scrutinizes. From many of the investigations in the earlier part of this book, *Hamlet* establishes itself as a transitional text, located at the intersection of changing cultural practices, political insecurity and the breakdown of older theatrical traditions. It is clear from later sections, however, that the play's transitional aspects lend themselves well to reinterpretations, and that *Hamlet* was resurrected in response to new challenges, as a belief in the transcendent subject foundered, as paternalistic values were thrown into disarray and as states collapsed, to be replaced by unprecedented political organizations.

The overriding concern of this collection is to return to perennial questions about *Hamlet* rather than attempting to provide comprehensive answers. Abundantly evident in the volume is *Hamlet*'s refusal to fit into neat categorizations, its resistance to generic classifications and its unwillingness to affirm cherished ideals. The play's interrogations are frequently demonstrated in the meditations on identity and in the question and answer sessions that are its distinguishing hallmarks. Its balanced rhetorical structures, and its characteristic fondness for doubling characters and situations, belong to this impulse to cast into doubt, to undermine and to deny the closure that is only ever promised but never delivered. At the same time, the contributors to *New Essays on 'Hamlet'* generally agree that these inconsistencies can be contextualized from a variety of theoretical viewpoints, and that the play's aesthetic features can be productively reinterpreted by taking into account a diversity of ideological approaches. Although the essays have been grouped according to the preoccupations addressed, therefore, this is not to suggest that they are streamlined or univocal in their arguments. More often than not, the opposite is the case; there are as many differences as correspondences. Younger scholars as well as more established figures from various parts of the academy, the contributors begin the process of undoing the mythic status of the play, questioning its canonicity and its place in current critical activity. Their efforts constitute a potent means of reassessing the influences that *Hamlet* continues to exercise.

A Note on the Text

Unless otherwise stated, the Arden edition of *Hamlet* edited by Harold Jenkins has been used for all citations.

Sources and Symbologies

TWO NOTES ON *HAMLET*

HAMLET AND HONOUR

In the first scene of *Hamlet*, after the appearance of the older Hamlet's ghost and the watchers' secret sharing of dark superstitions, come the lines

> So have I heard and do in part believe it.
> But look, the morn in russet mantle clad
> Walks o'er the dew of yon high eastward hill.

(I. i. 170-2)

As H. E. Kavros remarks, responses to the passage have varied remarkably.[1] Stephen Booth writes of 'a great change from darkness to light, from the unknown and unnatural to the known and natural'; Joseph Hunter anticipates Milton's 'Now Morn her rosy steps in th'Eastern clime'; T. S. Eliot finds poetic immaturity; and Kavros himself sees an allusion to Matthew 16. 1-3, where red dawn 'heralds bad weather and doom'. Harold Jenkins, in his judicious edition, eschews such imaginings: for him the passage is simply 'a very literary description'.[2] His Longer Note goes almost to the nub of the matter: 'the *russet mantle* was traditional, and in Gawin Douglas ... had belonged to "Aurora"'.

Kavros's meteorological-apocalyptic suggestion is probably ruled out by the very different associations of 'red' and 'russet' — the two colours are actually contrasted by Langland.[3] Russet could range from dull red-brown to dark grey, 'somewhat lighter than black',[4] and was as much fabric as colour — 'A coarse homespun woollen cloth of a reddish-brown, grey or neutral colour, formerly used for the dress of peasants and country-folk'.[5] Indeed, the *Hamlet* instance is cited by *OED* under B. 2, adjectival: 'made of russet cloth';

although some detect a suggestion also of B. 4, 'homely', particularly in view of the image's function in restoring the 'known and natural'.

One may quickly agree with Jenkins about the passage's literary feel. Only, the Douglas analogue cited seems to merit more attention than to be merely listed as one illustration among many. Observe how closely Shakespeare's lines resemble it:

> When pale Aurora with face lamentable
> Hir russat mantill borderit all with sable
> Lappit about be hevinlye circumstance
> The tender bed and arres honorable
> Of Flora quene till flouris amyable
> In may I rays, to do my observance ...[6]

'Russet', 'mantle', and the wearer, morning: all match. Douglas is Shakespeare's source. Moreover, this is no casual appropriation of obscure material; Douglas's poem enjoyed a high reputation. Printed in London in 1553, *The palis of honoure* was still in 1601 a well-known work.[7] Nor is this all. Shakespeare echoes a very particular place in *The palis of honoure*: the opening. As such, the source would have been recognized by many of Shakespeare's hearers and readers. For in memory-art, openings were learned as *incipit* prompts, even if the work they opened was not to be memorized *verbatim*. Shakespeare knew this; so that he can be assumed to mean the Douglas reference as something fit hearers are expected to supply as an optimal association. Here one must take care: allusion in its modern sense had not yet won a secure place in the literary repertoire. Nevertheless — assuming the passage functions more or less like an allusion — what does it imply?

Making such an enquiry is a delicate activity, fraught with dangers of over-interpretation. Among unfamiliar, scarcely-mapped domains of assumption, the normal criterion of optimal relevance is not easy to apply. And, even when applied, it may perforce select implicatures of widely varying probability. At one extreme, it is strongly probable that Shakespeare's use of the *incipit* implies his anticipation that hearers will uptake at least some associated content of Douglas's poem — minimally, perhaps, its subject of honour. If Shakespeare echoed Douglas unconsciously, or his hearers did not consciously recognize the echo, the association might still be a relevant one for a modern critic, although less pressingly so. In any case, the relevance needs to be assessed in relation to context, themes, structure and the like.

As it happens, honour's salience among the topics of *Hamlet* is obvious to anyone who knows the play. Different conceptions of honour, indeed, strikingly differentiate several of the characters. For Fortinbras — in a scene where Prince Hamlet soliloquizes on the nature of honourable action —

> Rightly to be great
> Is not to stir without great argument,
> But greatly to find quarrel in a straw
> When honour's at the stake.

(IV. iv. 53-6)

In the denouement, Laertes's conventional (yet secretly *politique*) notion of honour lets him avoid full reconciliation with Hamlet at a crucial juncture:

> I am satisfied in nature,
> Whose motive in this case should stir me most
> To my revenge; but in my terms of honour
> I stand aloof, and will no reconcilement
> Till by some elder masters of known honour
> I have a voice and precedent of peace
> To keep my name ungor'd.[8]

(V. ii. 240-6)

And Hamlet's dying speech, almost, expresses concern for his 'wounded name' (V. ii. 349). He begs Horatio to absent himself from felicity — to remain alive — so as to salve the Hamlet honour. Honour or reputation ('name'), together with the actions involved in winning or preserving it, constitute a chief subject of the play.

One inference from all this might be that the Douglas allusion, made by Horatio (whose name itself alludes to honourable deeds), serves as an oblique *propositio*. That is to say, it may have had the function of announcing the play's subject — to those, at least, who knew to expect a *propositio* in a heroic work, and who recognized the allusion. The imitated passage, being the *incipit* of Douglas's Prologue, was after all closely associated with *exordium* topics. It would be characteristic of Shakespeare to fulfil the convention so implicitly, in a manner so subdued to his fiction, as to be now almost invisible.

Another probable inference might be that the morning succeeding the night of unnatural horror is not merely homely, but specifically one of moral honour.

Turning to weaker yet distinct implications, one may ask whether the literary qualities of *The palis of honoure* do not offer further relevant associations. Douglas's allegorical vision would have been felt as old-fashioned, if not necessarily, yet, in the mode of a different historical period. Perhaps, then, Shakespeare means to link honour (or Horatio's sort of honour) with older *mores* — a way of life that was passing, or that seemed in danger of passing, away? If so, *Hamlet* would be addressing an insight also developed in several other of his plays, notably *Henry IV* (acted *c.* 1596-7; printed 1598) and *Troilus and Cressida* (acted 1602-3; printed 1609), where oppositions between Hotspur and Hal, or chivalrous Trojans and Machiavellian Greeks, polarize older and newer conceptions of the honourable life. In *Hamlet*, however, Shakespeare is specially concerned with honour as a way of life problematically divergent — as in the duty of revenge — from Christian morality.

Notes

1. H. E. Kavros, 'The Morn in Russet Mantle Clad', *Notes and Queries*, 224 (1979), 119-20.

2. *Hamlet*, ed. Harold Jenkins (London and New York: Methuen, 1982), p. 177.

3. B-text xv. 162.

4. Gerard Legh, *The accedens of armory* (London, 1597; S.T.C. 15392), p. 116.

5. *OED*, s. v. *Russet*, sb. A. 1.

6. Prologue 1-6. *The palis of honoure* (London, 1553?; S.T.C. 7073), sig. A2^v.

7. There were three edns in the sixteenth century: Edinburgh, *c.* 1535; London, 1553; Edinburgh, 1579.

8. See also I. iii. 29-30, where Laertes advises Ophelia, 'weigh what loss your honour may sustain / If with too credent ear you list his songs'.

SHAKESPEARE'S INSET STYLE

The beginning of the inset play in *Hamlet*, the *Murder of Gonzago*, stands out from the neighbouring dialogue by virtue of what Harold Jenkins calls 'artificial elaboration of style characteristic of an older period':

> *Full thirty times hath Phoebus' cart gone round*
> *Neptune's salt wash and Tellus' orbed ground,*
> *And thirty dozen moons with borrow'd sheen*
> *About the world have times twelve thirties been*
> *Since love our hearts and Hymen did our hands*
> *Unite commutual in most sacred bands.*

(III. ii. 150-5)

Jenkins compares the 'time-formulae' here with those in Robert Greene's *Alphonsus, King of Arragon* (acted *c*. 1587-8; printed 1599) —

> Thrise ten times *Phoebus* with his golden beames
> Hath compassed the circle of the skie,
> Thrise ten times *Ceres* hath her workemen hir'd,
> And fild her barnes with frutefull crops of Corne,
> Since first in Priesthood I did lead my life: [1]

— and in the anonymous *Selimus* (acted *c*. 1591-4; printed 1594), perhaps also by Greene:

> Twice fifteen times hath fair Latona's son
> Walked about the world with his great light
> Since I began, — would I had ne'er begun! —
> To sway this sceptre.[2]

Earlier critics thought the Shakespearean passage a parody or burlesque of Greene. But an exemplary article by Carol Replogle establishes beyond dispute its serious character. As he shows, a distinctive style was characteristic of inset plays not only throughout Shakespeare's oeuvre, but in those of other Elizabethan dramatists. He writes of 'a style ... traditionally employed by well-born characters' — a 'logical choice' for Shakespeare, since 'time settings were frequently used to start any work.' Moreover, the style 'met Shakespeare's dramatic needs most effectively, because its ornate texture and archaic flavour were particularly appropriate for setting apart a play within a play from the main action.'[3] Decisive as Replogle's argument is, it prompts one or two further reflections.

Replogle writes of 'frequent and even indiscriminate use' of *chronographia* in Chaucer and Spenser, followed by its acquiring 'traditional, formal and literary connotations'. It is not quite true, however, that *chronographiae* 'were frequently used to start any work'. As a periphrastic amplification, the device normally indicated elevation of style. It was a distinctively high-style figure, generic to epic and to heroic modulations in other kinds.[4] Indeed, when the chronographical style appears as parody or burlesque, this is precisely because of the target's heroic pretension.[5] While there is no question of Shakespeare's parodying Greene, it should be noticed that both *Alphonsus* and *Selimus* are heroic plays.[6]

The notion of a retrospective, 'traditional' association, important as it is, also needs to be qualified. This becomes obvious as soon as one adduces two instances of *chronographia* not discussed by Replogle. The first is in Joshua Sylvester's 'The Maiden's Blush' (ll. 1173-80):

> Thrice through the *Zodiak* had *Hyperian* pranc't,
> And fourthly now his fiery Teem advanc't
> When quiet stretcht upon his Ivory bed,
> In sweetest sleep, well toward morning-sted,
> To mighty *Pharaoh* the Almighty sent
> A double *Dream*, of so deep Consequent,
> That wondring much, the King awoke withall,
> Conceiving it some high *Prognosticall*.[7]

Sylvester's biblical epic, although not always dependable in its stylistic registers, undeniably aims here at a high level of heroic seriousness. But it is hardly retrospective; the aim of biblical epics like this, on the contrary, was either timeless immediacy, or, as here, contemporaneity.

Perhaps even more significant is this rhyme-royal stanza of Michael Drayton's:

> Now full seaven times, the Sunne his welked waine
> Had on the top of all the Tropick set,
> And seaven times descending downe againe,
> His fiery wheeles, had with the fishes wet,
>   Since malice first this mischiefe did beget:
> In which so many courses hath been runne,
> As he that time celestiall signes hath done.[8]

Printed in Drayton's 'Mortimeriados' in 1596, it was rewritten as *ottava rima* for *The Barons Warres* (1603), and subsequently reprinted, with variants, in 1605, 1608, 1610, 1613, 1619, 1630 and 1631. It probably enjoyed its main vogue in the 1630s: clearly the chronographical style Shakespeare adopted was eminently viable.

The analogues suggest two comments. First, it seems very probable that the style Shakespeare uses for his inset play is not merely traditional or archaic, but specifically 'high'. It is a style not so much generic to serious inset plays (although that may also be true), as indicating modulation to a heroic mode. Associated with heroic plays like *Tamburlaine* and *Alphonsus*, it belongs to the vogue of epic in the late sixteenth and seventeenth centuries. Outside literature, it may be related to the neogothic vogue of the 1590s and beyond.

This is not, of course, to deny the archaizing flavour of the Shakespearean passage, but rather to insist on its generic thrust. There can be no doubt that Shakespeare's use of *chronographia* to begin *The Murder of Gonzago* would have established a tone of heroic tragedy. And the inset scene it initiates delivers the challenge of high behaviour — not in the past, but in the present. The honour of an idealized and privileged past challenges a response in the present, which the characters in *Hamlet* itself attempt but tragically fail to achieve.

Notes

1. *Alphonsus, King of Arragon*, IV. i. 9-13 in *The Plays and Poems of Robert Greene*, ed. John Churton Collins, 2 vols (Oxford: Clarendon, 1905), I, 113, ll. 1152-6.

2. *The Tragical Reign of Selimus ...*, ll. 41-4, ed. Alexander B. Grosart (London: Dent, 1898), p. 2.

3. Carol Replogle, 'Not Parody, Not Burlesque: the Play Within the Play in *Hamlet*', *Modern Philology*, 67 (1969), 158.

4. Ernst Robert Curtius, *European Literature and the Latin Middle Ages*, tr. Willard R. Trask (Princeton: Princeton University Press, 1973), pp. 275-6, with many examples.

5. Curtius, *European Literature*, pp. 275-6, wrongly sees the *Hamlet* passage as an example of such parody.

6. Despite the latter's title, which announces a 'comical history'.

7. *The Complete Works of Joshua Sylvester*, ed. Alexander B. Grosart, 2 vols (1880; New York: AMS Press, 1967), II, 115.

8. 'Mortimeriados', ll. 1296-1302 in John William Hebel et al., eds, *The Works of Michael Drayton*, 5 vols (Oxford: Blackwell, 1931-41), I, 346.

SYMBOLA AND *EMBLEMATA* IN *HAMLET*

JOHN MANNING

Emblematic forms and structures impinged on every aspect of the literary and visual culture of Europe from the publication of the first emblem book in 1531 until the advent of Romanticism. Over two thousand printed emblem books were published during this period, and emblems were reproduced in decorative schemes in tapestry, plaster work and paintings. Emblematic images and structures may be discerned in all sixteenth- and seventeenth-century literary forms. Of these, the drama has a particular claim on our attention, since, of its very nature, it combines most strikingly the visual and the verbal to procure its effects.[1] As Glynne Wickham has shown, the properties of this theatre were frequently non-naturalistic and symbolic, 'emblematic' in the largest sense.[2]

It should come as no surprise, therefore, that *Hamlet* like other dramatic work of the period has been seen as indebted to this emblematic tradition. Henry Green's *Shakespeare and the Emblem Writers* points to some eighteen references to Devices and emblems in *Hamlet*.[3] These parallels are, admittedly, rather general or far-fetched — analogues rather than sources. But despite, or even perhaps because of these very general, superficial resemblances and parallels, Green succeeds in establishing the fact that *Hamlet* along with Shakespeare's other plays emerges from and belongs to an essentially emblematic culture, and draws upon a common stock of commonplaces, proverbial lore and iconographic convention. 'The cock, that is the trumpet to the morn' (I. i. 155), 'the steep and thorny way' of Virtue (I. iii. 48), the backward-moving crab (II. ii. 203-4), 'Hercules and his load' (II. ii. 358), the squeezing of the sponge (IV. ii. 11-20), the Janus posture, 'Looking before and after' (IV. iv. 37), 'giant-like' rebellion (IV. v. 121), 'the kind life-rend'ring pelican' (IV. v. 146), the 'quills upon the fretful porpentine' (I. v. 20), not to mention the language of flowers and herbs, are all recognizable in various sixteenth-century collections of emblems and *imprese*.

Modern commentators frequently invoke such iconographic conventions in interpreting and annotating the play. In explicating 'the strucken deer' (III.

ii. 265), Jenkins follows Green in citing Peacham's *Minerva Britanna* (1612), which uses such an image to represent a man with a guilty conscience, even though this book is too late to have served as a source.[4] In commenting on 'Let her not walk i' th' sun' (II. ii. 184), Jenkins refers more generally to 'the sun as a royal emblem'; 'symbolism felicitously combines with realism' in the account of the circumstances of Ophelia's death (IV. vii. 165-82), and frequently it is 'difficult to deny the possibility of some further significance attaching' to objects cryptically mentioned in the play.[5] Ophelia's flowers, Hamlet's sword, Yorick's skull, the poisoned chalice with its dissolved 'union' have all elicited iconographic commentary.

This seems appropriate, since the play itself insistently invokes various emblematic forms and structures: badges, cognizances, liveries, tokens, heraldic devices, icons and signs. Character is sometimes presented in emblematic and iconic terms:

> He is the brooch indeed
> And gem of all the nation.

(IV. vii. 92-3)

The royal image, the *icon principis*, is retailed as a 'picture in little' (II. ii. 362); Hamlet is (or was) the conspicuous image of the state, 'observ'd of all observers' (III. i. 156), the 'glass of fashion and the mould of form' (III. i. 155).[6] Laertes appears 'like the painting of a sorrow' (IV. vii. 107).

There are allusions to courtly devices and ornaments in, for instance, the carriages 'very dear to fancy ... and of very liberal conceit' (V. ii. 148-50).[7] Seals,[8] heraldic marks and signs are often referred to: 'a seal'd compact / Well ratified by law and heraldry' (I. i. 89-90); 'letters seal'd' (III. iv. 204); 'everything is seal'd and done' (IV. iii. 59); 'every god did seem to set his seal / To give ... assurance of a man' (III. iv. 61-2); 'the stamp of nature' (III. iv. 170); Pyrrhus' '*sable arms*' (II. ii. 448) and '*heraldry more dismal*' (II. ii. 452).

Since 'the apparel oft proclaims the man' (I. iii. 72), we find that nearly all the characters refer to emblematic trappings and significant, identifying attributes: the dawn's 'russet mantle' (I. i. 171); Hamlet's 'inky cloak' of 'solemn black' (I. ii. 77-8); 'customary suits' (I. ii. 78), 'trappings' and 'suits' (I. ii. 86) of woe. A 'look' may 'purport' (II. i. 82), and therefore reliance is placed on outward show, 'Nature's livery' (I. iv. 32), to declare what is hidden within. This frequently is a matter of 'Custom', which 'gives frock or livery / That aptly is put on' (III. iv. 166-7), and prescribes to each station in life its needful, 'importing' attribute:

> A very ribbon in the cap of youth —
> Yet needful too, for youth no less becomes
> The light and careless livery that it wears
> Than settled age his sables and his weeds
> Importing health and graveness.

(IV. vii. 76-80)

Alternatively, the authority for reading such defining signs is drawn from old saws or traditional ballads:

> *How should I your true love know*
> *From another one?*
> *By his cockle hat and staff*
> *And his sandal shoon.*

(IV. v. 23-6)

Elsewhere, as with '*the spokes and fellies*' of Fortune's wheel (II. ii. 491), the symbolism is common and conventional.[9]

Gesture frequently bears meaning in the play, as an expression of the forms which suit and embody a state of mind or 'conceit' (II. ii. 551). There are 'forms, moods, shapes of grief' (I. ii. 82) bodied forth in 'vailed lids' (I. ii. 70) and 'windy suspiration' (I. ii. 79). Elsewhere fingers, knees, ears, and, even more appropriately, the 'secret parts', insistently and cryptically body forth moral abstractions and personifications.[10] Fortune (II. ii. 228-36) is only one of such figures so anatomized.

Much of the play is taken up with the proverbial lore, 'common' themes (I. ii. 103), 'precepts' (I. iii. 58-80), and 'saws of books' (I. v. 100), which form the stuff and substance of moralizing emblems.[11] The play, like much emblem literature, constantly refers to consolatory topics, or the morality found in advice literature.

Events and characters in the play are not seen simply as themselves, but as bearers of a meaning, which is for the present hidden or occluded, but which may in future be revealed: figures are 'portentous' (I. i. 112) or '*ominous*' (II. ii. 450); they are prologues

> to the omen coming on,
> Have heaven and earth together demonstrated
> Unto our climatures and countrymen.

(I. i.126-8)

Hamlet himself employs emblematic devices, as may befit the character of a Renaissance prince who has benefitted from German academic training.[12] He expresses familiarity with the 'posy' genre (III. ii. 147)[13] and has recourse to images and portraits to make his instructive points: 'Look here upon this picture' (III. iv. 53). Further, the practice of enforcing moral exhortation by means of two contrasting icons is frequent in some emblematic Protestant polemic, as may be seen in the notorious Simon Rosarius's *Antithesis Christi et Antichristi.*

Hamlet forms his own *impresa*:

> Now to my word.
> It is 'Adieu, adieu, remember me.'

(I. v. 110-11)

Upon its invention, he applies the Latin tag, *'Hic et ubique'* (I. v. 164). His 'word' is his motto, his watchword, one of the constituent parts of the *impresa* or *symbolum*. In this case it passes from father to son, and is appropriate to a noble prince. And it is altogether appropriate that Hamlet's mind should run to the formulation of a device at this point in the play when he receives the ghost's commission:

> The practice of constructing *imprese* was derived from the military custom of the English, who entered upon, undertook and proposed the execution of some famous deed within a prescribed and limited period of time. It was at this point that they constructed a certain new *impresa*.[14]

The *impresa* was designed to commemorate the task undertaken, and to speed the bearer to its execution.

He seals his confederates in his plot with the sign of the ancient god of the mysteries, Harpocrates: 'still your fingers on your lips, I pray' (I. v. 195). He uses emblematic forms in the furtherance of his plot: the dumb show and inserted dramatic speeches are both emblematic in kind.[15] Idealistically, Hamlet sees the function of drama as essentially emblematic: 'to hold as 'twere the mirror up to nature; to show virtue her feature, scorn her own image, and the very age and body of the time his form and pressure' (III. ii. 21-4). Drama images or bodies forth moral abstractions or forms (Virtue, Scorn) and provides an image of the time. Many contemporary emblem writers saw themselves similarly as providing 'Theatres': van der Noot's *Theatre for voluptuous worldlings*; La Perrière's *Theatre des bons engins*; Boissard's *Theatrum vitae humanae*. Generically drama belongs in Hamlet's eyes, like so many emblem books, to the *Speculum* tradition,[15] and he proceeds like the emblematist to set up 'a glass / Where you may see the inmost part of you' (III. iv. 18-19).[16]

Later, Hamlet will indulge in another emblematic theatre, the *Theatrum funebre*,[17] when he catalogues the famous dead from antiquity up to his recent past. The emblematic machinery thus set up is soon to overtake him, when he becomes himself a part of an emblematic *pegma*, an icon of death placed 'high on a stage' (V. ii. 383).

Since *emblema* was defined by contemporary theorists as *quicquid inseritur* (something inserted or set in),[18] Hamlet's decision to 'insert' a 'speech of some dozen or sixteen lines' (II. ii. 535-6) must be regarded as an emblematic procedure. Indeed, the composition of the whole play, or at least, the preparation of the copy for the printing of the early editions of the play, might also be seen as being taken up with the insertion or removal of particular parts of the text: I. iv. 75-8, IV. iv. 9-66, IV. vii. 67-80 and IV. vii. 113-22 may all be justifiably seen as inserted portions of the text, which could be later removed in the 'Bad Quarto' or Folio versions. II. ii. 239-69 may justifiably be seen as a Folio insertion.

The emblem as a kind of detachable ornament to speech or writing characterizes some of the inset images in the speeches of the play. The following could all be removed from the speeches in which they are contained without any violence being done to the sense:

> 'tis an unweeded garden
> That grows to seed; things rank and gross in nature
> Possess it merely.

> (I. ii. 135-7)

> A violet in the youth of primy nature ...

> (I. iii. 7)

> The canker galls the infants of the spring
> Too oft before their buttons be disclos'd ...

> (I. iii. 39-40)

Yet for all the play's insistence on these emblematic forms and conventional iconographies, the action of the play seems to pay little heed. Polonius's fund of proverbial wisdom only makes him appear a fool. If Hamlet was ever intended to serve as an illustrious emblematic 'mirror for princes', the play soon announces that this 'glass' is 'quite, quite down!' (III. i. 155-6). 'Examples gross as earth exhort' (IV. iv. 46), but are ignored and neglected. Symbolic forms and rituals are by-passed: 'we have done but greenly / In hugger-mugger to inter him' (IV. v. 83-4); 'Antiquity' is 'forgot, custom not known' (IV. v. 104). Symbolic accoutrements are not applied as decorum demands:

> No trophy, sword, nor hatchment o'er his bones,
> No noble rite, nor formal ostentation —

> (IV. v. 211-12)

In spite of Hamlet's best efforts at emblematic composition, it remains 'inexplicable' whether Claudius even sees the dumb show. The effect it procures is at best dubious. Hamlet's 'word' is never fulfilled, and degenerates into 'Words, words, words' (II. ii. 192); Claudius acknowledges the hypocrisy of his 'most painted word' (III. i. 53).[19]

Although Ophelia invokes the emblematic attributes and signs by which one might recognize a true lover, these are hardly reliable: the '*cockle hat*, '*staff*'and'*sandal shoon*' and are scarcely evident in this play. Poor Ophelia, 'Divided from herself and her fair judgment,' becomes a picture (IV. v. 84-6) to which only pity, not meaning, can be attached. Any 'eternal blazon' (I. v. 21) is withheld from mortal eyes.

These advertized departures from and neglect of forms and conventions have much to do with the procuring of the life-like effect of the play. But even more, one can observe in its procedures an attempt by the text to deconstruct the very emblematic forms on which the society of the play once depended to make meaning and significance. In so doing, the play itself becomes an emblem, involving its readers and its spectators in an effort to puzzle out its riddles and its mysteries.

Notes

1. See the classic studies of Albrecht Schöne, *Emblematik und Drama im Zeitalter des Barock* (Munich: Beck, 1968) and Peter M. Daly, *Literature in the Light of the Emblem: Structural Parallels between the Emblem and Literature in the Sixteenth and Seventeenth*

Centuries (Toronto and London: University of Toronto Press, 1979), especially pp. 134-67.

2. Glynne Wickham, *Early English Stages*, 2 vols (London: Routledge, 1966).

3. (1870; New York: Burt Franklin, n.d.), p. 540. He refers to I. ii. 71; I. v. 13; II. ii. 295; III. i. 62; III. i. 70; III. i. 76; III. ii. 259; III. iv. 53; III. iv. 205; IV. iv. 33; IV. v. 135; IV. vii. 84; V. i. 73; V. i. 86; V. i. 191 and V. ii. 8.

4. Jenkins's Arden edition of *Hamlet*, p. 508.

5. Jenkins, p. 511, on Hamlet's cloud.

6. The contemporary fashion for *Icones illustrium* and *Icones principium* is attested to by the following partial list of publications: Theodore de Bèze, *Icones* (Geneva, 1580); Jean Jacques Boissard, *Icones diversorum hominum ... illustrium* (Metz, 1591) and *Bibliotheca ... in quo continentur illustrium ... virorum effigies* (Frankfurt, 1628-32); Hubert Goltz, *Imperatorum imagines* (Antwerp, 1557); Hendrik Hondius, *Icones* (The Hague, 1680); Marco Mantova Benavides, *Illustrium imagines* (Padua, 1559); Nicolaus von Reusner, *Icones ... imperatorum, regum, principum* (Leipzig, 1597); Valentin Thilo, *Icones heroum* (Basle, 1589).

7. For the use of emblem books as patterns for ornamenting belongings, including swords, see see Hessel Miedema, 'The Term Emblema in Alciati', *Journal of the Warburg and Courtauld Institutes*, 31 (1968), 248-9, who cites Filippo Fasanini's translation of *Horapollo*, where he speaks of the 'short sayings or marks, which they may apply to swords, rings ... and by which, in combination with painted or scupted figures, they can wrap the secrets of their minds in shrouds', and the prefatory epistle, *Ad lectorem* in Rouillé's edn of Alciato's *Emblemata* (Lyons, 1550): 'is ex Emblematum libello ... armis, gladio ... inscribere, et impingere possit'.

8. For *signum* and *sigillum* as synonyms for *emblema*, see Miedema, 'Emblema in Alciati', 239 and n. 30.

9. Probably so conventional that it does not require annotation. The attribute goes back to classical times. Guy de Tervarent, *Attributs et symboles dans l'art profane 1450-1600* (Geneva: Droz, 1958), s.v. Roue I. Attribut de la Fortune, cites Claudian, *De bello Gothico*, l. 632, Ammianus Marcellinus, *Res gestae*, XXXI, 1 and XXVI, 8, and Boethius, *De consolatione philosophiae*, II, 2, 28-31. The motif was, of course, handled in many emblem books and mythographic treatises of the Renaissance.

10. Cesare Ripa's *Iconologia*, first published 1593 with frequent reprintings, most famously made exclusive use of depictions of the human form to embody to abstract concepts and principles.

11. On *sententia* and emblem, see Miedema, 'Emblema in Alciati', 248 and n. 68.

12. On the role of the emblem in the German education system, see Frederick John Stopp, *The Emblems of the Altdorf Academy: Medals and Medal Orations 1577-1626* (London: The Modern Humanities Research Association, 1974).

13. On posies as emblems, see my Introduction to *The Emblems of Thomas Palmer: Two hundred poosees* (New York: AMS Press, 1988), pp. xxixf.

14. See Abraham Fraunce, *Symbolicæ philosophiæ liber quartus et ultimus*, ed. John Manning and tr. Estelle Haan (New York: AMS Press, 1991), pp. 26-7 and 137.

15. Rosemary Freeman was among the first to draw attention to the relationship between the emblem and the dumb show. See her *English Emblem Books* (London: Chatto and Windus, 1948), p. 15. For the emblematic nature of Hamlet's dumb show, see Jenkins, pp. 501-5.

16. See, for instance, the titles of the following emblem books, which advertize their function as 'mirrors': Jakob Masen, *Speculum imaginum* (Cologne, 1650); Jakob de Zetter, *Speculum virtutum et vitiorum* (Frankfurt, 1619); H. G., *The mirrour of maiestie* (London, 1618); Hendrik Laurenszoon Spieghel, *Hartspiegel* (Amsterdam, 1650), Jan David, *Duodecim specula* (Antwerp, 1610). On the mirror for princes tradition, see Dietmar Peil, 'Emblematische Fürstenspiegel im 17. und 18. Jahrhunderts: Saavedra —Le Moyne —Wilhem', *Frühmittelalterliche Studien*, 20 (1986), 54-92.

17. The most monumental emblematic catalogue of this kind is Otto Aicher, *Theatrum funebre* (Salzburg, 1674). See also, for example, *Il teatro del dolore* (Turin, 1664).

18. On emblem as insert, see Miedema, 'Emblema in Alciati', 240 and nn. 32-8.

19. On the emblem and 'painted words', see John Manning, 'Alciati and Philostratus's *Icones*', *Emblematica*, 1 (1986), 207-10.

Politics and Performance

THE 'HEART OF MY MYSTERY': *HAMLET* AND SECRETS

MARK THORNTON BURNETT

When Elizabeth I passed through the city in 1559 to be crowned in Westminster, Londoners were treated to a magnificent spectacle. A calvacade of pageants crowded the streets; children staged dramas in which the virtues of chastity and grace were celebrated; and respected members of civic corporations showered upon the young queen gifts and presents. But the coronation entry was more than a display of citizen exuberance; it was a carefully orchestrated episode designed to dissolve factions and to bring together disparate elements at a time of political crisis, and the various stages of the procession were arranged in consultation with Elizabeth herself. A contemporary recorder recognized the implications of the event, observing 'shee [knew] ... right well that in pompous ceremonies a secret of government doth much consist, for that the people are naturally both taken and held with exteriour shewes.'[1] The comment offers one way of assessing the mechanisms used by Elizabeth in securing and maintaining her royal power. Throughout her reign she practised what might be called a politics of secrecy, which involved cultivating a distant inscrutability even as she presented herself as open and vulnerable in matters of state. Recalling 1568 and the difficulties surrounding Mary Stuart, William Camden wrote, 'By means of these Letters, and ... words, Queen Elizabeth seemed (for who can dive into the secret Meanings of Princes? and wise men do keep their Thoughts locked up within the Closet of their Breasts,) seriously to commiserate the most afflicted Princess her Kinswoman'.[2] Sly suggestion and feigned impartiality join in the description, a telling instance of Elizabeth's exercise of control masquerading as apparent weakness. On many occasions, Elizabeth would employ such tactics to her advantage, and they extended to claiming a comprehensive acquaintance with political affairs in order to contain potentially damaging influences. She rankled in 1595 at the charge that she owed James VI money, and was quick to accuse him of dishonesty: 'Suppose you that so long a raigne as mine hath so fewe frends ... that ... dealings made by

such as ought most have helped you, could be kept secret from my knowledge?'[3] A shrewd manipulator of counsellor and ruler alike, Elizabeth
encouraged an illusion of defencelessness while remaining aloof and
guardedly impenetrable.

Much has been written about the function of secrets in social organizations.
Etymologically the word 'secret' has its roots in the Latin *secernere*, meaning
to put apart or to divide, and *secretus*, the past participle, connotes being separated, solitary or private.[4] These meanings suggest the ways in which secrets
establish boundaries, areas of autonomy which are inaccessible to those excluded from the possession of privileged information or not privy to special-
ized knowledge. They recall, too, the icy reserve of Elizabeth in her speeches
when she registered disapproval of the prying questions of members of parliament. Secrecy betokens the ownership of power. It should come as no surprise, therefore, that the exercise of secrecy was not the sovereign's province
alone. Closed associations (or 'secret societies' as they are sometimes termed)
traditionally yoke together the members of particular groupings, operating as
apparatuses of control and promoting cohesion in the place of fragmentation
and difference.[5] In a Renaissance context, there were elaborate methods
which evolved in order to disseminate the transmission of secrets, the techniques used by scribes or the mysteries of apprenticeship, for example. And
the *arcana imperii* of the monarch had a counterpart in the coded systems of
communication enlisted by dissidents; during the period of the English Civil
War and the Interregnum, emblems, ciphers and secret discourses marked the
writings of royalists wishing to escape the restrictions of censors anxious to
stamp out the broadcasting of subversive political messages.[6]

Perhaps more than Shakespeare's other plays, *Hamlet* has attracted readers
and playgoers who have attempted to account for the fascination the central
character exercises. Criticism, to adapt Hamlet's angry words to Guildenstern, has occupied itself with plucking out the 'heart' of the hero's 'mystery'
(III.ii.356-7), and as Catherine Belsey notes, the 'interiority, this essence, the
heart of Hamlet's mystery, has been the quarry not only of Rosencrantz and
Guildenstern, agents of the king's surveillance, but of liberal-humanist criticism of the nineteenth and twentieth centuries.'[7] Such is the volume of these
exegetical endeavours, *Hamlet* has become a text about which no agreement
seems to be possible. The more it is studied, the more obscure it appears to
become. Frank Kermode writes: 'Shakespearians may find explanations of
the mysteriousness ... of *Hamlet*, by considering instead the ur-*Hamlet* ...

Once a text is credited with high authority it is studied intensely; once it is so studied it acquires ... secrecy ... Shakespeare is an inexhaustible source of occult readings'.[8] While these are useful comments which go some way towards contextualizing the status of the play and its cultural resonances, they can be pushed further and redirected towards other modes of inquiry. One of the reasons for the interest generated by *Hamlet* is the play's overriding preoccupation with what is hidden and secret. Shakespeare's text primarily concerns itself with secrets, with their function, inception, management, continuation and exposure, in ways which are historically specific and politically active. The scenes of private conference, the metatextual details, the rites of initiation, and the stress upon sexuality, espionage and inheritance in *Hamlet* all point to a fascination with secrets and to questions of political moment in the period. Taking into account the various discourses of secrecy circulating in the English Renaissance makes possible a deeper appreciation of a play, which debates arguments concerning the usefulness of perpetuating a system dependent upon supporting the 'mysteries of state', and is informed by anxieties about an Elizabethan order spiralling towards its inevitable demise.

Illusions of Privacy

Why Hamlet's subjectivity has provoked such comment is worth pausing over for a moment. In exploring this aspect of the play, the warnings of Katharine Eisaman Maus might be heeded; she summarizes recent views on subjectivity in the period and arguments which claim that, despite a highly developed rhetoric of inwardness, the concept of privacy hardly existed.[9] The twentieth-century vocabulary of interiority is hardly congruent with terms popular in the sixteenth and seventeenth centuries where 'secrets' most effectively conveyed a sense of the mysteries of the contents of the heart. Self-conscious metaphorical languages and representational systems took the place of concepts now assumed to be normative. Nevertheless, it is possible tentatively to suggest that part of the impact of *Hamlet* can be traced to its delineation of characters who struggle to hide what is within, to subordinate a sense of self by keeping secrets, and who agitate to achieve authentic subject positions. The frustrations suffered by Hamlet, incapacitated from articulating 'that within which passes show' (I. ii. 85), is duplicated in a series of mirror images or doubles. In some respects Hamlet's reflection, Laertes undergoes com-

parable experiences. The long lesson in moral discipline given to him by
Polonius has as its principle the importance of remaining separate and refusing to divulge in public secrets which may have disruptive consequences. No overt political allusions to England or Scotland rupture the texture
of *Hamlet*, a play which only hints at the larger world of politics to which
it belongs, and gestures towards the rhythms and routines of the court. Its
scenes of repression, however, would seem to enact a peculiarly Renaissance phenomenon, and look forward to the circumstances of a monarch
such as James I whose most intimate bodily functions were public events
at which there was in attendance a substantial royal entourage. The sexual practices of his favourites, and the ailments which affected them, were
all publicly discussed in a ceaseless round of gossip and social exchanges.
A private realm, where such matters were not offered up for general consumption, was essentially inconceivable.[10]

Linked to the illusion of interiority in *Hamlet* is a parallel situation involving characters who appear alone on stage or who engage in 'private' conference. 'Privy' and 'private' are key terms, recurring at salient moments, as
when Horatio contemplates the terrifying possibility that the ghost may be
'privy to thy country's fate' (I. i. 136). In addition, few scenes contain large
groups of characters; the action, although it moves outside Denmark from
time to time, is dominated by Elsinore, and *Hamlet* must rank among the more
claustrophobic of Shakespeare's plays, one which is full of incident but which
figures experiences of an essentially solitary and isolated nature. Under duress Ophelia admits that Hamlet has given her 'private time' (I. iii. 92); later,
when counselled by her father, she remains on her own having denied Hamlet 'access' (II. i. 110). Privacy is defined by Sissela Bok as 'the condition of
being protected from unwanted access by others ... Claims to privacy are
claims to control access to what one takes - however grandiosely - to be one's
personal domain. Through such claims, and the counterclaims they often
generate, people try to reinforce or expand this control. Privacy and secrecy
overlap whenever the efforts at such control rely on hiding.'[11] But in *Hamlet*
privacy is not a matter of choice: the condition is induced, introduced through
or denied by political pressure. Eavesdropping makes a mockery of bids for
privacy as Ophelia overhears Hamlet's soliloquies and Polonius, killed by
Hamlet in Gertrude's chamber, is replaced as eavesdropper by the ghost. Af-
fections are annexed, and characters dictated to by the demands of a society
which roots out concealment to ensure its continued survival.

Writing Secrets

A text that looks in upon itself, *Hamlet* occludes the meanings of which it is constituted. The play's closest relative is the legend of Pandora's box, the mythic jar containing the gifts of misery and hope in classical accounts of the creation. Vigorously suggestive in this respect, the language of *Hamlet* clusters about ideas of locking, covering and shutting away material which, if released, could have disastrous ramifications. Ophelia locks up Laertes's advice in her 'memory' (I. iii. 85) and acts upon Polonius's order to 'lock herself from' Hamlet's 'resort' (II. ii. 143). As characters in the play withold or resist expressing what they know, so do they shield themselves by adopting roles and false identities. When he puts 'on' his 'antic disposition' (I. v. 180), it is as if Hamlet wears his madness like a garment; Gertrude dons a disguise more substantial than this, and her heart is described as being encased in armour (III. iv. 35-8). At times it appears, indeed, that nothing is in the open in Elsinore, the castle and its environs taking on the properties of a baffling, metaphysical, labyrinthine gaol.[12]

What is secret in *Hamlet* cannot easily be comprehended or embraced: either it is rarely articulated or it is the privileged possession of a single character. These secrets are unspoken, silent; they are also difficult to see or to perceive. Nor can they be read; in this respect, *Hamlet*, like other Shakespearean plays, displays a preoccupation with metatextual questions. At the level of writing, secrets are implied in the number of references to sealed documents. 'Upon his will I seal'd my hard consent' (I. ii. 60) says Polonius of Laertes's petition; Rosencrantz and Guildenstern bear 'letters seal'd' (III. iv. 204) to England; 'everything is seal'd and done' (IV. iii. 59) thinks Claudius of his scheme to have Hamlet assassinated; and Hamlet's decision to 'unseal' (V. ii. 17) this 'grand commission' (V. ii. 18) saves him from becoming the intended victim of the same plot. Whether the letters reach their ostensible destination or are substituted in an effort to forestall political conspiracy, they can still have a deadly effect: Rosencrantz and Guildenstern are murdered when they become ensnared in a web of textual communications.[13]

One of the motivating energies of *Hamlet* is Claudius's anxious desire to have established the foundations of his rule; it is a concern of such weight that he is eventually precipitated into attempting to wipe out those who block the path towards dominion. In this connection *Hamlet* seems to implicate itself in the kinds of political activities which characterized the period, and which shaped struggles for supremacy in the later sixteenth century. Only in the 1580s James had conducted a clandestine correspondence with various elder statesmen in England in order to cement a Scottish-English alliance and possibly to seal his own claims to one or other of the crowns. A letter of 1584 to Mary Stuart shows James rejecting his mother's design for an association under which she and her son would share the Scottish kingdom; James wrote reprovingly about the 'secret instructions that Your Majesty forbids me to ever reveal to any one'.[14] Later in the year, courted by Cecil this time, he was prepared to contemplate abandoning his mother and siding with English forces, and James ensured that the bearer of the letters expressing his enthusiasm for the project was 'directed ... with more special and secret commission than any I ever directed before'.[15] The scrupulous attention to the transmission of these documents was entirely necessary, for when the intrigue came before Elizabeth, she was furious, writing in 1585, 'we old foxes can find shiftes to saue ourselves by others malice, and come by knowledge of greattest secreat, spetiallye if it touche our freholde.'[16] This chastening experience appears to have instilled in James a fastidious regard for secret texts; lest his private thoughts be known, everything he wrote thereafter he subjected to strict protective regulations. Even *Basilikon Doron*, published in 1599, had to answer to these requirements, James at first permitting only seven copies *'to be printed, the Printer being first sworne for secrecie'*.[17] The lesson of misdirected political aspirations had been learned.

The timely exposure of James's clumsy manoeuvrings checked his predilection for intrigue, at least while his mother was still alive. With the reading of the letters in *Hamlet* (their contents being, as it were, textualized) comes the series of revelations that brings about the unravelling and partial resolution of its complications. For if the play obsessively folds up information into itself, simultaneously it illuminates and brings secrets to light. The reflections of Foucault on sexuality may be relevant here: he argues that secrets are forced into hiding so as to make possible their eventual discovery.[18] Entering into a critical relationship with *Hamlet* entails interpreting acts of repression and equally powerful representations of unburdening, showing and disclosing. The first we hear is for Barnardo to 'unfold' (I. i. 2) himself as he cannot be seen in the darkness. The Queen asks for Hamlet to 'cast' his 'nighted colour off' (I. ii. 68), to put aside his funereal garb and to present himself in brighter hues. Although constriction is associated with Ophelia, tied to her is an antithetical idea of unchecked movement: Polonius will 'loose' (II. ii. 162) her to Hamlet and exploit her innocence in a plan to have demonstrated the causes of his mad, melancholic malady. If *Hamlet* is a drama of cloistered communications, failed missives and tortured intellects, it is also one in which frustrations strive towards a climactic release.

Demonic Awakenings

Nowhere is this dialectic between hiding and unearthing or manifesting made more apparent than in the appearance of the ghost. This figurative unearthing provides the play with one of its most potent moments of unlocking as the tomb is broken to release the restless spirit. Typically the ghost is surrounded in mystery: 'This to me / In dreadful secrecy impart they did' (I. ii. 206-7) Horatio states, informing Hamlet of the supernatural visitation. In his reply, Hamlet urges his friends to consign the ghost to an area of unseen, unspoken phenomena — 'If you have hithero conceal'd this sight, / Let it be tenable in your silence still ... Give it an understanding but no tongue' (I. ii. 247-50) — although when the apparition is confronted, metaphors of unclasping and expulsion dominate, replacing the veiled occurrences of the previous scenes:

> but tell
> Why thy canoniz'd bones, hearsed in death,
> Have burst their cerements, why the sepulchre
> Wherein we saw thee quietly inurn'd
> Hath op'd his ponderous and marble jaws
> To cast thee up again.

> (I. iv. 46-51)

At last the ghost's voice rings out, but one of the revelations which has been anticipated is tantalizingly postponed. Promising to deliver unknown truths, the ghost only hints at secrets which will not be broken:

> But that I am forbid
> To tell the secrets of my prison-house,
> I could a tale unfold ...

> (I. v. 13-15).

For Hamlet, though, the story he hears is enough to impel him to make certain again of his friends' confidence: 'Never make known what you have seen tonight' (I. v. 149).[19]

Considering the ghost's appearance permits several broad patterns to emerge. As he listens to the disclosure and learns the fantastic secret, Hamlet's antipathy towards Claudius hardens and he elects himself co-conspirator in the execution of revenge. His conduct is a dramatic realization of the ways in which secrecy, according to Sissela Bok, can 'fuel gross intolerance and hatred towards outsiders. At the heart of secrecy lies discrimination of some form, since its essence is sifting, setting apart, drawing lines.'[20] Bok's observations are similarly helpful in contextualizing Hamlet's swearing his friends to secrecy with frantic, elaborate insistence immediately after the ghost's departure. Confidentiality helps to explain 'the ritualistic tone in which the duty of preserving secrets is repeatedly set forth in professional oaths and codes of ethics', she writes. 'Still more is needed, however, to explain the sacrosanct nature often ascribed to this duty.'[21] Professional dimensions of secrecy are not too far removed from *Hamlet*. An ecstatic fervour marks Hamlet once the ghost has made its pronouncements, and the urgency with which he guarantees the silence of Horatio and Marcellus smacks of the ceremonial of an arcane religious ritual. Now that he owns the ghost's knowledge, it is as if the transformed Hamlet has successfully passed through an initiation rite.

In *The History of Carolina* (1714), John Lawson describes the practice of '*Husquenawing*' common to some native American tribes. During the ceremony, which is intended to instil reverence towards superiors, young men are imprisoned in a house of correction where they are starved in darkness:

> Besides, they give them Pellitory-Bark, and several intoxicating Plants, that make them go raving mad as ever were any People in the World; and you may hear them make the most dismal and hellish Cries, and Howlings, that ever humane Creatures express'd; all which continues about five or six Weeks, and the little Meat they eat, is the nastiest, loathsome stuff, and mixt with all manner of Filth it's possible to get. After the Time is expired, they are brought out of the Cabin, which never is in the Town, but always a distance off, and guarded by a Jaylor or two, who watch by Turns. Now, when they first come out, they are as poor as ever any Creatures were; for you must know several die under this diabolical Purgation. Moreover, they either really are, or pretend to be dumb, and do not speak for several Days; I think, twenty or thirty; and look gastly, and are so chang'd, that it's next to an Impossibility to know them again, although you was never so well acquainted with them before.[22]

Many cultures have elaborated rites of passage during which the adolescents of the community are separated, tested and finally granted a more mature status, often being offered secret gifts of wisdom and experience that accompany the shedding of old dependencies and the assumption of new responsibilities. Through ceremonies of induction, the novice enters the adult world in a ritualized enactment of the movement from one stage of development to the next.[23]

Celebrations of the young person's incorporation into a new community are charged with local meanings and associations. It would be unwise to argue for generalized patterns which overcome historical contingencies. However, prudence cannot totally foreclose a discursive correspondence between the broad outlines of Lawson's description, whose general features reappear in countless other accounts, and Hamlet's behaviour. Quickly following upon the ghost's revelation is Ophelia's report of Hamlet's appearance in her chamber:

> Lord Hamlet, with his doublet all unbrac'd,
> No hat upon his head, his stockings foul'd,
> Ungarter'd and down-gyved to his ankle,
> Pale as his shirt, his knees knocking each other,
> And with a look so piteous in purport
> As if he had been loosed out of hell
> To speak of horrors, he comes before me.

(II. i. 78-84)

Apart from the suggestions of sexual assault and the familiar metaphors of exposure, the passage is striking as it enlists initiation rite motifs — the dirt, pallor, dumb language, seeming madness and infernal connotations. It is as if Hamlet, no longer in the first flush of youth, has belatedly undergone a rude, cathartic awakening, and has been admitted to terrifying realities. In Joel Fineman's elegant but enigmatic phrase, 'Placed between maternal presence and paternal absence, Hamlet learns, and becomes, the "secret" of the primal scene.'[24] The immediate mystery of the ghost resolved, Hamlet's fate is sealed.

Sexual Places

Hamlet abounds in secret places, whether they be Ophelia's chamber, Gertrude's closet or the 'removed ground' (I. iv. 61) from which the ghost announces to Hamlet its chilling injunctions. All of these spaces are connected, and Hamlet's experience of them leads him to a confrontation with sexual forces that lurk in hiding, pushed into concealment by Elsinore's political wrangles. As Foucault points out, from the Renaissance onwards, sex was presented as 'something akin to a secret ... [a] disquieting enigma: not a thing which stubbornly shows itself, but one which always hides, the insidious presence that speaks in a voice so muted and often disguised that one risks remaining deaf to it.'[25] In fairy tales, too, such as 'Bluebeard' or 'The Enchanted Pig', a child discovers forbidden information by unlocking the door of a secret place or room where are kept books or evidence of carnal knowledge.[26] About sex in *Hamlet* there gathers conflict, restriction and covert argument. Whatever secretively took place between Claudius and Gertrude prior to the murder of Hamlet senior is hedged about with silences, ambiguities and nervous speculations. In particular Ophelia suffers at the hands of a system which outlaws and straightjackets the expression of unhindered sexuality. She is advised by Laertes not to 'open' her 'chaste treasure' to Hamlet's 'unmaster'd importunity' (I. iii. 31-2); virginity is a precious item in a coffer's inventory, to be prized and removed from contact. Her beauty, similarly, should not be allowed to 'unmask' (I. iii. 37) itself, an ironic choice of word as this applies more to Hamlet who wishes to strip off the smooth urbanity that cloaks Claudius's villainy. The logical extension of these practices of sexual containment is Ophelia's madness and her song about Saint Valentine's day duplicity:

> Tomorrow is Saint Valentine's day,
>   All in the morning betime,
> And I a maid at your window,
>   To be your Valentine.
> Then up he rose, and donn'd his clo'es,
>   And dupp'd the chamber door,
> Let in the maid that out a maid
>   Never departed more.

(IV. v. 48-55)

Metaphorically, in the fateful chamber, Ophelia has yielded her treasure, and the knowledge gained contributes catastrophically to the sequence of events culminating in her death. A tone of sombre, chastened reflection informs these scenes which forcefully communicate the extremity of Ophelia's chaotic condition. The issues represented here also spill over into other parts of the play. The king's spies, Rosencrantz and Guildenstern, joke together saying that they live in the 'privates' (II. ii. 234) of Fortune, to which Hamlet replies: 'In the secret parts of Fortune? O most true, she is a strumpet' (II. ii. 235-6). Now a fickle woman replaces Ophelia's dissembling gentleman, but the idea of a sexuality that is or should be invisible or unintelligible is common to both types. Ballad and bawdy interchange unite in stimulating a suspicious interrogation of sexuality's enticing unknowability.[27]

The troubled soliloquies, whispered conversations and hushed, ghostly introductions that lend *Hamlet* its air of secrecy combine with constructions of woman in a dislocating anatomization of practices that are never clearly defined, but only hinted at through the use of euphemisms and rhetorical figures. Metaphor and metonymy rule the sexual discussion of *Hamlet*, miming the features of Renaissance legal treatments of the subject. The etymological roots of 'secret' and 'sex' are the same, and in contemporary judicial discourses 'secrets' indicated the sexual parts.[28] In addition, women were traditionally perceived either as themselves 'secrets', embodying the secrets of life, or as 'leaky vessels' incapable of respecting the confidences with which they were entrusted.[29] It is less the language of the courthouse which colours *Hamlet*, however, than the insecurities fostered in a society ruled over by a sovereign in whom the boundaries between male and female were indistinct. A woman occupying a traditionally male position, Elizabeth was princess and prince to her people at one and the same time. Although she played multiple sexual roles with delighted ease — idealized shepherdess, besieged mistress and chaste goddess — she was still mysterious, virginal, protective of her secret self.[30] The single status she maintained was her greatest political asset; consequently, negotiations for possible marriages were enveloped in secrecy and subterfuge. Anticipating a visit by Francis of Valois, the Duke of Alençon, one of her suitors, Elizabeth wrote to her ambassador in France in 1574: 'For that if there follow no liking between us after a view taken the one of the other, the more secretly it be handled, the less touch will it be to both our honours.'[31] But the idea Elizabeth popularized, that she was wife and mother to the nation, could not remain unchallenged. An unmarried woman was an ideological anomaly in the English Renaissance, a monstrous curiosity who would provoke salacious conjecture. Quarter sessions of the period overflow with seditious remarks, many of them directed against Elizabeth; in 1590, two Essex peasants came before the authorities for having claimed that the queen had secretly delivered two children, and that the Earl of Leicester, the father, had left them in a chimney to be burnt alive. A Colchester yeoman, Thomas Wenden, was punished in about the same year for alleging that Elizabeth was 'an arrant whore'.[32] These cases throw light on the predicament of a female ruler steering a course between wielding male prerogatives and performing the part of a delighted recipient of her courtiers' attentions. They convey a powerful sense of limited possibilities, of the constrictions of *Hamlet* and the embittered sexual comment which is its hallmark, and the contradictions with which Elizabeth wrestled as she sought to establish her political place in the face of forces both oppositional and intransigent.

Political Secrets

The sequestration of Ophelia and her accompanying collapse direct attention to the means by which Elsinore constructs itself as a political system. Most obviously, Claudius relies upon techniques of surveillance, arguing that they are legitimate ways of exerting authority as leader of a state. Contemporary thinkers approved in principle of espionage as a justifiable weapon to be employed by sixteenth- and seventeenth-century rulers, and also held that spies needed to be chosen with the utmost rigour and care. Giovanni Botero observed in *The Reason of State*, published in Italian in 1589, that since 'counsellors and ambassadors, secretaries and spies are those who deal most often with secret matters, they should be selected for their acute minds and for their taciturnity'.[33] Claudius takes this advice to heart and makes full use of the willingness of his servants to eavesdrop upon his subjects, but the transparent Rosencrantz and Guildenstern, and the garrulous Polonius, would seem to be unfit candidates for the model agents Botero recommends.

Foucault remarks that secrecy is 'indispensable to ... [the] operation [of power] ... power imposes secrecy on those whom it dominates'.[34] It is a formulation pertinent to *Hamlet*, to the desperate methods hatched by Claudius to tighten his tenuous hold on a kingdom threatened from within, by Hamlet, and from without, by Norwegian insurgences. With little compunction he dispatches Voltimand and Cornelius to Old Norway to work in secret to young Fortinbras's disadvantage. A similar partnership is shared by Rosencrantz and Guildenstern: they are appointed to find out about Hamlet's bizarre distemper, later assuming the mantle of hired murderers. Throughout, their behind-the-scenes conduct disrupts the flow of social intercourse; Hamlet attacks their 'secrecy to the King' (II. ii. 294) and maintains, since they have purposes which they do not reveal, that he enjoys an equivalent privilege: 'That I can keep your counsel and not mine own' (IV. ii. 10). Everything recovered in Elsinore falls prey to public scrutiny, and even Hamlet's private letters to Ophelia are not exempt from being read aloud in court.[35] The need to police, inform and control what are seen to be deviancies infects Denmark at every level, dislocating political and familial relationships: Polonius schools the aptly named Reynaldo in the arts of surveillance, and Laertes is obliged to return from France 'in secret' (IV. v. 88).

The mechanisms of surveillance in Elsinore express themselves in a number of ways. They are immediately apprehended in acts of secreting, and Polonius is the most diligent and enthusiastic of practitioners. With Claudius he decides to 'bestow' (III. i. 44) himself to overhear private conversations. Once discovered by Hamlet behind the arras in Gertrude's chamber, he is dispatched, taking his information with him in death.[36] As Hamlet says: 'This counsellor / Is now most still, most secret, and most grave, / Who was in life a foolish prating knave' (III. iv. 215-17). When it comes to Polonius's burial, he is put to rest 'hugger-mugger' (IV. v. 84) or secretively. The bumbling politician who prided himself on his skills in concealment is rewarded with an apposite tribute, an anonymous funeral at which no guest is present.

Articles which are secreted can turn rank and poisonous. The body decays, corrupts and becomes the feeding-ground for bacteria; politic worms make a meal of Polonius's corpse. Terms referring to opening and closing distinguish *Hamlet*'s exploration of secrecy; a similarly emphatic set of metaphors locates itself in disease and illness. 'Here is your husband, like a mildew'd ear / Blasting his wholesome brother' (III. iv. 64-5) says Hamlet, threatening Gertrude with images of his father and uncle. In a shrewd impersonation of ignorance born out of sympathy, Claudius pretends to have misled himself in his assessment of Hamlet:

> But so much was our love,
> We would not understand what was most fit,
> But like the owner of a foul disease,
> To keep it from divulging, let it feed
> Even on the pith of life.

> (IV. i. 19-23)

'Divulging' is being used richly, I think. The term carries the sense of 'becoming public', and there is the suggestion of a spreading infection, the existence of which has been carefully hidden from knowledge. The condition afflicting Claudius brings to mind Sissela Bok's remarks on the effects of nurturing secrets over a period of time:

> The fear of conspiracies, of revenge, and of the irreversible consequences of opening Pandora's box nourishes this view, as does awareness of the corruption that secrecy can breed. Thus Jung wrote that the keeping of secrets acts like a psychic poison, alienating their possessor from the community. Like other poisons, he wrote, it may be beneficial in small doses, but its destructive power is otherwise great.[37]

The strategies adopted by Claudius have as their objective the validation of what is already an uncertain claim to royal authority. But Hamlet flushes out or finds out his inefficient intelligencers; the rottenness in Denmark grows unabated, while a racked Claudius festers from within, consumed by an experience that he does not dare to put into words.

Stories and Confessions

Traditionally poison, infection and secrecy have formed an uneasy alliance. Keeping secrets is often regarded as a species of transgression which can only result in the owner being rewarded with eventual illness. It is a relationship which can be taken back to early hypnotists and doctors who, by bringing into the open painful secrets, aimed to cure the afflictions of their patients. Only by confession, the Christian fathers held, could such poisons be purged and the sufferer be restored to wholeness and grace.[38] Admitting to secrets entailed absolution, reintegration into the community and the banishment of intolerable, extreme experiences.

Not one but several confessions interlace the structure of *Hamlet*. The ghost's use of the word 'disappointed' (I. v. 77) suggests that the last rite of absolution was not ministered, and Hamlet is the first to hear its confessional revelations. Hamlet, intending to bring Claudius to justice at the performance of *The Murder of Gonzago*, later imagines an explosive disclosure prompted by an unbearable conflation of fiction and fact:

> I have heard
> That guilty creatures sitting at a play
> Have, by the very cunning of the scene,
> Been struck so to the soul that presently
> They have proclaim'd their malefactions.

> For murder, though it have no tongue, will speak
> With most miraculous organ.

> (II. ii. 584-90)

Tension mounts during the performance as Hamlet fears that the players will reveal the design: 'The players cannot keep counsel: they'll tell all' (III. ii. 137-8). But Claudius's longed-for confession is not forthcoming on this occasion; Hamlet must wait until he comes across the king at prayer, and even then he arrives too late. Claudius complains:

> Pray can I not,
> Though inclination be as sharp as will,
> My stronger guilt defeats my strong intent,
> And, like a man to double business bound,
> I stand in pause where I first begin,
> And both neglect.

> (III. iii. 38-43)

For Hamlet and Claudius, the confession backfires and is anti-climactic. The secret is confessed in secret; Hamlet enters only after the declaration has been completed, and there will be no public outcry to support him in his endeavour. Potentially a murderer, Hamlet here becomes an unpunctual father confessor, frozen into immobility by the possibility of the repentant Claudius gaining salvation.

Treacherous currents run through *Hamlet*, a play that comes perilously close to destabilizing monarchal power and the shibboleths that propped up its institutions. The possibility that there could be royal self-exposure instilled horror in most contemporary commentators on the traditions the ruler was expected to observe. In his essays, composed between 1597 and 1625, Bacon argued that '*an Habit of Secrecy, is both Politick, and Morall*', and went on to state: 'As to *Secrecy*; *Princes* are not bound to communicate all Matters, with all *Counsellors*; but may extract and select. Neither is it necessary, that he that consulteth what he should doe, should declare what he will doe. But let *Princes* beware, that the *unsecreting* of their Affaires, comes not from Themselves.'[39] Put briefly, the ruler was obliged to shun the counsellor attempting to delve too far into royal mysteries, and to concentrate instead upon preserving an imperviousness to external influences and a veneer of studied self-sufficiency. Both Elizabeth and James subscribed to these necessities with zealous commitment.[40] More keenly than his predecessor, James developed his sublime inaccessibility into a fine art. Only occasionally was a member of his circle admitted to his personal ruminations, as when he recommended to Elizabeth in 1585 the bearer of a letter, Sir William Keith, 'Whom I have directed, not as in any public message but priuatlye, to informe yow of my secret intention in all thinges.'[41] The theme dominated James's political transactions, reaching its completest statement in *Basilikon Doron*, published in 1599, in which he informed his son that 'a King will haue need to vse secrecie in may thinges: but yet behaue your selfe so in your greatest secrets, as yee neede not bee ashamed, suppose they were all proclaimed at the mercate crosse'.[42] Embodied in the injunction is the elaboration of a strict code of ethics which can nevertheless admit of the potential for fallibility and leakage. It is possible to pinpoint in *Hamlet*, therefore, moments of subversive discontent, and the scene in which Claudius almost uncovers himself throws off echoes of contemporary worries about the insubstantiality of the royal identity and the fragility of the barriers which separated monarch from subject. Hamlet's accidental intrusion is dangerous. As Louis Adrian Montrose states: 'To "discover" the nakedness of the prince is both to locate and reveal — to demystify — the secrets of state.'[43] Balancing itself between attempts to obscure realities and equally urgent impulses to have them illuminated, *Hamlet* cuts across the fears that animated a Renaissance ruler's darkest fantasies.

In quick, narrative strokes, Shakespeare sketches patterns of concealment and exposure in *Hamlet*. One scene delineates Polonius rushing to hide behind the arras; the next shows Claudius describing his crime for the first time. An alternating between hiding and revealing is the play's structural principle, the basis of its rhythm, the chief characteristic of its movement and procedure. At many points a secret is contracted in such a way as to suggest that its contents will immediately be broadcasted, or the play implies that vital intimacies hover on the brink of discovery. No sooner has Hamlet committed himself to the trust of Horatio and Marcellus — 'But you'll be secret?' (I. v. 127) — than he refuses to publish his secret: 'There's never a villain dwelling in all Denmark / But he's an arrant knave' (I. v. 129-30). When he visits Gertrude in her closet, Hamlet warns her not to reveal his pretence of madness, and threatens drastic consequences: 'No, in despite of sense and secrecy, / Unpeg the basket on the house's top' (III. iv. 194-5). That Gertrude confirms to Claudius that Hamlet is, indeed, insane signals either her incomprehension or her confidence. In a curious grammatical construction that echoes the ghost, Hamlet promises finally to show up the seedy operations that contaminate Elsinore but retracts at the last moment:

Had I but time — as this fell sergeant, Death,
Is strict in his arrest — O, I could tell you —
But let it be.

(V. ii. 341-3)

The confession is never made and indefinitely held in abeyance. Hamlet withdraws the promise to Horatio he has only just contracted. Like the ghost, he undertakes to tell a story which fails to materialize.

Secrets and Succession

A narrative of deeper consequence was coming to an end in the later sixteenth century, and another was about to commence. The last decades of Elizabeth's reign were tense and unstable, plagued by conspiracy, rebellion, economic distress and harvest failure. Contemporaneous with *Hamlet*, usually dated 1599-1601, was widespread speculation about how long the queen's health could last, and how soon a successor might be chosen. Although the question of the succession had monopolized the early parliaments, and continued to surface at moments of crisis in the ensuing years, by 1600 it seems to have fallen dormant. There was no 'golden speech' in which Elizabeth categorically identified a replacement, but few could doubt the most likely candidate. That James VI of Scotland would ascend to the throne appears to have been an open secret. Or perhaps not. After the ill-fated affair of the 1580s, James had quelled his Machiavellian dissimulations. But the 1590s show him renewing scheming contrivances, commending himself indiscriminately to various catholics, and corresponding with Florence and with Tyrone, in anticipation of being elected to the English monarchy.[44] Most intriguing were the letters that passed between James and Cecil in which preparations were made for the Scottish king's assumption of duties and London arrival. Complex numerological codes prevented the identities of the writers from being known; they constituted a private language designed to foil Elizabeth's intercepting agents. In 1601 James wrote to Cecil, concluding 'And in the meantime ye may rest assured of the constant love and secrecy of Your most loving and assured friend, 30.'[45] When in 1602 he brought into the plan a new recruit, possibly Charles Howard, Earl of Nottingham, James wrote: 'so have I for the present no other recompense to send you for your goodwill but my faithful promise that all my dealing with you shall ever be accompanied with these three qualities: honesty, secrecy, and constancy.'[46] The final days of Elizabeth were fast approaching. At first, her illness was kept secret but, when it became obvious that she would not live, her condition was made public. Without voice as death neared, she nominated with signs her successor, James, who may now have been able to convince himself that his furtive ventures had resulted in a tangible achievement.

Pages of critical exegesis have dwelt upon the eerie conjunction of Elizabeth's nomination of James, and Hamlet's election of Fortinbras with his dying voice. The house of Hamlet, like the house of Tudor, labours under a sentence of death. It is not the uniqueness of the parallel to which I am drawn, however; rather, the process whereby Hamlet comes to elect the Norwegian prince is what prompts interest. As the play proceeds, an audience is bombarded with conflicting messages concerning the Danish monarchy, not one of which appears to be privileged. On the issue of the succession, *Hamlet* prevaricates; in the same way, Elizabeth's reign was characterized by a singular insecurity about the continuation of her royal line. For much of the play, who precisely is the rightful heir is not made clear, although it seems that Hamlet will be king eventually. But cryptic remarks continually disallow such a straightforward reading, as in the second scene when Claudius refers to Gertrude as a 'jointress' (I. ii. 9), implying that she, too, has a legitimate claim. The hint, voiced later, that Claudius usurped the throne (III. iv. 96-101) adds to the confusion, as do passing comments in act four which suggest that Hamlet may accede with the help of popular protest. In a startling *volte-face*, act five abruptly establishes that Denmark is an elective rather than a hereditary system. What galls Hamlet is that Claudius 'Popp'd in between th'election and my hopes' (V. ii. 65), and Fortinbras offers corroboration of the elective process on taking control (V. ii. 402). Until this point, the subject of the future of the state has been shrouded in obscurity. As E. A. J. Honigmann states: 'the mystery of the Danish succession only yields its secret' in the final scene.[47] His observation invites a reconsideration of the plight of England as the Elizabethan period drew to a close. Years of uncertainty culminated in the investment of James at Elizabeth's death; the knowledge that Hamlet, having been deprived of the opportunity to assume power, can elect Fortinbras, finally resolves the play of its contradictions. It is as if the doubts riddling *Hamlet* follow the contours of the questions never answered by Elizabeth, a sovereign destined to die, like Hamlet, without issue, unable to pass on her inheritance to a direct descendant.

Often Shakespearean plays cast glances ahead to the restitution of order when they close, but critical argument can only confine itself to the evidence presented within the parameters of the text. However, Horatio's pat summary to Fortinbras of the action does not bode well for the unravelling of difficulties. As Terence Hawkes suggests, Horatio's rehearsal 'mocks at the subtleties, the innuendoes, the contradictions, the imperfectly realized motives and sources for action that have been exhibited to us.'[48] Another Claudius, it seems as if Horatio will only obscure secrets rather than allowing them to see revealment. Fortinbras, the arch-exponent of what Sissela Bok terms 'military secrecy', as he relies upon 'surprise and stratagems', is bent more upon removing the carnage and proclaiming his victory.[49] While Horatio is determined that events in Elsinore be generally known — 'let me speak to th'yet unknowing world' (V. ii. 384) — Fortinbras cleverly manages to make sure that the story will first be heard by a select, private gathering, thereby suppressing what might constitute threatening political secrets: 'Let us haste to hear it, / And call the noblest to the audience' (V. ii. 391-2).[50] What that audience hears is not for the ears of the spectators in the theatre; the play ends with the shadowy Fortinbras stifling elucidation, not encouraging it, and with another act of deferral.

Conclusions

The text of *Hamlet* covers and exposes its meanings (it dilates and contracts with the diastole-stystole beat of a heart), but it also teases phenomenologically, constantly promising to show itself but usually yielding only a glimpse of its secret interior. With reference to *Hamlet*, Patricia Parker has touched upon this aspect, writing: 'Derrida's punning "différance" is silent on this third term from that single Latin root, that of *dilatio* or dilation, which in Renaissance usage in its verbal form meant not only to expand, disperse, or spread abroad but also to put off, postpone, prolong, or protract — meanings that still linger in the modern English "dilatory".'[51] To identify the postponements of *Hamlet* is a prolegomenon to a longer critique. What I have attempted to illustrate is the relationship between *Hamlet*'s deferrals and politics, the ways in which the play thematizes the various secret processes whereby power was perpetuated in the English Renaissance. My reading is that Shakespeare's drama has a charged place in a culture in which notions of privacy were being hotly debated, in which dangerous letters concerning the state of the kingdom circulated, and in which the strains and stresses of a monarchy in eclipse fuelled deep-seated political tensions. *Hamlet* coincides with floods of espionage in the later sixteenth century, with gloomy forebodings about the condition of the nation, with scurrilous insinuations about the queen's sexual status, and with anxieties about her vulnerability — activities and preoccupations which impinge upon the course of the play's trajectory. Embedded in *Hamlet* are radical energies, a dissatisfaction with the politics of secrecy, and a demythologizing, dismantling treatment of arcane royal ceremonies. Two questions would seem to arise from this critical stance. What was the 'fate' of England, and who was 'privy' to it? Yet Shakespeare does not pose dilemmas so baldly, nor does he often deal in the currency of direct political allusions. More diffuse and subtler effects are achieved by the dramatist. The rhythms of the play, however, continually lead back to matters of contemporary import, to Elizabeth's hesitancy to name a successor, to the rituals that would surround her death, to the awakening of a new Stuart dynasty, and to the rites that James, in his inauguration as king, would experience. This is the sense in which it might be possible to begin to talk about the prophetic soul of the play, not the prince.

Both Elizabeth and James had frequent recourse to an identical formula. When they needed to put off answering delicate questions, they argued that God alone knew all secrets and could bring them from the gloom where they lurked into brightness. Angrily responding to parliament in 1586 on the subject of Mary Stuart, Elizabeth stated: 'If there be any that think I have prolonged the time of purpose to make a counterfeit show of clemency, they do me the most undeserved wrong, as He knoweth, which is the Searcher of the most secret thoughts of the heart.'[52] Likewise, in *Basilikon Doron* (1599), James observed that '*the deepest of our secrets, cannot be hidde from that all-seeing eye, and penetrant light, piercing through the bowels of very darkenesse it selfe.*'[53] Most sixteenth- and seventeenth-century reformers would have endorsed these sentiments, although they might have added that every secret would be revealed with the second coming of Christ.[54] There is not the merest suggestion of such justice informing *Hamlet*. The last scene offers little divine comfort to dispel the grim truths it reinforces. Towards an intensification of confusion and a thickening of mystification is the direction in which the play tends. Hamlet's spiritual fate is in doubt, as Horatio's worried invocation of the flights of angels indicates. Horatio muddles his unfolding of the secrets of Elsinore, and Fortinbras's political programme remains chillingly sketchy and enigmatic. No final word of judgement cuts through the clouds of uncertainty. No revelation is at hand, no key available to unlock the contents of the heart. The only assurance is engulfment by an ineluctable darkness.

Notes

1. Sir John Hayward, *Annals of the First Four Years of the Reign of Queen Elizabeth*, ed. John Bruce, Camden Society, 7 (1840), p. 15.

2. William Camden, *The History of the Most Renowned and Victorious Princess Elizabeth, Late Queen of England: Selected Chapters*, ed. Wallace T. MacCaffrey (Chicago and London: Chicago University Press, 1970), p. 89.

3. John Bruce, ed., *Letters of Queen Elizabeth and James VI of Scotland*, Camden Society, 46 (1849), p. 169. See also George P. Rice, ed., *The Public Speaking of Queen Elizabeth: Selections from Her Official Addresses* (New York: Columbia University Press, 1951), pp. 66, 90.

4. For derivations, see Page duBois, *Torture and Truth* (New York and London: Routledge, 1991), p. 129; Rudolf Ekstein and Elaine Caruth, 'Keeping Secrets' in Peter L. Giovacchini, ed., *Tactics and Techniques in Psychoanalytic Theory* (London: Hogarth, 1972), p. 200; Albert Gross, 'The Secret', *Bulletin of the Menninger Clinic*, 15 (1951), 38; Arnaud Lévy, 'Évaluation Étymologique et Sémantique du Mot "Secret"', *Nouvelle Revue de Psychanalyse*, 14 (1976), 117-29; Russell Meares, 'The Secret', *Psychiatry*, 39 (1976), 261; William W. E. Slights, 'Secret Places in Renaissance Drama', *University of Toronto Quarterly*, 59 (1990), 364; Gérard Vincent, 'The Secrets of History and the Riddle of Identity' in Antoine Prost and Gérard Vincent, eds, *A History of Private Life: Riddles of Identity in Modern Times* (Cambridge, Mass: Harvard University Press, 1991), p. 163.

5. On secrets and closed associations, see F. G. Bailey, *Gifts and Poison: The Politics of Reputation* (Oxford: Blackwell, 1971), p. 291; Gordon Hutner, *Secrets and Sympathy: Forms of Disclosure in Hawthorne's Novels* (Athens and London: University of Georgia Press, 1988), pp. 3-4; Douglas H. Johnson, 'Criminal Secrecy: The Case of the Zande "Secret Societies"', *Past and Present*, 130 (1991), 170-200; Evelyn Fox Keller, 'From Secrets of Life to Secrets of Death' in Mary Jacobus, Evelyn Fox Keller and Sally Shuttleworth, eds, *Body / Politics: Women and the Discourses of Science* (New York and London: Routledge, 1990), p. 178; D. A. Miller, 'Secret Subjects, Open Secrets', *Dickens Studies Annual*, 14 (1985), 17-38; J. M. Roberts, *The Mythology of the Secret Societies* (London: Secker & Warburg, 1972).

6. Elizabeth L. Eisenstein, *The Printing Press as an Agent of Change: Communications and cultural transformations in early-modern Europe*, 2 vols (Cambridge: Cambridge University Press, 1979), I, 270; Lois Potter, *Secret rites and secret writing: Royalist lit-

erature, 1641-1660 (Cambridge: Cambridge University Press, 1989); Stephen R. Smith, 'The London Apprentices as Seventeenth-Century Adolescents', *Past and Present*, 61 (1973), 149-61.

7. Catherine Belsey, *The Subject of Tragedy: Identity and difference in Renaissance drama* (London and New York: Methuen, 1985), p. 41.

8. Frank Kermode, *The Genesis of Secrecy: On the Interpretation of Narrative* (Cambridge, Mass: Harvard University Press, 1979), pp. 79, 144. Kermode's views are elaborated in his 'Secrets and Narrative Sequence' in W. J. T. Mitchell, ed., *On Narrative* (Chicago and London: University of Chicago Press, 1981), pp. 79-97.

9. Katharine Eisaman Maus, 'Proof and Consequences: Inwardness and Its Exposure in the English Renaissance', *Representations*, 34 (1991), 29-30. See also Anne Ferry, *The 'Inward' Language: Sonnets of Wyatt, Sidney, Shakespeare, Donne* (Chicago and London: University of Chicago Press, 1983), pp. 8-9, 29; Bruce R. Smith, *Homosexual Desire in Shakespeare's England: A Cultural Poetics* (Chicago and London: University of Chicago Press, 1991), p. 235.

10. See Jonathan Goldberg, *James I and the Politics of Literature: Jonson, Shakespeare, Donne, and Their Contemporaries* (Baltimore and London: The Johns Hopkins University Press, 1983), p. 150.

11. Sissela Bok, *Secrets: On the Ethics of Concealment and Revelation* (Oxford and Melbourne: Oxford University Press, 1984), pp. 10-11.

12. The metaphor of Denmark as a prison is made explicit in the version of *Hamlet* printed in the first folio; see *Mr. William Shakespeares comedies, histories, & tragedies* (London, 1623; S.T.C. 22373), p. 262.

13. Margaret W. Ferguson, '*Hamlet*: letters and spirits' in Patricia Parker and Geoffrey Hartman, eds, *Shakespeare and the Question of Theory* (New York and London: Methuen, 1985), p. 300.

14. G. P. V. Akrigg, ed., *Letters of King James VI and I* (Berkeley, Los Angeles and London: University of California Press, 1984), p. 56.

15. Akrigg, ed., *Letters*, p. 59.

16. Bruce, ed., *Letters*, p. 17. It has not been categorically established that Elizabeth is responding in this letter to the correspondence of the previous year, and any argument attached to her indignation must be necessarily conjectural. Some historians hold that James deliberately encouraged policies that would have led to his mother's death; the correspondence relating to this theory is rife with references to secrets. See Robert S. Rait and Annie I. Cameron, *King James's Secret* (London: Nisbet, 1927), pp. 11, 51, 120, 131, 157, 173, 191, 197.

17. *Basilikon Doron* (1599) in Charles Howard McIlwain, ed., *The Political Works of James I* (Cambridge, Mass: Harvard University Press, 1918), p. 5.

18. Michel Foucault, *The History of Sexuality: An Introduction*, tr. Robert Hurley (Harmondsworth: Penguin, 1990), p. 42.

19. On the secrets associated with death, see Michel Foucault, *The Birth of the Clinic: An Archaeology of Medical Perception*, tr. A. M. Sheridan (London and New York: Routledge, 1989), pp. 122, 172; Thomas Whythorne, *The Autobiography*, ed. James M. Osborn (Oxford: Clarendon, 1961), p. 3.

20. Bok, *Secrets*, p. 28.

21. Bok, *Secrets*, p. 123.

22. John Lawson, *The History of Carolina; Containing the Exact Description and Natural History of that Country* (London: W. Taylor and J. Baker, 1714), p. 233.

23. M. R. Allen, *Male Cults and Secret Initiations in Melanesia* (Melbourne: Melbourne University Press, 1967), pp. 6-7; Bruno Bettelheim, *Symbolic Wounds: Puberty Rites and the Envious Male* (London: Thames and Hudson, 1955), pp. 117-19, 205, 227; Arnold van Gennep, *The Rites of Passage*, tr. Monika Vizedom and Gabrielle L. Caffee (London: Routledge & Kegan Paul, 1960), pp. 78, 81. See also Foucault, *History*, p. 57, who describes the process whereby a master instructs a disciple in the secrecies of the *ars erotica*.

24. Joel Fineman, 'Fratricide and Cuckoldry: Shakespeare's Doubles' in Murray M. Schwartz and Coppélia Kahn, eds, *Representing Shakespeare: New Psychoanalytic Essays* (Baltimore and London: The Johns Hopkins University Press, 1980), p. 106. The 'initiation' aspect of *Hamlet* has been discussed by Marjorie Garber, but she does not consider the implications of the scene in which Hamlet appears in Ophelia's chamber. See her *Coming of Age in Shakespeare* (London and New York: Methuen, 1981), pp. 198-205.

25. Foucault, *History*, p. 35. See also Michel Foucault, 'Technologies of the Self' in Luther H. Martin, Huck Gutman and Patrick H. Hutton, eds, *Technologies of the Self: A Seminar with Michel Foucault* (London: Tavistock, 1988), p. 16; Jacques Revel, 'The Uses of Civility' in Roger Chartier, ed., *A History of Private Life: Passions of the Renaissance* (Cambridge, Mass: Harvard University Press, 1989), p. 188.

26. Bruno Bettelheim, *The Uses of Enchantment: The Importance and Meaning of Fairy Tales* (New York: Vintage Books, 1977), pp. 300, 302.

27. Jacques Lacan makes a similar point about the play: 'The object of desire is essentially different from the object of any need [*besoin*]. Something becomes an object in desire when it takes the place of what by its very nature remains concealed from the subject: that self-sacrifice, that pound of flesh which is mortgaged [*engagé*] in his relationship to the signifier. This is profoundly enigmatic, for it is ultimately a relationship to something secret and hidden.' See his 'Desire and the Interpretation of Desire in *Hamlet*' in Shoshana Felman, ed., *Literature and Psychoanalysis* (Baltimore and London: The Johns Hopkins University Press, 1982), p. 28.

28. G. R. Quaife, *Wanton Wenches and Wayward Wives: Peasants and Illicit Sex in Early Seventeenth Century England* (London: Croom Helm, 1979), p. 176; Lyndal Roper, 'Will and Honor: Sex, Words and Power in Augsburg Criminal Trials', *Radical History Review*, 43 (1989), 51. See also Francis Beaumont, 'Salmacis and Hermaphroditus' (1602) in Nigel Alexander, ed., *Elizabethan Narrative Verse* (London: Arnold, 1967), l. 848.

29. Keller, 'From Secrets of Life', p. 178; Slights, 'Secret Places', 365. It is interesting to note that in *All the Kings Short Poesis*, composed in 1616-18, James writes: 'Euen so all wemen are of nature vaine / And can not keepe no secrett vnreuealed'. See James Craigie, ed., *The Poems of James VI of Scotland*, 2 vols (Edinburgh: Blackwood, 1955 and 1958), II, 92.

30. Patricia Fumerton, '"Secret" Arts: Elizabethan Miniatures and Sonnets', *Representations*, 15 (1986), 58.

31. G. B. Harrison, ed., *The Letters of Queen Elizabeth* (London, Toronto, Melbourne and Sydney: Cassell, 1935), p. 122.

32. Joel Samaha, 'Gleanings from Local Criminal Records: Sedition amongst the "Inarticulate" in Elizabethan England', *Journal of Social History*, 8 (1975), 69.

33. Giovanni Botero, *The Reason of State*, tr. P. J. and D. P. Waley (London: Routledge & Kegan Paul, 1956), p. 48. For the use of spies by Elizabeth and James, see Roland Mushat Frye, *The Renaissance 'Hamlet': Issues and Responses in 1600* (Princeton: Princeton University Press, 1984), pp. 39-40; Harrison, ed., *Letters*, pp. 64, 91. Also useful are recent studies of the Elizabethan secret service: John Bossy, *Giordano Bruno and the Embassy Affair* (New Haven and London: Yale University Press, 1991); Alan Haynes, *Invisible Power: The Elizabethan Secret Services, 1570-1603* (Far Thrupp: Allan Sutton, 1992); Charles Nicholl, *The Reckoning: The Murder of Christopher Marlowe* (London: Cape, 1992); Alison Plowden, *The Elizabethan Secret Service* (Hemel Hempstead: Harvester Wheatsheaf, 1991).

34. Foucault, *History*, p. 86.

35. As Sissela Bok points out, secrecy and property are connected: 'At its root, it is closely linked to identity, in that people take some secrets, such as hidden love letters, to *belong* to them more than to others, to be *proper* to them. We link such secrets with our identity, and resist intrusions into them' (Bok, *Secrets*, p. 24). The public world of Elsinore fuels Hamlet's ruminations on his own identity.

36. Pierre Bourdieu has noted that '"Behind" is naturally associated with "inside", with ... all that is private, secret and hidden'. See his *The Logic of Practice*, tr. Richard Nice (Stanford: Stanford University Press, 1990), p. 90.

37. Bok, *Secrets*, p. 8.

38. Henri F. Ellenberger, *The Discovery of the Unconscious: The History and Evolution of Dynamic Psychology* (London: Allen Lane, 1970), p. 44; Foucault, *History*, p. 35; Neil Hertz, *The End of the Line: Essays on Psychoanalysis and the Sublime* (New York:

Columbia University Press, 1985), pp. 122-43; C. G. Jung, *Memories, Dreams, Reflections*, ed. Aniela Jaffé (London: Collins and Routledge and Kegan Paul, 1963), p. 118; C. G. Jung, *Modern Man in Search of a Soul* (London: Routledge and Kegan Paul, 1961), pp. 39, 41; Origenes Adamantius (Origen), *Hom. in Lucam* in Henry Bettenson, ed., *The Early Christian Fathers: A Selection from the Writings of the Fathers from St. Clement of Rome to St. Athanasius* (London, New York and Toronto: Oxford University Press, 1956), pp. 349-50.

39. Sir Francis Bacon, *The Essayes or Counsels, Civill and Morall*, ed. Michael Kiernan (Oxford: Clarendon, 1985), pp. 21, 65. For comparable ideas, see Sir William Cornwallis, *Essayes* (London, 1600; S.T.C. 5775), sig. E3ᵛ; Thomas Wright, *The Passions of the Minde in Generall: A Reprint based on the 1604 edition*, ed. Thomas O. Sloan (Urbana, Chicago and London: University of Illinois Press, 1971), p. 119.

40. For comparisons between Elizabeth and James on this issue, see *Secret History of the Court of James I*, 2 vols (Edinburgh: James Ballantyne, 1811), I, 69, 77, 320. Most illuminating on James's cult of secrecy is Goldberg, *James I*, pp. xii, 56, 65, 83.

41. Bruce, ed., *Letters*, p. 25.

42. *Basilikon Doron* in McIlwain, ed., *Works*, p. 44. For the fate visited upon those who were too inquisitive, see John Chamberlain, *The Letters*, ed. Norman Egbert McClure, 2 vols (Philadelphia: The American Philosophical Society, 1939), II, 14.

43. Louis Adrian Montrose, 'The Elizabethan Subject and the Spenserian Text' in Patricia Parker and David Quint, eds, *Literary Theory / Renaissance Texts* (Baltimore and London: The Johns Hopkins University Press, 1986), p. 328.

44. David Harris Willson, *King James VI and I* (London: Cape, 1966), pp. 142, 147, 148.

45. Akrigg, ed., *Letters*, p. 180. See also John Bruce, ed., *Correspondence of King James VI of Scotland*, Camden Society, 78 (1861), pp. 2, 15, 17, 18, 43, 57, 69, 72; Goldberg, *James I*, p. 70.

46. Akrigg, ed., *Letters*, p. 195.

47. E. A. J. Honigmann, 'The Politics in *Hamlet* and "The World of the Play"' in John Russell Brown and Bernard Harris, eds, *Hamlet*, Stratford-upon-Avon Studies 5 (London: Arnold, 1963), p. 139. See also Lisa Jardine, '"No offence i' th' world": *Hamlet* and unlawful marriage' in Francis Barker, Peter Hulme and Margaret Iversen, eds, *Uses of history: Marxism, postmodernism and the Renaissance* (Manchester and New York: Manchester University Press, 1991), pp. 130, 133, 138; A. P. Stabler, 'Elective Monarchy in the Sources of *Hamlet*', *Studies in Philology*, 62 (1965), 654-61.

48. Terence Hawkes, '*Telmah*' in Parker and Hartman, eds, *Shakespeare*, p. 311.

49. Bok, *Secrets*, p. 191.

50. Horatio here invokes the theory that the 'public has a right to know', itself a fallacy. 'How can one lay claims to a right to *know the truth* when even partial knowledge is out

of reach concerning most human affairs, and when bias and rationalization and denial skew and limit knowledge still further?' (Bok, *Secrets*, p. 254).

51. Patricia Parker, 'Deferral, Dilation, Différance: Shakespeare, Cervantes, Jonson' in Parker and Quint, eds, *Literary Theory / Renaissance Texts*, p. 182. Parker has in mind, I think, Derrida's essay 'Différance' which is reprinted in Peggy Kamuf, ed., *A Derrida Reader: Between the Blinds* (Hemel Hempstead: Harvester Wheatsheaf, 1991), pp. 61-79. Others have pointed out that to refuse to fix meaning is anti-theological as it implicitly resists God's word, an argument which pertains to *Hamlet*. See Roland Barthes, *Image, Music, Text*, ed. Stephen Heath (London: Fontana, 1990), p. 147; Gerald L. Bruns, *Inventions: Writing, Textuality, and Understanding in Literary History* (New Haven and London: Yale University Press, 1982), p. 18.

52. Rice, ed., *Public Speaking*, p. 93.

53. McIlwain, ed., *Works*, p. 5.

54. John E. Booty, ed., *The Book of Common Prayer 1559: The Elizabethan Prayer Book* (Charlottesville: University of Virginia Press, 1976), p. 291; John Rogers, *The displaying of an horrible secte of grosse and wicked heretiques* (London, 1579; S.T.C. 21182), sigs N1[r-v].

HAMLET'S THING

Hamlet is a play, it is to be performed.[1] And in the performance, it will unfold before the eye and for the ear. It has long been noticed that *Hamlet*
thematizes the notion of performance, with its 'play within the play'. Yet
it is less often noted that that performance is interrupted by a demand for
'Lights!', a demand that the drama end and some light be cast upon its
folds. The Oedipal drama invokes blinding, the actual murder the poisoning of the ear. By tracing the folds of the eye and the ear in the text, and
asking how they relate to the unfolding of the drama, I hope to throw some
critical light upon the enigma of *Hamlet* as a play caught between the lure
of visual representation and the grip of (the obligation to) the heard command of the Father. In each case, the play is about a certain failure of representation, an inability to *show* the enigmatic 'thing' that compels action
or grounds representation. This thing is not simply the hidden or absent
truth of a representation (a Lacanian phallus); it is a persistent irrepresent-
able presence that deconstructs representation.[2] The other name for this
'thing' is Ghost, but it may also be called language, or the Unconscious.
It names that in representation which cannot be represented, that in action
which cannot be acted out.[3] Not a signifier of difference, but a difference
with signification. The play remains for us as an enigma, not as a solution,
and that is because it stages a certain refusal, a refusal to deliver the thing
as idea (even as absent idea or idea of absence).[4] *Hamlet* is thus a founding critique of the *saturation of representation* promised by a modernist
technology that fuses seeing and hearing, *son et lumière*, the technology
that leads from the Shakespearean stage to Disneyland and the simulation
booth.

Kings and Things

'Pity me not, but lend thy serious hearing / To what I shall unfold' (I. v.
5-6). Unfolding, the demand with which the play opens: 'Stand and unfold yourself', says Francisco (I. i. 2). What will be unfolded in this most

enigmatic of plays? Two kinds of things seem to be unfolded in the play:
you may unfold a tale or a name. Barnardo responds to Francisco's demand, not with his own name, but with the name of an other, a name which
it is the business of the play to undermine:

> FRANCISCO: Nay, answer me. Stand and unfold yourself.
> BARNARDO: Long live the King!
> FRANCISCO: Barnardo?
> BARNARDO: He.
>
> (I. i. 2-5)

Under which king? Speak or die. Perhaps a king still fresh, if not in memory, at least in the grave, since as the Grave-digger tells us, your 'whoreson
dead body' (V. i. 166) 'will last you some eight year' (V. i. 161). A king who
will appear, on the stage and under it, and who will yet never be named in his
presence, who can only be named in his absence, as old Hamlet. Unless he is
named by one who bears his name, and for whom his naming is the mark of
the uncertainty of that presence: 'I'll call thee Hamlet, / King, father' (I. iv.
44-5). This is a king who remains, threatening a superfluity, both of those
called kings, and of those called Hamlet. The opening of the play introduces
a series of problems to do with naming, identity and kingly authority.

Or perhaps the king referred to by the phrase 'Long live the King!' is a king
who will not live long, a king who will never be named in the play, never
named beyond his first speech heading and entry direction. A king who is an
usurper, who relies for his kingship upon the death of that which will not stay
dead. Or maybe a player King. Or a popularly acclaimed king, the kind of
king whose power would be being invoked by the cry of a subject:

> They cry, 'Choose we! Laertes shall be king.'
> Caps, hands, and tongues applaud it to the clouds,
> 'Laertes shall be king, Laertes king.'
>
> (IV. v. 106-8)

Or a king who looked like a king, a king who found himself as monarch in
representation. A king of the stage, of the space within which these two soldiers seek their names: young Hamlet, borne to the stage:

> For he was likely, had he been put on,
> To have prov'd most royal.
>
> (V. ii. 402-3)

Or a king of action, Fortinbras, strong in arm, who is absent throughout, who enters at the end. What does 'Long live the King!' unfold? Which king? Some-body is king. 'The body is with the King, but the King is not with the body. The King is a thing', says Hamlet (IV. ii. 26-7). The king is a thing.

Point one. That which gives names is itself a thing which cannot be named except in death. Barnardo will simply identify himself following the uttering of the nameless name of the living king, 'Long live the King!' 'The play's the thing' (II. ii. 600). What sort of thing? The 'thing / Wherein I'll catch the conscience of the King' (II. ii. 600-1). To catch the conscience of the king is both to discover whether the monarch has a clean or a guilty conscience, and it is also to come to a consciousness of who is king. To catch the consciousness of kingship. Which is what Hamlet does, discovering the anonymous Claudius not to be a rightful king, but a usurper of kings who should be called Hamlet, but who are called either princes (if their name is Hamlet) or Ghost (if they are kings). At the opening of the play, 'Long live the King!' should unfold an identity, the identity of a (loyal) subject. But the king's subject, Barnardo, is not subjectively identified. He is named by the other (Francisco), and identifies himself, not in the first person, but in the third, not as 'I', but 'he'. He identifies himself in the third person, which is to say by analogy with the other. As a thing, perhaps?

The king is a thing, and the play has as many kings as it has dead bodies. One only has to enter Denmark, it seems, to be acclaimed as king, whether one is a ghost, a Norwegian rebel or a Parisian student. The problem of kingship is the problem of naming the thing that is king, 'A thing, my lord?' 'Of nothing' (IV. ii. 27-8). 'Bring me to him' (IV. ii. 28) says Hamlet, bring me to nothing. Which is what the play does. Names are ascribed, from the opening of the play, in function of this thing, the king. Yet the thing which gives names cannot itself be named, not until the last scene, not until the dying voice of Hamlet lights on Fortinbras.

Point two. The function of naming is identified as unfolding. What is to be unfolded, what is wrapped up, what is the figure in the carpet, or behind the folds of the arras? Whatever it is, it is not a simple identity. The secret of Hamlet is not, despite centuries of critical characterology, a problem of understanding, or even curing, a subjective psychosis.[5] ''Tis ... Hamlet's character', says Claudius (IV. vii. 49), but he says it of writing, of Hamlet's writing. And we know how Hamlet writes, how he signs and seals his subjectivity, the 'character' or handwriting of his messages:

HORATIO: How was this seal'd?
HAMLET: Why, even in that was heaven ordinant.
          I had my father's signet in my purse,
          Which was the model of that Danish seal,
          Folded the writ up in the form of th'other,
          Subscrib'd it, gave't th'impression, plac'd it safely,
          The changeling never known.

(V. ii. 47-53)

Hamlet signs, subscribes, but what he signs is not specified. He signs in the name of the King, but that name (especially if it is *Claudius Rex*) is never given. What is given is the form in which the letter is written, the form in which the letter is folded, 'the form of th'other'. Hamlet's character writes, and it writes fair, successfully, only insofar as it writes *in the form of the other*. The other, the thing which is nothing, which cannot be named.

The king is other to a subject. Just as for Barnardo, the naming effect of kingship is a move from subjective character to an order of thingness, an inscription of objects. Hamlet has given up his handwriting, his character, to be a king:

          I once did hold it, as our statists do,
          A baseness to write fair, and labour'd much
          How to forget that learning, but, sir, now
          It did me yeoman's service.

(V. ii. 33-6)

Point three. The thing to be unfolded is not the core of an identity. As Nicolas Abraham puts it, 'Don't most of the persons in the tragedy seem to be motivated by the stranger within them?'[6] The secret of *Hamlet* is not the depth or hidden centre of a character. The mystery of Hamlet's madness, which gives rise to so much psychologizing, both within and without the play, cannot be fathomed by an appeal to a core of identity. It lies *within* the centre of the subject, which is to say that it is not the same thing as the centre of the subject. *Hamartia*, the tragic flaw of the hero, is ignorance of circumstances. Polonius is a good Aristotelian in his attempts to read Hamlet the tragic hero, a reading which displaces the enigma of Hamlet from the centre of Hamlet's subjectivity to the question of what other thing it is which lies within that centre:

> If circumstances lead me, I will find
> Where truth is hid, though it were hid indeed
> Within the centre.

(II. ii. 157-9)

Hamlet concurs that his enigma is not that of the heart of a subject, but the enigma of the thing, other to a subject, which lies within the heart of a subject. If he is a noble hero, if his is a worthy enigma for a tragic hero, then attempts to understand his tragedy in terms of the recording of his character are a travesty, 'how unworthy a thing you make of me. You would play upon me, you would seem to know my stops, you would pluck out the heart of my mystery' (III. ii. 354-7). Such an analysis tries to make Hamlet speak like a recorder, like 'this little organ' (III. ii. 359). Yet 'murder, though it have no tongue, will speak / With most miraculous organ' (II. ii. 589-90). The heart of the mystery cannot be spoken by the subject as recorder of its own heart; a more miraculous organ is required, since truth is not the centre, but is hid indeed, as Polonius suspects, 'Within the centre' (II. ii. 159). If Hamlet were to speak his mystery, he would speak as a thing, made a thing by the other, Guildenstern. The heart of the mystery is something other than the expression of a subject. Witness Hamlet's madness:

> I will be brief. Your noble son is mad.
> Mad call I it, for to define true madness,
> What is't but to be nothing else but mad?

(II. ii. 92-4)

What is that thing, that 'it' that Polonius calls 'mad'? True madness? Then true madness is to be nothing but mad. To Define? Then to define madness is to be mad. To get to the heart of the mystery, to define true madness, is madness.

If the heart of Hamlet's mystery lies within the centre of Hamlet, it is not the centre of Hamlet as subject; Hamlet will only be unfolded by the logic of an 'it' or thing, to name or to define which is 'to be nothing else but mad'. 'Thus it remains; and the remainder thus' (II. ii. 104).

Hear Hamlet trying to speak of what lies within his centre, 'In my heart's core, ay, in my heart of heart, /As I do [wear] thee. Something too much of this' (III. ii. 73-4). At the heart of the heart is not a heart, but something too much, some thing which is too much, other to a subject that might speak it, some thing that remains. 'Thus it remains; and the remainder thus' (II. ii. 104).

The Drama Unfolds

For there is not within the play an 'idea of the play', as Ann Righter might wish.[7] The play is not an idea, it has no nature, it cannot function as the simple referent of the play, for to define a true play, what is't but to be nothing else but a play? Not that we shall just stop here, internalizing the endless self-referentiality of the literary, for that self-referentiality can only inhabit a subject, even a literary critic, as an otherness, a thing which remains and which, as it remains, is madness. The play is a thing, not an idea, nor is it neatly enfolded at the centre of the play (III. ii.), but it remains. Ghostly, it returns, upon the beating of a drum, in Horatio's feverish stage management of corpses and narration at V. ii.

What is being unfolded in this thing that is the play? It is not a self, but a thing, a nameless operation of naming, a madness it would be madness to define, a play inhabiting itself as a ghostly otherness. The name cannot be unfolded from within, and similar difficulties attend, it seems, the unfolding of tales:

> But that I am forbid
> To tell the secrets of my prison-house,
> I could a tale unfold whose lightest word
> Would harrow up thy soul, freeze thy young blood,
> Make thy two eyes like stars start from their spheres,
> Thy knotted and combined locks to part,
> And each particular hair to stand an end
> Like quills upon the fretful porpentine.

>   (I. v. 13-20)

The Ghost cannot tell, cannot unfold, but unfolds the picture of one in torment. He claims that the tale which might have this effect will not be told. Yet the effect of the appearance of the Ghost upon Hamlet is described by the Queen at III. iv.:

> Your bedded hair, like life in excrements,
> Start up and stand an end.

>   (III. iv. 121-2)

What cannot be told, it seems, can be seen. Repetitions of 'start' and 'stand an end' insist that the Ghost seems to be causing, by his image, the effect that he is forbidden to cause by his telling in I. v. There is an interdiction which enforces a disjunction of seeing and hearing:

> But this eternal blazon must not be
> To ears of flesh and blood.

(I. v. 21-2)

A blazon is, primarily, something to be seen, a heraldic image, the image of the tormented soul which is given to Hamlet as image of the effects of telling, and as effect of the image of the teller. What must not reach the ear works upon the eye of Hamlet. Hamlet has been told to 'lend thy serious hearing / To what I shall unfold' (I. v. 5-6), but nothing has been unfolded, and Hamlet seems only to have lent his eye. No wonder that the Ghost insists, 'List, list, O list' (I. v. 22), 'Now, Hamlet, hear' (I. v. 34). Does the thing, the thing which is to be unfolded, perhaps owe its resistance to this disjunction of seeing from hearing; is that distance perhaps the source of the complex web of delay, interruption, hesitation, which is the unfolding of the play? Abraham notes, against Freud, the disjunction of Hamlet from Oedipus.[8] Might we call Hamlet a failed Oedipus: one who has omitted to tear out his eyes the better to hear the command of the dead father, and who thus permits a discontinuity between the seen and the heard which would thus be the space of Hamlet's inflationary delay of murder? Let us follow up a suggestion of Jean-François Lyotard, in 'Jewish Oedipus', that 'Oedipus fulfils his desire in non-recognition; Hamlet un-fulfils his desire in representation'.[9] And this will be a tale of two organs, of what kind of organ might be miraculous enough to unfold the tale, to cry out murder (II. ii. 590), to reveal the heart of Hamlet's mystery (III. ii. 359), of what kind of organ Laertes would have to be for action to be unfolded, when he asks that it may be so devised, 'That I might be the organ' (IV. vii. 69). And the organs upon which the play constantly plays are the eye and the ear, 'the whole ear of Denmark' (I. v. 36), 'the porches of my ears' (I. v. 63), 'All given to mine ear' (II. ii. 127), 'our duty in his eye' (IV. iv. 6), 'In ear and ear' (IV. v. 94), '*to see your kingly eyes*' (IV. vii. 43-4). Something too much of this.[10]

The play opens with two unfoldings, that of Barnardo, heard but not seen, and that of the Ghost, seen but not heard. When the Ghost finally speaks and is heard by Hamlet, it is when no one but Hamlet can see it, not Horatio and the officers, in whose presence it remains mute, nor Gertrude, to whom it remains invisible, even as its command to Hamlet is to let her hear its commands, 'Speak to her, Hamlet' (III. iv. 115). Polonius hides behind the arras, not to be unseen, but to be unheard, 'I'll silence me even here' (III. iv. 4). Enfolded, he is heard but not seen, and killed because of that disjunction between the eye and the ear.

Commands are received by the ear; the mere appearance of the Ghost would not have been enough for Hamlet, 'Say why is this? Wherefore? What should we do?' (I. iv. 57). It is through the ear that we are impelled to action. The ear receives the command of the father; it is bound:

> HAMLET: Speak, I am bound to hear.
> GHOST: So art thou to revenge when thou shalt hear.

(I. v. 6-7)

The ear moves to action, and Hamlet appears to be prepared to respond to the call, steeled for the action which the Ghost's call demands:

> My fate cries out
> And makes each petty artire in this body
> As hardy as the Nemean lion's nerve.
> Still am I call'd.

(I. iv. 81-4)

Why is it that Hamlet, called repeatedly, does not act? What transforms the continued calling of the dead father ('still am I called') into a call to stillness, to inaction? Well might we call him 'still'. What is this call that takes prisoner his ear, only to leave him inactive, leading to the Pyrrhic victory of the denouement, in which revenge is achieved only at the cost of so many deaths including his own?

'I will be brief' (II. ii. 92). 'Brief let me be' (I. v. 59). This very long play constantly returns to the theme of brevity, interrupts itself to demand brevity. And Hamlet delays. The play's perhaps the thing here:

> *Th' unnerved father falls. Then senseless Ilium,*
> *Seeming to feel this blow, with flaming top*
> *Stoops to his base, and with a hideous crash*
> *Takes prisoner Pyrrhus' ear. For lo, his sword,*
> *Which was declining on the milky head*
> *Of reverend Priam, seem'd i' th' air to stick;*
> *So, as a painted tyrant, Pyrrhus stood,*

> *And like a neutral to his will and matter,*
> *Did nothing.*

(II. ii. 470-8)

There is only one fall here, that of the father, Priam, who is metonymically Ilium (a metonymy enforced by the gendered pronoun 'his' for the city-state). That the sound should move Pyrrhus to inaction, given that his return to making mincemeat of the aged follows immediately, might seem inexplicable, unless we were to take note of a certain shift of organs which the death of the father seems to impose upon Pyrrhus in this speech chosen by Hamlet. *'For lo'*, this sound at once becomes a visual image: Pyrrhus is imprisoned by the sound only insofar as he fails to listen, as silence intervenes *'As hush as death'* (II. ii. 482), to leave the actor a figure of purely figural representation, *'a painted tyrant'*. The shift from the ear to the eye suspends activity.

Hesitations: The Eye and the Ear

Hamlet's problem is perhaps that he responds to the Ghost as image, not as command, that he sees rather than hears. 'List, list, O list!' (I. v. 22) says the Ghost, who won't have told anything, but will have provided Hamlet with an image, will have turned Hamlet into the 'blazon' of his message which Hamlet's ears can't hear. And Hamlet does not so much listen to the Ghost, as list, make lists. The Ghost dwells not in his ear, but in 'the book and volume of my brain' (I. v. 103):

> My tables. Meet it is I set it down.

(I. v. 107)

Hamlet hears, but moves at once not to act, but to sit and write, to reduce the heard command into something for the eye, something which may be scanned and read, a representation. Likewise, when at the play, Hamlet insists upon the textuality of the action, 'The story is extant, and written in very choice Italian' (III. ii. 256-7). At this point, we can underline the fact that the split between the eye and the ear is not isomorphic with that between the performance and the reading of the play. Indeed, the play is not primarily either to be performed or to be read. Rather, the primacy of either form of apprehending the text is riven by the split between eye and ear. Performance offers a seeing that asks us whether we should believe our eyes when it shows us a ghost, and it offers us a hearing that tells us that the truth cannot be told, but must have recourse to dumbshow. Likewise, those of us reading the play are invited to consider the bathos of Hamlet's recourse to his 'tables'.[11]

For all his insistence on textuality, Hamlet himself is a valued figure as well as a specular image: the compliments paid to him concern his status as a fixed visual representation:

> The glass of fashion and the mould of form,
> Th'observ'd of all observers.

> (III. i. 155-6)

It is in these terms that Hamlet praises Laertes, his rival, seeking to make him his rival in specular representation, 'to make true diction of him, his semblable is his mirror and who else would trace him his umbrage, nothing more' (V. ii. 117-20).

Hamlet is told by the Ghost upon its second appearance in III. iv. to speak to his mother, an admonition which might seem strange, since that is all he has been doing to her up until the Ghost's entry. But he has not been speaking, in the sense that he has not been speaking to put words into her ear that might move her, but to leave her fixed and immobile before a specular visual image:

> QUEEN: Nay, then I'll set those to you that can speak.
> HAMLET: Come, come, and sit you down, you shall not budge.
>   You go not till I set you up a glass
>   Where you may see the inmost part of you.

> (III. iv. 16-19)

Hamlet seems obsessed by pictures, by the fact that erstwhile malcontents under his father's rule will now pay handsomely 'for his picture in little. 'Sblood, there is something in this more than natural, if philosophy could find it out' (II. ii. 362-4). Hamlet seems to have been involved in this unnatural art market, since he presents his mother with a pair of such images in III. iv., further provocation to the exasperated Ghost that he should 'Speak to her' (III. iv. 115):

> Look here upon this picture, and on this,
> The counterfeit presentment of two brothers.
> See what a grace was seated on this brow,

Hyperion's curls, the front of Jove himself,
An eye like Mars to threaten and command.

(III. iv. 53-7)

This was your husband. Look you now what follows.
Here is your husband, like a mildew'd ear
Blasting his wholesome brother. Have you eyes?
Could you on this fair mountain leave to feed
And batten on this moor? Ha, have you eyes?

(III. iv. 63-7)

Hamlet shows images, contrasting the wholesome image of Hamlet, with its 'eye like Mars' to the 'mildew'd ear' of Claudius. The move is not so much from one to another, since they are both husbands and brothers, as from eye to ear, the move which Hamlet seeks to redress. 'Have you eyes?' No, Gertrude has had no eyes, only ears, 'Eyes without feeling, feeling without sight, / Ears without hands or eyes' (III. iv. 78-9). Eyes deprived of sense and of sensation, all ears, no eyes. Speak to her, Hamlet.

There's something in this, if philosophy could find it out. 'There are more things in heaven and earth, Horatio, / Than are dreamt of in your philosophy' (I. v. 174-5). What thing more? What, more things? The play's the thing. 'What, has this thing appear'd again tonight?' (I. i. 24). The play is not an idea, but a thing, and in the play within the play, within the centre of the centre, we find the same uneasy shifting from ear to eye, as Hamlet struggles to bring the Ghost's command to visual representation. To hear would not have been enough; unfolding must take place in the visual:

I prithee, when thou seest that act afoot,
Even with the very comment of thy soul
Observe my uncle...
 .   .   .   .
                    Give him heedful note;
For I mine eyes will rivet to his face.

(III. ii. 78-85)

To psychologize here would be to make Hamlet's mistake, to identify an eye, or an I, which might bring everything to representation. To psychologize would be a viewing of the play which wouldn't be doing anything. The critic who reads the tragedy in terms of Hamlet's character can never escape mere identification or description of what comes to the eye, can never hear the command of the some thing more than the eye or the I which lies at the centre of the centre of the representation of the play, at the heart of the heart of the self. Just to perceive would be to mistake the Ghost's command for a representation, to replace a value with a sign or coin:

O good Horatio, I'll take the ghost's word for a thousand pound. Didst perceive?

(III. ii. 280-1)

Hamlet takes the Ghost's heard word to be visually representable, a sum of money which might be perceived, just as he had earlier sought to set it down in his 'tables'. Moses, on Sinai, hears the divine command, the Law of the Father, sets it down on tables. Returning, he finds the people grouped around the golden calf, and breaks the tables, mindful of the way in which the attempt to represent the heard command of the Father will result in a negligence of the command to action in favour of immobility before the representational quality of the visible object. Hamlet's play remains unfinished, once it has been seen; no more is to be spoken, and we are referred to the (visible) text, to what we 'shall see anon' (III. ii. 257). The play within the play is not a command; it is 'the image of a murder' (III. ii. 233). Hamlet's play is the constant effort to reduce the spoken: beginning in dumb show, and ending on a stage direction for unspoken action. If you are worried that it does contain speech, and that the remainder that we shall see is reported orally, remember that Hamlet's *Mousetrap* is distinguished from Shakespearean dramatic practice, and is very like its contemporary dramas, in its use of a dumb show, the dumb show Hamlet ridicules as 'inexplicable' at III. ii. 12. The dumb show is inexplicable, even if it tells the whole story; it marks a distinction from the ear, which is linked to judgement throughout the play — Claudius says to Laertes, 'your wisest friends ... / shall hear and judge' (IV. v. 201-2); the 'knowing ear' (IV. vii. 3) is contrasted to the susceptibility to mere appearances of the seeing eye. The purpose of the play, according to Hamlet, is to reduce nature to the visible, to the specular image, 'the purpose of playing, whose end, both at the first and now, was and is to hold as 'twere the mirror up to nature' (III. ii. 20-2). Hamlet's play, at the centre of the play, is a drive to representation, to the visible, a drive to make visible the heard command. And in this shift from the eye to the ear lies a hesitation.

There is a thing, a resistance to representation, a hesitation between the eye and the ear, something which will not be seen. If the ear impels to act, if the eye impels to specular immobility, in between them there is a hesitation. Hamlet's hesitation. As Hamlet says, 'I do not know / Why yet I live to say this thing's to do' (IV. iv. 43-4). The play's the thing. The play is always, in a sense, yet to do. The play is not an action, it is a delay, a hesitation between two organs.

It would be a work requiring more space than is at my disposal here to chart the interruptions, the suspensions, the hesitations, the delays, so frequent in Hamlet as not to impede the play so much as to make it up. And what might be seen or heard would be that those interruptions are linked to a shifting between the ear and the eye. I will be brief concerning interruptions. Let us take one example. Ghosts, by definition, don't 'really' exist, don't exist as real, so that it is always difficult to be sure that a seen ghost is not merely an illusion. On this question, the judgement of Horatio is already divided, poised and hesitating, between eye and ear:

> BARNARDO: It would be spoke to.
> MARCELLUS: Question it, Horatio.
> HORATIO: What art thou that usurp'st this time of night,
>   Together with that fair and warlike form
>   In which the majesty of buried Denmark
>   Did sometimes march? By heaven, I charge thee speak.
> MARCELLUS: It is offended.
> BARNARDO: See, it stalks away.
> HORATIO: Stay, speak, speak, I charge thee speak.   *Exit Ghost*
> MARCELLUS: 'Tis gone and will not answer.

(I. i. 48-55)

The encounter with the Ghost is described entirely in terms of an imperative or set of imperatives from the Ghost, and from those who see it, to speak. Yet when Horatio speaks, shifts from the seen to the heard, the Ghost is offended, and its appearance interrupted. This will happen again, when the Ghost will refuse to speak and to appear at the same time, except to Hamlet, who thus carries within his centre the dire discontinuity between seeing and hearing, inaction and action, which is hesitation itself.

The second appearance of the Ghost likewise suspends the unfolding of a tale to the ear: as Horatio seeks to prepare a narrative of the future (like Barnardo's suspended narrative of the past), the Ghost enters to be greeted as a visual event demanding silence. However, once that silence is modulated by a movement rather than a specular stillness, Horatio seeks to recall it to either the visual or the audible, to escape the hesitation between them:

Enter GHOST.

HORATIO: But soft, behold. Lo, where it comes again.
I'll cross it though it blast me.   *Ghost spreads its arms.*
                              Stay, illusion:
If thou hast any sound or use of voice,
Speak to me.
If there be any good thing to be done
That may to thee do ease, and grace to me,
Speak to me;
If thou art privy to thy country's fate,
Which, happily, foreknowing may avoid,
O speak;
Or if thou hast uphoarded in thy life
Extorted treasure in the womb of earth,
For which they say your spirits oft walk in death,
Speak of it, stay and speak.   *The cock crows.*

(I. i. 129-42)

Speech would involve action; it would be a command to do some good thing, and hence the Ghost cannot stay, and speak, at the same time. Let us pause for one more example of delay, of pause, of interruption, intervening as the gap between the organs. When Claudius sends Hamlet away, to England, he insists that it must seem 'Deliberate pause' (IV. iii. 9) because the people have shifted from the ear, the organ associated with judgement, to the eye. They won't listen to what Hamlet has done, they only recognize him as a specular image, they 'like not in their judgment but their eyes' (IV. iii. 5). This produces neither action nor inaction, but an action which is not an action, that paradoxical deliberate pause, a hesitation.

Why then does Hamlet hesitate? Because he cannot reconcile the heard command with visual representation. He has heard a tale which cannot be told, as the Ghost says, as his secrecy proves, and he seeks to reduce it to a visible representation, in his own hair style, in dumb show, in pictures. Caught between the ear, impelling to kinesis, and the eye, impelling to stasis, he hesitates.

Unfolding Names: Idea and Play in Language

How can we define this madness of hesitation, what name can we unfold for this thing? Let us see whether philosophy might find it out, what we might find enfolded in the name of the naming function of the two kings.

Hamlet the soliloquizer, he who says 'I'. Laertes, the people's choice, he to whom the people say 'you', whom they choose. Hamlet who says, 'I am dead', Laertes who says, 'thou art slain'. Laertes. Woven in the arras of that name, we hear, or perhaps we see, an ear, an ear that lets, that lets in sound, that listens. He listens to the voice of his father, hears Polonius's advice, and acts upon it. He listens to the voice of the people, who name him king. And in Hamlet, we find His Majesty, H. M., his majesty the ego, late, who speaks late, with a dying voice, 'I am dead', he repeats, His Majesty's tale. From Hamlet's name we can unfold his majesty's tale, to which serious hearing might be given, but only late, in death. Only in death, not 'To ears of flesh and blood' (I. v. 22). At which point my reader may be tempted to remark that this isn't reading, this is just playing with words. 'Words, words, words' (II. ii. 192).[12]

The thing, the enigma of *Hamlet*, is thus not merely the king, the Ghost, the Unconscious, but also language. This is because the linguistic subject cannot appear as itself, since the language it speaks is always that of others. That which wounds the self. Perhaps, then, if we are to look for it, we should look more closely at wounded names. Let us then return to Hamlet, His Majesty, whose name is wounded to find the 'tale' which will prevent a 'wounded name' (V. ii. 349) and 'Report me and my cause aright' (V. ii. 344). What is this insane hypogrammatization which ignores the proper reference of proper names, which finds their sense as figures, material elements, making words into objects and distinguishing the referent of the name from its signification?

The linguistic thing causes the madness of thinking words as words, as objects, as things. The madness of language in its non-referential materiality, which allows us to find a gap, a gap between the ear and the eye, between a proper name (which should refer to a unique and therefore nameable thing) and a common noun, a hesitation between Hamlet and His Majesty's tale. A figure of antonomasia, perhaps, the figure which takes the objective materiality of the word as a figure. To cross this gap, to make words of proper names, figures of discursive referents, is perhaps to hear the call of the thing that is nothing, the unnameable name. This thing would perhaps be that sense which language has in excess of any univocal signified meaning, that play (of language) which resists psychological incorporation as an idea (of meaning), which means more than it says and says more than it means. If we seek to confine language within a closed discursive system, even a system of tropes, the otherness of figurality will always appear as a tendency of words or letters to thicken into objects alien to the transparency of that system. If we seek to adhere to the visible immediacy of things, they will always appear as events, demanding to be placed within the space of a narrative. We cannot just listen, we cannot just see. We cannot live inside language, or outside with the objects, but only on the knife edge which separates them. And if we try both to see and hear at the same time, then this thing appears, this figure of difference, deviation, error, which deconstructs the opposition we seek to fuse. Hamlet is not about Hamlet, nor about H.M. tale, it is about staging the radical incommensurability of the two, which appears as a scandalous hesitation. That difference, which is improper, even in the most proper of proper names, which refuses to be recognized, and insists upon reading, upon a multiplicity of readings, that thing which always appears again, but never as itself.

But should not a play present an idea by means of staging, the fusion of hearing and seeing? Fortinbras, king of action, he who is strong in arm, enters at the end, when all of the bodies have been killed, when all of the bodies can 'High on a stage be placed to the view' (V. ii. 383), so that Horatio can tell a tale, a tale which will be the story of the play,

> So shall you hear
> Of carnal, bloody, and unnatural acts,
> Of accidental judgments, casual slaughters ...

> (V. ii. 385-7)

At the end of the play we shall both see and hear, and this will allow us to know who is king, which king will live and act, which will allow a king to be remembered, out of the dismembered heap of bodies, which will allow memory to work in the election of a monarch. This thing as play to be seen and heard would be the dialectical sublation of the paralyzing opposition of ear and eye. Remember me. As Fortinbras puts it:

> I have some rights of memory in this kingdom,
> Which now to claim my vantage doth invite me.

> (V. ii. 394-5)

This drama must be played, it is imperative that we both see and hear, see the heap of bodies in a space of public representation where it will not show 'much amiss' (V. ii. 407) as it does in the private space of the court, hear the tale which Horatio will 'Truly deliver' (V. ii. 391). It must be heard, now: 'Let us haste to hear it' (V. ii. 391). It must be seen, now: 'But let this same be presently perform'd' (V. ii. 398). It must be heard so that Hamlet's dying voice (V.

ii. 361) may light on Fortinbras, so that the strong in arm, the man of action, may become king. It must be seen

> Even while men's minds are wild, lest more mischance
> On plots and errors happen.

(V. ii. 399-400)

This tale which I, Horatio, shall truly 'deliver' will comment upon events, will be the tragedy of Hamlet, prince of Denmark, will arouse pity and fear, provoking catharsis, and thus providing dramatic closure, no more piling on of mischance upon plots and errors. Pathos as the *Aufhebung* of the hesitance-inducing opposition of eye to ear. And yet, 'Pity me not', the Ghost has said, if serious hearing is to be lent to what shall be unfolded. The union of seeing and hearing must not be reduced to an attitude of mind, a state of conscious pity and fear. The play is not an idea, it is a thing. The play is a thing which inhabits itself as an otherness. We see and hear at the same time, which does not mean that we achieve the fusion of an idea.

To close the play would be to see and hear the play at the same time with the univocity of an idea as dialectical sublation. If that were possible, then the play would not have been necessary: Hamlet's peculiar fate, which was to see and to hear the Ghost at the same time, would not have produced his hesitation. Perhaps so much critical dissatisfaction comes from the fact that critics have failed to understand Hamlet's error in seeking to unify a heard command and a visual representation, have faced the ending of the play and sought to believe that Horatio's version of the play could provide a homogenization of the seen and the heard as the representable idea of the play: an image which would unproblematically subsume both the heard and the seen, the discursive and the figural. The thing would no longer appear as the heterogeneity or disjunction between the two, there would be no more thing, no more play, just the idea of what had been seen and heard. If the history of criticism is the history of a drive to that fusion of an idea of the play of Hamlet, we may be inclined to characterize the progress of criticism as hesitant.

Criticism hesitates because this thing appears again tonight, every night that *Hamlet* is read or performed.

Notes

1. This paper was, in its initial form, a performance at the Oxford University Renaissance Seminar, following an invitation from John Carey. This is the least of my many debts of gratitude to him.

2. This sense of the thing as that which resists representation (resists becoming an object for a subject) owes much to Martin Heidegger. As Heidegger puts it in 'The Origin of the Work of Art', 'we never know thingness directly, and if we know it at all, then [we know it] only vaguely and thus require the work' [Martin Heidegger, *Poetry, Language and Thought* (New York: Harper and Row, 1971), p. 70]. See also the essay 'The Thing' in the same volume. My difference with Heidegger would be that I am less inclined to link the appearance of the thing to a notion of 'earth' (still less one of 'blood and soil'), even when that notion is nuanced as the conflict between the earth in its self-closure and the earth as it thrusts itself into a world.

3. It does *not* name Lacan's phallus as signifier of lack, an all too theatrical underpinning for representation. The thing is not an absence to which all representation seeks to become adequate, it is the uncanny presence of the *heimliche unheimliche* that representation seeks to repress when it directs itself towards an external absence, to become merely the signifier of something else. For a more detailed discussion of the theatricality of the Lacanian phallus, see my *Introducing Lyotard: Art and Politics* (London and New York: Routledge, 1991), chapter three.

4. Another reference to the Lacanian phallus as signifier of castration (loss, absence).

5. See Ernest Jones, *Hamlet and Oedipus* (New York: Norton, 1976) for a classic technical diagnosis.

6. Nicolas Abraham, *L'Écorce et le noyau* (Paris: Aubier-Flammarion, 1978), p. 448 (my translation).

7. Ann Righter, *Shakespeare and the Idea of the Play* (London: Chatto and Windus, 1962).

8. Abraham, *L'Écorce*, p. 447.

9. Jean-François Lyotard, *Driftworks*, ed. and tr. R. McKeon (New York: Columbia University Press, 1984), p. 47.

10. On the involutions of the ear in *Hamlet*, see N. Royle, 'The Distraction of "Freud"', *Oxford Literary Review*, 12 (1990), 101-38.

11. Some may be inclined to argue that Shakespeare did not write to be read. To which I would reply that the argument is simply contradictory, since it accords an authority to the author as determining instance of the production *and* reception of texts that belongs precisely to the modern age of printed books and private reading (or essentially private viewing of theatrical spectacles by spectators who are primarily *individuals*). Such a description of the subject establishes the text as virtually printed for public consumption. So, if 'Shakespeare' is what counts, then it doesn't matter whether or not he knew it was

going to be printed. For my own part, I find the question of Shakespearean prescience absolutely irrelevant to the obligation of responding to the text or performance of *Hamlet* that I have read or attended.

12. After all, what is it to anagrammatize, or more accurately, to hypogrammatize Hamlet's name, if not to see H. M. Tale at the same time as we hear 'Hamlet'? This is to see and to hear at the same time whilst being forced to recognize that the operations are distinct. At this point the name of the 'thing' is language, in its brute non-equivalence with the world of which it is both a part and an entire mirror. Hamlet the phoneme is being comprehended in a manner incommensurate with the grapheme H. M. Tale. That is, the heard 'Hamlet' is heterosemic to the seen H. M. Tale; the one is read or heard as a discursive element, a term in an unmotivated or arbitrary linguistic system, and the other is seen as a figure, a visible object whose contours are considered as motivated (though not necessarily by an intentional subject). An easy way of thinking this distinction between the unmotivated term and the motivated object is simply to consider the fact that it would make little difference to the heard significance of Hamlet were he called Piglet throughout, whilst the seen sense of the motivated object should be radically altered. This disjunction makes clear the qualitative incommensurability of the two modes of comprehension, discursive and figural, which I am assigning to the ear and to the eye.

HAMLET AND THE POLITICS OF INDIVIDUALISM

ANDREW MOUSLEY

> 'Tis not alone my inky cloak, good mother,
> Nor customary suits of solemn black,
> Nor windy suspiration of forc'd breath,
> No, nor the fruitful river in the eye,
> Nor the dejected haviour of the visage,
> Together with all forms, moods, shapes of grief,
> That can denote me truly. These indeed seem,
> For they are actions that a man might play;
> But I have that within which passes show,
> These but the trappings and the suits of woe.

> (I. ii. 77-86)

What content might we assign to that 'within', that interiority of Hamlet's? One of the problems for any exploration of the politics of individualism in *Hamlet* is the danger of homogenizing concepts of self by assuming their correspondence with later Romantic or 'liberal humanist' versions of them. If one of the functions of ideology is to produce single meanings and unitary histories for otherwise contestable terms, then perhaps one effect of an ideology of the self as author and origin of meaning has been to obscure the possibility of differently conceptualizing, and differently reading the history of, individualism.[1] It is as though the individual and the attendant notions of agency and choice inevitably belonged to the (equally homogenized) category of 'bourgeois liberal humanism' and cannot be re-defined or re-articulated.[2] So it can often appear that the only available history of the self is of the self as author, origin and separate consciousness.

Hamlet has itself recently been assigned a central role in this history, sited as a key moment in the formation of the modern subject. For Catherine Belsey in *The Subject of Tragedy*, *Hamlet* 'has begun to define an interiority as the origin of meaning and action, a human subject as agent'. Yet the play, she continues, 'cannot produce closure in terms of an analysis which in 1601 does not yet fully exist'. Belsey's enabling insistence on the *difference* of Hamlet's subjectivity from an emergent liberal humanist individualism does not, however, generate an account of any other form of subjectivity in the play. The alternative to an emergent sovereignty of the self is not another version of individualism but various residual voices of morality which are seen as speaking through the prince:

> Alternately mad, rational, vengeful, inert, determined, the Hamlet of the first four acts of the play is above all *not* an agent. It is as if the hero is traversed by the voices of a succession of morality fragments, wrath and reason, patience and resolution. In none of them is it possible to locate the essential Hamlet. In this sense Hamlet is precisely not a unified subject.[3]

How are we to move beyond what can often appear to be an irredeemable opposition between a subject-less language (here a Hamlet spoken or 'traversed by' morality fragments) and a language-less human subject (an 'essential' Hamlet)? How can we articulate subjectivity and individualism differently? The pre-modern interiority represented in *Hamlet* may provide some answers to these questions, as long as we are prepared to attend to its differences.

*

Hamlet may be seen as dramatizing the failure of ideologies fully to interpellate or precisely to 'speak through' the individual. Attempts to ascribe and determine social identity must accommodate potentially resistant individualisms and interiorities which have not yet been contracted to any particular class ideology.

The production of social identities from above thus has to reckon with a subjective dimension to politics. This is evident in the first of the play's scenes at court. In his opening speech, Claudius projects himself as the unifying representative of the new court and nation, in an attempt to effect a smooth transfer of allegiance from the old to the new regime:[4]

> Though yet of Hamlet our dear brother's death
> The memory be green, and that it us befitted
> To bear our hearts in grief, and our whole kingdom
> To be contracted in one brow of woe,
> Yet so far hath discretion fought with nature
> That we with wisest sorrow think on him
> Together with remembrance of ourselves.

Therefore our sometime sister, now our queen,
Th'imperial jointress to this warlike state,
Have we, as 'twere with a defeated joy,
With an auspicious and a dropping eye,
With mirth in funeral and with dirge in marriage,
In equal scale weighing delight and dole,
Taken to wife. Nor have we herein barr'd
Your better wisdoms, which have freely gone
With this affair along.

(I. ii. 1-16)

The situation of a new monarch attempting to establish himself as the embodiment of a new social and political unity is familiar from several other of Shakespeare's plays. The focus upon this key moment of *formation* of a new regime signals an instability, a need for continual construction and re-construction of social order. Order, it seems, is never something which can be relied upon, or which can be established once and for all. As Machiavelli's *The Prince* advises, the successful leader must employ a variety of strategies to gain and maintain a fragile stability, a precarious consensus.

Central to this legitimization crisis is the problem of the individual. As a new king, Claudius cannot afford to be complacent about his subjects. Given the prospect of individuals aligning themselves differently (with the old regime, for example), the loyalty of subjects and their place in the social scheme of things have themselves to be continually reconstructed. Claudius has to take account of and contain a potentially subversive individuation, which makes allegiance anything but automatic.

The attempt by Claudius to contain the possibility of non-identification with the new regime is made by coaxing his would-be subjects into sharing a view of the past, present and future which seems to come as much from them as from him: it is their 'better wisdoms' which encouraged the marriage with Gertrude. Claudius is obliged, in other words, to use rhetoric: to deploy a variety of persuasive strategies in an effort to win allegiance in the face of the potential multiplication of allegiances. His speech balances a sense of loss with the sense of a new beginning; it plots for its audience a controlled narrative of transition from past to present; and it constructs a sense of a collective national identity. The successfully interpellated subject will identify him or herself in the 'one brow of woe' presented by the king, and consequently recognize the new monarch's right to initiate and then terminate national mourning for the old monarch. At the end of this speech Claudius uses a more explicitly authoritative language: 'we here dispatch / You, good Cornelius, and you, Voltimand' (I. ii. 33-4); but the opening appeal to the special ability of the king to give a sense of identity to his subjects exposes the need for authority to take account of the potentially non-aligned individual.

Hamlet epitomizes the problem and possibility of individuals refusing the identities ascribed to them from above. Claudius's speech, encouraging at the same time as limiting public mourning for the dead king, does not have the desired effect on the person whose transfer of allegiance to the new realm is especially required. Despite the personal attention given to the dead king's son further on in the scene, the attempt to coax Hamlet into the identities of 'chiefest courtier, cousin, and ... son' (I. ii. 117) is a spectacular failure. But the question of how the gap between self and social identity is then to be marked receives a variety of different answers in the play. There is no ready-made ideology of the individual waiting patiently in the wings to be called on stage at the moment when Hamlet tells his mother that Claudius's 'one brow of woe' has failed to reach *him*. Such is the gestural nature of Hamlet's appeal to inwardness that it is open to a variety of interpretations and / or production choices.[5] A 'Hamlet' confidently substituting an interior reality for external appearances, private truth for public untruth, might well have the effect of constituting the individual as a ready-made alternative to the inauthentic world of the court. It might then be possible to claim the play as one of the birthplaces of the modern bifurcation between public and private selves.

But there are other possibilities here, suggested in part by the paradoxically formal nature of that speech in which Hamlet claims to 'have that within which passes show':[6] an obviously declamatory, 'public' appeal to interiority, for example, would produce subjectivity, not as a form of consciousness separated or separating itself entirely from public discourse, but as a refusal of that very separation or marginalization. Rather than placing, or attempting to place his 'self' totally beyond the reach of social authority in a private world of its own, Hamlet could be seen as publicizing and politicizing the very failure of authority to interpellate him. Amongst the corollaries of this failure are then the problems and the possibilities, amidst competing classifications and identifications, of classing himself.

The ghostly return of the father promises an early resolution to these difficulties and options, however. This spectral authority from a past which Claudius had hoped to have left behind offers a complete explanation of the cause of Hamlet's grief and alienation, and at the same time re-joins him to a recognizable social identity: that of dutiful son and loyal subject in a more legitimate-looking social and patriarchal order. Hamlet sees in the ghost's explanation and incitement to revenge the prospect of an uncomplicated version of self. Erasing traces of all other inscriptions, the memory of the ghost will provide a single source from which to derive his 'true' identity:

> Remember thee?
> Ay, thou poor ghost, whiles memory holds a seat
> In this distracted globe. Remember thee?
> Yea, from the table of my memory
> I'll wipe away all trivial fond records,
> All saws of books, all forms, all pressures past
> That youth and observation copied there,
> And thy commandment all alone shall live
> Within the book and volume of my brain,
> Unmix'd with baser matter. Yes, by heaven!
> O most pernicious woman!
> O villain, villain, smiling damned villain!
> My tables. Meet it is I set it down
> That one may smile, and smile, and be a villain —

> (I. v. 95-108)

A series of simplifying translations of the play and of Hamlet's character are offered here: from an overcrowded, heterogeneous 'globe' to a simple play in which to act; from an over-determined self faced with the problem / possibility of choice to a commanded subject; and from 'baser matter' to heavenly causes. Where Claudius failed to contract the kingdom into 'one brow of mourning', the ghost of Hamlet's father is apparently so successful in reducing heterogeneity that he will achieve total interpellation. He will 'speak through' Hamlet and in so doing displace all other speech.

What revenge represents in the play is, however, far from simple. As Belsey usefully puts it:

> Revenge exists in the margin between justice and crime. An act of injustice on behalf of justice, it deconstructs the antithesis which fixes the meanings of good and evil, right and wrong. Hamlet invokes the conventional polarities in addressing the Ghost, only to abandon them as inadequate or irrelevant.[7]

Looked at from the point of view of the competing versions of subjectivity and agency represented in the play, revenge is additionally problematic. For if, on the one hand, the incitement to revenge promises to put an end to *any* form of individualism by (re)turning the subject to a questionably higher structure of command, then, on the other, revenge, as an extreme act of self-assertion, serves to pluralize the meanings of individualism still further. Hamlet may represent revenge as an all-determining imposition: 'O cursed spite, / That ever I was born to set it right' (I. v. 196-7); but the excess of revenge consists in individuals taking, or appearing to take matters into their own hands. As with Hamlet's interiority, however, the individualism of revenge is inflected in very different ways by the play.

Hamlet's self-recriminations, after the First Player's impassioned recital of the story of Pyrrhus, present one version of the individualism of revenge. Hamlet's comparisons between himself and the player are based on his own inability as an 'actor'. He can neither act in the sense of being able to absorb himself in a role as convincingly as the player:

> What would he do
> Had he the motive and the cue for passion
> That I have?

> (II. ii. 554-6)

Nor can he act in the sense of being or becoming (a certain kind of) agent:

> I,
> A dull and muddy-mettled rascal, peak
> Like John-a-dreams, unpregnant of my cause,
> And can say nothing.

> (II. ii. 561-4)

Taken together, these two failures add up to an unmanly inability to act with conviction: 'Am I a coward?' (II. ii. 566);

> it cannot be
> But I am pigeon-liver'd and lack gall
> To make oppression bitter.

> (II. ii. 572-4)

The form of masculine agency and heroic self-assertion appealed to here is taken on by both Laertes and Fortinbras in the play, and simultaneously admired and called into question by Hamlet. Fortinbras's invasion of Poland, 'to gain a little patch of ground / That hath in it no profit but the name' (IV. iv. 18-19), illustrates the pointless bravado of the man of action prepared to sacrifice lives 'for an eggshell' (IV. iv. 53).

The individualism of revenge can be seen from this perspective as the expression of a macho aristocratic code of personal honour. As Robert Watson has recently written, this form of self-assertion was coming under increasing threat in the late sixteenth and early seventeenth centuries from a centralizing state bureaucracy:

> Duels of honour would become a serious problem among the Jacobean aristocracy, but they are probably a secondary manifestation of a more basic shift that was already troubling the Elizabethan populace. Local justice, based in the competing interests of families, was rapidly giving way to a centralized legal bureaucracy in which personal passions and honour counted for little and patronage and rhetorical skill became all-important. Little wonder that the revenger is usually a powerless outsider avenging an inflammatory offence to a lover or close kin.[8]

The *ad hoc* surveillance system operated by Claudius — the desire to have Hamlet 'in the cheer and comfort of our eye' (I. ii. 116) — could be seen as the play's symbolic analogue for this centralizing society. Hamlet's 'aristocratic' response, however, is ambiguous. It is difficult to tell whether he is increasingly drawn to a form of heroic self-assertion, or whether he, and through him the play, parody to the end what is to be seen as an anachronistic form of masculine agency.

Perhaps as a result of this sense of anachronism, heroic self-assertion is accompanied by a more rhetorically dependent revenger, looking to persuade others and himself of the metaphysical and moral certainties to which he simultaneously clings. But if Hamlet's notorious 'wordiness' and hesitation suggest an equivocal attitude towards revenge, then the vestigial self-assertive hero in him responds to the substitution of *verba* for military *res* (or in Watson's terms, rhetorical skills for personal honour), by treating words themselves as phallic weapons. Preparing himself for a confrontation with Gertrude after the revelations of the play within the play, Hamlet proposes to 'speak daggers to her, but use none' (III. ii. 387). This use of language as a weapon to penetrate to the heart of things signals the revenger's dependence on rhetorical skills, which, like Claudius's rhetoric, may fail to impress, at the same time as it ascribes to that rhetoric a virile potency.

A similar ambivalence informs Hamlet's theory of acting and his use of a play, a fiction, to find out truth. The very recourse to such an indirect strate-

gy itself suggests that truth is beyond the compass of any simple heroic assertion. Yet Hamlet is at the same time keen to place acting in the service of an
idealist form of mimesis, a simple truth-revealing form of theatre. The 'purpose of playing', he tells the actors, 'was and is to hold as 'twere the mirror
up to nature; to show virtue her feature, scorn her own image, and the very
age and body of the time his form and pressure' (III. ii. 20-4). And it is again
acting with conviction — 'Be not too tame' (III. ii. 16), he advises — which
will produce this accurate reflection of moral, metaphysical and social truths.

The use of complex strategies to reveal elusive truths is not, of course, peculiar to Hamlet. The maintenance of Claudius's court itself relies as much
upon a form of indirect panoptic surveillance as upon direct coercion or the
spectacular use of violence. But the conception of truth appealed to in both
Hamlet's advice to the players and in the court informer's promise to 'find /
Where truth is hid, though it were hid indeed / Within the centre' (II. ii. 157-
9) has the simplicity of a kind of heroism or force. Hamlet's advice on acting
rests upon the conviction or hope that self-evident, already given truths can
simply be mirrored or dis-covered, while Polonius's promise relies upon a
similar premiss. There is a further congruence, here, between Polonius's assumption that truth has a centre or single source, and Hamlet's derivation of
his revenging self from an authoritative, patriarchal origin.

The preoccupation with truth and knowledge on the part of those in or as-
piring to positions of authority indicates an anxiety similar to the anxiety
about social order. That truth, like public grief, might not be solely derivable
from or definable by those in or near to authority, suggests the further sense
of a breakdown of ascriptive identities and knowledges. The outcast figure of
the revenger at once symbolizes and offers a solution to that breakdown. Resistant to what he sees as false values, he sets out on an heroic mission to restore truth to a fallen world. Such an enterprise again obviously requires the
revenger to act with conviction.

These various elements of Hamlet's self-conception as a revenger and
moral actor combine in the scene with Gertrude (III. iv.) to construct a powerful form of agency for Hamlet. There he aggregates the aristocratic heroism
of revenge to ideas of mission and truth, representing himself as the agent of
retribution, the heroic purger of a corrupt society:

> heaven hath pleas'd it so,
> To punish me with this and this with me,
> That I must be their scourge and minister.

(III. iv. 175-7)

The question of who is speaking, Hamlet or a higher authority, returns here, though it is the sense of the revenger attempting to justify an excess of power, knowledge and agency which prevails. Holding his truth-revealing mirror up to Gertrude, Hamlet aspires to a complete monopoly over knowledge. And as others have attempted to identify Hamlet's true role as courtier, dutiful son and revenger, so he now, assuming the truth of the role of revenger, prescribes a series of rules and a moral identity for his mother:

> Confess yourself to heaven,
> Repent what's past, avoid what is to come;
> And do not spread the compost on the weeds
> To make them ranker. Forgive me this my virtue;
> For in the fatness of these pursy times
> Virtue itself of vice must pardon beg,
> Yea, curb and woo for leave to do him good.

(III. iv. 151-7)

The form of moral agency and self-empowerment taken on here by Hamlet has the effect, or at least aim, of once again reducing others to ciphers.

*

I suggested earlier that there is no singular form of individualism to be extracted from the play, as different answers to the question of what it means or might mean to be an 'individual' are presented. The code of revenge effectively illustrates this, for the set of representations which Hamlet draws upon to construct himself as soothsayer, purger and self-assertive hero are complicated and called into question by a more reflexive or parodic version of the revenging 'self'. The way in which Hamlet self-consciously prepares himself for the scene with Gertrude, for example, arguably has the effect of putting the idea of the self as avenging angel (or scourge) in quotation marks:

> 'Tis now the very witching time of night,
> When churchyards yawn and hell itself breathes out

Contagion to this world. Now could I drink hot blood,
And do such bitter business as the day
Would quake to look on. Soft, now to my mother.
O heart, lose not thy nature. Let not ever
The soul of Nero enter this firm bosom;
Let me be cruel, not unnatural.
I will speak daggers to her, but use none.

(III. ii. 379-87)

This speech could be delivered seriously or jestingly depending on what kind of subject and subjectivity 'Hamlet' is seen to represent. Is he 'really' acting with conviction, becoming the impassioned scourge of man- and womankind? Or is the self as autonomous moral agent, familiar from previous revenge plays, being deliberately sent up and quoted in order to make room for other selves and subjectivities? Here I want to consider two key alternatives: Hamlet's 'antically disposed' self, which transposes him, his ideas of acting, and the play as a whole onto a meta-theatrical level; and his reflexive, contemplative self, which I shall argue is in productive tension with his 'antic disposition' (I. v. 180).

The manly form of mimesis propounded and practised by a morally pretentious Hamlet could be seen as yielding in the above speech and in the play as a whole to an antic mimicking of any discourse or form of subjectivity with aspirations to 'truth'. Belief in the ability of the scourge to hold an undistorting mirror up to either nature, the times, himself or others, cedes place to a Hamlet exposing through parody and quotation the way figures of authority (himself included) attempt to have their fictions accepted as truths. The very idea of searching for truth, whether metaphysical, religious or social, is itself exposed by the mimic as a kind of (masculine) fiction.

These emphases might lead to a reading of the play as undermining the basis for any kind of mimesis. The self-conscious theatricality of the play in some ways supports such a reading: if there are no self-evident truths, but only representations and mediations which get taken or mistaken for realities, then self-conscious theatricality offers a way breaking those mimetic illusions. The version of 'self' which might be seen as appropriate to this non- or anti-mimetic mode is precisely that ironic, parodic self of Hamlet's: a self endlessly quoting roles and personae which are only ever half engaged. The idea of being true to a self is, from this point of view, another mimetic illusion masking the fictiveness of the concept. The answer to the question of how, amidst competing roles and identites, to class or identify oneself might then take the form of a rebuff: the very notion of a self to which one can finally be committed or true is itself a fiction.

The explicitly political dimension to Hamlet's antic disposition consists in the resistance it offers to any imposition of role, self or knowledge. Pretending to identities like the love-sick lover (for the benefit of Polonius) or the ambitious courtier (for the benefit of Rosencrantz and Guildenstern), Hamlet strings along those who would truly know and fix his character only to evade their authoritarian reach. As Terry Eagleton suggests:

> Hamlet loiters hesitantly on the brink of the 'symbolic order' (the system of allotted sexual and social roles in society), unable and unwilling to take up a determinate position within it ... As fluid as his father's ghost and as fast-talking as any Shakespearian clown, Hamlet riddles and bamboozles his way out of being definitively known.[9]

In these respects, and as Eagleton indicates, Hamlet joins the traditions of carnivalesque and clowning. Falstaff-like, he refuses and makes mockery of high- level politics, releasing himself and the play from their high mimetic aims and ambitions. The revenger's sense of mission and agency is equally a casuality in this carnivalisation of meaning.

Eagleton himself somewhat teasingly goes on to suggest that the character of Hamlet 'would not be the most secure foundation on which to construct a political order'.[10] That may be so, but only if Hamlet's antic disposition is (paradoxically) taken as the definitive representation of a 'character' to which yet further versions of self and subjectivity can be attributed.

It seems to me that Hamlet's antic self-irony coexists with a version of self still actively engaged with the problems of agency and mimesis, though at a more complex level than the self-assertive revenger. The idea of the play as drastically non- or anti-mimetic can therefore be qualified, by suggesting that *Hamlet* 'reflects' for its audience the pressing problem of how to act, of what kind of agency to pursue, in the fraught social, political and ethical situation inhabited by its central character. Acting 'antically' is in other words only one response to this situation.

Of course the problem of knowing how to act is bound up with the problem of discovering the truth of that situation. Hamlet is offered and himself constructs a variety of different accounts of his position: from the ghost's construction of the play as a simple morality play with individual villains held responsible for society's fall from grace, to Hamlet's own construction of women in general as scapegoats for society's ills: 'Frailty, thy name is woman' (I. ii. 146). The action, identity and form of agency he pursues thus depends on the view he takes of his situation. The attempt to piece together the truth of that situation from the various accounts and simplifications of it constitutes Hamlet's and arguably the play's own complexly mimetic aspirations. Where a consistently parodic, antic Hamlet might be content to 'quote the fragments', to mimic the multiple permutations of his situation and self without attempting to do anything with or about them, the early modern detective cum social reformer in Hamlet requires him at least to struggle with these fragmentary truths and perceptions.

It is at this point that we can invoke a reflexive, contemplative, 'sensitive' Hamlet, abandoning or at least half-abandoning an heroic, manly pursuit of truth in favour of an attempt to piece together truths in a more pluralistic, less authoritarian way. Hamlet's 'experimentalism', his testing of received truths and accounts of events for himself, and the extension of this questioning to his own sense of self, informs this more complex, less heroic sense of agency. His calling into question of the knowledge and identity prescribed by the ghost of his father makes reference to his own 'weakness' and 'melancholy' at the same time as it maintains a degree of confidence in the ability of and need for individuals to try out and test truths for themselves:

> The spirit that I have seen
> May be a devil, and the devil hath power
> T'assume a pleasing shape, yea, and perhaps,
> Out of my weakness and my melancholy,
> As he is very potent with such spirits,
> Abuses me to damn me. I'll have grounds
> More relative than this. The play's the thing
> Wherein I'll catch the conscience of the King.

(II. ii. 594-601)

Hamlet's running commentaries upon the social and political intervention he has been called upon to make entail the continual revision and re-revision, not only of his practical strategies but of his self-conception as an agent. Having once brought into question the ghost's capacity fully to authorize his intervention, Hamlet is obliged to keep on questioning the grounds, the justification for his actions. Because truth is no longer simply derivable from a single source or authority, it becomes a problematic, questionable term, which demands active scrutiny and reflection on the part of the individual.

The difficulty of separating action from contemplation, practice from an enquiry into the grounds of practice, occasionally brings Hamlet to a sense of impasse:

> And thus the native hue of resolution
> Is sicklied o'er with the pale cast of thought,
> And enterprises of great pitch and moment
> With this regard their currents turn awry
> And lose the name of action.

(III. i. 84-8)

This nostalgia for a simple, heroic kind of agency can be seen as a response to the complicating but also liberating pluralization of concepts of agency presented in the play. The taxing question of who or what authorizes Hamlet to take action is open-ended precisely because of Hamlet's loss of faith in the single authority of his absent-present father. The loss of patriarchal origins and single sources means that the action and agency once derivable from a simple heroism become equally problematic and open-ended.

Thus the question of authorization is turned over again and again by a reflexive, contemplative Hamlet, as it becomes increasingly difficult for him and us to align his intervention and agency with any one politics or authority. Is he seeking to restore the old patriarchal order of his father? In pursuing a bloody revenge will he be re-enacting a displaced feudal ethic of personal honour and violence? Or is his revenge to be understood as an enactment of a populist form of justice, made necessary because of the corruption and breakdown of justice at the top of society? Further ethical and political questions, such as whether the revenger remedies or contributes to injustice, follow on from these. But the main point I want to emphasize is the way in which the play sustains very different readings of the politics of intervention and agency. Hamlet's character and actions can be understood in different ways because the political and social orientation of his individualism is open-ended, extended beyond a traditional heroism but not yet determined by an essentializing liberal humanism.

*

By way of conclusion, I want to underline the sense of the connectedness of these questions of agency and mimesis to the play's Elizabethan / Jacobean audiences. For isn't the play's dramatization of different ways of acting (antically, reflexively, nobly, heroically and so on) mimetically related to the actual or potential agencies of those audiences? And isn't the play's extension or pluralization of concepts of agency, of what it means or might mean to 'act', again intimately related to the mixed heterogeneous nature of those metropolitan audiences? While princes and courtiers may have had more opportunities to intervene in political and social life than the 'ordinary' playgoer, the question of who or what the prince is acting for (or, in a literally theatrical sense, who he is playing to) places an otherwise distancing princely agency within the orbit of other less exalted individuals / audience members. Thus what the play reflects back to those 'vociferously participating audience[s]'[11] of the Elizabethan and Jacobean periods is perhaps a complex sense of their own differentiated potentialities as social and political actors.

The extent to which a play places issues within the orbit and control of an audience can itself be seen as informing the kinds of agency that play is able to imagine or construct.[12] Agency in *Hamlet* is not free-floating, but 'situated'. It does not correspond with that version of individualism which conceives of the self as an essence or as a totally free agent. Abstracted from social relations, emptied of social and discursive content, the concept of the self as free-floating paradoxically deprives the individual of any meaningful social and political agency.[13] Contrastingly, agency in *Hamlet* is defined in terms of the range of possible responses to a concrete social and political situation which thereby constitutes but which does not wholly determine 'the self'.

Questions like 'What would you do if ...' or 'How would you act in a situation where ...' form the basis nowadays for certain kinds of games (computer adventure games, for example); they also appear in personality assessment questionnaires, in some job application procedures, or as possible 'leisure' activities in newspapers and magazines. If such questions, partly because of the few contexts in which they now appear, seem rather meaningless, unchallenging questions for *the* most canonized text of English literature to be asking, then that perhaps reflects the diminution of our sense of what they might involve.

Notes

1. For discussions of ideology, see Jorge Larrain, *The Concept of Ideology* (London: Hutchinson, 1982); and Terry Eagleton, *Ideology: An Introduction* (London and New York: Verso, 1991).

2. For a similar critique of the use of the category 'liberal humanist subject' as a catch-all category, see David Aers, 'Reflections on Current Histories of the Subject', *Literature and History*, Second Series, 2 (1991), 20-34.

3. Catherine Belsey, *The Subject of Tragedy: Identity and difference in Renaissance drama* (London and New York: Methuen, 1985), pp. 41-2. For a similar reading of the history of the self and the place of *Hamlet* in that history, see Francis Barker, *The Tremulous Private Body* (London and New York: Methuen, 1984), pp. 25-40.

4. This worry about the transfer of power can be specifically related to the Elizabethan/Jacobean succession crisis; i.e., to the problem of determining who had the most legitimate claim to the throne after Elizabeth.

5. Barker also discusses the gestural nature of Hamlet's interiority in *The Tremulous Private Body*. For Barker as for Belsey, however, the gesture is exclusively towards an 'essential subjectivity' (p. 38).

6. For further discussion of the declamatory nature of this speech seen in relation to pre-modern concepts of character and rhetorical identity, see Edward Burns, *Character: Acting and Being on the Pre-Modern Stage* (London: Macmillan, 1990), p. 141 and *passim*.

7. Belsey, *The Subject of Tragedy*, p. 115.

8. Robert Watson, 'Tragedy' in A. R. Braunmuller and Michael Hattaway, eds, *The Cambridge Companion to English Renaissance Drama* (Cambridge: Cambridge University Press, 1990), p. 318.

9. Terry Eagleton, *William Shakespeare* (Oxford: Blackwell, 1986), p. 71.

10. Eagleton, *Shakespeare*, p. 73.

11. Graham Holderness, *Shakespeare's History* (Dublin: Gill and Macmillan, 1985), p.13.

12. For a suggestive discussion of drama and questions of intervention/agency, see Bernard Sharratt, 'The Drama of Raymond Williams' in Terry Eagleton, ed., *Raymond Williams: Critical Perspectives* (Oxford: Polity, 1989), p. 139 and *passim*.

13. A similar point, in a differently focused article on individualism, is made by Peter Stallybrass in 'Shakespeare, the Individual, and the Text' in Lawrence Grossberg, Cary Nelson and Paula Treichler, eds, *Cultural Studies* (New York and London: Routledge, 1992), p. 610.

TELMAHS: CARNIVAL LAUGHTER IN HAMLET

ROBERT BARRIE

Telmahs is *Shamlet* spelled backwards. In an essay entitled '*Telmah*', Terence Hawkes explores the conservative ideological context of John Dover Wilson's well known study, *What Happens in 'Hamlet'*.[1] Hawkes's perspective suggests an absurd and recursive mode, a reversal of logical structure. *Telmah*, as the literal mirror image of *Hamlet*, reveals the non-rational aspects of reality which he understands to be encoded in the play. Such reversal offers only slight, if any, demotion of *Hamlet* as serious intellectual stuff, however — the 'right stuff' of tragedy. Yet 'pluralizing' Hawkes's reversal turns *Hamlet* into *Shamlet* and mocks the ideological earnestness of Dover Wilson *and* Terence Hawkes — mocks, in fact, the ideological earnestness of tragedy itself as a serious literary genre, mocks most certainly my serious efforts in this essay.[2]

Setting aside his high blood's royalty, Hamlet shares with the Fool/Vice such attributes as an association with the devil, improvisational wit, special speech and body languages, an association with music and dancing, cynicism regarding women, and roles as Presenter, Chorus, plotter, and swordsman. Thus he recalls the Fool/Vice figures of earlier popular drama in all of their playful, anarchic, pagan, diabolic, topsy-turvy functions.[3] While granting most of these associations, however, traditional (i.e., humanist) interpretations of Shakespeare's *Hamlet* have nevertheless tended to centre the play in some tragic, moral order, thus privileging hierarchical values. Hence the play may be seen to reinforce the Tudor Myth, the 'Elizabethan World Picture', the 'Great Chain of Being', and related conservative cultural paradigms, including notions of a free, morally responsible, independent self. Seen in the context of *Hamlet*'s nearly unchallenged position as the supreme English tragedy, the predominance of such 'readings' is hardly surprising. But Hamlet, as his own Fool, can be seen to subvert *Hamlet* so thoroughly as to reduce to laughter the very idea of serious tragedy.

It surely comes as no surprise to Derridian-influenced academics that *Hamlet*'s text can be shown to deconstruct itself. New historicism, however, encourages a further question: might some significant segment of Shakespeare's audience have participated in such a deconstruction? When Shakespeare's *Hamlet* first played at the Globe, that theatre represented a rich mixture of cultural assumptions. Since the time of those first performances, however, the festive, carnival discourse of *Hamlet* has been largely suppressed or co-opted, and few have explored very far how Hamlet's Fool aspect (as opposed to Hamlet's madness) might be seen to influence the play's meaning. Among those who *have* undertaken such study are Harry Levin, Michael Graves, Arthur McGee, David Wiles and Michael Bristol.[4]

Levin interprets Hamlet's foolish behaviour to be a manifestation of Erasmian humanism. For Levin, such folly is actually a type of traditional Socratic wisdom. Thus Hamlet, like Erasmus's Folly, stoops to foolishness merely as a means to criticize the world, and Hamlet, in his essential self, 'stands apart, a solitary, sane individual.'[5] Such a Hamlet, while critical of official corruption, poses no real threat to official values.

Graves, while sympathetic to Levin's analysis, focuses primarily on aspects of Hamlet's language to extend the associations of Hamlet's foolishness to the 'grand Shakespearean' fool and to Death 'the antic', the stylized, joking skeleton who leads Hans Holbein the Younger's *Dance of Death*.[6] Graves emphasizes the Christian aspect of this figure, so once again Hamlet the Fool is seen to support orthodox values, in this case 'reliance on the Providence of Christ'. Indeed, according to Graves, Hamlet's 'resemblances to Christ ... grow more noticeable as the play nears its end'.[7]

McGee's *The Elizabethan Hamlet* also emphasizes the Christian context of Hamlet's foolishness. McGee sets Hamlet squarely in the Vice tradition, but he considers that tradition from the moral perspective of Protestant religious doctrine exclusively. Thus he sees Hamlet to be a spiritually damned revenger enticed into evil by the devil-Ghost. McGee's evil Hamlet contrasts starkly with the Hamlets of Levin and Graves. However, McGee's *Hamlet* supports the same orthodox value structure which sees good and evil as absolutes.

Wiles also contends that in *Hamlet* Shakespeare combined the roles of hero and Fool, but suggests that Hamlet's 'one unifying consciousness' successfully co-opts the comic, anarchic energies of the Fool, so that 'in *Hamlet*, symbolically, we see the jig being swallowed up and dissolved within the play' in such a way that 'the celebration of anarchy ceases, necessarily, to be an admissible complement to the play'.[8] Hamlet's all-inclusive totality, then, in

Wiles's scheme, 'swallows up' the subversive impulses in the play to under-gird the humanist, 'monologic' view of *Hamlet* as an icon of orthodox wisdom.

The Hamlet-as-Fool interpretations of Levin, Graves, McGee and Wiles, then, all support the commonly held humanist assumption that *Hamlet* reinforces some hierarchical structure of moral order upon which the stability of the official culture (then and now) rests, and upon which the seriousness of tragedy depends.

Bristol offers a more radical point of departure for an exploration of *Hamlet*'s carnival context. He contends that Hamlet's antic response, when Claudius asks him to reveal where dead Polonius is hidden, turns 'Temporal authority and indeed all political structures of difference ... inside out'.[9] And in a sense, he argues, qualifying his assertion *even* as he makes it,

> even Hamlet's death is a laughing matter, the result of miscalculation and farcical bungling that leave the succession to Fortinbras and his 'rights of memory'. The transfer of authority is solemnized by Hamlet's ceremonial removal. Like all other similar removals, this one has a funny side disclosed by grotesque laughter which refuses to understand the unfathomable contradictions of political succession.[10]

How loudly might this laughter have resounded in the Elizabethan theatre? How deeply might it be seen to subvert the 'official' meanings of the play? How aware is Hamlet (as his own Fool) of this subversive aspect of his own drama?

By insisting on an essential distinction between Hamlet and the Grave-digger, with whom Hamlet talks 'at cross-purposes because the clown does not make the same assumptions about authority and ownership that Hamlet does', Bristol mutes the very laughter he posits.[11] But from a Bakhtinian point of view the merger of Hamlet with the Fool turns all official hierarchies topsy-turvy, for the Fool's mask grants its wearer certain unalienable rights, among them,

> the right *not* to understand, the right to confuse, to tease, to hyperbolize life; the right to parody others while talking, the right to not be taken literally, not 'to be oneself'; ... the right to act life as a comedy and to treat others as actors, the right to rip off masks, the right to rage at others with a primeval (almost cultic) rage— and finally, the right to betray to the public a personal life, down to its most private and prurient little secrets.[12]

The resonances with Hamlet leap to the foreground.

I wish to emphasize Hamlet in his Fool's aspect, then, without interpreting his function in that aspect as serving the ends of the official culture exclusively (as do Levin, Graves and Wiles) and without defining that function simply as evil and thus co-opting it to serve the exclusive purpose of the official culture (as does McGee). I choose to foreground *Hamlet*'s Fool neither as an ironic champion of orthodox morality nor as a negative moral example, but rather as one who challenges official culture at the level of its most basic value assumptions, which include the assumptions of tragedy.[13]

The Fool's relationship with the audience was interactive and competitive, and his theatrical improvisation frequently led to 'anarchic upstaging'.[14] Such upstaging becomes a theme of Shakespeare's *Hamlet* when Hamlet runs completely amuck during *The Mousetrap*, doing exactly what he has warned the visiting actors' clowns (conspicuously absent from the stage) against, i.e., speaking 'more than is set down for them' (III. ii. 39). Just as Hamlet in the role of spectator-*provocateur*, might be seen to turn the supposedly neoclassical tragedy of *The Mousetrap* topsy-turvy, so in the roll of Fool-*provocateur* he might be seen to collaborate with some part of his audience to turn his own popular tragedy topsy-turvy. The Fool, as Hamlet well knew, represented a likely menace to those necessary questions upon which tragedy depends.

In the 'Bad Quarto' of 1603, Hamlet's admonition to the actors to control their clown(s) is extended:

> And doe you heare? let not your Clowne speake
> More then is set downe, there be of them I can tell you
> That will laugh themselues, to set on some
> Quantitie of barren spectators to laugh with them,
> Albeit there is some necessary point in the Play
> Then to be obserued: O 't is vile, and shewes
> A pittiful ambition in the foole that vseth it.
> And then you haue some agen, that keepes one sute
> Of ieasts, as a man is knowne by one sute of
> Apparell, and Gentlemen quotes his ieasts downe
> In their tables, before they come to the play, as thus:
> Cannot you stay till I eate my porrige? and, you owe me
> A quarters wages: and my coate wants a cullison:
> And, your beere is sowre: and, blabbering with his lips,
> And thus keeping in his cinkapase of ieasts,
> When, God knows, the warm Clowne cannot make a iest
> Vnlesse by chance, as the blinde man catcheth a hare:
> Maisters tell him of it.[15]

Though Hamlet decries such havoc with writers' scripts as the clowns were known to use, nevertheless, this passage, as a possible memorial construction, very likely *preserves* an example of just the sort of anarchic upstaging which Wiles suggests had gone out of style by the time of the play.[16] Thus the probably spurious 'Bad Quarto' suggests that at least one Elizabethan actor playing Hamlet *did* subvert tragic decorum through comic ad-libbing.

Andrew Gurr echoes the view of Wiles in his contention that after Tarlton theatre audiences valued more highly, 'the dramatic illusion in the self contained play', and psychologically unified characters, than Tarlton's type of clowning.[17] But, if Tarlton's less illusionistic, more improvisational style of performance relying more on collaboration with the audience went out of style in the 1590s, then what are we to make of the career of Will Kempe, an exceedingly popular member of the Lord Chamberlain's Company right up to the time of *Hamlet*? Even Gurr admits that

> Will Kempe's departure from the Shakespeare company in 1599 was one of a complex series of adjustments which started the company on a road leading firmly away from the jigs and knockabout clowning which stayed on as citizen staples at the northern playhouses until the 1640s. In 1599, when they were just starting in a costly new playhouse, Kempe's departure left the company hazardously poised for a new beginning in conditions of unprecedented competition.[18]

Will Kempe had taken up the mantle laid down by Richard Tarlton.[19] But why would Kempe's departure have left the Lord Chamberlain's Company 'hazardously poised' if, as Gurr asserts, 'Tarlton's kind of audience … united by comedy into intimacy with the players, did not long outlast the 1580s'?[20]

Gurr's image of a 'hazardously poised' acting company seems to me to reflect an obvious ambivalence in *Hamlet*, 'hazardously poised' itself between neoclassical realism (emphasizing psychological consistency of character, poet-playwright as AUTHORity, and separation of actor from audience) and ritualistic action (emphasizing dramatic function, native ritual and a more improvisational and collaborative audience rapport). Wiles and Gurr regard *Hamlet* as signalling the more sophisticated fare for which the Globe became known in the seventeenth century. Perhaps so. But the play also appears to look back to an older, more improvisational style of theatre.

Wiles contends that Shakespeare's purpose in doubling Hamlet as the Fool was to acknowledge Will Kempe's departure from the Lord Chamberlain's Company. Though the reason for Kempe's departure is not known, Wiles speculates that Kempe left Shakespeare's company because Falstaff was cut from *Henry V*.[21] I wonder, conversely, if Kempe's sudden departure from the Lord Chamberlain's Company might not be the reason that Shakespeare omitted the character of Falstaff from *Henry V*. Wiles argues that

> when Shakespeare fails to bring on a clown amongst the 'tragedians of the city' in *Hamlet*, he deliberately reminds the Globe audience that the real tragedians who play before them have lost the services of Kempe. The relevance of this reminder emerges when Hamlet casts himself as the fool of both 'The Mousetrap' and *Hamlet*.[22]

But why would the Lord Chamberlain's Company have wanted to call attention to its loss (for whatever reason) of so popular an actor as Will Kempe? Wiles does not say. Nor does Gurr, who contends that 'Shakespeare's fellows may well have shared Hamlet's view of clowns', and that under such circumstances Kempe's departure from the company may have been an unwilling one. According to Gurr, 'the Globe seems never to have returned to that kind of clowning.'[23] Perhaps not, but the company could not have foreseen this. Even *if* 'Shakespeare's fellows' did share 'Hamlet's view of clowns', it seems unlikely that the majority of Shakespeare's audience, commoners or privileged, did so. 'Balanced precariously', then, uncertain of its future success, the Lord Chamberlain's Company, in casting Burbage as Hamlet, the tragic hero and comic fool, made virtue of necessity. The company was not, as Wiles argues, deliberately drawing attention to Kempe's absence. What purpose could that have served? Comic geniuses the likes of Dick Tarlton and Will Kempe were exceedingly popular and difficult to replace.

Surely the mass of London's rural immigrants attending the London professional theatre loved the Fool as much as their country cousins. And if Tarlton's and Kempe's popularity are any indication, citizens, gentry and nobles loved the Fool as well. Shakespeare's company would not have wanted to advertize Kempe's departure. It would have wanted to disguise it, even *if*, for whatever reason, Kempe had been let go.

At the time when *Hamlet* was first performed, then, the Lord Chamberlain's Company lacked the ever-popular Fool. But the company is unlikely to have regarded this situation as anything other than a predicament. What *Hamlet* reveals, given this predicament, is not, as Gurr suggests, a confident new style of play but a boldly ambivalent play uncertain of its own identity, an uncertainty which legions of critics analyzing *Hamlet* primarily as a Hamlet character study have taken to be a realistic portrayal of human psychological complexity. Gurr contends that *Hamlet* broached psychological complexity as a new theatrical interest, and that Burbage did indeed convince his audience 'of the reality of the roles he played.'[24] But Gurr's logic on this point seems somewhat circular, citing *Hamlet*, a play assumed *realistically* to depict psychological complexity as evidence of a new theatrical interest. That the Lord Chamberlain's Company chose to present at this 'precarious' time in its history a reworking of an old revenge play suggests an intention to satisfy its audience's conventional taste for broad sensationalism, while perhaps at the same time satirizing the generally recognized excesses of such old-fashioned stuff. This could be accomplished *without* Will Kempe because Richard Burbage could be pressed into double duty — tragic Hero and jig-maker Fool. Burbage was perhaps the only actor still available to the company with the requisite comedic skills.

The documents reprinted in Appendices C and D of E. K. Chambers's *The Elizabethan Stage* clearly suggest that what made the Elizabethan theatre particularly troublesome to authority was its topsy-turvy tradition of carnival laughter.[25] The theatres functioned as deconstructing temples of carnival laughter. There, nothing in the official culture was sacred. According to Bakhtin, carnival laughter defeats awe of the sacred, of death, 'of earthly kings ... of all that oppresses and restricts'.[26] Indeed, reading over the many documents reprinted in Chambers's *The Elizabethan Stage* containing the often vivid complaints of the Puritans and the London City Fathers against the theatres, it is possible to hear, between the lines, the roaring crescendos of carnival laughter rising from the groundlings and the stinkards, rising also from the so-called 'privileged playgoers', safe all in their theatre sanctuaries, safe in the same way that pot smokers are safe today in the carnival sanctuary of a rock concert arena.

The subversive (but academic and intellectually élite) traditions of much postmodern critical theory seem clearly to reinforce such popular Elizabethan attitudes insofar as both might be seen to deconstruct the high seriousness of *Hamlet*. But postmodernism has yet to offer such a radical challenge to the play. James L. Calderwood, for example, explores fairly thoroughly the implications of the metadrama in *Hamlet* as a device for subverting meaning and character as absolute truths in the play. Calderwood asks some wonderfully fresh questions of the play, particularly regarding the problem of Hamlet's identity, but in the last analysis his Hamlet is, after all, a tragic, existential hero who succeeds finally in discovering his 'tragic self' as 'Hamlet, the Dane.'[27] Such an assertion supports the sort of orthodox truth hierarchies which both Tudor myth and humanist criticism might be seen to support, but which carnival laughter as understood by Bakhtin would challenge.

How can Hamlet assert — with all the line implies regarding his assumption of regal authority, in the graveyard of all places — that 'This is I, / Hamlet the Dane' (V. i. 250-1)? Such an assertion must be made above carnival laughter's deafening roar. One wonders if Hamlet has been paying attention to anything he has just been saying regarding Alexander and Caesar:

> Why, may not imagination trace the noble dust of Alexander till a find it stopping a bung-hole?

(V i. 196-8)

> Imperious Caesar, dead and turn'd to clay,
> Might stop a hole to keep the wind away.
> O that that earth which kept the world in awe
> Should patch a wall t'expel the winter's flaw.
> But soft, but soft awhile. Here comes the King.

(V. i. 206-10)

Hamlet's ironic cue for the King's entrance (along with the rest of Ophelia's funeral party) suggests emphatically that he has *not* been paying his earlier words much attention. Annabel Patterson contends that Hamlet, as a consequence of his encounter with the Grave-digger, discards his alienation to rejoin 'the culture of the court'.[28] But once the radical nature of Hamlet's popular associations have been established, they are not so easily wished away. How can the audience be expected to forget as quickly as Hamlet seems to the insignificance of the self, even a royal self, in the context of the graveyard? Even when Hamlet's 'identity' *seems* finally once and for all established, when he no longer *seems* to be playing the Fool but to have centred himself as 'Hamlet the Dane', is the audience, nevertheless, invited to laugh at the comic erasure of his 'official' identity? Almost certainly some significant segment of the Elizabethan audience was so moved. If, as Bristol supposes, Hamlet's ceremonial removal 'has a funny side disclosed by grotesque laughter', then why do we today not hear more people laughing at the end of the play?

We don't dare. *Hamlet* is, after all, the greatest play by the greatest playwright who ever lived, perhaps the single most sacred icon in the entire canon of English, if not world, literature. Not even Stephen Booth, arguing for the presence of an audience-bewildering multiplicity of inconsistent meanings in *Hamlet*, encourages such deconstructing laughter. Rather, Booth posits an intellectually serious audience unable to make up its mind about the play and taken 'to the brink of intellectual terror.'[29] The essence of *Hamlet*'s 'value', for Booth, lies in the play's heroic transcendence of the contradictory frames of reference it inhabits. Nevertheless, Booth understands *Hamlet* to have 'put Western man into a panic.'[30] Small wonder, in the context of such pronouncements, that modern audiences feel intimidated. But the Elizabethan context of the play could not have been so constituted. Elizabethan audiences would have approached the play as just another *Hamlet*, another popular revenge tragedy, a genre so thoroughly familiar to them already, perhaps, as to have actually predisposed them to laughter. Elizabethan popular audiences participated (at times irreverently) in the play of the play. The typical modern audience, even if it is invited to do so through an unusually intimate physical proximity to the stage and an unusually intense emotional intimacy with the actors, does not dare. A modern theatre-goer, fearful of being locked out of the theatre altogether and thus forfeiting the considerable price of the ticket, does not even dare to arrive late.

Ironically, a postmodern 'reading' of *Hamlet*, perhaps in a style and vocabulary as baffling to most modern popular audiences (as opposed to the official clique of 'knowing' academic audiences) as *Hamlet* itself, can be made to support a subversive interpretation of the play which popular Elizabethan audiences might have collaborated with but which popular modern audiences would surely find inimical. There may be no such thing as a popular audience for *Hamlet* today since the major portion of such audiences is there largely to 'get cultured' and is thus extraordinarily submissive to the play's function as a vehicle of official culture. Thus *Hamlet* is popularly seen to explore the 'absurd' or the 'irrational' by such audiences but is not popularly seen as a celebration or debunking of the *Angst* associated with these. Queen Elizabeth could only covet such docility from audiences of 'her' popular theatre.

According to Wiles, the Elizabethan theatre 'stood at a point of transition between the modern concept of theatre as part of a leisure industry and the medieval or pre-urban concept of drama as part of an inversionary or carnivalesque mode of living life'.[31] The so-called groundlings, at least, some of them recent immigrants from the country, would have arrived at the theatre in a carnivalesque, participatory mood which theatrical convention encouraged. Contemporary references to the ur-*Hamlet* suggest that Hamlet was popularly *known* for a 'ham' and was thus a likely — perhaps even a traditional — source of such irreverent parody. Thomas Nashe's Preface to Robert Greene's *Menaphon* (1589), well known among Elizabethan scholars for its sarcastic allusion to an earlier *Hamlet* play, possibly by Thomas Kyd, supports such an assumption:

> [Y]et English *Seneca* read by Candlelight yeelds many good sentences, as *Blood is a begger*, and so forth; and if you intreate him faire in a frostie morning, hee will affoord you whole Hamlets, I should say handfuls of Tragicall speeches.[32]

Thomas Lodge's irreverent allusion seven years later, probably to the same play, further suggests the critical contempt in which the earlier *Hamlet* was apparently held. One of Beelzebub's several offspring, Hate-Vertue by name, is described:

> [H]e is a foule lubber, his tongue tipt with lying, his heart steeld against charity, he walks for the most part in black vnder colour of grauity, & looks as pale as the Visard of ye ghost which cried so miserably at ye Theator like an oisterwife, **Hamlet, reuenge**.[33]

But it is not only the ur-*Hamlet* which comes in for such contemptuous contemporary allusion. The great majority of explicit allusions to Shakespeare's *Hamlet* from the first decade of the seventeenth century cited in *The Shakespere Allusion-Book*[34] also take on a facetious ring, tending toward a demystification of *Hamlet* as tragic icon. Such allusions might be understood as part of the give and take of the War of the Theatres, but such a context does not seem to me to disqualify them as evidence of one variety of actual audience response to *Hamlet*.

Hamlet's insults to the groundlings everywhere seem double-edged, in the 'authorized' text as well as the 'Bad Quarto' passage. Claudius claims not to have proceeded publicly against Hamlet because of 'the great love the general gender bear him' (IV. vii. 18). Perhaps Hamlet was so regarded by the 'general gender' of the Globe audience as well, which might have interpreted his insults to them as rough intimacies intended to elicit something other than their meek acquiescence.

*

Hamlet as tragedy, as ritual enactment of a royal prince's personal death and rebirth (in the arms of a troop of singing angels), effecting a sympathetic rebirth for the whole of Denmark from its former rank moral / spiritual condition, shares a mythic resonance with the primitive custom of ritual sacrifice. And here, too, the folk tradition of the Fool bears relevance. Citing Frazer's *The Golden Bough*, Chambers writes:

> The victim in a human sacrifice was not originally merely a man, but a very important man, none other than the king, the priest-king of the tribe. In many communities, Aryan-speaking and other, it has been the principal function of such a priest-king to die, annually or at longer intervals, for the people.[35]

With time, according to Chambers, the common association of madness with divine possession apparently contributed to make the village fool or natural seem a suitable substitute king / victim. When the sanctity of human life forbade *any* human sacrifice, the temporary king was still chosen, but his slaying was symbolic.[36] This explains the traditional association of the May-king with foolery as well as agricultural rebirth. Hamlet, then, as his own tragic Fool, dying so that Denmark may be cleansed of rank regicide and royal incest, may be seen in the context of these rituals. The folk dramas derived from the sword dance

> have a common incident, which may reasonably be taken to be the central incident, in the death and revival, generally by a Doctor, of one of the characters. And in virtue of this central incident one is justified in classing them as forms of a folk-drama in which the resurrection of the year is symbolized.[37]

Hamlet is brought back to life in two different aspects. He is spiritually reborn, as signified by the angels; he is physically reborn in Fortinbras, emblem of resurrected Denmark, also the son of a defeated king, also prevented from succeeding his father by an uncle. In this context, young Fortinbras almost literally has young Hamlet's 'dying voice'. But the sombre resonances of Hamlet's princely death ritual are mocked by the 'substitute' Fool. Conceivably, the play *was* viewed as a celebration of death in the 'gay' carnival sense by some segment of its original audiences. The 1980 BBC *Hamlet* production features Emrys James as a fat (pregnant?) Grave-digger with a skinny companion.[38] The Grave-digger is a jester, an associate of Yorick perhaps, who 'poured a flagon of Rhenish on [his] head once' (V. i. 173-4). Here is an image of 'fat Death', the carnival figure explored by Bakhtin, under whose influence Hamlet seems to realize that all ambition must come to the same low, comic conclusion (death/erasure). Fortinbras in the final act reminds the audience of this lesson: 'O proud Death, / What feast is toward in thine eternal cell?' (V. ii. 369-70). We *are* witnessing a *feast*, and not necessarily a cold one like Gertrude's second wedding feast.

What does Hamlet mean by his final words, 'the rest is silence' (V. ii. 363)? What does 'silence' mean? Does it mean *peace*? Or does it mean *nothing*, that there *is nothing more*? Hamlet has played his final scene, spoken his final lines (until the 'put on' of the next performance). If he lives on, he lives on not in the identity of Hamlet but in the 'voice' of Fortinbras. This is enough. The King is dead. Long live the King! Horatio, however, does not let matters rest there. He seems to contradict Hamlet: 'Good night, sweet prince, / And flights of angels sing thee to thy rest' (V. ii. 364-5). Maybe the audience should laugh here because Hamlet isn't going anywhere with any singing angels! Just ask the Grave-digger. Just ask the Fool. *Hamlet* invites its audience's imagination to 'trace the noble dust' (V. i. 197) of Hamlet as well as Alexander to a 'bung-hole' (V. i. 198). The image is that of a cork stopper in a beer-barrel. The image also suggests a stuffed mouth. A 'bung' can also be a pickpocket or 'bung-nipper', and as an adjective 'bung' can mean 'tipsy, fuddled'.[39] The carnival associations seem inescapable. Do Horatio and Fortinbras, standing for the official, neoclassical, serious view of *Hamlet* as tragedy, think, because they themselves are virtuous, that there shall be no more cakes and ale? In the teeth of such official seriousness, the context of the native tradition of the Elizabethan, popular theatre suggests that some significant portion of Shakespeare's audience surely felt otherwise.

Perhaps the metadramatic echoes of the final lines continue to undercut the claims of official culture regarding the tragedy. Horatio says to Fortinbras:

> give order that these bodies
> High on a stage be placed to the view,
> And let me speak to th'yet unknowing world
> How these things came about. So shall you hear
> Of carnal, bloody, and unnatural acts,
> Of accidental judgments, casual slaughters,
> Of deaths put on by cunning and forc'd cause,
> And, in this upshot, purposes mistook

> Fall'n on th'inventors' heads. All this can I
> Truly deliver.

(V. ii. 382-91)

But how can he? Why should Fortinbras trust Horatio's prologue? Terence Hawkes comments on the above lines:

> We know, from what we have seen, that the story which he [Horatio] proposes to recount ... was not as simple, as like an 'ordinary' revenge play, as that. His solemnity — 'All this can I / Truly deliver' — mocks at the subtleties, the innuendoes, the contradictions, the imperfectly realized motives and sources for action that have been exhibited to us.[40]

As Calderwood points out, the messengers in this play consistently foul up their messages, and Horatio is not any different. Polonius earlier has offered to 'Truly deliver' Hamlet to Claudius as though Hamlet's truth were a simple matter:

> Hath there been such a time — I would fain know that —
> That I have positively said ''Tis so',
> When it prov'd otherwise?
>
> . . . .
> If circumstances lead me, I will find
> Where truth is hid, though it were hid indeed
> Within the centre.

(II. ii. 153-9)

What truth does Horatio intend 'Truly' to deliver that Fortinbras would 'haste to hear' (V. ii. 391)? Do we hear (perhaps in the 'wings') the laughter of Death and the Fool? In the *voice* of his newly acquired authority, Fortinbras commands:

> Let four captains
> Bear Hamlet like a soldier to the stage,
> For he was likely, had he been put on,
> To have prov'd most royal ...

(V. ii. 400-3)

Hawkes writes that Fortinbras's summation of Hamlet's potential here 'must, surely, wring a tiny gasp of disbelief at the very least from us. Nobody, so far as we have seen ... was likely to have proved less royal.'[41] What's more, from a metadramatic perspective, *Hamlet* / Hamlet has already been 'put on', and in that 'put on' proven a sham, a 'put on' ludicrously analogous to the central character's antic 'put on' disposition. Hamlet doesn't need to be borne *to* the 'stage'. He needs to be borne *from* the stage. Unless Hamlet is not at present on the stage but down among the groundlings. The 'stage' here, though, most probably refers to some upper, more distant and formal position.[42] 'Stage' does not *necessarily* have explicit reference to a theatre, but its theatrical resonances would have been (and are) impossible to blot out. Perusal of its usages recorded in the *OED* support this. A 'stage' was a platform structure on a pageant wagon or a 'pulpit'.[43] Chambers identifies the first raised 'stages' in the early miracle plays as church *pulpita* which served as platforms from which the more formal speeches would have been delivered.[44] These *pulpita* stood upon a broader playing area called the *platea*, where there was broader actor/audience interaction.[45] In other places where Shakespeare uses the word 'stage' as a noun he means that platform in a theatre where performances take place.[46] Here 'stage' seems to mean some higher and more honoured place 'off stage'. But 'stage' also suggests, in the present case, some structure (*locus, domus, sedes, pulpita, tentus*) elevated above the general surface of the 'playne' or '*platea*'. In this sense 'stage' refers to that part of the playing area reserved for the most important characters. By implication then, Hamlet, until his death, has been 'downstage', at the edge of that broad portion of the Elizabethan stage analogous with the medieval *platea*, interacting antically, as the Fool was wont to do, with the spectators. Thus considered, Fortinbras would remove Hamlet from the burlesque associations of the *platea* to the more formal, mimetic associations of the 'stage' or *pulpita* objectifying his high rank. And that is where the humanist tradition of scholarship and interpretation has placed him.

Fortinbras, for what it is worth, does not imagine any singing angels, only feasting death. The only singing in this play comes from the mad Ophelia and the Grave-digger (and perhaps from Hamlet in the jig following *The Mousetrap*). The Grave-digger sings not, as Hamlet suggests, because he has 'no feeling of his business' (V. i. 65) but because (to use Bakhtin's terminology) he sees through his business to its 'gay', 'regenerative' side. Hamlet never *appears* to penetrate that far. In fact, tragedy, by definition, cannot penetrate that far. But the social perspective of the graveyard scene, taken with the metadrama generally, particularly if considered in the context of the native tradition, does penetrate so far, and, in so doing, has the power to challenge the tragedy.

What of Hamlet's stoic friend? Can Horatio be to the formal, royal Hamlet what Polonius was to Claudius, an ineffectual advisor? What is the possibility that the same actor might have doubled the parts of Polonius and Horatio? Is Horatio about to assume the ineffectual advisor role in his relationship to Fortinbras? In the graveyard scene Horatio stands awkwardly by, mute for the most part, except for a few one-line responses honouring the seemingly morbid, philosophical whimsies of his prince: 'Ay, my lord' (V. i. 86) and 'E'en so, my lord' (V. i. 195). Though young Fortinbras imagines the death scene before him as a feast, he does not laugh nor appear to comprehend, either, the intimations which the grave-digging clown suggests to Hamlet; but then Fortinbras, too, is worldly and ambitious. There does seem to be an aspect of the play, however, that, as Bristol suggests, invites us to laugh with Death, and in this sense Shakespeare's *Hamlet*, this most ambitious of tragedies by the 'immortal Bard', appears to erase itself not merely through metadrama or other linguistics-based critical theory, but through the laughter of Death, which is not satirical laughter but the inclusive, absolute, all-affirming, feasting, social laughter of the folk (*all* the people), the laughter of carnival.

Notes

1. See Terence Hawkes, '*Telmah*' in Patricia Parker and Geoffrey Hartman, eds, *Shakespeare and the Question of Theory* (New York and London: Methuen, 1985), pp. 310-32; J. Dover Wilson, *What Happens in 'Hamlet'* (Cambridge: Cambridge University Press, 1935).

2. Throughout this essay I rely broadly on the work of E. K. Chambers, Robert Weimann, M. M. Bakhtin, Michael Bristol and David Wiles.

3. I interpret the Fool tradition broadly here to include the Vice and clown, for by Shakespeare's time the separate identities of Fool, Clown, and Vice had to some significant degree merged. See L. W. Cushman, *The Devil and the Vice in the English Dramatic Literature before Shakespeare* (Halle: Max Niemeyer, 1900), p. 70; E. K. Chambers, *The Mediaeval Stage*, 2 vols (London: Oxford University Press, 1903), I, 214, II, 141, 203-5; Charles Read Baskervill, *The Elizabethan Jig and Related Song Drama* (Chicago: University of Chicago Press, 1929), p. 92; Robert Weimann, *Shakespeare and the Popular Tradition in the Theatre: Studies in the Social Dimension of Dramatic Form and Function*, ed. Robert Schwartz (Baltimore and London: The Johns Hopkins University Press, 1978), p. 12; Andrew Gurr, *Playgoing in Shakespeare's London* (Cambridge: Cambridge University Press, 1987), p. 117; Arthur McGee, *The Elizabethan Hamlet* (New Haven: Yale University Press, 1987), pp. 81, 84-5; David Wiles, *Shakespeare's Clown:*

Actor and Text in the Elizabethan Playhouse (Cambridge: Cambridge University Press, 1987), pp. 1, 12.

4. See Harry Levin, *The Question of Hamlet* (New York: Oxford University Press, 1959); Michael Graves, 'Hamlet as Fool', *Hamlet Studies*, 4 (1982), 72-88; McGee, *The Elizabethan Hamlet*; Wiles, *Shakespeare's Clown*; and Michael D. Bristol, *Carnival and Theatre: Plebeian Culture and the Structure of Authority in Renaissance England* (New York and London: Routledge, 1989).

5. Levin, *The Question of Hamlet*, p. 126.

6. Graves, 'Hamlet as Fool', 73-4.

7. Graves, 'Hamlet as Fool', 82-3.

8. Wiles, *Shakespeare's Clown*, pp. 59-60.

9. Bristol, *Carnival and Theatre*, p. 187.

10. Bristol, *Carnival and Theatre*, p. 193.

11. Bristol, *Carnival and Theatre*, p. 191. François Laroque, *Shakespeare's festive World: Elizabethan seasonal entertainment and the professional stage*, tr. Janet Lloyd (Cambridge: Cambridge University Press, 1991), p. 184, also concedes carnival's radical ground to a conventional understanding of tragedy, contending that 'in the great tragedies of [Shakespeare's] ... middle period the meaning of festivity is reversed, coming to signify chaos and darkness'.

12. M. M. Bakhtin, *The Dialogic Imagination: Four Essays*, ed. Michael Holquist, tr. Caryl Emerson and Michael Holquist (Austin: University of Texas Press, 1981), p. 163.

13. Steven Mullaney, *The Place of the Stage: License, Play, and Power in Renaissance England* (Chicago and London: The University of Chicago Press, 1988), contends that the popular theatres, located as they were in the margins and liberties of London, were in a unique position to offer such challenges.

14. Wiles, *Shakespeare's Clown*, p. viii.

15. Horace Howard Furness, ed., *A New Variorum Edition of Shakespeare:'Hamlet'*, 2 vols (1877; New York: American Scholar Publications, 1965), II, 64-5.

16. The phrase is from Wiles, *Shakespeare's Clown*, p. viii.

17. Gurr, *Playgoing*, p. 128.

18. Gurr, *Playgoing*, p. 151.

19. Thomas Nashe dedicated *An Almond for a Parrat* (1590) 'To That Most Comicall and conceited Caualeire *Monsieur du Kempe, Iestmonger and* Vice-gerent generall to the Ghost of Dicke Tarlton.' See Ronald B. McKerrow, ed., *The Works of Thomas Nashe*, 5 vols (Oxford: Blackwell, 1958), III, 341.

20. See Gurr, *Playgoing*, p. 128.

21. Wiles, *Shakespeare's Clown*, p. 117.

22. Wiles, *Shakespeare's Clown*, p. 57.

23. Gurr, *Playgoing*, p. 152.

24. Gurr, *Playgoing*, pp. 139, 127.

25. See E. K. Chambers, *The Elizabethan Stage*, 4 vols (Oxford: Clarendon Press, 1923), IV, 184-345.

26. M. M. Bakhtin, *Rabelais and His World*, tr. Hélène Iswolsky (Bloomington: Indiana University Press, 1984), p. 92.

27. James L. Calderwood, *To Be And Not To Be: Negation and Metadrama in 'Hamlet'* (New York: Columbia University Press, 1983), p. 104.

28. Annabel Patterson, *Shakespeare and the Popular Voice* (Oxford: Blackwell, 1989), p. 95. See also pp. 99-104.

29. Stephen Booth, 'On the Value of *Hamlet*' in Norman Rabkin, ed., *Reinterpretations of Elizabethan Drama* (New York and London: Columbia University Press, 1969), p. 151.

30. Booth, 'On The Value of *Hamlet*', p. 175.

31. Wiles, *Shakespeare's Clown*, p. xii.

32. Nashe, *Works*, III, 315.

33. Thomas Lodge, *Wits miserie, and the worlds madnesse* (London, 1596; S.T.C. 16677), p. 56.

34. See C. M. Ingleby, Toulmin Smith, and F. J. Furnivall, eds, *The Shakspere Allusion-Book: A Collection of Allusions To Shakspere From 1591 To 1700*, 2 vols. Re-issued with a preface by Sir Edmund Chambers (London: Oxford University Press, 1932).

35. Chambers, *The Mediaeval Stage*, I, 134.

36. Chambers, *The Mediaeval Stage*, I, 137-8.

37. Chambers, *The Mediaeval Stage*, I, 207.

38. *Hamlet*, dir. Rodney Bennett, PBS Stations, U.S.A., 10 November 1980.

39. *OED* sb. 11; sb. 2; a1.

40. Hawkes, '*Telmah*' in Parker and Hartman, eds, *Shakespeare*, p. 310-11.

41. Hawkes, '*Telmah*' in Parker and Hartman, eds, *Shakespeare*, p. 311.

42. See *OED* sb. I. 4.

43. *OED* sb. I. 1. a and I. 4. d.

44. Chambers, *The Mediaeval Stage*, II, 134-6.

45. See Weimann, *Shakespeare and the Popular Tradition*, pp. 73-85.

46. Excluding the two occurrences under discussion here (*Hamlet*, V. ii. 383 and 401), John Bartlett's *A Complete Concordance to Shakespeare* (London: Macmillan, 1937) cites twenty occurrences of the word 'stage' in Shakespeare's plays. All but two clearly suggest a theatrical reference.

Psychoanalysis and Language

POLONIUS, THE MAN BEHIND THE ARRAS:
A JUNGIAN STUDY

ELIZABETH OAKES

All of Shakespeare's plays, especially *Hamlet*, have something rumbling below the action, characters and images, something attributable neither to his sources nor his culture, something even the dramatist himself could not, in T. S. Eliot's words, 'drag to light'.[1] It is this level that lends itself to an analysis informed by Jungian psychology. Archetypal critics have done some excavation work on the play, especially on Hamlet and the two women.[2] However, more remains, for *Hamlet* is composed of a panopoly of archetypes, Jung's term for those 'inborn forms' common to all mankind that erupt in madness and in dreams, myths and literature.[3] Hamlet is the hero and scapegoat, Gertrude the terrible / great mother, Ophelia the anima, Claudius the shadow, and the elder Hamlet the racial father. One character, however, occupies a more substantial position on the archetypal level than his function on the literal level would at first suggest. Polonius embodies three important figures: wise old man, fool and scapegoat. His degeneration within these roles is crucial to the play; for the sacrifice of the fool contrasts, through symbols connected with the mother archetype, with that of the hero, which is preceded by the archetypal night sea journey. After the trip to England, a reoriented and reborn Hamlet sacrifices himself and, in so doing, makes possible the resurgence of a new order. On the archetypal level, Polonius is an instrumental character, for his truncated sacrifice, the climax of the action, contrasts with the transcendent one of Hamlet, the climax of the symbolic level.

Polonius as Wise Old Man

On the literal level of the play, Polonius is a father whose fears that the young prince will seduce and abandon his daughter turn to opportunism, when he mistakenly diagnoses Hamlet as lovesick. On the archetypal level, he functions as the wise old man, whose positive and negative sides alternate in the triad he makes with Hamlet and Ophelia of wise old man, hero and anima. Amidst her talk of young men and Valentine's day, Ophelia 'speaks much of her father' (IV. v. 4), describing him as having a *'beard ... as white as snow'*, a *'flaxen ... poll'* (IV. v. 192-3). By calling attention to this detail, she unconsciously links her father with the wise old man figure; as Jung pictures him, he has a white beard and a bald head ringed with white hair.[4] Although in life Polonius in no way performs with the wisdom of, say, Prospero, whom Alex Aronson identifies as a wise old man figure in his relation to Miranda,[5] in her madness Ophelia rectifies the situation, replacing the father she had with the one she needed. Feminist critics rightly decry Polonius's patriarchal control of his daughter, but the play presents them as intertwined on the archetypal plane. 'I would give you some violets, but they withered all when my father died' (IV. v. 181-3), Ophelia says, annexing the loss of herself to the death of her father. Laertes's question,

> is't possible a young maid's wits
> Should be as mortal as an old man's life?

> (IV. v. 159-60)

is rhetorical, for the answer is definitely affirmative.

As Hamlet's anima — 'she is the human screen upon which Hamlet's unconscious anima is projected', says H. R. Coursen[6] — Ophelia is linked with him, as well as Polonius, in death. After losing the two men closest to her, her father and Hamlet, who represent her animus (Jung's term for the male side of the female psyche),[7] Ophelia falls 'like a creature native and indued / Unto' water (IV. vii. 178-9), the element most associated with the anima figure.[8] Thus, her madness and death not only reflect her archetype but also parallel Hamlet's 'antic disposition' (I. v. 180). Earlier in the play, Horatio adumbrated the similarity in his warning to Hamlet about following the ghost ('What if it tempt you toward the flood, my lord?' [I. iv. 69]), for in these lines falling, madness and drowning are linked, just as they are at Ophelia's death. Hamlet, however, emerges reborn after 'falling' into his unconscious, while Ophelia does not.[9] Thus, appropriately, when Hamlet returns from England, he encounters Ophelia's funeral train. Representative of his female side, she has gone mad and died as Hamlet regained his rationality. Indeed, in her all his sins are remembered.

It is the responsibility of the wise old man, with his superior insight, to instruct and guide the hero when he is unable to help himself.[10] With Hamlet, however, Polonius inverts the figure; Hamlet's psyche has cast him in the role of spiritual leader, but he will not play it. Polonius's failure does not lie in his not having some insight, but in his overriding concern for his position in the court at the expense of helping either his prince or his daughter. Hamlet conveys his frustration at Polonius's inadequacy in his jibes, especially in his calling him a 'fishmonger' (II. ii. 174). Although on the literal level the epithet seems so unapt for the chief aide to a king as to be meaningless,[11] on the archetypal level the term resonates. A wise old man is present, says Jung, in many dreams in which fish symbolize the unconscious particles of the mind.[12] But instead of fulfilling his role and helping Hamlet achieve psychological and spiritual insight, Polonius *uses* these unconscious elements to secure his position in court. Instead of 'fishing' for them, he 'peddles' them; thus he is a fishmonger instead of a fisherman. Such expedience marks Polonius as the fool, a role he plays until after he dies, when he finally resembles the wise old man that Hamlet needed him to be. Polonius is in death, Hamlet says, no longer a 'foolish prating knave' but 'most still, most secret, and most grave' (III. iv. 216-17), as befits the wise old man figure.

Polonius as Fool and Scapegoat

In the ritual of sacrifice, the community transfers all its sins to a chosen figure and then kills him or her, thereby purifying itself. Not confined to classical antiquity, the practice 'seems not to have been wholly extinct' in medieval Europe and survived into Shakespeare's time transmuted into holiday entertainment.[13] Shakespeare's dramatic use of these remnants, the effectiveness of which is dependent upon subtlety, was possible only when they were ceremonial, not actual, or, as C. L. Barber says, 'still in the blood but no longer in the brain'.[14] One of the ways in which archetypal energy erupted in community practices, scapegoating forms a basis for several of Shakespeare's characters, especially Falstaff, as Barber shows.[15] But one figure – Polonius – whose embodiment of the scapegoat is subtle but integral to *Hamlet*, needs to be added to the company.

Polonius becomes the scapegoat when he is killed behind the arras, with the role deriving much of its mana from Shakespeare's 'supersubtleties', Harold Goddard's term for those words or phrases that create an atmosphere not attributable to the action alone.[16] For instance, Hamlet's calling Polonius a calf (III. ii. 104) before the play within the play links him to the scapegoat tradition, for, as Shakespeare and his audience would have known from the Old Testament, calves were commonly chosen as sacrificial animals.[17] Additionally, in drawing 'apart the body' (IV. i. 24), as Gertrude says he does, Hamlet completes the process of sacrifice, as the enacters of the ritual cut the animal apart in specified ways. Although those executed in Shakespeare's society were sometimes drawn and quartered, and the words obviously relate to that practice, and serve to build up the submerged meaning of the play.

Polonius's death incurs added meaning from his substituting for the king.[18] Immediately after killing Polonius, Hamlet says, 'Is it the King?' (III. iv. 25). Later, Claudius, realizing his danger, says to Gertrude:

> It had been so with us had we been there.
>
> (IV. i. 13)

He is suited for this role because of his incarnation of the fool, the one traditionally chosen as a substitute for the king in ritual.[19] Although Polonius is not in motley, Hamlet calls him a fool often enough, although nowhere more significantly than in the closet scene after the murder:

> Thou wretched, rash, intruding fool, farewell.
> I took thee for thy better.
>
> (III. iv. 31-2)

Polonius is not the source of evil in the society, however, so not only must the king's substitute die, but also the king.

This aspect of Polonius's death partakes of the movement from fool to king and king to fool that recurs several times in the play.[20] It occurs, for instance, in Claudius's ordering Polonius's body to be found and taken into the chapel (IV. i. 36-7). Here the two men exchange places, for Claudius was in the chapel right before the closet scene. The same polarity from fool to king is also evident when Hamlet holds Yorick's skull and ponders the meaning of death (V. i. 74-209). His mind wanders from the fool to heroes and kings. And as he speaks of death in terms of the fool and the king, so has he recently killed a fool and will soon kill a king. Aptly, the graveyard scene closes with the entrance of the king, Claudius. Given this pattern, then, the death of Polonius portends the death of Claudius.[21] Not confined to the action, the movement between opposites is also alluded to figuratively when Hamlet says, 'Your fat king and your lean beggar is but variable service — two dishes, but to one table' (IV. iii. 23-4), a riddle that suggests that the king, as well as the fool, will be eaten by 'a certain convocation of politic worms' (IV. iii. 19-20) that Hamlet says are gnawing at Polonius.

Just as the death of the fool who stands in for the king resonates archetypally, so does the actual death of the king. To kill the king, Hamlet must distance himself from him, a difficult task, as Claudius personifies all that is wrong in Denmark to Hamlet, all he does not want to be – and perhaps fears he is.[22] Hamlet projects onto him his shadow self, which is, as Frieda Fordham describes it, 'all those uncivilized desires and emotions that are incompatible with social standards, and our ideal personality, all that we are ashamed of, all that we do not want to know about ourselves.'[23] To Hamlet, a certain part of himself, the instinctual part, is no better than Claudius. For instance, he tells his mother that she has married a man who is no more like her first husband than he 'to Hercules' (I. ii. 153), putting himself on the same level with Claudius: both are unlike the idealized father. Claudius represents to Hamlet, as Jung says the personified shadow always does, 'everything that the subject refuses to acknowledge about himself and yet is always thrusting itself upon him directly or indirectly'.[24] Crucially, unlike Claudius, Hamlet tries to conquer these drives in himself. He, who can be described as a 'child of violence and lust',[25] tries to set himself right as well as his society. However, when an individual tries to reject the shadow self,

> a part of our own personality will remain on the opposing side. The result is that we shall constantly (although involuntarily) do things behind our own backs that support this other side, and thus we shall unwittingly help our enemy.[26]

It is only after his return from England that he separates himself from Claudius. Enumerating the king's trespasses to Horatio (V. ii. 63-70), Hamlet now sees his stepfather as a person whose evil originates in and is confined to his own actions, and in the last scene he dispatches him.

Much as Polonius blends with the king on the social level, he also incorporates the fathers in the play into one figure whom Hamlet can confront. The conflated father figures in the play are a staple of psychoanalytic criticism especially,[27] with most commentators seeing the elder Hamlet as the idealized father and Claudius as his evil *alter ego* or the part of the father whom the Oedipal son fears. In archetypal terms, however, the biological father and the stepfather together comprise the racial father, who

> is the representative of the spirit, whose function it is to oppose pure instinctuality. That is his archetypal role, which falls to him regardless of his personal qualities;

hence he is very often an object of neurotic fears for his son. ... The paradox lies in the fact that ... the father apparently lives a life of unbridled instinct and yet is the living embodiment of the law that thwarts instinct.[28]

Not only is the dominant aspect of the elder Hamlet brought out in the play in the emphasis on his being a warrior, but also Hamlet immediately dedicates himself to carrying out the ghost's command. Thus, the elder Hamlet in a way usurps his son's life, and, significantly, in the following lines, the words 'dearest foe' remind Hamlet of his father:

> Would I had met my dearest foe in heaven
> Or ever I had seen that day, Horatio.
> My father — methinks I see my father .

(I. ii. 182-4)

Indeed, his father is most dear to him, and, also, his dearest (worst) foe. For this latter aspect of the father – as foe – Claudius easily serves, as he also shares in some of the disciplinary side of the racial father. Although Hamlet directs opposite emotions – idealized love and rabid hatred – toward the two men, he attacks only the father as dotard, that is, in the form of Polonius, whose age he stresses.[29] Through Polonius Hamlet triumphs for a time over his fathers.[30] They are only 'guts' (III. iv. 214) to him in the closet scene, food for worms and for his own jests.

The Contrasting Sacrifices

As Erich Neumann observes, those chosen as scapegoats usually do not fit into the society because of either inferiority or superiority.[31] Like Polonius, Hamlet may play the fool at times but, unlike the older man, he is a fool with a conscious purpose. He is a scapegoat, too, but a heroic, not an accidental one. Hamlet's sacrifice completes the process begun at Polonius's death: there he struck the first blow at the old order,[32] but by his own willingness to give his life he cleanses his society of evil. The different effects the deaths have on the community derive from the nature of the two individuals' sacrifices. Through symbols connected with the mother archetype, Hamlet's sacrifice is, both individually and in its effect on the community, consummate, while Polonius's is void.

On the archetypal level, the mother figure, which is 'inconceivably complex', says Jung,[33] is embodied in Gertrude in several aspects. First, she is what Jung calls the 'terrible' or 'devouring' mother who 'gives life and then takes it away'. On this level, Jung stresses, it is not the real mother who causes the fixation, although she may 'seriously injure her child by the morbid tenderness with which she pursues it into adult life, thus prolonging the infantile attitude beyond the proper time. It is rather the mother-imago',[34] that is, the subjective perception by the child of the mother that is influenced by the store of archetypes in the mind as well as by the actual relationship. Significantly, Hamlet does not leave his mother until he sets sail for England, the journey that generates his extrication from the terrible mother in his rebirth from water.

Besides this negative aspect, the mother can represent security on the archetypal level as well as she often does on the personal level. Having just suffered a terrible shock, Hamlet wishes to return to the paradisal state of the womb where no decisions have to be made. This regressive wish makes it impossible for him to function as an adult — he must renege on his promises of love to Ophelia, he must hedge on his promise to the ghost and he must let his speech sometimes take the form of nonsense. This longing for security can also take the form of a death wish for, Jung says, death can also be a symbol of the maternal womb:[35] ''tis a consummation / Devoutly to be wish'd' (III. i. 63-4), says Hamlet, welding the sexual and the mortal together. In this aspect of the mother archetype also, even though it is seemingly positive, the mother who gives birth incapacitates the child, turning him toward death instead of life.

In her psychoanalytic study, Janet Adelman posits Hamlet's *Angst* in his fear of being engulfed by 'the sexualized maternal body', whose gift of life carries with it the grossness of flesh and the certainty of death. The business of the play then becomes not revenge for the father but the reformation of the mother; the 'main psychological task that Hamlet seems to set himself is ... to remake her in the image of the Virgin Mother who could guarantee his father's purity, and his own, repairing the boundaries of his selfhood'. His task, as Hamlet sees it, is to overcome his own and his mother's solid or sullied flesh — one presupposes the other. In this analysis Adelman locates the mother not so much in the actual character of Gertrude that we see on the stage but in the adult Hamlet's reactivated infantilism. The 'threats to the self' Hamlet suffers emanate from 'the earliest stages of emergent selfhood, when the nascent self is most fully subject to the mother's fantasied power to annihilate or contaminate'. Like Adelman, I am interested in Gertrude less as an 'independent character than as the site for fantasies larger than she is,'[36] but I approach her from a different angle. The mother can symbolize something in the personal unconscious (death, for instance, as she does in Adelman's study), but there are also elements in the play that symbolize the mother, and these are recoverable by the archetypal approach. Besides being embodied in Gertrude, the mother archetype is present in the play in symbolic form in the contrasting elements of water, from which Hamlet is mysteriously reborn, and earth, from which there is no rebirth. Hamlet transcends, through symbols,[37] the aspect of the mother archetype – the terrible mother – that most affects him. In fact, this is the reason for the Oedipal element, whose presence in the play is a point of agreement among psychoanalytic commentators:[38] it gives impetus to and provides energy for the complex symbol formation needed for Hamlet's rebirth. The following archetypal study thus adds to the psychoanalytic by examining the dynamics of Hamlet's individuation from the maternal matrix.

To discuss the Oedipal element on the symbolic level, it is necessary to examine, in addition to Freud's theories on incest (which are sufficient for a psychoanalytic examination of the play, based as they are on the personal unconscious), Jung's more inclusive formulations based on his study of the collective unconscious.[39] Refuting Freud's contention that symbol formation could be explained completely as a substitute for incest, Jung argues that the basis of the incest wish is not literal but 'the strange idea of becoming a child again, of returning to the parental shelter, and of entering into the mother in order to be reborn through her'. Jung also says that although the unconscious mind is much greater than the mother, the mother is its symbol. Regression thus leads back to the mother insofar as she is the 'gateway into the unconscious'. If allowed to go on, he continues, the regression will go back beyond the mother 'to the prenatal realm of the "Eternal Feminine", to the immemorial world of archetypal possibilities'. In this deep, unconscious part of the mind, he concludes, one finds:

> possibilities of 'spiritual' or 'symbolic' life and of progress which form the ultimate, though unconscious, goal of regression. By serving as a means of expression, as bridges and pointers, symbols help to prevent the libido from getting stuck in the material corporeality of the mother. Never has the dilemma been more acutely formulated than in the Nicodemus dialogue: on the one hand the impossibility

of entering again into the mother's womb; on the other, the need for rebirth from 'water' and 'spirit'.[40]

Through symbols, the individual goes beyond the personal and literal realization of a desire which involves the prohibited act of incest. The basic schema of Hamlet's symbolic rebirth involves the archetypal night sea journey. It is a rebirth of the self not through the mother but through the unconscious which stands for her. In *Complex / Archetype / Symbol*, Jacobi details these precise characteristics:

> A hero is devoured by a water monster in the West (*swallowing*). The animal travels with him to the East (*sea journey*). Meanwhile, the hero lights a fire in the belly of the monster (*fire-lighting*), and feeling hungry, cuts himself a piece of the heart (*cutting off of heart*). Soon afterwards he notices that the fish has glided to dry land (*landing*): he immediately begins to cut open the animal from within (*opening*); then he slips out (*slipping out*).[41]

Although some of the specific actions are, of course, different, Hamlet's journey to England by sea matches the overall pattern. 'I'll have him hence tonight' (IV. iii. 58), Claudius says, on the literal level expressing his impatience to have him gone, but on the symbolic level denoting the journey as one into the unconscious. Then, when Hamlet returns to Denmark, having saved himself by his own ingenuity, as does the hero in the *ur*-journey, he writes to Claudius, '*High and mighty, you shall know I am set naked on your kingdom*' (IV. vii. 42-3). One is born naked, and, although the word also means destitute, the connotation reinforces the symbolic rebirth. '"Naked"' (IV. vii. 50), exclaims Claudius, in his consternation implying that Hamlet is not using the term in an ordinary, or, in the terms of this study, a literal way.

Unfortunately, however, says Jung, this heroic deed 'has no lasting effects. Again and again the hero must renew the struggle, and always under the symbol of deliverance from the mother'. The second return to the mother and the consequent rebirth occur at Hamlet's death, as death can also be seen as a return to the mother.[42] During the night sea journey, Hamlet moves beyond the personal to the communal, a step that is shown in the play by his being surprised at Laertes's anger (V. i. 283-5). The concept of personal vengeance is far behind him; instead, he sees revenge, which he must now wreak on Claudius, in the context of the community. 'This is I, / Hamlet the Dane' (V. i. 250-1), he says, signifying not only that he has regained his identity but also that he considers himself an agent of the Danish people. Then, in another step, by his death, Hamlet moves beyond the communal to the spiritual; he transcends even the most complicated symbolic meaning that can be contained in physical acts, existing now entirely on the spiritual plane. After his death, Hamlet exists as a realized ideal, having importuned Horatio to 'in this harsh world draw [his] breath in pain / To tell [his] story' (V. ii. 353-4).

Polonius, however, achieves no such transformation. Although Hamlet will be buried with ceremony and remembered in Horatio's story of him, the court inters Polonius 'hugger-mugger' (IV. v. 84). Even his earthly line — his children — dies out, Ophelia also being buried without full rites. It is to the earth as mother that Polonius returns,[43] a fate made explicit in the play by the details concerning his corpse. 'I'll lug the *guts* [italics mine] into the neighbour room' (III. iv. 214), Hamlet says. 'Compounded it with dust, whereto 'tis kin' (IV. ii. 5), he answers, when asked by Rosencrantz what he has done with the body. Hamlet emphasizes Polonius's physical body, not his spirit, after his death just as he did before it,[44] an emphasis that may even extend to another character. Much has been made by critics of the various 'character-splits' in the play,[45] and in Polonius's case, the skull of Yorick graphically illustrates his fate. Polonius slips from wise old man to fool to scapegoat, and the skull shows dramatically the futility, on the spiritual level, of his sacrifice. In contrast, Hamlet can leap into Ophelia's grave and emerge, an action that not only graphically illustrates his rebirth but also foreshadows his spirit's victory over death at the end of the play.

In addition to the theatrical, literary, historical and personal ones, Shakespeare's 'source' was the archetypes that in this play vibrate beneath the surface. By tapping these 'healing and redeeming forces of the collective psyche',[46] Shakespeare transmutes the play's involvement with the corporeal world of nature, which Hamlet describes as 'gross' (I. ii. 136; IV. iv. 46) into a vision of the spiritual. Indeed, what fascinates us about *Hamlet* may be, as Gilbert Murray says, the same things which

> set our forefathers dancing all night on the hills, tearing beast and men in pieces, and joyously giving up their own bodies to the most ghastly death, to keep the green world from dying and to be the saviours of their own people.[47]

From the same stirrings that prompted such ancient rituals, Shakespeare created a work of art that, in its effect, begins to resemble a religious ceremony. And when this last stage begins, Polonius, the man behind the arras, has played out his role.

Notes

1. T. S. Eliot, '*Hamlet*' in *Selected Essays* (New York: Harcourt, 1932), p. 123.

2. For Hamlet, see Gilbert Murray's *Hamlet and Orestes: A Study in Traditional Types* (New York: Oxford University Press, 1914); Francis Ferguson's *The Idea of a Theater: A Study of Ten Plays* (New Jersey: Princeton University Press, 1968), pp. 127-33 especially; and Sven Armens's *Archetypes of the Family in Literature* (Seattle: University of Washington Press, 1966), pp. 125-8, 135-7. H. R. Coursen identifies Ophelia as an anima figure in *The Compensatory Psyche: A Jungian Approach to Literature* (New York: University Press of America, 1986), pp. 83-5, 91-3, as does Alex Aronson in *Psyche and Symbol in Shakespeare* (Bloomington: Indiana University Press, 1972), pp. 177-80. Armens also describes Gertrude as the Terrible Mother (p. 126). One other study deserves mention. W. I. D. Scott suggests the following schema: 'It is possible to visualize the main characters according to the conception of Jung, as components of Hamlet's total psyche. Polonius and Gertrude thus appear as distorted forms of the archetypal wise old man and great mother; Ophelia is the anima, Claudius the dark shadow and the ghost the persona. Only Horatio, as the helpful shadow, promotes any satisfactory stability in the psyche, and this structure expresses quite well the flaws responsible for the imperfect integration which we observe in Hamlet, and which is largely responsible for his failure to cope with the situation confronting him.' See *Shakespeare's Melancholics* (1920; Folcroft, Pa: The Folcroft Press, 1969), p. 106. However, Scott does not elaborate upon this outline of the archetypal figures in the play.

3. C. G. Jung, *Symbols of Transformation*, tr. R. F. C. Hull (New York: Pantheon, 1956), p. 408, and *The Archetypes and the Collective Unconscious*, tr. R. F. C. Hull (New York: Pantheon, 1959), pp. 5, 285. Since Maud Bodkin's pioneering *Archetypal Patterns in Poetry: Psychological Studies of Imagination* (1934; London: Oxford University Press, 1974), literary commentators have utilized Jung's theories to delve into what the psychologist calls visionary literature. In one kind of work, Jung specifies, a writer raises the details of daily life 'from the commonplace to the level of poetic experience'. In another kind, however, the artist creates out of the elements of 'primordial experience' (*Modern Man in Search of a Soul*, tr. W. S. Dell and Cary F. Baynes (New York: Harcourt, 1933), pp. 155-7). The impetus and shaping force for this second type of work emerge from the collective unconscious, that stratum of the psyche that contains the 'supra-individual' qualities which were not acquired but inherited, Jung says in *Contributions to Analytical Psychology*, tr. H. G. Baynes and Cary F. Paynes (New York: Harcourt, 1928), p. 275.

4. C. G. Jung, M.-L. von Franz, Joseph L. Henderson, Jolande Jacobi and Aniela Jaffé, *Man and His Symbols* (New York: Doubleday, 1964), p. 198.

5. Aronson, *Psyche*, pp. 175-80, 189-92.

6. Coursen, *Compensatory Psyche*, p. 93.

7. C. G. Jung, *Aion: Researches into the Phenomenology of the Self*, tr. R. F. C. Hull (New York: Pantheon, 1959), p. 141.

8. The anima is often associated with water and its figures, says Frieda Fordham, so it is fitting that Gertrude refers to Ophelia's skirts as 'mermaid-like' (IV. vii. 175). See *An Introduction to Jung's Psychology* (Baltimore, Md: Penguin, 1966), p. 54. It is also appropriate that it is Gertrude who describes her death, for the anima figure in its maiden aspect is the counterpart of the mother archetype (Jung, *The Archetypes*, p. 82).

9. In contrast, Aronson believes that although Ophelia's death 'appears to be a regression into insanity and suicide, her association in death with water, flowers, and spring points toward rebirth,' as, he continues, Shakespeare later resurrects her in the forms of Cordelia, who fulfils 'her fate as her father's anima', and Miranda, who rises 'out of the water into which Ophelia had sunk' (*Psyche*, p. 180). However, I would describe the three women as variations on a basic pattern rather than as one fluid character.

10. 'The old man always appears when the hero is in a hopeless and desperate situation from which only profound reflection or a lucky idea ... can extricate him. But since, for internal and external reasons, the hero cannot accomplish this himself, the knowledge needed to compensate the deficiency comes in the form of a personified thought, i.e., in the shape of this sagacious and helpful old man' (Jung, *The Archetypes*, pp. 217-18). Also see Jolande Jacobi, *Complex / Archetype / Symbol in the Psychology of C. G. Jung*, tr. Ralph Manheim (New York: Pantheon, 1959), p. 71.

11. Harold Jenkins glosses the term as 'ridiculously inappropriate' in the Arden edition of the play (p. 246). Interpretations on the literal level abound. Believing the term means procurer or pimp, Eric Partridge adds it to his list of Shakespeare's bawdy terms in *Shakespeare's Bawdy* (New York: Dutton, 1960), p. 113. Also, M. A. Shaaber suggests that it may mean something closer to 'wencher' in 'Polonius as Fishmonger', *Shakespeare Quarterly*, 22 (1971), 179-81; and Jean Jofen believes the term may connote one who spies out secrets, since a fishmonger, being all over town, would know all the gossip. See 'Polonius the Fishmonger', *Notes and Queries*, 19 (1971), 126-7.

12. Jung, *Aion*, pp. 152-3.

13. See Sir James Frazer, 'The Scapegoat' in John Vickery and J'nan M. Sellery, eds, *The Scapegoat: Ritual and Literature* (Boston: Houghton Mifflin, 1972), p. 12.

14. C. L. Barber, *Shakespeare's Festive Comedy: A Study of Dramatic Form and Its Relation to Social Custom* (Cleveland, Ohio: Meridian, 1967), p. 11.

15. Barber, *Festive Comedy*, pp. 192-221.

16. Harold Goddard, *The Meaning of Shakespeare*, 2 vols (Chicago: University of Chicago Press, 1951), I, 340n.

17. For verses detailing the sacrifice and dismemberment of calves, see Exodus 24: 5 and 29: 10-15, and Leviticus 9: 2-22. The festival fool in England sometimes wore a calf's skin. See Enid Welsford, *The Fool: His Social and Literary History* (1935; New York: Doubleday, 1961), p. 72. The epithet may also have reminded Shakespeare's audience of an entertainment called 'Killing the Calf', in which a performer pretended

to kill a calf behind a curtain. See Elizabeth Oakes, 'Killing the Calf in *Hamlet*', *Shakespeare Quarterly*, 34 (1983), 215-16.

18. In an Oedipal reading of the play, Polonius represents Claudius as father; Hamlet, says Ernest Jones, combines the two men with 'ease'. See his classic *Hamlet and Oedipus* (New York: Doubleday, 1954), pp. 154-5.

19. Welsford, *The Fool*, pp. 68-75.

20. For instance, Hamlet's vacillation between the two poles of hero-prince and fool is part of this design.

21. 'The death of kings is the beginning and the end of Hamlet's study in this play. Polonius offers him an imaginative link between the live king ... and the dead king', says John Hunt in 'A Thing of Nothing: The Catastrophic Body in *Hamlet*', *Shakespeare Quarterly*, 39 (1988), 33.

22. In Freudian terms, Claudius is, as Jones calls him, Hamlet's 'other self'; Hamlet cannot exact revenge because Claudius has achieved the Oedipal son's 'horrible wishes' (*Hamlet and Oedipus*, pp. 99-100). However, the shadow self incorporates aspects of the adult personality as well as the infantile.

23. Fordham, *An Introduction*, p. 50. The shadow self always projects onto another person of the same sex, says Jung in *Aion*, pp. 8-10.

24. Jung, *The Archetypes*, pp. 284-5.

25. Goddard, *Meaning*, I, 351.

26. Jung, *Modern Man*, p. 173.

27. For instance, see Janet Adelman, *Suffocating Mothers: Fantasies of Maternal Origin in Shakespeare's Plays, 'Hamlet' to 'The Tempest'* (New York and London: Routledge, 1991), pp. 18-23.

28. Jung, *Symbols*, p. 261.

29. See II. ii. 196-204, 219, 378-9. Also, K. R. Eissler interprets Polonius's and Hamlet's banter about the older man's enacting Julius Caesar as indicating that in Hamlet's unconscious even an 'elevated father', of whom Julius Caesar is an example, 'will one day fall into a decline and become a dotard' in *Discourse on Hamlet and 'Hamlet'* (New York: International Universities Press, 1971), p. 449.

30. Hamlet's words after he kills Polonius — 'Thou wretched, rash, intruding fool, farewell! / I took thee for thy better' (III. iv. 32-3) — assume an added dimension. For in addition to implying Claudius's social superiority, the word 'better' also pertains to the elder Hamlet, since he is the only one Hamlet reveres enough to consider better than the other people in Elsinore.

31. Erich Neumann, 'The Scapegoat Psychology' in Vickery and Sellery, eds, *The Scapegoat*, p. 47.

32. For instance, Ivor Morris says, 'Polonius is the embodiment of Hamlet's Denmark' in *Shakespeare's God: The Role of Religion in the Tragedies* (New York: St Martin's Press, 1972), p. 378.

33. Jung, *Modern Man*, p. 25.

34. Jung, *Symbols*, pp. 261, 298.

35. Jung, *Symbols*, pp. 390, 328.

36. Adelman, *Suffocating Mothers*, pp. 27, 31, 29, 30.

37. One can approach the collective unconscious mind only through the symbol, which acts as 'a kind of mediatory between the incompatibles of consciousness and the unconscious, between the hidden and the manifest' (Jacobi, *Complex*, p. 98).

38. See Norman N. Holland, *Psychoanalysis and Shakespeare* (New York: McGraw-Hill, 1964), p. 193.

39. Jung locates the collective unconscious beneath Freud's personal unconscious, the 'gathering place of forgotten and repressed contents' of the individual, which is a *tabula rasa* at birth (*The Archetypes*, p. 3).

40. Jung, *Symbols*, pp. 223-4, 298, 330, 330-1.

41. Jacobi, *Complex*, p. 180.

42. Jung, *Symbols*, pp. 348, 218, 439.

43. This symbolic linking, apart from being a common one, is found several places in Shakespeare, though perhaps most explicitly in the following lines from *Romeo and Juliet*, ed. Brian Gibbons (London and New York: Methuen, 1980):

> The earth that's nature's mother is her tomb:
> What is her burying grave, that is her womb;
> And from her womb children of divers kind
> We sucking on her natural bosom find.
>
> (II. iii. 5-8)

44. It may even be a requirement of the scapegoat figure, at least in Shakespeare, that this be so. Not only does Hamlet chronicle Polonius's physical infirmities, but he also castigates the weakness of his own flesh. Likewise, Hal details Falstaff's infirmities and weaknesses in his jests.

45. See Holland, *Psychoanalysis*, p. 193.

46. Jung, *Modern Man*, p. 272.

47. Murray, *Hamlet*, p. 25. It may also be the presence of the archetypal level that makes, as Murray says, 'Aeschylus, Euripides, and Shakespeare ... strikingly similar in certain points which do not occur at all in Saxo or Ambales or the Greek epic' (p. 17).

TRAGIC ALTERNATIVES: EROS AND SUPEREGO REVENGE IN *HAMLET*

JOANNA MONTGOMERY BYLES

Hamlet tells us, he has 'that within which passes show' (I. ii. 85). We become intensely aware of Hamlet's inner life through his soliloquies, which externalize and dramatize his inner conflicts so powerfully. How to denote these inner tensions, and his all-pervasive feelings of powerlessness and rage, and to express them truly is Hamlet's problem throughout the play.

In this essay I should like to focus on some of the psychological origins of revenge in *Hamlet*. I acknowledge that what I have to say leaves out many other problems, but from the perspective of psychoanalysis we might pose the following questions: what is the psychological object of mimesis in revenge tragedies, particularly in *Hamlet*? Why are many of Hamlet's actions motivated by impulse rather than reason? What is being represented? What role do destructive and self-destructive impulses play in Hamlet's destiny? What part does the socialized and / or individual superego play in creating the revenge tragedy in *Hamlet*? Is tragic revenge different from tragi-comic revenge? Is there some basic dynamic pattern of psychic action that Shakespearean tragedy dramatizes as revenge? How can Freud and other theorists help us to understand this dynamic pattern?

The concept of the superego, both individual and cultural, is important to our understanding of the dynamics of aggressive destruction in Shakespeare's tragedies involving revenge. The Freudian superego is usually thought of as heir to the Oedipus complex, the internalization of parental values and the source of punitive, approving and idealizing attitudes towards the self.[1] In drama, the tragic hero's superego is, of course, separate from the cultural superego. Superego aggression may be directed against the self or the external world; the operative feeling in this unconscious aggression is externalized and dramatized as revengeful hatred. Revenge is an important means of dramatizing this dynamic and its cultural significance within family relationships in the drama.

On one level, *Hamlet* is a play about conflict between the generations; within the play, parents and children are often enemies. All the younger generation are manipulated by the older generation for selfish ends. Clearly, *Hamlet* invites reflection on the proper relation between generations and the significance of inter-generational conflict.[2] After the death of his father, Hamlet cannot leave his family until he is forced into exile; he cannot separate from them, not just geographically but emotionally. Laertes is the only one to escape from Elsinore of his own free will. Ophelia is in much the same position as Hamlet until she takes her own life. Hamlet thinks constantly of suicide or murderous revenge; at times, he is totally absorbed by these deathly desires. Further, in this play two sons are slain, a daughter commits suicide, a mother and two fathers are murdered, and one, old Norway, is killed. The Pyrrhus speech with its arrested sword of vengeance first '*Repugnant to command*' (II. ii. 467) and then '*Aroused*' (II. ii. 484) falling on old Priam, whose sons had ambushed and murdered Pyrrhus' father, Achilles, extends this appalling pattern, metaphorically, to a fourth murdered father. The allusion looks back to the long ritual of revenge in literature. And, of course, it foreshadows Hamlet's own actions. Hamlet has already recalled the dire effect of this ancient revenge story on families in his earlier prompting of the chief Player: Pyrrhus is described as

horridly trick'd
With blood of fathers, mothers, daughters, sons

(II. ii. 453-4)

In *Hamlet*, Shakespeare subverts the essential logic of the revenge form by representing revenge as an inward tragic event, reinforced by destructive family relationships whose psychic energies violate and destroy the protagonist's psychic wholeness, fragmenting and ultimately dissolving the personality. In Hamlet himself, hate and destructiveness are consuming passions; the deep movement of superego aggression that motivates revenge carries him towards death.

I necessarily assume that tragic action directly links the protagonist's suffering and death to the vengeful destructiveness of his superego and that of the community he exists in, especially his family. Tragic revenge dramatizes qualitative differences between various forms of superego aggressiveness. Ultimately, it is the tragic revenge hero's fate to satisfy the conflicting demands of the socialized and his own superego; when these demands coalesce, we have a definitive tragic image: the destruction and self-sacrifice of the tragic hero.[3]

In *Hamlet*, Osric is the agent of this coalescence. The wager represents the poisonous revenge of both Laertes and Claudius; it is Hamlet's death warrant, but Hamlet has surrendered himself to its treachery and, more importantly, to his own death. The devoted Horatio guesses Hamlet's terrifying and deep resignation:

> If your mind dislike anything, obey it. I will forestall their repair hither and say you are not fit.

(V. ii. 213-14)

But Hamlet is ready to 'Let be' (V. ii. 220). At the end of the tragedy, there is a deathly co-operation between the protagonist and his environment in which destructive aggression is resolved and guilt atoned.

The theatre supplies the external frame onto which the internal struggle of the ego and superego is most commonly projected. The tragic hero involved in revenge acts out the inner conflict of the ego's struggle against the cruel demands of both his own and the socialized superego. The play represents the author's working out of this unconscious conflict which is transformed, with all its identifications into the play. The question of the socialized superego, or the communal or cultural superego, allows us to shift from the inner dynamics of the hero to those who surround him, the external figures in the social world of the play, who not only influence his inner life, but his entire tragic history, especially his family history. For example, at the beginning of the play Hamlet is mourning his lost father, and, in another sense his lost mother; what he needs to do is to refashion his emotional attachments to them. However, the circumstances of the play, the 'rottenness' in the State of Denmark and the crucial command to revenge, prevent Hamlet from identifying himself as the new heir; the demand to revenge intensifies his introjection of his father whose ideal he cannot live up to, and whose demands he cannot carry out. Instead of feeling the support and love of his father, he feels the fear, separation and anxiety of frustration and hostility. Added to all this is the general menacing atmosphere of the court, covered, of course, by a courtly show of good manners, in which nearly everyone seems to spy on him; the play is full of licit and illicit listening, secrecy and anxiety. The command to murderous revenge denies Hamlet the possibility of developing the healing processes of mourning whereby the lost loved one is internalized. Moreover, Hamlet's dead father's revelations cause Hamlet cruelly to reject Ophelia, who might have saved him from himself, and would, in fact, have prevented the separation of Eros and aggression in Hamlet's psychodynamic story.

Ophelia, too, is a victim of parental authority. She allows her father to deny what for her is her most crucial reality: her love for Hamlet and its history.[4] Although she is in love with Hamlet and has encouraged his intimacies, Ophelia allows her father to deny this emotional reality:

> OPHELIA: My lord, he hath importun'd me with love
> In honourable fashion.
> POLONIUS: Ay, fashion you may call it. Go to, go to.
> OPHELIA: And hath given countenance to his speech, my lord,
> With almost all the holy vows of heaven.
> POLONIUS: Ay, springes to catch woodcocks. I do know,
> When the blood burns, how prodigal the soul
> Lends the tongue vows.
>
> .   .   .   .
>   This is for all.
> I would not, in plain terms, from this time forth
> Have you so slander any moment leisure
> As to give words or talk with the Lord Hamlet.
> Look to't, I charge you. Come your ways.
> OPHELIA: I shall obey, my lord.

(I. iii. 110-36)

Polonius is clearly not at all interested in what Ophelia feels or how she perceives her relationship with Hamlet. Moreover, he forces her to be untrue to herself: to deny her love for Hamlet. He forces her into an invidious position and uses her to entrap Hamlet, so that he can prove himself right about Hamlet's 'madness', which then allows Claudius to take advantage of Hamlet's 'madness'.[5] But it is the poor, motherless Ophelia, who actually goes mad. All the fathers in the play, including the Ghost, without the slightest compunction gratify their own needs by manipulating their children.

Why, many critics have asked, does Hamlet accept the role of revenger?[6] Ethically and morally, it may be considered right or wrong; but, from a psychoanalytic perspective, it is the *only* thing he can do, mobilized as he is by the traumatic effects of his family predicament. He must identify with his dead father's outrage, and rescue his mother from her incestuous marriage, if he is to recover an integrated self and the integrity he needs to become his father's rightful heir:

> Remember thee?
> Ay, thou poor ghost, whiles memory holds a seat
> In this distracted globe. Remember thee?
> Yea, from the table of my memory
> I'll wipe away all trivial fond records,
> All saws of books, all forms, all pressures past
> That youth and observation copied there,
> And thy commandment all alone shall live
> Within the book and volume of my brain
> Unmix'd with baser matter.

(I. v. 95-104)

But all this unconsciously involves the murderous and self-murderous superego, dramatized as delay. The inward traumatic pressures of the past cannot so easily be wiped out.

In one sense, we might consider the characters in *Hamlet* as agents of the Ghost's hate. Or the Ghost may be a dramatic means of externalizing Hamlet's desire to kill Claudius, since the command to kill Claudius seems to come from outside himself. Daniel E. Schneider writes that a play is like a dream turned inside out — and an interpretation at the same time, the success and coherence depending upon the talents of the dramatist to organize and interpret fantasies so that they resonate with the fantasies of the audience. The dream's conflicting pain / pleasure principle made paramount and explicit is the emotional force of the drama; and the interpretation subsidiary and implicit is in its action, in plot, the exposition and motivating force of the drama's story, the dynamic of the author's conflict as it is externalized and interpreted into the fully realized social world of the drama.[7] I find this idea interesting and useful because it unites three essentials: the dramatist's psychic conflicts, the drama itself in all its identifications and the psyche or psyches of the audience. It takes account of the complexity of the tragedy as a work of art and the variety of reactions it stimulates in its audience, from the release of passion under the protection of aesthetic illusion, to the highly complex process of recreation under the dramatist's guidance, of a series of processes of psychic discharge that take place in the audience, including pity and fear. The audience must be drawn into the drama and its resistances overcome; Shakespeare forces the audience to identify and act out in their minds his interpretation of inner conflict and disturbing fantasies that provide the unconscious dynamic as the action moves through conflict, crisis, climax and resolution. In Shakespeare's tragedies involving revenge, the action is nearly always fatal, and we, too, must experience this pressure, recognizing with terror the cruel power of superego aggression, of the dynamic that powers hateful revenge, in ourselves as well as in our representatives on stage, in life as well as in the drama. One reason why revenge tragedies were popular in Shakespeare's culture and are still popular in our own, is that revenge is profoundly disturbing; for an audience the projection of revenge is extremely therapeutic.[8]

A definitive image of tragi-comedy is of forgiveness, reconciliation and regeneration. The endings of tragic revenges are quite otherwise, and perhaps relate to an earlier or more primitive form of psychic conflict (such as scapegoating) than to the life-asserting endings of many tragi-comedies, the underlying dynamic of which is shame, not guilt. Guilt, and the hateful destructiveness and rage which accompany it, are at the centre of Hamlet's experience. The superego is a highly important factor in illustrating the fate of the protagonist in revenge tragedy; he is one for whom the conscious and / or unconscious sense of guilt, with the corresponding need for punishment, satisfied through suffering and eventually through an honourable death, plays a decisive part in his will and willingness to die. In revenge tragedy, as opposed to tragi-comedy involving revenge, the protagonist's superego is a cruelly persecuting agency which his ego has good reason to dread, and much of the tragic hero's motivation, once he has renounced Eros (defusion), derives from the struggle either to avoid or to submit to its claims. When the hostile elements in the external world of the play are directed against Hamlet, he not only internalizes them, but they combine with his own self-destructive tendencies to produce a deep need for inner punishment: death. But this is the final dynamic of Hamlet's psychic journey; the dramatic action covers much ground before that ultimate act.

Tragic Alternatives: Eros and Superego Aggression

To some extent, it is the denial of Eros and the destructiveness of family attachments which largely contribute to the fate of Hamlet, Othello, Macbeth and King Lear. All these tragic figures make the initial mistake of rejecting a crucial and sustaining love relationship. These tragic heroes fail in love, are usually unsuccessful in their ambition, which often includes a powerful and fatal desire for revenge, and suffer from a highly developed superego, whose effect is to produce a pronounced sense of guilt. As I have already suggested, when this inner dynamic of guilt combines with the hostile tendencies of the cultural superego within the social world of the drama, we have a definitive generic marker of tragedy: the self-sacrifice of the tragic figure.

There are two Freudian concepts which might help us to understand these psychodynamics of tragic action and how Shakespeare dramatizes them in the revenge motif of *Hamlet* in particular:

(1) Defusion of the dual instincts of Eros and Death, and

(2) Superego aggression, which is one aspect of the death instinct.[9]

Freud employs the idea of Eros, from Plato's *Symposium*, in his final instinct theory (1930), to connote the whole of the life instincts, as opposed to the death instinct. According to Freud, the dual instincts are usually mingled with one another or fused. 'Normally,' Freud says, 'the two kinds of instincts seldom appear in isolation from each other, but are alloyed with each other in varying and different proportions, and so become unrecognizable to our judgment'.[10] It is important to understand that Eros neutralizes aggression, and that the ego must find objects for Eros and aggression. Usually, aggression is modified in its impact

(1) by displacement to other object;

(2) by restriction of its aim;

(3) by the sublimation of the aggressive energy; and

(4) through the influence of fusion.

Ultimately, none of these modifications applies to Hamlet.

The tragic process (which includes the total environment of the play, with all its hostilities and hatreds, its failures in loving, and its tremendous emphasis on guilt and the corresponding need for punishment and suffering), instead of strengthening the ego in its task of regulating Eros and aggression so that they do not clash with reality and defuse (separate), is one in which the ego is destroyed by the undermining of its total organization. Fusion represents an integrated ego, one which is functioning well, and, with the aid of Eros, able to modify aggression in the four normal ways just mentioned. The failure of Eros results in complete defusion (separation) of the dual instincts and the dominance of the aggressive death instinct, whose agency is the harsh, self-abusive superego. It is then the task of the ego to defend itself by keeping the aggression directed outward in the interests of self-preservation. According to Freud, 'It would seem that aggression when it is impeded entails serious injury, and that we have to destroy other things and other people in order not to destroy ourselves, in order to protect ourselves from the tendency to self-destruction.'[11] As long as the protagonist can displace his inner aggression onto others, usually through hating and revenging, he survives. After separation of the dual instincts (defusion), the erotic component no longer has the power to bind the whole of the destructiveness that was combined with it, and this releases much of the cruelty and violence that is so characteristic of superego aggression and of Shakespeare's tragedies involving revenge, as we see in *Hamlet*.

Sources, Formation and Function of Superego

The superego is the psychic agency that produces the sense of the ideal, of the way things ought to be, not the way they are, and so it is not always oriented towards reality. Freud thought the source of the superego was the internalization of the castrating Oedipal father. He also thought the superego was one aspect of the death instinct (thanatos) in its aggressive need for punishment. Freud theorized that the cruel superego was also the revengeful aggressor that produces not only the need to idealize, but also the need for aggressive self-abuse when the ideal fails: for suicide or murder.[12] Although the formation of the superego is grounded in hostile Oedipal wishes and in the renunciation of loving, it is subsequently refined, according to Freud, by the contributions of social and cultural requirements (education, religion, morality).[13]

In her chapter on superego formation, Edith Jacobson states that the core of the superego is 'the law against patricide and matricide and the incest taboo'; she then goes on to say that superego fear continues and replaces castration fear, but that some people may 'unconsciously equate the superego with the threatening paternal — or their own — phallus'. She also points out that 'there is a tremendous step between the simple moral logic of castration fear, fear of punishment and hope of reward, to the abstract moral level of a superego which has expanded from the taboo of incest and murder to a set of impersonal, ethical principles and regulations for human behaviour.'[14] Melanie Klein traces the beginning of the superego back to early (infant) oral fantasies of self-destruction, which is a direct manifestation of the death instinct.[15] In his re-interpretation of the death instinct, Jean Laplanche sees the death drive 'not as an element in conflict but as conflict itself substantialized, an internal principle of strife and disunion.'[16] In his chapter on the death instinct, Paul Ricoeur sees the superego as an essential instinct problem for the philosophy of art.[17]

The death instinct is a useful concept in many ways: it represents a decomposition of the ego under attack by the superego; it tends to weaken object relations, and it tends to narcissistic withdrawal. In other words, the person in whom the aggressive tendencies of the death instinct are dominant over the life instincts has a weakened ego, and in an effort to regain the strength of self-esteem and self-confidence, he / she tries narcissistically to withdraw from persons and conflicts altogether. This is particularly true if the person's love relations have failed. If one thinks of Eros as a life-preserving force (the ego needs Eros to carry out its intricate life-preserving functions), and if one thinks of the idealistic superego as the self-aggressor, promoting life-denying tendencies, then the beloved may become a means whereby the ego is defeated. More often than not, Shakespeare dramatizes sexuality as a destructive force, and this is especially true of *Hamlet*.

One striking collusion between the dynamics of character and the universe of Shakespearean tragedy is that the protagonist chooses the wrong lover, or his perception of the loved one is disastrously flawed, or his family relationships are intimately destructive. The ability to relate to the other/s is an immense difficulty, if not to say impossibility for Hamlet. This may be because, as Richard P. Wheeler and others have suggested, men are less able to merge their identity with the other/s, than women are (i.e., men have more definite boundaries to the self than women), or because tragedy dramatizes the inability to steer a relationship through loving betrayal to survival.[18] D. W. Winnicott describes these phases in psychoanalytic object-relations terms as using, destroying and surviving.[19] Winnicott's idea applies more to tragi-comedy than to tragedy. A definitive image of tragi-comedy is forgiveness, reconciliation and regeneration; that of tragedy is self-sacrifice and death.

Perhaps narcissism is relevant here.[20] The aim of the narcissist is to be loved, and the narcissistic lover is usually dangerously dependent on his beloved. One who loves in this way has 'expropriated' part of his narcissism, which can only be replaced by his being loved. There is a constant need to replenish the amount of self-love the narcissistic lover gives the other. If, instead of being loved, the narcissistic person is betrayed, it is as if he had betrayed himself; he feels a painful lowering of self-esteem and is full of self-pity. He does not, however, hate himself as the idealist does in similar circumstances. On the contrary, betrayal usually leads to a compensatory increase in narcissism; instead of being fixated on the loved one, the narcissist regresses to a previous point in his life when he loved only himself. In other words, a narcissistic lover who is betrayed is often sustained by his narcissism, whereas an idealistic lover feels utterly worthless and hates himself sometimes to the point of suicide. The idealist lover is driven by superego demands either to murder his beloved and / or himself.

It is only fair to say that there has been enormous resistance to Freud's idea of a death instinct since he first formulated it. Perhaps this resistance has something to do with our unwillingness to accept the violence of self-destructive and revengeful tendencies within ourselves. It seems it is easier to bear punishment inflicted from the outside than to face internal self-destructive tendencies. Possibly the origin of the superego also represents a similar attempt at externalization. Ehrenzweig suggests that instead of being rent by internal tensions, it is as if the ego projects its self-destructive aggression onto a split-off part, the superego, and prefers to submit to its attacks which now come to it from outside.[21] Superego aggression also projects itself into the outside world and onto the figures of punishing parents, punitive laws, repressive political regimes, conquest and invasions.

The superego's function is to induce guilt and to repress; openness (not closure) requires a weakening of the superego power of repression. Yet a lifting of repression, or recognition of repressed material, may produce extreme anxiety, even panic. For example, on one level of interpretation, the Ghost represents the unrepressed hostility Hamlet feels for his father. The hostility Hamlet feels for his father is externalized as revengeful hatred not only for Claudius, his 'uncle-father', but also for Gertrude, his 'aunt-mother', and for Ophelia. These internal processes are externalized and dramatized in the soliloquies, where the thought is frequently revengeful, sadistic and self-destructive. Hamlet's soliloquies are also expressions of superego conflict: to die or to live; to honour or to revenge; duty to oneself or to one's father. On one level, Hamlet is ashamed of his father's command to revenge, and, at the same time, ashamed of his inability to fulfil the command.

Eleanor Prosser suggests the Ghost is an idea Hamlet has long been waiting for.[22] It is possible that the Ghost is not only a projection of Hamlet's hostile feelings towards his father, but also serves as a projection of his murderous feelings about his mother's husband:

> O villain, villain, smiling damned villain!
>
> . . . .
>
> So, uncle, there you are.

(I. v. 106-10)

If the command to murder Claudius is another instance of repressed wishes surfacing into conscious intention, then it is obviously less threatening that the revengeful need seems to come from outside, from the superego demands of authority, of the outraged father, husband and king. The Oedipal theory clearly works here. Hamlet has been thinking, on some pre-conscious level, about his uncle-father; and that is why at first he thrills to the command to revenge and murder: 'O my prophetic soul! My uncle!' (I. v. 41).

By creating the Ghost, Shakespeare creates a father-son-mother confrontation at the heart of the play. The play dramatizes a crisis in Hamlet's identification with his idealized, murdered, heroic father, who returns from the dead to demand Hamlet revenge his death, and in so doing, rescue his mother from her second, and incestuous marriage. At first Hamlet responds with alacrity to his ghostly father's demands; then with paralyzing reluctance: 'O cursed spite, / That ever I was born to set it right' (I. v. 196-7). Everything hinges on Hamlet's struggle to identify with his father's superego demands that he revenge; that is, after all, justice within the revenge genre, and it coincides with one aspect of the cultural superego — it is the right thing to do — but Shakespeare sets up the problem of revenge in such a disruptive way that the action on moral, ethical and psychic levels is blocked. The conflict of revenge engages the action on many levels, delaying revenge through ambiguities in psychological motivation, language and action.

The creation of the Ghost is itself a piece of theatrical aggression for it stops Hamlet's initial fierce self-restraint; allows him to express his deeply conflicted feelings about Claudius, and his desire to kill him. The Ghost's revelation of murder, incest and adultery — 'Ay, that incestuous, that adulterate beast' (I. v. 42) — is a validation of Hamlet's suspicions and justification of his loathing of Claudius the man who, with 'traitorous gifts' (I. v. 43), seduced his mother, that 'seeming-virtuous queen' (I. v. 46). 'Seeming', as we learn earlier from Hamlet, can cover all kinds of deception and crime. The revelation is also conclusive and irreversible affirmation of his intense feelings about his mother: 'O most pernicious woman!' (I. v. 105). The Ghost and Hamlet share the same obsession: Gertrude. Together they comprise an ancient and often cursed triangle. The acting of *The Mousetrap*, as arranged by Hamlet, is, in fact, a fantasized murder in which Hamlet revenges by doubling as 'one Lucianus, nephew to the King' (III. ii. 239). As actor-manager, Hamlet externalizes or projects his inner conflict about revenge onto the directing and acting of the entire scene of his father's murder, which, by pure chance (or dramatic device!) parallels *The Murder of Gonzago*:

> I'll have these players
> Play something like the murder of my father
> Before mine uncle

> (II. ii. 590-2).

The play reaches its climax with Hamlet ferociously urging Lucianus on: 'Come, the croaking raven doth bellow for revenge' (III. ii. 247-8). As director, actor, chorus and audience, Hamlet is ecstatic at the end of this performance, because it is as if he *had* avenged his father. The successful displacement of inner aggression affords Hamlet immense relief. Moreover, he has made public the entire story, from known beginning to wished-for conclusion.

The Ghost is the means of dramatizing Hamlet's deep-seated inner fears and anxiety, his hatred of Claudius and his unconscious desire to kill the man who has 'whor'd' (V. ii. 64) his mother, murdered his father and has

> Popp'd in between th'election and my hopes.

> (V. ii. 65)

The Ghost's foul imaginings about Gertrude's lustful sexuality anticipate Hamlet's own image of 'incestuous sheets' (I. ii. 157). There is very little evidence in Gertrude's dialogue that she is as lustful as her first husband and Hamlet would have us suppose. Just as Iago voices Othello's disturbing, destructive, jealous fantasies, so the Ghost does Hamlet's. It may be objected that the Ghost tells Hamlet to leave his mother 'to heaven' (I. v. 86). In the closet scene, he pleads with Hamlet to 'step between her and her fighting soul' (III. iv. 113). But it is too late. And Hamlet's father knows it. He has timed his intervention perfectly; for, in his passionate and deeply conflicted interview with his mother, Hamlet has already used enough verbal daggers to cleave her 'heart in twain' (III. iv. 158). It is needless to labour the Oedipal basis of the closet scene. It is a famous piece of psychoanalytic criticism frequently incorporated into contemporary productions.[23] It is clear that Hamlet is torn between love and loathing for his mother, and that the destructive impulses of his own superego are displaced temporarily in trying to be her conscience.[24] This affords him some relief from the intense anxiety and painful tension of inner aggressiveness, just as his cruel treatment of Ophelia did, and for similar reasons. But what chance does Hamlet have of keeping the crucial love of Ophelia, which might have sustained him? None. Hamlet is irretrievably trapped in a parental relationship involving murder, adultery and incest. What chance is there of detaching himself from this overwhelming guilt? None. He has been made responsible for wiping it out; moreover, he has promised to do so. And Hamlet is a responsible person; his superego sees to that, even if he curses his masculinity in being 'born to set it right' (I. v. 197). Yet Hamlet cannot become his father's avenger because that would involve him and his mother still further in family guilt. His repudiation of her makes clear the powerful family knot of emotional attachments that ruin their relationship:

> You are the Queen, your husband's brother's wife,
> And, would it were not so, you are my mother.

> (III. iv. 14-16)

The superego, then, is a revengeful force which seeks to punish. Hamlet tries to become his father's superego, but because he cannot act on it, his own superego takes revenge on him — tortures him, kills him eventually. He cannot consciously question the morality of avenging his father's murder, because that would be to challenge his father; moreover, part of him is torn by the moral discrepancy involved in committing murder as a solution to the problem of murder. In a conscious effort to gain control over the destructiveness of the superego, the tragic hero tries to project his sense of guilt, through his ambition or revenge, onto others. Hamlet channels his vengeful aggression in a variety of ways: through his constant cruelty to others, his verbal hostility and his 'antic disposition' (I. v. 180).

Barber and Wheeler write of Hamlet's need to use his hostility to 'protect his integrity against acquiescence in the corrupt world, on the one side, or acquiescence in self-loathing, on the other'.[25] These critics also see Hamlet's 'need for revenge as the core of a need for expression and vindication'.[26] Certainly Hamlet's aggression finds frequent relief in his violent expressiveness, especially when he turns love into hateful violence in the nunnery and closet scenes. The command to revenge is itself a directive to transform love into violent and vengeful hatred. It is a superego command from the idealized father to his son to hate and destroy the bestial father-figure of Claudius, that heap of 'garbage' (I. v. 57), that 'nasty sty' (III. iv. 94). Initially, the command to revenge displaces some of Hamlet's superego aggression outward in his attempts to 'catch the conscience of the King' (II. ii. 601) and to be his mother's conscience, but the failure to achieve revenge, to murder Claudius, and so be at one with his father, fills him with deep dismay and self-contempt, as his soliloquies reveal. Furthermore, his attempts to act out his inner conflicts, his desire to rescue his mother and kill Claudius, have resulted in the regrettable, accidental killing of Polonius and the devastating suicide of Ophelia. Moreover, his mother still shares his uncle's bed, continues to sleep between those 'incestuous sheets' (I. ii. 157). He suffers acute mental agony for these blunders.

No wonder Hamlet seems resigned to his own death upon his return from England; all his displacements have failed; the immense energy attached to his sense of guilt turns inward, there is nowhere else for it to go. Hamlet becomes a victim of his own desire for punishment — his need to end his life. He takes revenge upon himself; he accepts the wager from the absurd Osric: ''Tis a chuff, but, as I say, spacious in the possession of dirt' (V. ii. 88). This is the same anguished, grief-stricken Hamlet who, standing in Ophelia's open grave, has willed 'Millions of acres' to be thrown on him so that he may be buried quick with her (V. i. 276). His ego yields to his superego and takes on the suffering the self-abusive superego produces. In these circumstances, the ego collapses under the weight of so much revengeful self-hatred; the pain and anxiety produced by the murderous superego become unendurable. Hamlet submits his person to a duel arranged by one he knows to be his mortal enemy.

Freud's view of instinctual fusion between erotic and aggressive instincts suggests an admixture of erotic quantities even in destructive processes, and this may explain any masochism there might be in the tragic hero's self-sacrifice, as well as the sadism in superego aggression. In Shakespearean tragic drama, the protagonist's sense of guilt (superego aggression) and need for punishment are so pronounced that the ego is not strong enough to be independent of the superego, or to control it. In normal living, this unconscious aggressive energy is displaced or sublimated. In this kind of tragedy, the ego seems unable to defend itself from the severity of the revengeful demands of the superego by such normal activities as repression, denial or rationalization. The function of the plot is to make sure the protagonist's displacements eventually fail. The ultimate aim of the tragic hero is to act out the compulsive nature of his guilt, both the guilt he feels for his own personal wrong-doing, and the generalized guilt which the social demands represented by the drama have required him to internalize. He is compelled to submit to the deathly demands of his own superego and those of the community.

In dying, Hamlet's psyche is cleansed of the burden of failed love, familial outrage and grief. As I suggested at the beginning of this essay, in *Hamlet*, Shakespeare represents revenge as an inward tragic event which is externalized, dramatized, and then reinforced by destructive family relationships whose psychic energies violate and eventually destroy the psychic wholeness of the tragic person. The conflict between ego and superego constitutes the dynamic action of *Hamlet* on many levels, creating revenge and its delay through acute inner anxieties and mental anguish, as well as ambiguities in action, language and thought. But, in the end, although the superego wins, because Hamlet must die, it is with Hamlet's / Shakespeare's total acceptance, as long as revenge is revealed for what it is: a dynamically hostile, hateful, destructive force, and, in *Hamlet*, an unbeatable enemy, as well as an Oedipal foe.

Through his conscious articulation and dramatization of the unconscious dynamics which drive stories of poisonous revenge, Shakespeare invites our reflection, invites us to hold the mirror up to our own deepest conflicts and desires. The resolution of *Hamlet* leaves us not only moved, but challenged and enlightened. Hamlet's fatal story is a lesson we must not ignore, but keep in our hearts, too:

> If thou didst ever hold me in thy heart,
> Absent thee from felicity awhile,
> And in this harsh world draw thy breath in pain
> To tell my story.

(V. ii. 351-4)

The mimetic power of violent revenge in *Hamlet* depends on the reality of those psychic conflicts Shakespeare dramatizes as revenge.

Notes

1. See J. Laplanche and J.-B. Pontalis, 'The Oedipus complex plays a fundamental part in the structuring of the personality and in the orientation of human desire' (*The Language of Psycho-Analysis* (London: Hogarth Press, 1980), p. 283).

2. See Coppélia Kahn, *Man's Estate: Masculine Identity in Shakespeare* (Berkeley, Los Angeles and London: University of California Press, 1981), pp. 132-40.

3. J. Montgomery Byles, 'A Basic Pattern of Psychological Conflict in Shakespearean Tragic Drama', *University of Hartford Studies in Literature*, 11 (1979), 58-71.

4. J. Montgomery Byles, 'The Problem of Subjectivity in the Language of Ophelia, Desdemona and Cordelia', *Imago*, 46 (1989), 37-59.

5. David Leverenz suggests that there is little sense in Ophelia's madness: 'Not allowed to love and unable to be false, Ophelia breaks. She goes mad rather than gets mad' ('The Woman in *Hamlet*: An Interpersonal View' in Murray M. Schwartz and Coppélia Kahn, eds, *Representing Shakespeare: New Psychoanalytic Essays* (Baltimore and London: The Johns Hopkins University Press, 1980), p. 119). I would argue that there is much subject sense in her language when mad. See also Harry Morris, 'Ophelia's "Bonny Sweet Robin"', *Publications of the Modern Language Association of America*, 73 (1958), 601-3.

6. Over the past twenty years or so, many feminist critics have identified the 'man-hon-our-fight' content of revenge as 'morally bankrupt'. See Linda Bamber, *Comic Women, Tragic Men: A Study of Gender and Genre in Shakespeare* (Stanford: Stanford University Press, 1982); Marilyn French, *Shakespeare's Division of Experience* (New York: Summit Books, 1981); Coppélia Kahn, *Man's Estate*; Carolyn Ruth Swift Lenz, Gayle Greene and Carol Thomas Neely, eds, *The Woman's Part: Feminist Criticism of Shakespeare* (Urbana, Chicago and London: University of Illinois Press, 1980); Marianne L. Novy, *Love's Argument: Gender Relations in Shakespeare* (Chapel Hill: University of North Carolina Press, 1984); and Linda Woodbridge, *Women and the English Renaissance: Literature and the Nature of Womankind, 1540-1620* (Urbana, Chicago and London: University of Illinois Press, 1984).

7. *The Psycho-Analyst and the Artist* (New York: Mentor Books, 1950), p. 164.

8. Susan Jacoby asks how audience sympathy for the revenger is gained, lost or compromized, and also what dramatic and rhetorical techniques operate to affect sympathy, mostly in modern literature and film in *Wild Justice: The Evolution of Revenge* (New York: Harper and Row, 1983). See also Linda Anderson's helpful introduction to the history of revenge in *A Kind of Wild Justice: Revenge in Shakespeare's Comedies* (Newark: University of Delaware Press, 1987). See also Erich Fromm, *The Anatomy of Human Destructiveness* (New York: Holt, Rinehart and Winston, 1973), especially pp. 268-99.

9. Sigmund Freud, 'Instincts and their Vicissitudes' in *The Standard Edition of the Complete Psychological Works*, tr. James Strachey, Anna Freud, Alix Strachey and Alan Tyson, 24 vols (London: Hogarth Press, 1953-74), XIV; 'Beyond the Pleasure Principle' in *Complete Works*, XVIII; 'The Ego and the Id' in *Complete Works*, XIX; and 'Civilization and its Discontents' in *Complete Works*, XXI.

10. Freud, 'The Ego and the Id' in *Complete Works*, XIX, 41-2; see also 'Civilization and its Discontents' in *Complete Works*, XXI, 119.

11. Freud, *Complete Works*, XXI, 107.

12. Freud, *Complete Works*, XXI, 64-149.

13. Laplanche and Pontalis, *The Language of Psycho-Analysis*, p. 437.

14. *The Self and the Object World* (New York: W. W. Norton, 1966), p. 127.

15. Juliet Mitchell, ed., *The Selected Melanie Klein* (New York: Macmillan, 1986), pp. 80-3.

16. *Life and Death in Psychoanalysis* (Baltimore: The Johns Hopkins University Press, 1976), p. 122.

17. *Freud and Philosophy* (New Haven: Yale University Press, 1970), pp. 281-309.

18. '"Since first we were dissevered": Trust and Autonomy in Shakespearean Tragedy and Romance' in Schwartz and Kahn, eds, *Representing Shakespeare*, pp. 150-69.

19. *Playing and Reality* (New York: Basic Books, 1971).

20. Freud, 'On Narcissism' in *Complete Works*, XIV, 73-105. See also Otto Kernberg, *Borderline Conditions and Pathological Narcissism* (New Jersey: Jason Aronson, 1975), and J. M. Byles, '*The Winter's Tale, Othello*, and *Troilus and Cressida*: Narcissism and Sexual Betrayal', *Imago*, 36 (1979), 80-93.

21. Anton Ehrenzweig, *The Hidden Order of Art* (Berkeley: University of California Press, 1967), p. 192.

22. *Hamlet and Revenge* (Stanford: Stanford University Press, 1967), p. 134.

23. Although Freud related Hamlet to Oedipus in 1897, and subsequently published the idea in *The Interpretation of Dreams* in 1900, Ernest Jones developed it fully in '*Hamlet*: The Psychoanalytic Solution' (1910). See M. D. Faber, ed., *The Design Within* (New York: Norton, 1970). See also in the same anthology, pp. 113-20, F. Wertham's 'Critique of Freud's Interpretation of *Hamlet*'. For a comprehensive survey of the ramifications of the Freud-Jones view, see Norman Holland, *Psychoanalysis and Shakespeare* (New York: Octagon Books, 1976).

24. Janet Adelman concentrates on the maternal point of the triangle between Hamlet, his father and his mother: 'As in a dream, the plot-conjunction of father's funeral and mother's remarriage expresses this return: it tells us that the idealized father's absence

134 Joanna Montgomery Byles

releases the threat of maternal sexuality, in effect subjecting the son to her annihilating power' (*Suffocating Mothers: Fantasies of Maternal Origin in Shakespeare's Plays: 'Hamlet' to 'The Tempest'* (New York and London: Routledge, 1992), p. 18.

25. C. L. Barber and Richard P. Wheeler, *The Whole Journey: Shakespeare's Power of Development* (Berkeley: University of California Press, 1986), p. 262.

26. Barber and Wheeler, *The Whole Journey*, p. 263.

LOSING THE NAME OF ACTION

VALERIA WAGNER

T'have seen what I have seen, see what I see

One can but wonder at the number of critics producing 'new' readings of *Hamlet*. One feels they must believe that their readings are somehow exceptional.[1]

Nicolas Abraham states that 'a ghost returns to haunt with the intent of lying: its would-be "revelations" are false by nature. This is what the spectators and critics alike have, for nearly four hundred years, failed to consider.'[2] The assertion begs two questions: does Abraham really *know* the truth he affirms; and how has he arrived at the knowledge that so many people have failed to consider. He certainly has not read all *Hamlet* criticism, nor has he listened to the comments of countless spectators: his certitude is not grounded on a knowledge of what *has* been noticed about *Hamlet*. He must then lay claim to a unique knowledge of the text, unavailable to any other reader. The text, perhaps, is simply not the same text as the one that others have — there might be more words, even more passages, in it; there might be, yes, an additional scene. Yes: Abraham's text is not the same as others because he has himself written a sixth act, wherein the ghost's lies are uncovered and the mystery of *Hamlet* played out. This sixth act is consequently 'missing' from current copies of *Hamlet*.

I want to suggest that the exceptional quality of 'new' readings of *Hamlet* resides in how their '*Hamlet*' compares to *Hamlet*. The urge to read aloud to others might well be a function of the critics' uncanny sense that they are in fact reading another *Hamlet*, a copy nobody else has read before. Hence they notice things — words — which can only have gone unnoticed by others. Not all critics go to the extreme of reproducing their visionary readings, of course; but in my experience of essays on *Hamlet*, critics tend to believe that they have seen what nobody else has seen, their surprise echoing Ophelia's expression of woe: 'T'have seen what I have seen, see what I see' (III. i. 163).

The visionary vein in *Hamlet* criticism can doubtless be understood in terms of the history of the text: the fact that *Hamlet* has definitely been over-read has certainly changed the text, as the text has changed its readings. The ensuing instability of *Hamlet* accounts for the readers' sense that the text has been under-read, or overlooked, and that they are dealing yet again with a 'new' one. Contemporary trends in reading can also account for the critics' symptoms, since we now assume that texts are unstable and fragmentary entities in the first place and that readings are consequently necessarily partial, a metonymic process — hence the possibility of ever new essays. It is possible, however, to engage with *Hamlet*, this dubious text and play, as specifically participating in its own recurring reemergence as a 'new' text.

Before I discuss the play itself, I will try to identify the form such 'newness' takes in *Hamlet* criticism, by identifying the critical operations that screen the critics' vision. This I will do very cursorily through Lacan's seminar, 'Desire and the Interpretation of Desire in *Hamlet*'.[3] Lacan's seminar is an ideal case study in 'reading *Hamlet*', because it combines the two moves that we saw in Abraham's article: the location of the 'unread' text, of the omission in other critics' readings (or copies of *Hamlet*); and the rewriting of the newly 'read' lines (or text). In particular, I would like to concentrate on the two moments in his seminar when he refers to other readers' omissions.

The first instance is clearly a joke, and therefore, not just a joke: 'I'm just surprised that nobody's pointed out that Ophelia is *O phallos*'.[4] The joke resides in the self-suggestive reading, in the name 'Ophelia', of the phallus, a reading which adds to 'the sort of hogwash that psychoanalytic texts are full of'.[5] In order to make this association, however, the association of Ophelia with the missing phallus must already have been made. Thus Lacan's joke might well reveal his surprise at the obvious link not having been made before him, or even the suspicion that it has, without his knowledge. The seriousness of the joke is supported by the second instance of Lacan's referring to other readers' lack of insight, which actually concludes the published text:

He [Hamlet, the subject] speaks these words which up till now have remained as good as sealed to the commentators: "The body is with the king" – he doesn't use the word "corpse" please notice – "but the king is not with the body." *Replace the word "king" with the word "phallus," and you'll see that that's exactly the point* – the body is bound up [*engagé*] in this matter of the phallus – and how – but the phallus, on the contrary, is bound to nothing: it always slips through your fingers.
Hamlet: The king is a thing -

Guildenstern: A thing, my lord?
Hamlet: Of nothing.[6]

I find it significant that the two omissions Lacan finds in other readers'
texts should constitute the precise knot binding (*engageant*) *Hamlet* for his
(Lacan's) time. I also find that the move of replacing the king by the phallus
is exactly the point at which Lacan's reading of *Hamlet* joins those 'other'
readings, in his provision of the 'missing' element which is, ultimately, made
of 'nothing'. Lacan's assumption that the text is 'patched up' — that the missing phallus has been covered, if not recovered — echoes Abraham's own
'patching up' of *Hamlet* — his addition of a sixth act — in that both 'see' the
founding omission of their reading as the possibility of substituting: what is
'there' (the king) for what is not 'there' (the phallus), what is not (the sixth
act) for what is (no sixth act at all).

I hope to show in this essay that both the writing of additional acts and the
reckless replacement of protagonists (and words) are encouraged, if not demanded, by the text itself.

Of 'purposes mistook'

Throughout the first scene of *Hamlet* we are led to believe that the play
will be about young Fortinbras, who is talked of as being the cause of the
ghost's — another Hamlet's — unrest. At the end of the play, Hamlet dies
and young Fortinbras steps in to replace him, as if to recover 'his' plot.
Thus Hamlet, before he dies, asks Horatio to report him and his 'cause
aright / To the unsatisfied' (V. ii. 344-5). Young Fortinbras is certainly to
be included among the latter, but they are more generally the 'mutes or
audience to this act' (V. ii. 340) — those who witness Act V of *Hamlet*
and who may think it is Act V of *Fortinbras*.

The demonstrative qualifying 'act', however, sounds odd when uttered on
stage: what is Hamlet pointing out — at — as 'this act'? How can an act be
shown? We realize a few lines later that Hamlet is here anticipating his own
death, with which his story is definitely arrested in time. This 'act' is the
'sight' about which Fortinbras questions Horatio when he enters, as well as
the ambassadors' dismal 'sight'. The transition from Hamlet's 'act' to Fortinbras's 'sight' is not only a function of the passing of time, but a function of
two specific positions:[7] Hamlet's, involved in the act and still in its time, and
Fortinbras's, for whom the act is concluded and transformed into a sight and

who thus stands outside its temporality and field of subjectivity. In fact, as I will argue in later sections of this paper, the transition from 'act' to 'sight' — a recurrent issue in *Hamlet* — is a function of the passing of time.

Acts are seen, but what is seen are not acts. This is what Horatio's questioning answer to Fortinbras seems to suggest:

> What is it you would see?
> If aught of woe or wonder, cease your search.

(V. ii. 367-8)

Horatio has granted himself the life which Hamlet lacked to dispel this wonder, so he proceeds to satisfy the 'unsatisfied' (V. ii. 345). He announces he will explain, 'How these *things* came about' (V. ii. 385, my emphasis), ostensibly referring to the dead bodies he wishes staged, and 'placed to the view':

> give order that these bodies
> High on a stage be placed to the view,
> And let me speak to th'yet unknowing world
> How these things came about. So shall you hear
> Of carnal, bloody, and unnatural acts,
> Of accidental judgments, casual slaughters,
> Of deaths put on by cunning and forc'd cause,
> And, in this upshot, purposes mistook
> Fall'n on th'inventors' heads. All this can I
> Truly deliver.

(V. ii. 382-91)

Horatio's task, we remember, is to report Hamlet and his cause aright. By referring to the staged bodies, Horatio presumably hopes to particularize his otherwise general account, endowing the action with proper agents. The 'sight' thus promises to be the ground for the 'act', the bodies the stage of the action. Accordingly, the creation of a stage within the stage can also be seen as an attempt to demarcate the plot of Hamlet's revenge from that of young Fortinbras's claims on Denmark, setting the end of the first at Hamlet's death and breaking any possible continuity between them. Thus the first step of Horatio's account is to identify the protagonists of his narrative and to define the proper limits of their actions. Then his correct and corrective reading of the play can begin, and the play can end.[8]

Without the staging, Horatio fears, the situation might go out of control, the play might even never end:

> But let this same be presently perform'd
> Even while men's minds are wild, lest more mischance
> On plots and errors happen.

(V. ii. 398-400)

His urgency suggests that errors and mischances have already so proliferated within his, the bodies' and the public's stage, that his efforts to control the dramatic and critical interpretation of the play may be bound to fail. In effect, Horatio's corrective plotting subverts itself: as it strives to appoint the previous action of the play to the stage of the dead bodies, it submits it to the interpretive gaze of what should in his reading be but the secondary plot, the stage of which indeed stages that of the 'central' plot. Consequently Horatio's retelling of Hamlet's revenge becomes *Hamlet*, a retelling which should account for Fortinbras's appropriation of Hamlet's role, as it articulates the two parallel plots and reverses their positions of centrality and marginality. Indeed, as Fortinbras inherits Hamlet's 'dying voice' and in all probability his kingship, Hamlet's vengeance is appropriated in order to bring to a successful conclusion the 'wrong' story, issuing from King Hamlet's and King Fortinbras's contract, which takes up the first scene of the play, but is discarded as irrelevant once the ghost confides in Hamlet.

If Hamlet's plans seem to forward young Fortinbras's interests, then Horatio's concern over the identity of the protagonists and over the limits of the action is more than justified. Who is the main character? What have we read / witnessed? Further 'mis-takings' confirm the reasonableness of Horatio's preoccupation. In Act III, Hamlet stages a play in order to accuse his uncle, but forgets his initial purpose and accuses his mother; later he kills Polonius instead of Claudius. In Act IV, Laertes, who wants to take revenge on Hamlet, murders Claudius, on whom Hamlet must take revenge. Hamlet himself transfers his death penalty to its ignorant bearers, Rosencrantz and Guildenstern, and thus deflects Claudius's intentions. A similar deflection occurs in Act V, when Claudius's desire that Laertes kill Hamlet is accomplished, but results in many more deaths as well.

In all these cases, revenge is blunted either by the substitution of the intended victim, or by an unintentional multiplication of victims: the conspiracy remains unaltered, but its victim is not always the only or the intended one. Whether this deflection is intended (e.g., Hamlet's exchange of letters), or not (e.g., the murder of Polonius), it implies a diversion of one character from his own interests in favour of the plot. Each character contributes to what may look like the purpose of the play through the pursuit of his or her 'own', 'independent' intentions, which are thus bound to be 'mistook', since they serve other purposes. Hence, even when the character's projects are realized, it is *not* because they 'have cause, and will, and strength, and means / To do't' (IV. iv. 45-6) — an apparent paradox of which Hamlet's revenge, achieved in spite and not because of himself, is a paradigm.

My reference to the *purpose of the play* requires some further qualification lest 'the play' be read as implying either 'the author' or some *deus ex machina* such as 'fate'. For both, 'purpose' would suggest that the action is the realization of a unified, if not unitary, agency. If we read the term 'purpose' also as 'end', however, we find that we cannot understand the 'purpose of the play' unproblematically as its 'intention'. As a synonym for 'purpose', 'the end' is not just the realization of an aim, or the point of arrival of a trajectory; it is also what *happens* to that notion of purpose — at its end, as it were. The end of purposes in this play is that they are displaced from individuals; what happens cannot be traced back to individual courses of action and intentions. Instead, the configuration of 'purposes mistook' results in a pattern of action that should be considered intersubjective.[9] In the play of action, the individual must give up the role of controlling agent.

In *Hamlet* the intersubjective pattern of action is articulated, unsurprisingly, by a contract: that between Kings Fortinbras and Hamlet, which Horatio recounts at the beginning of the play as the explanation of young Fortinbras's attack on Elsinore, and the ghost's midnight visitations:

> our last King
>
> .   .   .   .
> Was as you know by Fortinbras of Norway,
> Thereto prick'd on by a most emulate pride,
> Dar'd to the combat; in which our valiant Hamlet
>
> .   .   .   .
> Did slay this Fortinbras, who, by a sealed compact
> Well ratified by law and heraldry
> Did forfeit, with his life, all those his lands
> Which he stood seiz'd of to the conqueror;
> Against the which a moiety competent
> Was gaged by our King, which had return'd

> To the inheritance of Fortinbras,
> Had he been vanquisher; as, by the same cov'nant
> And carriage of the article design'd,
> His fell to Hamlet.

(I. i. 83-98)

The contract in question stipulates that at the death of either king the other will inherit his lands. This testament — will — of exchange, signed by both kings and 'ratified by law and heraldry', implies that they disinherit their respective sons; hence, in the long run, at the death of one, the other's son is entitled to inherit. Their joint 'will' thus interchanges their lines of descent. The first 'act' of this contract is that at King Fortinbras's death, King Hamlet inherits his lands; the second act might therefore well be that at King Hamlet's death, young Fortinbras inherits his, in the quality of contractual son — hence his claims on Elsinore, and hence the outcome of the play.[10] From this perspective, the ghost's claim for revenge, i.e., for King Claudius's death, can be read as the implementation of the logic of the original contract.

Whether this is the case ('true') or not is unimportant. My point is that it is a contract, as opposed to localized intentions, which can be seen as providing a frame for the 'unnatural acts' and 'purposes mistook' otherwise unbound and unleashed on particular characters. Horatio's preoccupation with the possible spreading of errors and mischances beyond and within the stage, as well as his own attempt to bind action to particular — because dead — bodies, shows that the need for containment is anything but trivial. The contract first contains or binds the plot in language, textually. Then, the contract provides a logical frame for the action: we could say that it sets the conditions for the play's formal closure. Thus Hamlet's vow of revenge is determined by his father's written contract with King Fortinbras, the subtext of which, we have seen, appoints young Fortinbras as the beneficiary in the quality, as it were, of adopted son. Finally, the contract frames the play in time by appointing Hamlet's revenge — deferment — as its mode of development, and Fortinbras's inheritance as its conclusion (and beginning).

We could say that these two contracts — let us consider Hamlet's vow as one for the moment — formulate Hamlet's disjunction from his acts by depriving him of a 'proper' (i.e., his 'own') intentions. Hence, though the continuity in Hamlet's actions (*Hamlet*'s action) is guaranteed by the two contracts, these presuppose a discontinuity — a substitution and duplication — of Hamlet the subject (and the subjects of *Hamlet*).

He seem'd to find his way without his eyes

The contracts bind the action for the reader or spectator, but they certainly do not bind it for the characters. They, however, attempt to make sense of what happens: characters constantly spy on each other, misread each other's acts, ponder on the relationship between 'playing' and 'acting' and are generally preoccupied with the elusive nature of action. In the following passage Ophelia struggles with this elusiveness, as she attempts to capture action with the net of intentionality.

A transfigured Hamlet has intruded upon Ophelia, as she was sewing in her closet. The encounter in turn sufficiently transfigures her — *her* term is 'affrighted' — for Polonius to notice her condition and question her. She has difficulty explaining what has happened, because Hamlet has said nothing to her, and action does not speak for itself.[11]

> POLONIUS: What said he?
> OPHELIA: He took me by the wrist and held me hard.
> Then goes he to the length of all his arm,
> And with his other hand thus o'er his brow
> He falls to such perusal of my face
> As a would draw it. Long stay'd he so.
> At last, a little shaking of mine arm,
> And thrice his head thus waving up and down,
> He rais'd a sigh so piteous and profound
> As it did seem to shatter all his bulk
> And end his being. That done, he lets me go,
> And with his head over his shoulder turn'd
> He seem'd to find his way without his eyes,
> For out o'doors he went without their helps,
> And to the last bended their light on me.
>
>   (II. i. 86-100)

How, then, can Hamlet's actions be understood? As Ophelia seems to realize, an account of Hamlet's acts solely in terms of bare movements unarticulated by 'reason' would be inadequate. Indeed, what is the act of holding someone's wrist hard, and how can it be read, without some knowledge of the purpose that inspires it or of the result that it attains?

Ophelia's interpretation is twofold: she groups Hamlet's movements in three distinct (narrative) sequences, and she concludes each of these with an alternative description. Hence Hamlet

(1) takes Ophelia by the wrist, goes to the length of his arm (or steps back an arm's length from her) and peruses her face with his hand over his brow.

After a long interval he

(2) shakes Ophelia's arm, 'waves' his head up and down three times and sighs.

'That done', he

(3) lets Ophelia go, turns his head over his shoulder and goes out of the door looking at her.

Articulated in this manner, Hamlet's movements appear to be intentional. They lead to each other and, most importantly, they end, conveying the impression that their purpose has been achieved. This sense is reinforced by the concluding redescriptions of each sequence, where intransitive verbs such as 'look at',[12] and 'go out' are interpreted as transitive ones. Hamlet looks at Ophelia's face, as if (because) he was *drawing* it; he does not go out, but *finds his way* (he goes out because he finds his way): in this manner an object — a purpose — is attributed to Hamlet's movements, and they result in something other than themselves. Similarly, Hamlet raises a sigh which seems to '*shatter* all his bulk / And *end* his being' (my emphasis): the intransitive act of sighing produces the (transitive) effects of shattering his body and of concluding his being.

Ophelia's rephrasings not only confirm our and Polonius's expectations that Hamlet has actually done something or acted intentionally, but, answering Polonius's question ('What said he?'), they also show an understanding of Hamlet's actions as being expressive of other actions (to *look* is to *draw*), and invite a reading of his silent performance as a 'substitute' for language. This view is supported by the ensuing dialogue between Ophelia and Polonius, where we learn that the former, on the orders of the latter, has repelled Hamlet's letters and denied him access to her. Consequently, Hamlet's dumb show is easily explained as a means to address Ophelia without violating the interdiction (now Ophelia's) against either talking to her or having access to her — in fact, his performance actually denies *her* access to *him*, his meaning and his language.

In her three redescriptions of Hamlet's actions, Ophelia reveals a growing uncertainty about what she is witnessing, as the terms 'as if' and 'seems to' suggest. But, more specifically, her account increasingly problematizes Hamlet's role as the *subject* of his actions. Whereas the movement from 'falls to such perusal of' to 'draw it' asserts Hamlet's agency, her next similes displace him from his actions. Thus Hamlet's sigh operates on its own upon his body, to the point that it seems to end his being, and, 'That done', his being consumed in a wordless sigh, *he seems* 'to find his way without his eyes'. But *he* may only *seem* to accomplish this action: in fact, his now beingless body leaves without his eyes, suggesting that the guidance of a knowing subject has become unnecessary. Ophelia has compelling reasons to fear that Hamlet's actions may well be exhausted in the shattering of his 'bulk', that his acts *seem,* and what they *show* is ultimately a subjectless and triumphant body.[13]

As she tries to render Hamlet's actions intelligible, mainly by attributing purposes to them, she finds that Hamlet disappears *in their semblance.* Either his acts are purposeful, and therefore he is not a subject, or he is a subject but does not 'act'. Temporally speaking, Hamlet the subject disappears in the 'sight' of his 'acts', because, as we will see, he 'passes show'.

Yet I, / ... unpregnant of my cause ... / can say nothing — no, not for a king

Polonius has no difficulty in making a choice. For him, Hamlet does not know what he is doing: 'That hath made him mad' (II. i. 110). For him, Hamlet's behaviour expresses the disturbance that Ophelia's rejection has produced, and its only significance lies in its cause. Beyond specifying his symptoms, Hamlet doesn't *do* anything, he cannot articulate his actions, he is not really himself but in 'ecstasy' — whatever he does is only madness. Polonius, however, confident of his reading and of the reversibility of the event, overlooks the implications of Hamlet's show.

We know what Polonius does not know: in the preceding scene Hamlet has given his word to the ghost. More specifically, the ghost has taken Hamlet's words through a skilful interpretive twist, and appropriated them for his / its own ends:

> GHOST: Pity me not, but lend thy serious hearing
>   To what I shall unfold.
> HAMLET: Speak, I am bound to hear.
> GHOST: So art thou to revenge when thou shalt hear.

> (I. v. 5-7)

Hamlet is doubtlessly 'bound' in all senses of the word to listen to the ghost, but what does not follow, of course, is that he should thereby be 'bound' to respond to the content of the speech. But the ghost's manipulation of Hamlet's language is effective:[14] Hamlet 'loses' his word, or is possessed by the ghost's, which 'enters' his body through his ears; Hamlet is thus bound to avenge his father's death by poison, which 'entered' *his* body through the ears as well. Henceforth Hamlet must follow his word and no longer has decisive power over his actions — he can only seem to carry them out. As his dumb show suggests: *he* is a fiction.

All this blatantly contradicts Hamlet's words to his mother in I. ii., before he 'loses' them to the ghost: before her, he claims a status of 'pure', unseeming being. The Queen has admonished Hamlet for still mourning his dead father. She argues that the King's is the common lot of human beings — they live and consequently die. Hamlet acknowledges this, whereupon the following dialogue ensues:

> QUEEN: If it be,
> Why seems it so particular with thee?
> HAMLET: Seems, madam? Nay, it is. I know not 'seems'.
> 'Tis not alone my inky cloak, good mother,
> Nor customary suits of solemn black,
> Nor windy suspiration of forc'd breath,
> No, nor the fruitful river in the eye,
> Nor the dejected haviour of the visage,
> Together with all forms, moods, shapes of grief,
> That can denote me truly. These indeed seem,
> For they are actions that a man might play;
> But I have that within which passes show,
> These but the trappings and the suits of woe.
>
>   (I. ii. 74-86)

The Queen suggests that Hamlet's excessive distress at his father's death might well be due to one, or two, logical mistakes, which she sketches by inverting the categories of seeming / being and common / particular. In the Queen's question, the common *is*, while the particular *seems*; whereas for Hamlet, the common has the appearance of the particular. We suspect that for the Queen all particulars are common, and what seems, is, in so far as it belongs to the realm of the common. The Queen objects to Hamlet's particular mourning, because the King's death is an event happening not to the King himself, as he is dead, but to all who witness his death. The King's death is in so far as it *seems* to all — it affects all living, not any one individual. The Queen, it could be said, obviously has no great faith in particularity — this might explain, or result from, her having just replaced one husband by another.

Her implicit argument, however, strikes a chord in Hamlet:

> Seems, madam? Nay, it is. I know not 'seems'.

(I. ii. 76)

The Queen's objection is thus reduced at a stroke to the categories of seeming / being, as Hamlet suppresses the validity of the common. Though he admits that his sorrow may 'seem' —and therefore not be his, but be feigned — because it is recognized in 'actions that a man might play', he insists that there is a coincidence between 'seeming' and 'being' which particularizes both the common and himself. He argues, basically, for the priority of 'being' over appearance, of the particular over the common. His move identifies the common with 'the other'. The coincidence he claims is formulated in terms of the disjunction of inside / outside and time: 'I have that within which *passes show*'. Hamlet obviously shares the well known view that we *are* within, within our bodies as it were, and that what we show, our 'outside', can manifest our being only partially. Hence that 'which passes show' is that part which cannot be shown, because it is most intrinsically ours, or our being. But the expression, 'passes show', is not exhausted in its spatial dimension. The verb 'passes' here has a temporal dimension — it occurs in time, and thus 'passes'. That which 'passes'— which both forwards 'seeming', undoes it as it forwards it, and outlasts it — is in the realm of time. Thus what is only accessible to himself is the 'passing of seeming' — the time of the action as opposed to the time of the appearance, of the 'sight'. Having time 'within', Hamlet's 'being' and 'seeming' coincide, in his time. This is not the other's time, which is the time in which appearance is beheld, and which turns appearance itself into some kind of otherness. He 'know[s] not "seems"' because only the other can know this, in another time; his knowledge is truer because it is that of the passing itself (as opposed to that of the show already gone) and this passes within, inside the subject.

Hamlet's vehemence might well betray an awareness of the frailty of his argument. Its 'spatial' aspect, that something remains un-shown to others, begs its corollary, that something shown to others remains unshown to him. Indeed, the ignorance of how one stands in another's gaze can undermine one's knowledge of what one *is* doing. When Hamlet asserts that he 'know[s] not "seems"', he unwittingly acknowledges the impossibility of the coincidence (between 'being' and 'seeming') which he claims. But it is the temporal aspect of his argument which will eventually convince him that he is not quite convincing. By the end of the play he has become aware that he has no time, that time is never had — 'Had I but time ... O, I could tell you' (V. ii. 341-2). He has no time because he is dying, but more specifically, he has no time to tell.

Hamlet realizes that he has no time shortly after the beginning of the play, when his (intended / internal) meaning is overpowered by the ghost: as he loses his word through its materiality, he is himself lost through his semblance. The ghost's intervention between what Hamlet says and what he 'means' is in effect an intervention of time between saying and doing, demonstrating that the coincidence of seeming and being in a mythical 'proper' time is impossible. The ghost asks Hamlet to set his story right; Hamlet asks Horatio to set *his* story aright; and Horatio doesn't have the time to begin doing it before the play — the action — closes. This implies the play's rejection of Hamlet's belief in the coincidence of seeming and being.

The time is out of joint. O cursed spite, / That ever I was born to set it right

If the contracts 'contained' the action of the play, the ghost, I suggest, is that within the play which 'passes' it. The ghost 'passes [the] show' in that, formally, its apparition 'precedes' the play and the anticipation of its re-apparition begins it. It also 'passes' the play in that its apparition — indeed, as will be seen, its appearance — disjoints the play at all levels except the contractual: the ghost creates and itself evades the two temporal orders of seeming and being, benefitting from the temporal disorder between saying and doing to split the plot in two. More precisely, the figure of the ghost effects the transition between the time of the actor and that of the character, that of the stage, and that of the staging.

As the play opens, characters dramatize the question of whether 'seeming' has already begun, or whether we still 'are'. Their uncertainty is figured by the series of 'blunders' at the moment substitution takes place. Barnardo assumes his office before Francisco bequeaths it to him, anticipating the conclusion of the exchange of guards we are to witness. Thus the 'identity quiz' that starts the play:

> BARNARDO: Who's there?
> FRANCISCO: Nay, answer *me*. Stand and *unfold yourself*.

(I. i. 1-2, my italics)

Francisco's reply is both a claiming of his role (*he* is the one assigned to ask questions) and a reminder to Barnardo that he is not playing *his* part, indeed, that the play has *begun*. Barnardo's question, 'Who's there?', seems to imply the underlying questions: 'Who am I?' 'What character am I playing?' He seems not to know whether he still 'is' (the actor / impersonator) or whether he already 'seems' (the character he should be playing). Finally Barnardo catches up with his role as he responds to Francisco's questioning call ('Barnardo?') with a 'He', as he identifies his own name and character in the third person. Thus an initial temporal anticipation (before the play) is echoed within the play and actually seems to result in the disorienting moment of substitution. Barnardo's confusion, revealing to the public gaze the duplicity implied in role-playing, is then overcome as he enters into 'full' seeming, displaying himself — now character — within the time and field of the theatre.

Having 'entered' into his character, however, Barnardo presumably 'forgets' he seems, as characters must, or rather, as actors must: he is thus playing at being through his playing at being unaware of seeming. Unsurprisingly, then, as the dramatization of the transition from being to seeming is concluded, the question becomes urgent again, if not for the particular sentinels, at least for the play. The rest of the scene pursues the identity quiz, as characters consider the identity of the ghost which comes

> In the same figure like the King that's dead.
>
> .   .   .   .
>
> Together with that fair and warlike form
> In which the majesty of buried Denmark
> Did sometimes march ...

(I. i. 44-52)

The ghost can only be *like* the king, because the king is dead. Who then, or what, is the figure like the king? What is the content of the 'form' of the King of Denmark? Horatio tries to clarify these questions: the ghost, he suggests to Marcellus, is like the King, 'As thou art to thyself' (I. i. 62).

Marcellus, however, a character, is not defined by his appearance: he is not physically like anyone but the (replaceable) actor impersonating his role. Similarly, Horatio affirms to young Hamlet: 'I knew your father; / These hands are not more like' (I. ii. 211-12), meaning that the 'form' of the ghost was as similar to the King as the King was to himself. But this formulation simply poses the question whether the ghost *is* the King himself in the same way that Horatio's hands are like themselves because they *are* themselves, or, more logically, whether the ghost is like the King in the way that one hand is like the other, i.e., a mirrored double. The latter option suggests, as Hamlet does, that 'The body is with the King, but the King is not with the body' (IV. ii. 26-7). The King is the image of the King.

Ironically, the ghost represents that coincidence between 'seeming' and 'being' that Hamlet passionately claims as his own: the ghost 'is', in that it 'seems'. Or rather, the ghost's unquestionable unity is based upon the assumption that it is what it seems — it looks like the king but cannot possibly be the king, it *is* the image of the king. The rest of the play unfolds through its various 'doubling devices' the irreducible paradox of the ghost being and not being something or somebody *else*. Most characters are paired: Ophelia with the Queen in Hamlet's eyes; Hamlet with his father via his name.

The status of the ghost can be explained through Hamlet's formulation of the coincidence of being and seeming as 'that within which passes show': we could say that the ghost passes show, because it is bodiless, but also because it has nothing *within*. It is within time: it even answers the call of time, when the cock crows. Being in time, the ghost cannot be and seem, as this duplicity would require two times in which to appear. Thus, in so far as it seems, it coincides with itself, it takes up time, and dispossesses others of time, as its demand for revenge shows: revenge not only skips the present, but threatens to turn the future into the past. Characters have no time, because their time is always past. The ghost inhabits a time they do not have.

Throughout the first scene, the ghost's identity is linked to the question, 'What is happening?' Its nightly performances coincide with young Fortinbras's attack on Elsinore. The sentinels try to account for the ghost's troubling apparitions and appearance by reference to young Fortinbras, but lose sight of the ghost's identity as they figure out its relationship to the continuing events.

The ghost is troubling because it resists the concept of identity and constitutes a danger to rational order. It is to guard 'the *pales* and *forts* of reason'

(I. iv. 28, my italics) that Horatio, a student of philosophy, is called upon to witness the unreasonable apparition of the 'image' (I. i. 84) of the 'last King' (I. i. 83). For reason's sake, Horatio, Marcellus and Barnardo strive to relate the ghostly visitation to young Fortinbras's military threat. Their successful effort transforms the irrational into a manifestation of the now reasoned fear of invasion. The logical manoeuvre is based upon the perception of the ghost itself as an invader, 'usurping' the night, and engaged in action, from which Horatio deduces that there will be 'some strange eruption to our state' (I. i. 72). The 'strange eruption' refers as much to the ghost's invasion of the castle wearing the king's armour as to young Fortinbras's foreign threat to Denmark. It is thus easy for Horatio to regard the latter first as the confirmation of the truth of the former, and then, in view of young Fortinbras's identity and his reasons for attacking Denmark, to consider the ghost as a warning of the danger he represents to the throne. Finally, young Fortinbras's attack becomes the reason and explanation of the ghost's agitated midnight rambles, no longer a threat in themselves:

> BARNARDO: Well may it sort that this portentous figure
> Comes armed through our watch so like the King
> That was and is the question of these wars.
> HORATIO: A mote it is to trouble the mind's eye.

(I. i. 112-15)

The status of the ghost changes as the argument advances. Initially the ghost is an independent entity, referrable to the fear it provokes as its reason or cause. Then the ghost becomes an omen, a purely formal reason for fear. Then, once the omen has been deciphered, or confirmed by reality (in the guise of young Fortinbras seeking to recover his lost inheritance), it is a direct manifestation of the state of affairs: either *because* Denmark is threatened (which involves a naturalization of the fantastic event, as the ghost reacts 'like one of us') or as silent expression of the conflict. As a 'side-effect' of young Fortinbras's attack, the ghost is an undesired 'outgrowth' of the plot. Uncontrollable, as side-effects are, it eventually unfolds the alternative and temporarily predominant story of young Hamlet's revenge. From this perspective, the revenge plot can be read as a 'rebellious' narrative, which is only reinserted in the original telos at the end of the play.

Horatio's and the sentinels' rationalization of the ghost's appearance as a side-effect of young Fortinbras's actions effectively discards the ghost's intentions, leaving it, like Hamlet, 'mad': a subject, but disjunct from its own acts. This is important, of course, because nobody wants ghosts to intervene actively within the 'forts' of life. As the ghost is marginalized from the action, it is assigned the position — shared by the sentinels — of spectator. Once it is further reduced to a redundant expression of the 'now' identified conflict — once what is happening is given a name — the ghost loses its status of subject and spectator.

O, woe is me / T'have seen what I have seen, see what I see

Ophelia, like Hamlet, is unable to set time right — she is caught between 'have seen' and 'see', the 'whats' of which are set apart by herself, as if her body was interposed between the two times she cannot reconcile. The attempt to link time, to join 'being' and 'seeming', 'sight' and 'act', can only succeed in the absence of bodies or thinking subjects — the bodies being subject to the time which the 'pale cast of thought' (III. i. 85) objectifies, construing the body into a yet larger obstacle to time. But this is the subject for another paper.

Hamlet only joins 'the time' at his death, when he passes on his 'dying voice'; Ophelia, whose disarticulated speech echoes Hamlet's dis-articulation from himself, dutifully drowns herself. The body, in so far as it stands for the subject, only links time when it is missing — it is the missing link. Observations of this kind may well be at the heart of the critics' conviction that they have found what nobody else has found, as if they were the link between the incomplete and complete versions of *Hamlet*. But what is 'missing' in *Hamlet*, as in all texts, is the moment of intersubjectivity which could reconstitute the text for us as one, simultaneous, happening, as it were, *all at once*. This moment, almost of the order of the sublime, and certainly of the order of reading, successive critics have thought they have momentarily lived, until they could only see they could not see what they had seen. Had the moment lasted, I suspect, the critics would have become ghosts — and there would have been an end to our story.

Notes

1. I would like to thank the doctoral reading group of the English Department of the University of Geneva for *their* exceptional reading of a previous version of this paper.

2. Nicolas Abraham, 'The Phantom of *Hamlet* or the sixth act: preceded by the inter-mission of "truth"', *Diacritics*, 18 (1988), 2-19.

3. Jacques Lacan, 'Desire and the Interpretation of Desire in *Hamlet*' in Shoshana Fel-man, ed., *Literature and Psychoanalysis* (Baltimore and London: The Johns Hopkins University Press, 1982), pp. 11-52.

4. Lacan, 'Desire', p. 20.

5. Lacan, 'Desire', p. 20.

6. Lacan, 'Desire', p. 52, emphasis mine.

7. To be more precise, we should replace the spatial metaphor of the subject for a temporal one, and talk about the *moments* of the subject instead of subject positions. I have chosen to leave the term 'position' in my discussion of time to 'test', as it were, its rhetorical resistance.

8. The appointment of the 'right' protagonists counters the fictionality of the play, which presupposes replaceable actors. But by countering it, of course, Horatio contains it within the boundaries of 'fiction', of the stage.

9. Intersubjective should be read here in opposition to trans-subjective, which would mean something like fate.

10. Young Fortinbras is a contractual son because he becomes the heir to King Hamlet's fortunes. In fact, it could be further argued that he also inherits the family name. This is in accordance not only with the end of the play, but with young Hamlet's and young Fortinbras's parallel progressions throughout the plot.

11. The fact that Hamlet's action has already concluded when Ophelia recounts it (and is usually not staged) further emphasizes the issue of the scene: how to name the action — arrest it in time — and subject it to a particular body when its occurrence surpasses (temporally) both the body and the attempt to articulate it.

12. I feel justified in replacing Ophelia's 'fall to perusal of' by 'look at' on the grounds that the intransitivity of the verb 'to fall' is reflected in that of 'look at'. Furthermore, the sense of abandonment which 'falls to' conveys is sufficiently developed in what follows of my argument.

13. From this perspective, Hamlet's conditional in his letter to Ophelia constitutes an explanatory note to the preceding scene: '*Thine evermore, most dear lady, whilst this machine is to him*' (II. ii. 122-3). The dumb show would then dramatize the loss of his 'machine' — his body, and his language — or his loss to it.

14. Its effectiveness is mediated by the illogicality of 'if you lend thy hearing, then you give your word', as if the act of listening somehow effected a transfer of wills, as if words irresistibly conquered subjects as they passed from mouth to ear. The logic of the ghost's illogicality is that words borrow bodies or subjects, invest them with action, and eventually restore them to themselves — for further investment.

PARISON AND THE IMPOSSIBLE COMPARISON

LISA HOPKINS

It is a critical commonplace that *Hamlet* is the most impenetrable play that Shakespeare ever wrote, a play the heart of whose mystery continues to baffle and elude after three hundred years. It is an equally celebrated fact that it is also the longest play which Shakespeare ever wrote, and virtually impossible to perform uncut in the theatre.[1] *Hamlet*'s length and its problematic nature are not, however, two disparate features of its identity: they are, in fact, intimately bound up together.

One of the reasons for the inordinate length of the play is its insistence on repeating elements of itself. It is true that there is a considerable amount of plot to be got through: Hamlet, informed that the uncle who has recently married his mother has also killed his father, first of all decides to test the truth of the allegation, then confronts his mother, accidentally kills Polonius, is banished to England, escapes, and returns to Denmark, where he duels with Polonius's son in a scene which brings about the death of all the principals. There is, however, at least as much narrative business to be dealt with in *The Comedy of Errors*, but this stands at the polar opposite of the Shakespearean canon from *Hamlet*, being in fact the shortest of his plays. What distinguishes them from each other is, primarily, the question of repetition. Whereas *The Comedy of Errors* works through each possible permutation of mistaken identity once and only once, *Hamlet* doubles and redoubles its situations, its characters, its events and, ultimately, its meaning. The psychological and psychoanalytic implications of this doubling have been repeatedly studied, drawing on the theories and observations of, amongst others, Freud, Rank and Lacan to comment on the significance of the repetition of roles and characteristics to be observed in, to name only some of the most obvious, Hamlet and Laertes, Hamlet and Fortinbras, Ophelia and Gertrude, and Old Hamlet and Claudius; and psychoanalytic approaches have been similarly brought to bear on the proliferation of mirror imagery in the play.[2]

Attention has also been paid to the fact that the play itself has doubles — its sources in Saxo Grammaticus, *The Spanish Tragedy* and the ur-*Hamlet*, its parallels with Greek tragedies such as *Oedipus Tyrannus* and the *Choephori*, its mysterious relationship with its contemporary analogues such as *Antonio's Revenge* and *The Revenger's Tragedy*, even its own survival in three different texts.[3] Rather less emphasis, however, has been placed on the systematic tracing of the patterns of linguistic doubling which riddle the play;[4] yet these are both equally insistent, and also impinge more directly on the actual experience of audiences in that it is they which directly contribute to *Hamlet*'s extraordinary length.

One of the most obvious of these linguistic doublings is a simple coupling of words, most usually nouns or epithets. This is a trait to which many of the characters are prone. Marcellus uses it: 'So hallow'd and so gracious is that time' (I. i. 169); so does Horatio: 'It is a nipping and an eager air' (I. iv. 2); Polonius, that outpourer of language, does not neglect it: 'The flash and outbreak of a fiery mind' (II. i. 33-4); and neither does the Queen: 'To show us so much gentry and good will' (II. ii. 22); Laertes also uses it: 'So crimeful and so capital in nature' (IV. vii. 7). But the character who most insistently employs the device is Claudius: 'Why, 'tis a loving and a fair reply' (I. ii. 121); 'This gentle and unforc'd accord of Hamlet' (I. ii. 123); 'The head and source of all your son's distemper' (II. ii. 55); 'My soul is full of discord and dismay' (IV. i. 45); 'Since yet thy cicatrice looks raw and red' (IV. iii. 63); 'That we are made of stuff so flat and dull' (IV. vii. 31); 'That I in forgery of shapes and tricks' (IV. vii. 88); 'That he could nothing do but wish and beg' (IV. vii. 103); 'Time qualifies the spark and fire of it' (IV. vii. 112); 'A kind of wick or snuff that will abate it' (IV. vii. 114); 'Should have a back or second that might hold' (IV. vii. 152); 'When in your motion you are hot and dry' (IV. vii. 156).

In each of these cases the second term of the two is effectively redundant. The sense has already been completely established by the first: the second can therefore act merely as a qualification or, more usually, perform the even more limited function of an amplification. Why use two words when one will do? It is, in one sense, a linguistic strategy particularly appropriate to Claudius, who says of himself that, like

> a man to double business bound,
> I stand in pause where I shall first begin,
> And both neglect.

> (III. iii. 41-3)

Hideously conscious of his psyche-splitting duality, Claudius has from the outset of the play been attempting to elide distinctions and differences. Just as he himself has attempted to collapse the separate roles of prince and king, husband and brother-in-law, brother and murderer, and uncle and father, so he tries to compress language together to distort the differences it creates:

> It shows a will most incorrect to heaven,
> A heart unfortified, a mind impatient,
> An understanding simple and unschool'd ...

> (I. ii. 95-7)

> Fie, 'tis a fault to heaven,
> A fault against the dead, a fault to nature ...

> (I. ii. 101-2)

> And we beseech you bend you to remain
> Here in the cheer and comfort of our eye,
> Our chiefest courtier, cousin, and our son.

> (I. ii. 115-17)[5]

Claudius's linguistic practice is especially interesting here because he is relying not just on the repetition and accumulation of words to blur distinctions, but also on the rhetorical trope of parison. A popular device in the Renaissance, this is defined by Gert Ronberg in *A Way With Words: The Language of English Renaissance Literature* as 'Repeating the same grammatical construction in successive clauses or sentences. If these are of identical length, the figure is sometimes called **isocólon**. *Parison* and *isocolon* were not distinguished by the Renaissance rhetoricians'.[6] Claudius shows himself notably fond of parison. Indeed, he employs the figure in his very first words of the play:

> Though yet of Hamlet our dear brother's death
> The memory be green, and that it us befitted
> To bear our hearts in grief, and our whole kingdom
> To be contracted in one brow of woe,
> Yet so far hath discretion fought with nature
> That we with wisest sorrow think on him
> Together with remembrance of ourselves.
> Therefore our sometime sister, now our queen,
> Th' imperial jointress to this warlike state,

> Have we, as 'twere with a defeated joy,
> With an auspicious and a dropping eye,
> With mirth in funeral and with dirge in marriage,
> In equal scale weighing delight and dole,
> Taken to wife.

(I. ii. 1-14)

Here the play of equally balanced clausal structures is sustained for an extraordinary thirteen lines. Within the matching 'yet ... yet' structure of the first sentence, further paralleling is achieved by the two clauses hinging on the twin infinitives, 'To bear' and 'To be contracted' (both interestingly insinuating overtones of marriage and children into a passage ostensibly concerned with death). Three descriptions of Gertrude accumulate more matching structures, which are completed by the even balancing of 'an auspicious and a dropping eye', 'mirth in funeral ... dirge in marriage', with its equal syllabic structures, and 'delight and dole'. Only in the last line is the smoothness of the rhetorical structuring eroded by the brutal simplicity, stressed by the abrupt caesura, of 'Taken to wife'. Until then Claudius's balancing act has not only imparted a sense of form and orderliness to the pattern of events he has been describing: it has also, in one sense, suspended not only judgement but meaning itself. And this, indeed, can be claimed to be the underlying effect of Claudius's constant generation of twinned structures: by offering two possible locations of meaning, they cancel out the possibility of any ultimate, single, authoritative interpretation or label. The actual signified is lost in the gap between the two synonymous yet not identical signifiers. Fullness and singleness of meaning are ultimately irrecoverable. This is a pattern that can be seen working not only in the shifting, elusive language of Claudius but in the play as a whole. Its presence is signalled from a very early stage, when we are offered some answers to the questions in which the play so liberally abounds:

FRANCISCO: I think I hear them.

Enter HORATIO *and* MARCELLUS.

Stand, ho! Who is there?
HORATIO: Friends to this ground.
MARCELLUS: And liegemen to the Dane.

(I. i. 15-16)

There are many puzzling features here to add to the disturbing character of this scene as a whole. Initially, Francisco is happy to put a definite label on the two newcomers: they are 'them'. Rapidly, however, his certainty gives way to the more questioning 'Who?' To this Horatio and Marcellus respond with some interesting definitions of their identities: instead of using their personal names, they offer two distinct responses which are, however, virtual paraphrases of each other. Once again the possibility of a whole and unified meaning is dissipated into its alternatives. The same effect recurs when the Ghost is first sighted:

> MARCELLUS:　　　　　　　　Is it not like the King?
> HORATIO:　As thou art to thyself.
> 　　　　　Such was the very armour he had on
> 　　　　　When he th'ambitious Norway combated.
> 　　　　　So frown'd he once, when in an angry parle
> 　　　　　He smote the sledded Polacks on the ice.[7]

> (I. i. 61-6)

To Marcellus's simple monosyllabic question Horatio replies in complex terms. Shifting initially from 'like' to 'as', he concentrates on two very specific aspects of the Ghost: its armour and its frown, both of which call up for him military associations. This is perhaps unsurprising, given the context of military preparation in which they have already decided to place the apparition, but it is nevertheless noticeable that Horatio attributes to the Ghost only a public, royal identity, instead of a private one, and that once again the focus is on twin rather than single identifying characteristics, suggesting that there is no one mark of identity. Even Marcellus's apparently innocuous question may perhaps be seen as having hidden depths, for the word 'like' is to recur significantly in connection with the Ghost:

> HAMLET: I shall not look upon his like again.
> HORATIO: My lord, I think I saw him yesternight.

> (I. ii. 188-9)

One obvious effect here is the bathos accompanying Horatio's matter-of-fact rebuttal of Hamlet's sweeping statement; but it may well also be relevant to recall the original derivation of the word 'like' from the Germanic word for 'corpse', which still survives in the English term 'lych-gate', for in a very literal sense his father's 'like' is exactly what Hamlet is going to see again, and

more than once at that. Any such possible pun would be again picked up shortly afterwards when Horatio affirms, 'These hands are not more like' (I. ii.
212). But like what? Horatio's hands may be like each other, but they are also
subtly different; and similarly all the affirmations of the Ghost's identity can
never quite affirm what it actually is, or how 'like' one's 'self' a 'self' can be.
Even the Ghost's own son surrounds it in a multiplicity of labels:

> Be thou a spirit of health or goblin damn'd ...

(I. iv. 40)

>   I'll call thee Hamlet,
> King, father, royal Dane.

(I. iv. 44-5)

Here identity is precisely not innate, or a property of person: it can only be
conferred by the vocative of another. In such a case, then, meaning, identity
and accurate signification are always going to be ultimately dependent on the
interpretative voice which interpellates the objects around it into a coherent
structure. For audiences of *Hamlet*, that voice has traditionally been that of
the Prince himself, who is both the most voluble and the most articulate of the
characters of the play (the extent to which critical analysis of both Ophelia
and Gertrude has been shaped by Hamlet's own opinions of them is, for instance, remarkable). It is his commentary and reactions that we are tempted
to be swayed by to interpret the events of the play; his journey that we attempt
to follow. And yet this is also precisely where the seeds of the play's
unfathomability are sown, for Hamlet no less than his uncle is caught in the
trap of doubled language and of doubled rhetorical structures, and most particularly in that of parison.
We hear it from him, as with Claudius, in his very first words of the play.

> A little more than kin, and less than kind.

(I. ii. 65)

Here the pun is compounded by the similarity of the grammatical structure,
and indeed the equality of the syllabic lengths of the two parts, which make
this not just parison but isocolon. Hamlet, so anxious to establish himself as
different from his uncle — as, indeed, his 'mighty' opposite (V. ii. 62) —
opens his account by using the very figure of speech which so distinguishes

that uncle's discourse. He does the same, too, when, in answer to his mother's question, he speaks at greater length:

> Seems, madam? Nay, it is. I know not 'seems'.
> 'Tis not alone my inky cloak, good mother,
> Nor customary suits of solemn black,
> Nor windy suspiration of forc'd breath,
> No, nor the fruitful river in the eye,
> Nor the dejected haviour of the visage,
> Together with all forms, moods, shapes of grief,
> That can denote me truly. These indeed seem,
> For they are actions that a man might play;
> But I have that within which passes show,
> These but the trappings and the suits of woe.
>
> (I. ii. 76-86)

The multiplication of similar structures serves here, as in the language of Claudius, to elide difference, creating a list-like effect which, together with the use of parison, homogenizes even as it ostensibly itemizes. This inevitably exerts a crushing and deadening effect on Hamlet's simultaneous attempt to create difference as he asserts the customary distinction between seeming and being: by the end of his parisonal listing, all that has happened is that 'that within which passes show' must stay within, unable to find show, since language itself has proved so disturbingly incapable of precision.

This tension between similarity and difference marks Hamlet's experiences through the play. Ignoring all the points of contrast between Ophelia and Gertrude, he perceives them as fundamentally the same; ignoring all the points of similarity between his father and Claudius, he perceives them as radically separate. His own identity becomes confused with Pyrrhus', Lucianus's, and of Fortinbras's; the exact parallel between his own situation and that of Laertes produces sharply contrasted reactions. As he struggles to articulate his own sense of his confused emotions, parison plays a crucial part in this blurring and overlapping of meanings:

> O what a rogue and peasant slave am I!
>
> (II. ii. 544)

> He would drown the stage with tears,
> And cleave the general ear with horrid speech,
> Make mad the guilty and appal the free,

Confound the ignorant, and amaze indeed
The very faculties of eyes and ears.
Yet I,
A dull and muddy-mettled rascal ...

(II. ii. 556-62)

Who calls me villain, breaks my pate across,
Plucks off my beard and blows it in my face,
Tweaks me by the nose, gives me the lie i'th'throat ...

(II. ii. 567-9)

Bloody, bawdy villain!
Remorseless, treacherous, lecherous, kindless villain!

(II. ii. 576-8)

Prompted to my revenge by heaven and hell ...

(II. ii. 580)

fall a-cursing like a very drab,
A scullion!

(II. ii. 582-3)

This soliloquy ostensibly revolves around differences — the distinction between heaven and hell, the distinction between the good dead father and the bad living uncle, the distinction between action and inaction, the distinction between Hamlet's inactivity and the passion of the player. And yet the obsessive use of parison means that these apparent opposites are continually yoked together and forced into a position of syntactic and rhetorical similarity which militates considerably against the fact of their semantic difference. It is thus little wonder that the soliloquy ends not with a decision for action but with a decision to legitimize further inaction by resolving to stage *The Mousetrap* — a further duplication, this time both of the murder and of the play itself — before anything more definite can be done. For the ultimate effect of the flattening, homogenizing trope of parison is to make meaningful comparison impossible.

This is seen even more vividly in the most famous of all Hamlet's soliloquies:

To be, or not to be, that is the question:
Whether 'tis nobler in the mind to suffer

The slings and arrows of outrageous fortune,
Or to take arms against a sea of troubles
And by opposing end them. To die — to sleep ...

(III. i. 56-60)

                    To die, to sleep;
To sleep, perchance to dream —

(III. i. 64-5)

For who would bear the whips and scorns of time,
Th'oppressor's wrong, the proud man's contumely,
The pangs of dispriz'd love, the law's delay,
The insolence of office, and the spurns
That patient merit of th'unworthy takes ...

(III. i. 70-4)

Thus conscience does make cowards of us all,
And thus the native hue of resolution
Is sicklied o'er with the pale cast of thought ...

(III. i. 83-5)

Here choice has become even more radically circumscribed. The repetition, reduplication and parisonal clauses which structure the speech force the ultimate annihilation of the apparent decision with which it opens; as one term slides under another, genuine differentiation proves utterly impossible. A soliloquy which opens with an assertion of polar opposites ends, like so many of Hamlet's rhetorical gestures, firstly with an overt admission of impotence and of inability actually to differentiate and, secondly, with his willing compliance with the distraction provided by the presence of Ophelia. Once again an attempt at semantic comparison has been blocked by the syntactic device of parison. The same pattern of thought equally bedevils Hamlet's final soliloquy:

                    Now whether it be
Bestial oblivion, or some craven scruple ...

(IV. iv. 39-40)

Sith I have cause, and will, and strength, and means ...

(IV. iv. 45)

> Witness this army of such mass and charge,
> Led by a delicate and tender prince ...
>
> (IV. iv. 47-8)
>
> That have a father kill'd, a mother stain'd,
> Excitements of my reason and my blood ...
>
> (IV. iv. 57-8)
>
> My thoughts be bloody or be nothing worth.
>
> (IV. iv. 66)

Again the process of the speech is marked by a determined effort to mark ideas conceived of as alternative into clearly separated demarcations: bestial oblivion or craven scruple, bloody or nothing worth. Once more, however, the insistent repetition of the syntactic pattern serves to undermine the semantic distinction. The ultimate effect of this soliloquy, as of all the others, is not one of progression — as might have been achieved by the use of a different rhetorical trope such as climax[8] — but of a stultifying circling in which not only the possibility of movement but the fixity of semantic meaning itself is called into question.

It is notable that Hamlet himself seems ultimately to become aware of the duplication of meaning that proliferates around his every attempt to establish distinction. This is apparent in his conversation with Osric:

HAMLET: Sir, his definement suffers no perdition in you, though I know to divide him inventorially would dozy th'arithmetic of memory, and yet but yaw neither, in respect of his quick sail. But, in the verity of extolment, I take him to be a soul of great article and his infusion of such dearth and rareness as, to make true diction of him, his semblable is his mirror and who else would trace him his umbrage, nothing more.

> (V. ii. 112-20)

HAMLET: What's his weapon?
OSRIC: Rapier and dagger.
HAMLET: That's two of his weapons. But well.

> (V. ii. 141-3)

HAMLET: What call you the carriages?

> (V. ii. 151)

Here, finally, a distinction is drawn and sustained: rapier and dagger are not the same. Osric's loose usage is, however, in one sense technically accurate, since rapier and dagger were habitually wielded together in Renaissance duelling as complementary weapons, and it is also a phrase which would have sat very comfortably on the lips of the majority of the characters, particularly of the elision-prone Claudius; and even Hamlet's parodic redundancy of language is not that far removed from his own earlier duplications in the soliloquies. Ironically, then, even as the play exposes the dangers of one of its major linguistic features, it does so by duplicating that feature.

In this closing scene of the play, language gives place to action as the pace speeds up and events overtake intentions; indeed, Hamlet's dying words signal a final retreat from language. Nevertheless, it is through the language of the play that generations of readers and audiences have attempted to approach the quest for meaning in it, and thus it is not surprising that they have so consistently failed to agree on a single, unified, consistent interpretation of the play, or that readings of it can continue to proliferate: for the parisonal structuring of many of its most crucial scenes and speeches means that, within them, a constant multiplicity of interpretation is generated as sense wars with sense and semantic meaning with syntactic structure, as distinction is eroded and signifiers slide into each other, so that no final single rendering of any one speech is ultimately ever possible. Each separate experience of reading or watching the play thus becomes a complex negotiation between a series of incompatible choices where meaning is first offered and then shifted or denied, and where its production is always a delicate balancing act

> Between the pass and fell-incensed points
> Of mighty opposites.

> (V. ii. 61-2)

Notes

1. There are, of course, three early versions of the play, all of differing lengths. For a discussion of the question of their relative lengths and of the associated staging difficulties, see Graham Holderness and Bryan Loughrey, eds, *The Tragicall Historie of Hamlet Prince of Denmark* (Hemel Hemstead: Harvester Wheatsheaf, 1992), p. 14 (this is a reprint of the so-called 'Bad Quarto'). The 1992/3 RSC production of the play runs at four and a half hours and has to have an early start-time.

2. Where there is a literature so extended as that on *Hamlet* it is obviously impossible even to skate the surface of the field, but some of the critical material on various forms of doublings in *Hamlet* includes Ralph Berry, 'Hamlet's Doubles', *Shakespeare Quarterly*, 37 (1986), 204-12; Marjorie Garber, *Shakespeare's Ghost Writers: Literature as uncanny causality* (New York and London: Methuen, 1987), p. 129; Ernest Jones on Hamlet and Oedipus, conveniently reprinted in John Jump, ed., *'Hamlet': A Casebook* (Basingstoke: Macmillan, 1968), pp. 51-63; David Scott Kastan, '"His Semblable is his Mirror": *Hamlet* and the Imitation of Revenge', *Shakespeare Studies*, 19 (1987), 111-24; Frank Kermode, *Forms of Attention* (Chicago: University of Chicago Press, 1985), pp. 35-63; and Anna K. Nardo, 'Hamlet, "A Man to Double Business Bound"', *Shakespeare Quarterly*, 34 (1983), 181-99.

3. For the relationship between *Hamlet* and other plays, the most convenient summary is the Arden introduction. See also William F. Hansen, *Saxo Grammaticus and the Life of 'Hamlet'* (Lincoln: University of Nebraska Press, 1983), and Scott McMillin, 'Acting and Violence: *The Revenger's Tragedy* and its Departures from *Hamlet*', *Studies in English Literature 1500-1900*, 24 (1984), 275-91.

4. Kermode, *Forms*, p. 49, comments interestingly on hendiadys in the play. A brief survey of language-based approaches to the text is found in Michael Hattaway, *'Hamlet'* (Basingstoke: Macmillan, 1987).

5. I feel the Arden editor is too peremptory in asserting that this must mean 'bend yourself'. It could read equally well as a reiteration of 'beseech'.

6. (London: Edward Arnold, 1992), p. 160. Ronberg also comments (p. 184) on the use of parison in *The Two Gentlemen of Verona*.

7. There is some interesting commentary on this phrase in Malcolm Evans's section, 'Jacques Derrida Meets the Sledded Pollax' in *Signifying Nothing: Truth's True Contents in Shakespeare's Text* (Brighton: Harvester, 1989), pp. 193-200.

8. For climax, see Ronberg, *Words*, p. 152, where an example from *The Spanish Tragedy* is given.

Renaissance Feminisms

HAMLET'S WHORES

KAY STANTON

'Get thee to a nunnery' (III. i. 121): in a play filled with memorable lines, this has been one of the most often quoted. As editors rarely fail to note in gloss, 'nunnery' was Elizabethan slang for 'brothel', so Hamlet *really* tells Ophelia to go to a whorehouse, where, he believes, she belongs. Why does the virtuous Ophelia belong, in Hamlet's judgement, in a whorehouse?[1] A frequent answer has been that Hamlet so relegates her because of his disillusionment with women resulting from the revelation of his mother's lustfulness; *Gertrude* belongs in a whorehouse, since she has been 'whor'd' by Claudius (V. ii. 64). Because Gertrude has become a whore, so will Ophelia — and so, in fact, will all women, in the estimation not only of Hamlet but also of those many men of various generations who have quoted — I would say prostituted — the line for the purpose of smugly concurring (and implying Shakespeare's concurrence) with Hamlet's estimation of woman's whorish nature.

A slightly more sophisticated reading of the passage in which the line occurs might recognize that both meanings of 'nunnery' are operating: Ophelia is too virtuous for this corrupt world, which will prostitute her to its ways if she does not retreat into a cloistered religious life. Hamlet is 'cruel only to be kind' (III. iv. 180). The world will corrupt Ophelia as it has corrupted Gertrude; Gertrude has become a whore, a fate that Hamlet wishes Ophelia to avoid, so he must therefore shock her, even by denying his feelings of love. This reading, however, still leaves Gertrude a whore, but it does also neatly reflect another comfortable misogynistic position that the play's commentators have often pandered it to: not all women are whores; some are Madonnas. Certainly the play as reflected through the male characters' perceptions seems to support this position. Women in *Hamlet* are allowed by the play's men to have two and only two choices: virgin or whore. Ophelia cannot, but Hamlet can, be 'indifferent honest' (III. i. 122). So far as the play provides evidence, Gertrude has indulged in sexual activity only in marriage, yet even legalized expression of sexuality merits her the label of 'whore':[2] she suffers from the 'plague' that Hamlet gives Ophelia for *her* dowry: 'be thou as chaste as ice, as pure as snow, thou shalt not escape calumny' (III. i. 136-8). Thus the second position on women doubles back into the first: there may seem to be two choices for women of virgin or whore, but if a woman tries to be virtuous *and* sexual in monogamous marriage, or even if a woman remains an unmarried virgin, she cannot escape the 'calumny' that will brand her a whore: all women are thus whores, either by action or by slander.[3]

Of course, although it seems to warn against slander from others, the passage is itself an exercise in such 'calumny': Ophelia's honour is verbally violated by Hamlet in his speech — and it may have already been done so in action: he may indeed have raped her in the offstage closet interlude that she reports, perhaps only in part, to her father in II. i. 75-110. The onstage Hamlet-woman-closet scene in III. iv. is usually staged, with good reason, to simulate a rape by Hamlet of Gertrude. If both Gertrude and Ophelia are whores, it is Hamlet himself who has made them so, in words if not deeds, by *his* calumny.[4] Although the other male characters may be seen to share Hamlet's misogyny, no male character not named 'Hamlet', elder or younger, *calls* either woman a whore.

Perhaps it may be granted, however, that what makes a woman a whore in the Hamlets' estimation is her sexual use not by one man but by more than one man: Gertrude seems not to have been a whore in old Hamlet's judgement until she bedded Claudius; Ophelia, even if she has been sexually used by young Hamlet, is not seen by him as a whore until she has been employed as a sex object by Polonius, her 'fishmonger' (II. ii. 174), or pimp. The rape of Ophelia by Hamlet may be more verbal than physical; the pandering of Ophelia by her father is more symbolic than literal, so its interpretation may be missed by the naive. Though I would concur with Hamlet that Polonius employs Ophelia's sexuality for his purposes, Polonius seems not to see himself as a 'fishmonger', and Ophelia certainly does not see herself as a whore — it is, again, primarily Hamlet's interpretation that makes them so, and, as he states later in the scene, 'there is nothing either good or bad but thinking makes it so' (II. ii. 249-50).

Hamlet's labels may put rather a strong point upon it, but what seems to enrage him in the 'nunnery' interlude is that Ophelia has put her sense of love and duty for another man above her sense of love and duty for him, just as Gertrude put her sense of love and duty for her new husband above her sense of love and duty for her old. Gertrude chose a brother over a dead Hamlet;

Ophelia chooses a father over a living Hamlet: both choices can be read as additionally sexually perverse in being, to Hamlet, 'incestuous'. And both choices, to Hamlet, result from male lying manipulation of female sexuality — although the female, not the male, is made to bear the sexual abuse of his language. Hamlet is as revolted at Polonius's perverse use of his daughter as he is at his uncle's perverse use of his mother and appalled that neither woman can see, as he can, that she has become a whore.

Hamlet is very skilled at detecting whorishness in women; he is less good (though not completely inept) in detecting it in himself.[5] If the innocent Ophelia has unwittingly been made a whore to her father's purposes, so has Hamlet been prostituted by his father. If Ophelia has betrayed her love for Hamlet for her loving duty to her father, so has Hamlet betrayed his love for her for submission of himself in loving duty to *his* father's unsavoury employment of himself for *his* purposes. Both offspring choose to sacrifice their chance for love to their fathers' desired machinations of power. Both fathers' employment of them forces the offspring to go against their own natural, if uninherited, inclinations. The life force of Hamlet's and Ophelia's love is sapped by an old man and a dead man, both of whom wish to live on the flesh of their children. The older generation incestuously prostitutes the innocence of the younger.

Thus Hamlet, like Ophelia, has been 'whored' by the father. But they are not the only members of the younger generation to be so prostituted. Laertes, too, is in a sense 'whored' by his father, as Polonius entreats Reynaldo to impune Laertes's reputation by going so far as to have him accused of 'drabbing' (II. i. 26), further prostituting his messenger Reynaldo's purpose by making him a spy. Although Reynaldo is reluctant to prostitute Laertes's reputation in this way, Rosencrantz and Guildenstern, in their prostitution by their symbolic father, the King, 'make love to this employment' (V. ii. 57) of spying on and trying to destroy the prince. Hamlet, of course, recognizes them as whores. When Guildenstern admits that he and Rosencrantz are neither the 'very button' (II. ii. 229) of Fortune's cap 'Nor the soles of her shoe' (II. ii. 230) but 'her privates' (II. ii. 234), Hamlet replies, 'In the secret parts of Fortune? O most true, she is a strumpet' (II. ii. 235-6). The representation of Fortune as a whore functions to provide a safe projection for the prostitution of Rosencrantz and Guildenstern. Their meaning seems to be that they sexually use Fortune for their pleasure — which is, of course, the manner of dealing with Fortune that Machiavelli recommends. But because the two previous metaphoric associations anatomically sited them on Fortune's body, this metaphor makes *them* Fortune's whorish pudendum. In attempting to make Fortune their whore, they whore themselves to Fortune. When Fortune's wheel turns against them and for Hamlet, they will be 'Hoist with [their] own petard' (III. iv. 209).

Later in the same scene, II. ii., we are given another passage regarding the *'strumpet Fortune'*, in the conclusion that the player makes of the Pyrrhus speech that Hamlet begins. As young Pyrrhus is described butchering old Priam, the *'strumpet Fortune'* is suddenly introduced, as though responsible for the horrifying act, and the gods are entreated, *'In general synod'*, to

> *take away her power,*
> *Break all the spokes and fellies from her wheel,*
> *And bowl the round nave down the hill of heaven*
> *As low as to the fiends.*

> (II. ii. 490-3)

The speech resumes, after interruptions from Polonius and Hamlet, with the description of the *'mobbled queen'* (II. ii. 498), Hecuba. Her description links her with Fortune. If blind Fortune is dispossessed and consigned to hell, Hecuba, blinded by being *'mobbled'* and / or by her *'bissom rheum'* (II. ii. 502), and dressed only in a blanket, runs through *'flames'* (II. ii. 501). If Fortune's wheel is lost, so is Hecuba's *'diadem'* (II. ii. 503). If Fortune's genitals have been much used because she is a *'strumpet'*, Hecuba's loins are *'all o'erteemed'* (II. ii. 504). As the speech continues, we are told:

> *Who this had this seen, with tongue in venom steep'd*
> *'Gainst Fortune's state would treason have pronounc'd.*

> (II. ii. 506-7)

Thus the goddess, Fortune, more so than Pyrrhus or the male-inflicted violence of war, is blamed for Hecuba's suffering: the whore's state ruins the Madonna's (just as, to Hamlet, Gertrude's state ruins Ophelia's). Oddly, onlookers are to regard Fortune as responsible for *'treason'*. The treason that has occurred is that the old king of Troy, Priam, has been killed, by a young Greek, in the course of war. Yet that Greek, Pyrrhus, had been fated to be the one whose participation was deemed necessary to end the war. In the same way, Hamlet, faced by the treason of regicide, senses that

The time is out of joint. O cursed spite,
That ever I was born to set it right.

(I. v. 196-7)

But in the Pyrrhus speech, Fortune takes the blame for the horrifying acts
of male violence, when all she has done, if anything, is to turn her wheel.
The fate that she is said to deserve is visited upon the innocent Hecuba.
The image of the mobbled queen is used to punish the very feminine representation that she enacts. She is both source of blame and victim, conveniently allowing male violence to be overshadowed.

The Pyrrhus speech is said to be part of Aeneas' tale to Dido. Although
Aeneas had supernatural help from Venus to make Dido fall in love with him,
his tale is said to have been enough to seduce her. He wins her sexual favours,
co-rules her kingdom, then betrays and leaves her, in a sense committing
'treason' against her love and her state. As he departs, she leaps into the
flames, just as Hecuba runs through flames distraught over the loss of her husband. Aeneas achieved rule over Carthage, as Claudius secured rule of Denmark, through sexual association with the widowed queen. Dido is sacrificed
to Aeneas' dynastic mission to found the Roman Empire, just as Ophelia is
deserted for Hamlet's dynastic responsibilities. Dido, as widowed queen and
rejected lover, is a model of both the women in *Hamlet*.

The portion of Aeneas' tale to Dido that Hamlet begins and the player continues also has a seductive effect, first detected on the player speaking it and
then on Hamlet. Polonius notes the physiological changes on the actor. As he
speaks the following lines, tears come to his eyes and his colour changes:

> *if the gods themselves did see her then,*
> *When she saw Pyrrhus make malicious sport*
> *In mincing with his sword her husband's limbs,*
> *The instant burst of clamour that she made,*
> *Unless things mortal move them not at all,*
> *Would have made milch the burning eyes of heaven*
> *And passion in the gods.*

(II. ii. 508-14)

The queen's grief at her husband's murder should move the gods, and does
move the actor speaking of it.

In Hamlet's soliloquy at the close of this scene, II. ii., he contrasts himself
to 'this player', who,

> But in a fiction, in a dream of passion,
> Could force his soul so to his own conceit
> That from her working all his visage wann'd,
>
> .   .   .   .
>
>   his whole function suiting
> With forms to his conceit.

(II. ii. 546-51)

A masculine-feminine interplay is in operation between soul and conceit. Hamlet considers it 'monstrous' (II. ii. 545) that this profound effect should be created 'all for nothing! / For Hecuba!', since 'What's Hecuba to him, or he to her, / That he should weep for her?' (II. ii. 551-4). A queen's horrified reaction to the murder of an old man (like Gertrude's response to Polonius's murder) is devalued in comparison to Hamlet's 'motive' and 'cue for passion' (II. ii. 555). The player, with his skill, can produce a reaction 'for nothing! For Hecuba!' (II. ii. 551-2); Hamlet, with his 'cue for passion',

> can say nothing — no, not for a king,
> Upon whose property and most dear life
> A damn'd defeat was made.

(II. ii. 564-6)

After accusing himself of cowardice, he returns to a theatrical image to make three consecutive comparisons of himself to a prostitute:

> Prompted to my revenge by heaven and hell
> Must like a whore unpack my heart with words
> And fall a-cursing like a very drab,
> A scullion!

(II. ii. 580-3)

It is curious that after he had lamented being able to 'say nothing' (II. ii. 564), the attribute of the female prostitute that he admits to in two of the comparisons is verbal. The third comparison in the 'Good Quarto' is not to a 'scullion', but to a 'stallyon' — Elizabethan slang for a male prostitute. This also links him to the Trojan horse, which Pyrrhus had been the first to enter. Directly after the three prostitution images, Hamlet sets his 'brains' to work (II. ii. 584), as the player had forced his soul to his conceit, and he comes up with his plan for *The Mousetrap*. Seducing himself with the effect of Aeneas' tale to Dido, Hamlet decides that a play can be the instrument to determine Claudius's guilt, and this love of theatre allows him to reinterpret the mission put upon him by the Ghost. First, he had a tremendous 'motive' and 'cue for passion' (II. ii. 555) and was 'Prompted to [his] revenge by heaven and hell' (II. ii. 580), but armed with a play, a means that, he has heard, has been known to strike 'guilty creatures'

> so to the soul that presently
> They have proclaim'd their malefactions,

(II. ii. 585-8)

he allows himself the freedom to doubt the Ghost and to regard it as his enemy:

> The spirit that I have seen
> May be a devil, and the devil hath power
> T'assume a pleasing shape, yea, and perhaps,
> Out of my weakness and my melancholy,
> As he is very potent with such spirits,
> Abuses me to damn me.

(II. ii. 594-9)

The only time in *Hamlet* when the eponymous character is happy is when he plans the play: it is the outlet for his imagination and creativity; it is the foundation for the most complex plan that he devises; to have anything to do with the players puts him in a state of what Rosencrantz calls 'joy' (III. i. 18). He is obsessively careful to have the actors speak his lines correctly — obviously, for him, the play, not violent revenge, is the thing. It is his great love, the one thing that he regards more highly than his father. The play could be his salvation, but, as we are informed by the three prostitution images, it is what he whores, just as he whores his other loves, Gertrude and Ophelia. In fact, we may see each of the prostitution images of himself as a brief statement of the whoring that he makes of each love relationship. With Gertrude he unpacks his heart with words; with Ophelia he curses, and with the play he is a stallion, as he makes it a kind of Trojan horse, brought into the court as a seeming peace offering that hides a surprise attack in the darkness.

Hamlet begins his whoring of the play by whoring the actors, in a manner similar to that employed by Claudius with Rosencrantz and Guildenstern and Polonius with Reynaldo and Ophelia, by perverting their purposes to his self-interested ends, putting words in their mouths (thereby also prostituting the actors to betray the play's and thus the original author's integrity) and coach-

ing their actions. In the scene — III. i., the 'nunnery' scene — just before
Hamlet's coaching of the actors, we see Rosencrantz, Guildenstern and Ophelia being coached by their 'bawds'. In fact, in III. i., as Polonius directs Ophelia to

> Read on this book,
> That show of such an exercise may colour
> Your loneliness,

(III. i. 44-6)

he has his one momentary flash of guilt over so using her:

> We are oft to blame in this,
> 'Tis too much prov'd, that with devotion's visage
> And pious action we do sugar o'er
> The devil himself.

(III. i. 46-9)

Yet Polonius frames this evil as a general fault of humanity, not as particular to himself. The combination of Ophelia's stage-directed show of piety and
Polonius's comment on it, however, provokes Claudius to reveal, in aside, his
first hint of guilt, and, interestingly enough, he expresses it in an image of
prostitution:

> O 'tis too true.
> How smart a lash that speech doth give my conscience.
> The harlot's cheek, beautied with plast'ring art,
> Is not more ugly to the thing that helps it
> Than is my deed to my most painted word.
> O heavy burden!

(III. i. 49-54)

The 'thing' referred to here is equated with Claudius's 'deed', but the
meaning of the 'thing' is ambiguous: it could mean the prostitute's genitalia,
desire for her expressed in the male organ, the act of prostitution itself, and
other 'things'. But his is the first use in the play of the word 'thing' after Hamlet's 'The play's the thing' (II. ii. 600). Whatever Claudius means by it, the
'thing' associated with the 'harlot' momentarily catches the 'conscience of the
King' (II. ii. 601), and once again, prostitution serves its turn for male pro-
jections of guilt.

Located where it is in the play, directly following the prostitution image of
Claudius and directly before Hamlet's 'nunnery' interlude with Ophelia, as
well as, in terms of Hamlet's agenda, between his resolution to use the play
to catch the conscience of the King and the performance itself, the 'To be or
not to be' speech (III. i. 56-90) strikes me as less a soliloquy than a performance. It is certainly expressed with more studied formality than his other soliloquies. Undoubtedly before the end of the 'nunnery' interlude Hamlet shows
his awareness of the presence at least of Polonius; he may indeed have been
aware from the time of his entrance in III. i. that he was being watched and
overheard. Before the arrival of the actors, he could (and did) consider suicide
as a way out of his problems, but a serious consideration of suicide at this moment seems highly unlikely, since, at this point in the play more than at any
other, he has something to live for — the performance of *his* play, for which
he has such high hopes. By seeming to consider suicide now, he could conceal his designs against Claudius, which would protect the play. If this speech
is a performance, it is also then a prostitution of Hamlet's feelings that had
previously been genuine — exactly the case as in his remarks to Ophelia that
follow the speech.

Hamlet's treatment of Fortune in the 'To be or not to be' speech may be in-
formatively compared to his previous uses of the image. In the speech, he
poses the question of

> Whether 'tis nobler in the mind to suffer
> The slings and arrows of outrageous fortune,
> Or to take arms against a sea of troubles
> And by opposing end them.

(III. i. 57-60)

Both of the previous uses of the word 'fortune' in the play were in personifications of a whore-goddess, instruments of misogynistic male projection, first for the whorishness of Rosencrantz and Guildenstern, and
then as scapegoated cause of Pyrrhus' butchery. Here Fortune has herself
become the wielder of weapons, directly rather than indirectly responsible
for violent action. In response a man may passively suffer (unlike Hecuba, who actively suffered and clamoured her protest), or he may himself
'take arms' against what seems like it should be Fortune, but turns out to
be 'a sea of troubles'. Fortune now seems to be a shape-shifter, like
Proteus, especially in view of the sea image. Proteus, the sea-god with the
ability to assume various shapes, was also gifted with prophecy, but could

only be made to speak truth when held by his captor, through a series of frightening metamorphoses. By proposing to meet Fortune in combat against her, one may 'take arms' in the sense of weapons, or 'take arms' in the sense of seizure, only to find her metamorphosed into a sea of plural 'troubles' before he can learn the truth of what is 'nobler in the mind'. But the image 'take arms against a sea of troubles' itself changes further, as taking arms against the sea is also an image of swimming — and indeed of swimming against the current, the sea's natural motion. One has as much of a chance in defeating the sea in this manner as in wresting the indicator of the motion of Fortune, her wheel, away from her — and yet, such a feat was imaged in the Pyrrhus speech. Of course, one defeats the sea in the 'To be or not to be' speech by defeating oneself, by killing oneself. As one is born to die, one can achieve a kind of existential triumph by controlling one's death, which is in a sense also 'taking arms' in embracing that death, making love to that employment. Thus to learn Fortune's secrets and to triumph over her, as well as to be noble, one must submerge oneself in her element and thereby die. 'To die', particularly as 'a consummation / Devoutly to be wish'd' (III. i. 60, 63-4), is, in the habitual Renaissance pun, a sexual climax. But by the end of the speech, the idea of suicide has been discarded, because of fear of

> The undiscover'd country, from whose bourn
> No traveller returns.

> (III. i. 79-80)

Hamlet uses the word 'country' only twice in the play: here and in the bawdy pun on 'cunt' in the 'country matters' interchange with Ophelia before the play performance that culminates in the 'fair thought to lie between maids' legs' (III. ii. 115, 117): 'Nothing' (III. ii. 119). 'Country' is in both cases the mystery of the thing of no thing,[6] the thing both desired and feared (as Claudius fears the harlot's 'thing') by its supposed power to annihilate man (or at least his masculinity). Although Hamlet says that 'No traveller returns' from the bourn of this 'undiscover'd country' of death, he has seen one who has, his father's Ghost. Of course, he may mean that no one returns to life, and there may be further possible interpretations of this contradiction, but it may give additional support to the idea that the speech is a performance, one in which it would be best not to mention the Ghost returning from his grave to accuse Claudius of murder. It is otherwise extremely curious that Hamlet, in an extended meditation on death during which he truly believes himself to be unheard, would not mention his father. In every other soliloquy, he does. His only references in the speech to the task assigned him by his father are in the ambiguous 'native hue of resolution / Is sicklied o'er with the pale cast of thought' (III. i. 84-5), and the equally ambiguous 'enterprises of great pitch and moment' (III. i. 86). In the first image, the 'pale cast of thought' is eerily similar both to Polonius's 'show' of piety that 'may colour ... loneliness' in the way that 'We' 'sugar o'er' the 'devil' with 'devotion's visage', and to Claudius's 'harlot's cheek, beautied with plast'ring art' and his 'deed' 'painted' with his 'word'. It is also like Hamlet's entreaty to Gertrude in the closet scene that she should not lay a 'flattering unction' to her 'soul', lest

> It will but skin and film the ulcerous place,
> Whiles rank corruption, mining all within,
> Infects unseen.

(III. iv. 149-51).

In each parallel, the surface covers the evil. So here too, we may assume, the 'native hue of resolution' is the real crime. The 'enterprises of great pitch and moment' whose 'currents turn awry' (III. i. 87) return to the sea metaphor, but if the sea's 'currents' can be turned awry by 'conscience' (III. i. 83), one can indeed successfully triumph over the 'slings and arrows of outrageous fortune' by taking 'arms against a sea of troubles', and the 'name of action' (III. i. 88) may be won, not lost. Hamlet's last use of the word 'conscience' had been in his stated intent to employ the play 'to catch the conscience of the King' (II. ii. 601); his next use of the word 'action' will be in his advice to the players to 'Suit the action to the word, the word to the action' (III. ii. 17-18).

Further evidence that the 'To be or not to be' speech prostitutes Hamlet's formerly held ideas may be seen in its very pretence to consider, by images that deconstruct themselves, what is 'nobler in the mind' (III. i. 57). The speech concludes with first a recognition of and then an address to Ophelia. When Ophelia offers to 'redeliver' Hamlet's 'remembrances' to her, and he denies that he ever gave her 'aught' (III. i. 93-6), she reasserts that he did. She further urges,

> Take these again; for to the noble mind
> Rich gifts wax poor when givers prove unkind.

(III. i. 100-1)

Although he had lied to her immediately before this speech, he does not become abusive until after she refers to the 'noble mind', which seems to set off the verbal sexual assault that begins with 'Ha, ha! Are you honest?' (III. i. 103) and continues over fifty lines, punctuated with *five* relegations of her to a nunnery. As Hamlet exits, on his last 'To a nunnery, go' (III. i. 151), Ophelia laments, 'O, what a noble mind is here o'erthrown' (III. i. 152). If consideration of a 'noble mind' sets the tone for the 'To be or not to be' speech, it also defines the bourn of the 'nunnery', and makes a powerful link between Hamlet and Ophelia. Her first use of the phrase was in association with herself; Hamlet's anger may be triggered by her claim to a quality that he attributes only to himself (or at least to masculine identity). His relegation of her to a 'nunnery', then, seems to express a subconscious desire to distinguish himself from her: *he* has a noble mind, she does not; *she* is a whore, he is not; he is at least 'indifferent honest' (III. i. 122), but she cannot be both honest and beautiful. Yet both are in some sense noble and honest and in some sense whores. The difference is that she can see male and female as possessed of the same qualities; he cannot. He can acknowledge the taint of prostitution in himself only potentially and indirectly and only as proceeding from her: 'the power of beauty will sooner transform honesty from what it is to a bawd than the force of honesty can translate beauty into his likeness' (III. i. 111-14).

This projection onto a female target of one's own male whorishness in the course of asserting a 'noble mind' also infects Laertes. If Hamlet has been seduced by the actor's effects on an audience to prostitute playacting to his purpose and then to scapegoat Ophelia, Laertes, upon his return from France, seems to be initially seduced to avow *his* revenge dramatically, in overstatement that 'out-Herods Herod' (III. ii. 14). His audience of rabble 'applaud it to the clouds, / "Laertes shall be king, Laertes king"' (IV. v. 107-8). After breaking into the court with his followers' aid, Laertes asserts:

> That drop of blood that's calm proclaims me bastard,
> Cries cuckold to my father, brands the harlot
> Even here between the chaste unsmirched brow
> Of my true mother.

(IV. v. 117-20)

This image, a totally needless and wanton implication of his mother, also echoes Hamlet's accusation of Gertrude, in the closet scene, of an act that

takes off the rose
From the fair forehead of an innocent love
And sets a blister there.

(III. iv. 42-4)

That accusation of his mother for whorishness follows fast on the heels of Hamlet's murder of Polonius; her supposed sin is made to overshadow his actual sin and somehow to justify it, just as Laertes employs his 'whorish' image of his mother to justify his murderous impulses. As Hamlet can easily switch between his mother and Ophelia as a convenient scapegoat, so can Laertes. When, later in IV. v., Ophelia enters, mad,[7] Laertes's question — 'is't possible a young maid's wits / Should be as mortal as an old man's life?' (IV. v. 159-60) — demonstrates the degree to which his love of his father has been exaggerated in service of his 'honour', and also expresses his blindness that his own wits have proved similarly mortal by his mad grasping for violent revenge. Ophelia handily absorbs the whore image of the mother in being a 'cause' for Laertes's revenge and sacrificially embodies both his and Hamlet's 'madness'. In life, Ophelia had interested both Laertes and Hamlet only in terms of her potential illicit expression of sexuality; in death, Ophelia switches from potential whore to worshipped Madonna as Hamlet and Laertes can then safely whore their own self-constructed images of pure love for her as rationale for violence against each other, both in their conflict in her grave in V. i.,[8] and in their fencing match in V. ii. As Hamlet himself notes in regard to Laertes, 'by the image of my cause I see / The portraiture of his' (V. ii. 77-8); yet he cannot help but add that 'the bravery of his grief did put me / Into a tow'ring passion' (V. ii. 79-80), and, within a few more lines, he will consent to meeting Laertes in the fatal fencing match. As both young men prostitute their love of a woman (such as it is, in an imagined image) in competition with one another, they symbolically replay the competition between old Hamlet and Claudius for Gertrude — Hamlet calls their match 'this brothers' wager' (V. ii. 249). In the same way, the 'portraiture' image recalls Hamlet's comparison for Gertrude of the portraits of old Hamlet and Claudius (III. iv. 53-88). In enticing Laertes into his plan to rid himself of Hamlet, Claudius also employs a portrait image:

> was your father dear to you?
> Or are you like the painting of a sorrow,
> A face without a heart?
>
> (IV. vii. 106-8).

The link between portraiture and painting suggests a connection as well with Hamlet's denunciation of women's painting: 'God hath given you one face and you make yourselves another' (III. i. 144-6). This image also harks back to Claudius's earlier comparison of his deed's 'painted word' to the harlot's cheek; indeed, he is in the process of seducing Laertes's love for fencing to self-interested use.

As we look upon the 'portraits' of Hamlet and Laertes, the painted and therefore 'counterfeit presentment of two brothers' (III. iv. 54), it becomes increasingly as difficult to differentiate between them — and between them and the harlot — as Hamlet thought it was for the harlot Gertrude to distinguish between old Hamlet and Claudius. And 'what a falling off was there' (I. v. 47) for Hamlet to descend to Laertes's level and for both to descend to that of Claudius.[9] Both have whored not only their love for a woman but also their love for their favoured pastime, to violent revenge. Hamlet has even been seduced to exchange his beloved activity, play-acting, for Laertes's, fencing. Yet, as noted above, Laertes's desire for violence expresses itself theatrically; so Hamlet's desire for theatre expressed itself rather violently. Hamlet calls himself Laertes's 'foil' (V. ii. 252), yet Laertes is a foil for Hamlet in terms of the play at large. Each may be seen to play the other's major key in a minor mode. Fencing is violence in its most artistic form; *The Mousetrap* art in its most violent form. Both play and match have an on-stage audience that comments on and to some degree participates in and / or is implicated in the action.

Thus the older generation, old Hamlet and Claudius, through perversions of loves, whores for its own purposes the younger generation, young Hamlet and Laertes. Young men are seduced to 'make love to this employment'. As Hamlet tells Gertrude, 'reason panders will' (III. iv. 88) — but with the result that each will 'couple hell' (I. v. 93). Laertes enthusiastically volunteers to be Claudius's 'organ' (IV. vii. 69). Hamlet, too, defines himself as an 'organ'. Though delivered in another context, his speech is applicable here:

Why, look you now, how unworthy a thing you make of me. You would play upon me, you would seem to know my stops, you would pluck out the heart of my mystery, you would sound me from my lowest note to the top of my compass; and there is much music, excellent voice, in this little organ, yet cannot you make it speak. 'Sblood, do you think I am easier to be played on than a pipe? Call me what instrument you will, though you can fret me, you cannot play upon me.

(III. ii. 354-63)

Rosencrantz and Guildenstern are incapable of plucking out Hamlet's 'mystery', but old Hamlet knew his son's 'stops' well enough to make him an 'unworthy thing', playing upon him to make him sound the old refrain of violent revenge. In this, Hamlet and his 'mystery' are not unique. The 'stops' are the same for him as for Laertes: the willingness to regard men as inherently noble, and women as inherently whorish; to prove oneself noble and male by asserting oneself competitively — even if suicidally — against another; to put duty towards the past, the patriarch and the patriarchal system above duty to the present, one's self and positive mutuality; to pervert one's love — whether of women or of one's favoured pastime — to service to an outmoded, self-destructive code of honour, and thereby to become its instrument, its organ, its weapon, its phallus. Although Hamlet and Laertes each allows these stops to be played upon in order to avoid seeming like a woman, and therefore whorish, each is most a whore when performing this siren song.

Directly after each has agreed to the fencing match, however, Laertes and Hamlet each identifies himself as a woman. In response to the news of Ophelia's death, Laertes states that although he struggles to 'forbid ... tears' (since his grief as well as his revenge will have appropriate male release in the fencing match), 'The woman will be out' (IV. vii. 185, 188). Hamlet confesses to Horatio 'how ill all's here about [his] heart' yet discounts his misgivings about agreeing to the match as 'a kind of gaingiving as would perhaps trouble a woman' (V. ii. 208-9, 211-12).[10] The 'woman' in both Laertes and Hamlet is the part that protests against his whoring rather than that which submits to it. Thus, at the fencing match, Hamlet and Laertes are each both phallus and pudendum, reduced to weapon and receptive vessel of poison,[11] with the match itself constituting a gruesome perversion of the sex act, whored by violence and the poisoning of noble instincts and love,[12] where the symbol of 'union' (V. ii. 269) — the pearl in the cup, representing marriage, the state, loving attachment and bonding — is no less poisonous than the organ of destruction, the sword-phallus. Gertrude is poisoned by the 'union', Hamlet and Laertes by the phallic weapon that each allows himself to be, but Claudius, 'The King' — the patriarch, representing the state and the past — is justly poisoned by both, in that he, the representative of patriarchy and its poisonous, prostituting male code, is 'to blame' (V. ii. 326).

Yet the whoring does not stop there. Dying, Hamlet in a sense 'whores' Horatio (whose name suggests 'whore' as well as 'orator'), as he posthumously compels his friend to speak his story.[13] But Fortinbras in his turn 'whores' Hamlet's story by reducing his 'mystery' in representing him as a 'soldier', his most 'unworthy' aspect. Hamlet's dying words, 'the rest is silence' (V. ii. 363), are contradicted by Fortinbras's final command: 'Go, bid the soldiers shoot' (V. ii. 408). The play ends with the new order to be determined by another 'bawd' — one with the most impressive record of employing the bodies of others to his self-interested purposes and who additionally controls the most potent weapons. Patriarchy is re-established among its ruins in even more forceful form — though in unfortunately familiar 'custom'. Yet we, the audience, should now be able to recognize, although we are 'native here / And to the manner born,' that 'it is a custom / More honour'd in the breach than the observance' (I. iv. 14-16).

As I hope to have demonstrated, *Hamlet* repeatedly reveals patriarchy's assumption of male superiority and female whorishness as poisonous, treasonous, and suicidal. Although each time it is asserted it is eventually 'Hoist with [its] own petard' (III. iv. 209), its proponents cling to it from fear of being regarded as 'womanish', and end up being either its prostitutes, its pandars or both. Most male characters pandar themselves and others besides being used as whores; if Gertrude and Ophelia become whores by men's exploitation of them, neither at least becomes a bawd to others. Male characters inhibit the self-expression of the female characters, define them in ways that have little to do with their reality, and yet punish them for even supposed or projected transgressions from the male-defined images of what they should be; the female characters do not inflict anything comparable on the males. Yet, although the poisons of the patriarchal system may be seen to be fundamentally responsible for the 'black and grained spots' (III. iv. 90) that are most ugly and destructive in *Hamlet*, it is too easy to assert with Laertes that 'The King — the King's to blame' (V. ii. 326) and thereby paint over the roles of his (actually *their*, since old Hamlet still functions as king to his son) willing subjects. If old Hamlet, Claudius and Polonius were 'bawds', young Hamlet, Laertes, Gertrude and Ophelia were obedient 'whores', and must take a share of the blame — as must we all.

In a controversial article on what he calls 'Feminist Thematics' in Shake-speare criticism, Richard Levin sneers at the idea that 'the dying Laertes could have ended his confession to Hamlet by exclaiming, "I can no more; the Pa-triarchie, the Patriarchie's to blame!"'[14] Although I consider much of Levin's attack unjust, I concur insofar as that to project sole blame for the problems in Shakespeare's tragedies onto patriarchy and / or masculinity is to over-simplify in a way 'Almost as bad' (III. iv. 28) as to project sole blame on femininity, as in 'Frailty, thy name is woman' (I. ii. 146). Patriarchy is the 'custom' by which the problem finds not only legitimized expression, but un-healthy encouragement — in that it soils 'our addition' and 'takes / From our achievements, though perform'd at height, / The pith and marrow of our at-tribute' (I. iv. 20-2). Yet the problem itself goes much deeper. It is a 'mole of nature' (I. iv. 24). Because of that 'mole', or 'defect' (I. iv. 31), 'our virtues else, be they as pure as grace' (I. iv. 33) may 'take corruption' (I. iv. 35) from a 'dram of evil' (I. iv. 36), and thereby our 'noble substance' (I. iv 37) may be poisoned.[15] This defect is our vulnerability to corruption and our tendency to spread that corruption by infecting others, as well as reinfecting ourselves, by penetrating them with our corruption. This mole or defect is that which makes us susceptible to becoming 'whores' and to 'whoring' others — and pa-triarchy exploits that susceptibility for its purposes.

Although the custom of patriarchy, with its strictly bounded gender roles, holds that the female is the vulnerable object and the male the penetrating, this 'mole' is not gender-specific, and the pudendum is not the only receiving organ — among the others are the heart and brain, and, most easily, the eye and ear. The play is filled with images of assault upon these organs. Hamlet speaks the speech about the 'mole of nature' before he sees the Ghost of his father. But when he actually encounters that 'old mole' (I. v. 170), he is him-self 'cozen'd ... at hoodman-blind' (III. iv. 77). Old Hamlet, asleep and vul-nerable, received penetrating poison in his ear; in his revenge, he pours the poison of his tale and command into the ear of his vulnerable son, to whom it is just as surely fatal.

Like the audience of the dumb show in III. ii., Hamlet the prince knows but does not understand, sees but does not perceive, hears but does not appre-hend — but *Hamlet* the play always does all of these. And just as old Hamlet whores young Hamlet to be the organ for his revenge, so *Hamlet* in a sense 'whores' Hamlet the prince to be the organ for its art, holding 'the mirror up to nature' (III. ii. 22) by making him the 'glass of fashion and the mould of

form' (III. i. 155), of poisonous penetration for Ophelia (which initially reflects for her the nunnery and ultimately shows her madness and suicide), and
the 'glass' for Gertrude to 'see the inmost part' of herself (III. iv. 18, 19) and
find in her soul 'such black and grained spots / As will not leave their tinct'
(III. iv. 90-1). Yet he cannot see the same and worse reflected in himself for
the 'mote' that troubles his own 'mind's eye' (I. i. 115).

The only other character specifically assigned a specular role in the play is
Laertes, and this is conferred by Hamlet himself, when he says in his mock-
ing conversation with Osric that Laertes's 'semblable is his mirror' (V. ii.
118). Even though earlier in the same scene Hamlet had recognized the 'portraiture' of Laertes's 'cause' by the 'image' of his own, he does not realize
how thoroughly he has degenerated to become Laertes's 'semblable', his own
glass: a mirror does not see itself reflected in a mirror. But one image reflected
against itself by double mirroring can yield multiple, seemingly infinite, versions of that image, and thus Hamlet and Laertes mirror one another, their
self-painted images of Ophelia and their mothers, Claudius and old Hamlet,
old Fortinbras and old Hamlet, young Fortinbras and young Hamlet, the head
and heart of revenge, patricide and fratricide, War and Murder, Force and Imagination, the art of violence and the violence of art, their own functions as
whores and organs, and very much more, as the opulence of commentary on
this play itself reflects.

If Hamlet is whored by *Hamlet*, so *Hamlet* is also whored by Hamlet when
he makes *The Murder of Gonzago* a perverse distorting mirror by transforming it into *The Mousetrap*, which is and is not *Hamlet*.[16] As indicated above,
Hamlet whores his love of the theatre to his revenge, and in so doing he corrupts art to violence. Most disturbingly, as well as most obviously whorishly,
he employs the play as his 'cue' for revenge in a virtually pornographic way,
as it seems to provide the erotic charge to stimulate the blood-lust of his behaviour in Gertrude's closet, for which he scapegoats his mother.[17] He imi-
tates the character of Lucianus, nephew to the king, pouring poison in Claudius's ear by summarizing the plot before it is enacted, thus prostituting the art
of the play; then, as Lucianus was to have done in the unacted part of the play,
he seeks control over the Queen's sexuality. In murdering Polonius in Gertrude's closet, he in a sense murders a Player King, as he had apparently believed Claudius to be behind the arras. He becomes more and more involved
in *The Murder of Gonzago*, beginning as an innocent member of the audience; he then becomes successively its patron, its collaborating author, its

stage manager-director, its historian, its Chorus, its interpreter, its villain and finally its victim. By whoring the actors, the play, and its audience, he becomes caught in the perverted version of *The Murder of Gonzago*: *The Mousetrap*. The play is the thing that catches his own conscience, and it whores him as he has whored it, making him no longer one of the innocent, but one of the 'guilty creatures' at and in the play.

But what of the other 'guilty creatures' at the play: ourselves, the audience of the play at large?[18] I am one who will confess my 'black and grained spots'. Certainly by reducing the play to its whore images and whoring them to my interpretation, I see by this mirror that I have made it a whore, just as I consider Hamlet to have done to Gertrude and Ophelia by his distorted mirroring to them. In doing so, as again I interpret Hamlet to have done, I have been caught in my own *Mousetrap* and proved myself a whore. But, dear reader, 'Are *you* honest?' Will you join Hamlet, *Hamlet*, Gertrude, Ophelia, and me in a 'nunnery'? And will that nunnery be a religious retreat or a brothel — or one of them painted to resemble the other? That is the question.

If we regard the play through the image of the whore in its double reflecting mirrors of Hamlet and *Hamlet*, we can see our own reflections as whore and whored. Actors and directors are 'whored' by the play when they are seduced by it enough to perform it; they in turn 'whore' the play and its characters to their interpretations, and the theatre then becomes the brothel-nunnery where they sell their painted image of it. Those of us who teach the play and offer critical interpretations of it do so in the 'nunnery' of the cloistered halls of Academe, but we are whored by and whore it in the same way. When we make the play our organ, play upon its stops and thereby seek to pluck out the mystery of it and its characters,[19] we make it our whore, and yet we are whored to it because it employs our love for it to give it continued life and perform its desires. Is there a noble escape, however, from this *Mousetrap* of whore and whored? We may as well ask if there was — and is yet — a noble escape for Gertrude and Ophelia, and thus for all women, from the whorish nunnery in which Hamlet (but not *Hamlet*) puts them. Perhaps, if there is, it would be by recognizing the play as reflecting ourselves in our best and worst images and acknowledging the mole in nature that tempts us to project our own faults onto *Hamlet* and thereby scapegoat it, painting our lack of understanding of the full range of its mystery as its blame. Perhaps, when we make love to our employment of interacting with the play, we could additionally at least try not to couple hell by raping it, exploiting and then demeaning it. If we greet the play as a lover rather than a whore and submit ourselves open-heartedly to its mystery, we perhaps could mate with it creatively rather than destructively and thereby have our lives enhanced by artistic mutuality. To this whore, at least, that would be a consummation devoutly to be wished.

Notes

1. For a discussion of prostitution in Shakespeare's time, see Wallace Shugg, 'Prostitution in Shakespeare's London', *Shakespeare Studies*, 10 (1977), 291-313.

2. In 'The Character of Hamlet's Mother', first published in 1957, rpt. in *Hamlet's Mother and Other Women* (New York: Columbia University Press, 1990), pp. 9-17, Carolyn G. Heilbrun objects to the critics' habit of reading Gertrude only as Hamlet depicts her and treating her as if 'weakness and lack of depth and vigorous intelligence' are 'the entire explanation' of her character (p. 10). She grants that Gertrude 'wishes to continue a life of sexual experience,' but states that 'it does not follow' that therefore 'her brain is soft or her wit unperceptive' (p. 13). Heilbrun's defence of Gertrude's intelligence and sexuality is well supplemented by Rebecca Smith's point that if she were dramatically represented 'as only her own words and deeds create her, Gertrude might become another stereotypical character: the nurturing, loving, careful mother and wife — malleable, submissive, totally dependent, and solicitous of others at the expense of herself' ('A Heart Cleft in Twain: The Dilemma of Shakespeare's Gertrude' in Carolyn Ruth Swift Lenz, Gayle Greene and Carol Thomas Neely, eds, *The Woman's Part: Feminist Criticism of Shakespeare* (Urbana, Chicago and London: University of Illinois Press, 1980), p. 207).

3. As Madelon Gohlke notes, 'The paradox of prostitution in the tragedies is based on the masculine perception of the prostitute as not so much the victim as the agent of exploitation. If women are classed as prostitutes and treated as sexual objects, it is because they are deeply feared as sexually untrustworthy, as creatures whose intentions and desires are fundamentally unreadable' ('"I wooed thee with my sword": Shakespeare's Tragic Paradigms' in Lenz, Greene and Neely, eds, *Woman's Part*, p. 153).

4. Linda Bamber suggests that 'Gertrude and Ophelia are psychologically and morally neutral characters who take on the coloration of the play's moods' (*Comic Women, Tragic Men: A Study of Gender and Genre in Shakespeare* (Stanford: Stanford University Press, 1982), p. 77). Bridget Gellert Lyons asserts that of all the characters in the play, Ophelia is 'most persistently presented in terms of symbolic meanings' ('The Iconography of Ophelia', *English Literary History*, 44 (1977), 61).

5. According to Joel Fineman, 'In *Hamlet* all women are prostitutes, and they are Hamlet-like to the extent that all of them are by nature in disguise' ('Fratricide and Cuckoldry: Shakespeare's Doubles' in Murray M. Schwartz and Coppélia Kahn, eds, *Representing Shakespeare: New Psychoanalytic Essays* (Baltimore: The Johns Hopkins University Press, 1980), p. 81).

6. See David Willbern, 'Shakespeare's Nothing' in Schwartz and Kahn, eds, *Representing Shakespeare*, pp. 244-63, for an excellent exploration of the implications, sexual and other, of Shakespeare's use of the word 'nothing'.

7. Carol Thomas Neely states that 'Ophelia's movement from submissive daughter to mad prophet reveals the combination of powerlessness and freedom that women in the tragedies achieve by virtue of their isolation from men and their position partly implicated in, partly outside of the violent conflicts of patriarchy' (*Broken Nuptials in Shakespeare's Plays* (New Haven: Yale University Press, 1985), p. 103).

8. Linda Boose describes both the 'nunnery scene' and the incident with Hamlet and Laertes in Ophelia's grave as perversions of the marriage ceremony ('The Father and the Bride in Shakespeare' in Robert P. Merrix and Nicholas Ranson, eds, *Ideological Approaches to Shakespeare: The Practice of Theory* (Lewiston, NY: Edwin Mellen Press, 1992), p. 14).

9. Harold C. Goddard, who considers the warrior old Hamlet to represent War and the murderer Claudius to represent Murder, suggests that Shakespeare indicates that War and Murder are brothers (*The Meaning of Shakespeare*, 2 vols (Chicago: University of Chicago Press, 1951), I, 350-2). The essential conflict throughout Shakespeare, Goddard asserts, is between Force and Imagination (*passim*). That conflict is perhaps nowhere more easily proved than in the match between Laertes and Hamlet.

10. For the woman in Hamlet, see David Leverenz, 'The Woman in Hamlet: An Interpersonal View' in Schwartz and Kahn, eds, *Representing Shakespeare*, pp. 110-28.

11. The poisonous sexual symbolism of Laertes's and Hamlet's match in a sense parallels *Hamlet*'s initial poisoning. Coppélia Kahn states that the Ghost 'depicts Claudius as a phallic serpent who poured poison into his victim's ear, an action that strongly suggests sexual penetration. The king, ignorantly "secure" and utterly passive and vulnerable in his sleep, is in the feminine position of being penetrated by the man who has already penetrated his wife' (*Man's Estate: Masculine Identity in Shakespeare* (Berkeley, Los Angeles and London: University of California Press, 1981), p. 135).

12. In making her case that the psychological centre of Hamlet and *Hamlet* is that 'The Queen, the Queen's to blame', Janet Adelman argues that Gertrude's sexualized body is the source of all poison: 'her body is the garden in which her husband dies, her sexuality the poisonous weeds that kill him, and poison the world — and the self — for her son' (*Suffocating Mothers: Fantasies of Maternal Origin in Shakespeare's Plays, 'Hamlet' to 'The Tempest'* (New York and London: Routledge, 1992), p. 30).

13. Peter Erickson reads Horatio as providing a defensive function for Hamlet, through which the prince can avoid both his father and his responsibilities to women and can construct a substitute bond of affection (*Patriarchal Structures in Shakespeare's Drama* (Berkeley, Los Angeles and London: University of California Press, 1985), pp. 74-80).

14. Richard Levin, 'Feminist Thematics and Shakespearean Tragedy', *Publications of the Modern Language Association of America*, 103 (1988), 127.

15. Most commentators interpret this passage as a statement concerning the Aristotelian 'tragic flaw'. Although the speech flows from discussion of 'custom' into consideration of the 'mole', these concepts are distinguished.

16. Robert Weimann argues that 'Hamlet's production of *The Mousetrap* can be seen as some dramatized metaphor of the appropriation of the world of the play through mimesis, which appropriation — as it affects Hamlet's position in the play — is itself turned into drama' ('Mimesis in *Hamlet*' in Patricia Parker and Geoffrey Hartman, eds, *Shakespeare and the Question of Theory* (New York and London: Methuen, 1985), p. 288).

17. Jacqueline Rose's 'Sexuality in the reading of Shakespeare: *Hamlet* and *Measure for Measure*' in John Drakakis, ed., *Alternative Shakespeares* (London and New York: Methuen, 1985), analyzing 'how the question of aesthetic form and the question of sexuality are implicated in each other' (p. 98), concludes that 'Failing in a woman, whether aesthetic or moral, is always easier to point to than a failure of integration within language and subjectivity itself. If we try to read Shakespeare in terms of the second, however, it might be possible to lift the onus off the woman, who has for so long now been expected to take the responsibility, and to bear the excessive weight' (p. 118) .

18. Phyllis Rackin notes that 'There was likely to be some ambiguity in Shakespeare's theatre about the identity of the guilty creatures sitting at the play, for if Claudius was watching the players, he was himself a "player king", and Hamlet and the Danish court watched him as well as the players.' Therefore the 'process of seeing undisclosed guilt here reaches beyond the confines of the stage to implicate the audience directly and painfully in the tragic action' (*Shakespeare's Tragedies* (New York: Felix Ungar, 1978), p. 54).

19. Elaine Showalter asserts that 'To liberate Ophelia from the text, or to make her its tragic centre, is to re-appropriate her for our own ends; to dissolve her into a female symbolism of absence is to endorse our own marginality; to make her Hamlet's anima is to reduce her to a metaphor of male experience' ('Representing Ophelia: women, madness, and the responsibilities of feminist criticism' in Parker and Hartman, eds, *Shakespeare*, p. 79).

HAMLET: A DOCUMENT IN MADNESS

ALISON FINDLAY

Some four hundred pages into *The Anatomy of Melancholy* Robert Burton comes close to admitting that his task is impossible:

> Who can sufficiently speak of these symptoms, or prescribe rules to comprehend them? ... if you will describe melancholy, describe a phantastical conceit, a corrupt imagination, vain thoughts and different, which who can do? The four-and-twenty letters make no more variety of words in divers languages than melancholy conceits produce diversity of symptoms in several persons. They are irregular, obscure, various, so infinite, Proteus himself is not so diverse ...[1]

This passage reveals the tensions that exist between language and mental disorder, between documents and madness. Words are inadequate to anatomize Burton's subject but remain the means of control and communication. One must 'speak of these symptoms' in order to 'prescribe rules to comprehend them', difficult though the task may be. Burton's own description of madness significantly uses the metaphor of language and problematizes the relationship between the two even further. He compares 'melancholy conceits' to 'the four-and-twenty letters', says the symptoms of mental illness are a 'variety of words' and describes the people who exhibit them as 'divers languages'. The extended metaphor suggests that identity and madness are verbally constructed. In reverse, it also implies that letters, words and languages are themselves mad. Like the symptoms of melancholy, they carry a plurality of meanings, an excess of interpretations. Although Burton begins the extract by stressing the importance of speech as a means of rational control, he ends it by implicitly eliminating the difference between language and the insanity it seems to subjugate.

The relationship between words, madness and the desire for order is the subject of my investigation into *Hamlet*. My aim is not to provide an analysis of the causes and symptoms of Hamlet's or Ophelia's madness *per se*. By comparing their roles, my essay will examine how gender dictates access to a language with which to cope with mental breakdown. It will consider how madness produces and is produced by a fragmentation of discourse.

Before proceeding to these detailed examinations, it is important to look at the court, the social context in which Hamlet and Ophelia speak. The world of Elsinore is particularly vulnerable to madness. Renaissance physicians, preachers and astrologers commonly cited fear and grief as the principle causes of mental disorder.[2] These emotions abound in Denmark, imperilling the sanity of society at large. Excessive mourning was regarded as particularly dangerous, so the moderate show of grief evident in I. ii. is a safeguard against madness as well as a disguise for crime. Gertrude's composure in response to her husband's death is not a type of insanity, a loss of the 'discourse of reason' (I. ii. 150), but a protection of it. For Claudius to consider his crime too deeply would also be dangerous. He ironically speaks the truth when he claims 'That we with wisest sorrow think on him / Together with remembrance of ourselves' (I. ii. 6). Hints in the text suggest that a preoccupation with the murder, combined with an increasing fear of Hamlet, threatens Claudius's sanity as the play continues (III. ii. 295-9 and IV. iii. 69-70).

Outside the immediate Hamlet family circle, the prison of Denmark is the asylum for a 'distracted multitude' of inhabitants (IV. iii. 4). At the opening of the play Francisco admits he is 'sick at heart' (I. i. 9), and the sighting of the ghost by Bernardo and Marcellus is regarded by Horatio as a symptom of mental instability (I. i. 26-8). The audience, who also see the ghost each time it appears, are included in the community of disordered consciousnesses. This is made explicit in V. i. when the Grave-digger refers to Hamlet's exile:

HAMLET: Why was he sent into England?
GRAVE-DIGGER: Why, because a was mad. A shall recover his wits there. Or if a do
not, 'tis no great matter there.
HAMLET: Why?
GRAVE-DIGGER: 'Twill not be seen in him there. There the men are as mad as he.

(V. i. 145-50)

The 'distracted globe' (I. v. 97) extends beyond Denmark to embrace the spectators.[3] Amongst the English audience, Hamlet's lunacy will not be noticed; he speaks the same language.

The death of King Hamlet puts the language of Elsinore out of joint as well as disrupting its emotional order. The characters struggle to rationalize their experiences in a court where discourse has broken down into a 'rhapsody of words' (III. iv. 48). At the top of the power structure a fissure is created: 'The King is a thing ... Of nothing' (IV. ii. 27-9). King Hamlet is a spirit without a form, a figment of madness or 'fantasy', whereas King Claudius is an empty letter of majesty. Neither has full presence in the play. As a result, the action can no longer be suited to the word nor the word to the action. With the death of King Hamlet, the network of close knit meanings and signs unravels so that all the characters become prisoners of an unstable and plural language. Claudius comments on the gap between 'my deed' and 'my most painted word' (III. i. 53). Words are no longer fixed by any palpable intention; the 'very soul' has been plucked out of the 'body of contraction' (III. iv. 46-7), and it is impossible to identify that which 'passes show' (I. ii. 85). In *Madness and Civilization* Foucault explains how these circumstances where 'Meaning is no longer read in an immediate perception' make a signifying system (like that of language) very accommodating to madness. Once the sign is detached from any authentic intention, it becomes 'burdened with supplementary meanings, and forced to express them. And dreams, madness, the unreasonable can also slip into this excess of meaning.'[4]

Elsinore constructs a courtly discourse characterized by verbosity and an anxiety to fix meaning by definition. In II. ii., Polonius's speeches provide an example. He introduces the subject of Hamlet's madness with the words:

> My liege and madam, to expostulate
> What majesty should be, what duty is,
> Why day is day, night night, and time is time,
> Were nothing but to waste night, day, and time.
>
> .   .   .   .
>
> I will be brief. Your noble son is mad.
> Mad call I it, for to define true madness,
> What is't but to be nothing else but mad?

> (II. ii. 86-94)

Polonius's oratory does, as Dr Johnson claimed, make mockery 'of prefaces that made no introduction, and of method that embarrassed rather than explained',[5] but it also displays an infinite 'deferral' of meaning. The opening lines are not about the nature of majesty, duty, day, night or time, but the failure of language as representation. Polonius may be tedious, but he is not stupid. He shows an awareness of his own mode of expression as a system of self-referring 'limbs and outward flourishes' (II. ii. 91). Like Burton, he recognizes a close relationship between language and madness in spite of their apparent opposition as embodiments of reason and non-reason. To define madness is to 'be nothing else but mad'. His insight into the nature of

words makes him appear as foolish as Hamlet. It displays 'an absurd agita-
tion in society, the mobility of reason'.[6]

It is in this disturbed environment that Hamlet and Ophelia are threatened
with mental breakdowns, rendering their need to define their experiences and
re-define themselves particularly acute. The extent to which they are able to
'put [their] discourse into some frame' (III. ii. 300) is an essential element in
the contrasting representations of madness that Shakespeare offers in these
two characters.

In the preface to *The Anatomy of Melancholy*, Burton explains that he
wrote the book not simply for the elucidation of others but as a cure for his
own mental illness:

> I might be of Thucydides' opinion, "To know a thing and not to express it, is all
> one as if he knew it not." When I first took this task in hand, *et quod ait ille, im-
> pellente genio negotium suscepi* [and, as he saith I undertook the work from some
> inner impulse], this I aimed at, *vel ut lenirem animum scribendo,* [or] to ease my
> mind by writing; for I had *gravidum cor, foedum caput,* a kind of imposthume in
> my head, which I was very desirous to be unladen of, and could imagine no fitter
> evacuation than this ... I was not a little offended with this malady ... I would ...
> make an antidote out of that which was the prime cause of my disease.[7]

Burton equates expression and knowledge, suggesting that the trauma-
tized individual can only become self-aware through the external articulation of a malady. Working with language allows him to step outside his
condition: 'to ease my mind by writing'. He uses his complaint as the raw
material for his book, and recording ideas about melancholy becomes a
treatment and cure.

After what must be Hamlet's most disturbing experience to date — the
ghost's revelation of the murder — the prince resorts to the same self-cure in
order to control his 'distracted globe'. The discourse of his mind has been
interrupted by a voice which speaks only to him and which introduces a range
of experience that could easily put him from 'th'understanding of himself' (II.
ii. 9), but writing and speech provide the means to couple 'all you host of
heaven', earth and hell (I. v. 92-3). To avoid a diagnosis of schizophrenia
(where the subject experiences voices not his own inserted into the mind from
outside), Hamlet responds to the ghost's news with a determination to document his experience and the ghost's voice:

> from the table of my memory
> I'll wipe away all trivial fond records,

All saws of books, all forms, all pressures past
That youth and observation copied there,
And thy commandment all alone shall live
Within the book and volume of my brain ...

(I. v. 98-103)

This mental record does not prove sufficient; thoughts of Gertrude and Claudius disorder the regular rhythm of Hamlet's speech and distract his mind again (I. v. 105-6). To control this outburst of emotion, Hamlet turns to external documentation — writing in his tables. Once Claudius has been 'writ down' a villain after the ghost's report, Hamlet can return to his own 'word' (I. v. 110). Further details in the play show how Hamlet uses his control over the written word to empower himself in emotionally disturbing situations. He writes to Ophelia, to Horatio and to Claudius, and re-writes his destiny by substituting his own letter to the English monarch. He adapts *The Murder of Gonzago* as *The Mousetrap* in order to 'catch the conscience of the King' (II. ii. 601), and even when he is reading a book he imposes his own meaning or 'matter' onto the words to mock Polonius (II. ii. 191-204).

The importance of re-wording to restore mental equilibrium is clear after Hamlet's second encounter with the ghost in III. iv. His initial responses to it convince Gertrude of his madness since his eyes look wild, his hair stands on end and his speech of spontaneous expression seems to be a discourse with the 'incoporal air' (III. iv. 118). As on the previous occasion, once the ghost has departed, Hamlet is ready to re-encode his experience in a language which will make it appear reasonable. He tells Gertrude

It is not madness
That I have utter'd. Bring me to the test,
And I the matter will re-word, which madness
Would gambol from.

(III. iv. 143-6)

Hamlet's ability to transpose experience from one language to another is shown at several points. Rosencrantz and Guildenstern say he is at once 'distracted' but using a 'crafty madness' to remain impenetrable (III. i. 5, 8). He tells them himself that he is 'but mad north-north-west' and that he can distinguish his sane speech from that of lunacy, knowing the difference between a hawk and a handsaw (II. ii. 374-5). Polonius and Claudius also recognize method in Hamlet's madness which, to Claudius, indicates a degree of self-awareness on Hamlet's part (III. i. 165-7). Hamlet's double voice bears similarities to contemporary cases of mental illness like that of Richard Napier's patient who would use 'idle talk' and cry out on devils in his distraction but could talk 'wisely until the fit cometh on him'. Popular accounts of melancholy pointed out that patients were frequently able to scrutinize their own abnormal behaviour from outside, whereas true lunatics could not.[8] Hamlet follows this pattern, describing himself as analyst and patient when he apologizes to Laertes at the end of the play:

> What I have done
> That might your nature, honour, and exception
> Roughly awake, I here proclaim was madness.
> Was't Hamlet wrong'd Laertes? Never Hamlet.
> If Hamlet from himself be ta'en away,
> And when he's not himself does wrong Laertes,
> Then Hamlet does it not, Hamlet denies it.
> Who does it then? His madness. If't be so,
> Hamlet is of the faction that is wrong'd;
> His madness is poor Hamlet's enemy.
>
> (V. ii. 226-35)

Hamlet refers to his madness as a 'sore distraction' with which he is currently afflicted (V. ii. 225), so his self-analysis is not a retrospective one except in the narrowest sense. He speaks both inside and outside his malady, as he has done earlier, making use of syntactic modification to explain and control his mental state.

As the play shows, Hamlet does not always talk so wisely. In comparison to the measured blank verse of the lines above, much of his speech is in a style which makes little immediate sense to the characters around him. Although Hamlet depends on 'Words, words, words' (II. ii. 192) to stay sane, the disturbing encounter with the ghost has made him inescapably aware of their plurality and artifice. This forces Hamlet to fall into a speech which will expose *différance*. He tells Rosencrantz and Guildenstern that he cannot make 'a wholesome answer'; his wit is diseased (III. ii. 313). His 'distracted' speeches suggest that it is language as much as female sexuality, neglected love, or grief that has made him mad. His conversation with Ophelia about beauty, honesty and discourse (III. i. 103-15) links his emotional concerns and his awareness that speech is common to a multitude of meanings rather than honest to one. Hamlet demonstrates this blatantly in his use of puns. His 'antic disposition' (I. v. 180) uses a style which Irigaray would term 'feminine' since it is a direct contradiction of the authoritative power of language used to maintain patriarchy. His 'mad' speeches exploit a lack of unity in the subject and 'undo the unique meaning, the proper meaning of words'.[9]

Hamlet's distrust of language is dangerous since it threatens to invalidate the very means which he uses to avoid breakdown. It is like the patient realizing that his cure is a poison to drive him further into madness. Discussing Plato's use of the ambiguous word *pharmakon* to describe writing, Derrida points out that *pharmakon* means both 'poison' and 'remedy'.[10] Hamlet is in the position of seeing both sides of this paradox at once. He recognizes the need for language to construct sanity but cannot escape his awareness of its essential folly. What allows him to reconcile the two and avoid complete mental collapse is his use of theatre. It is not surprising that he welcomes the players so warmly. By virtue of their status as performers they are able to provide a register of speech which allows Hamlet to tell the truth of his father's murder while demonstrating the artificial nature of all utterances. The players are able to 'Suit the action to the word, the word to the action' (III. ii. 17-18) within a signifying system, a play whose social construction is obvious. J. L. Austin's theory of speech acts would discredit their performative utterances as 'parasitical' by pointing out that their fictional nature would abrogate the speaker's responsibility and deny them the required 'serious' intention.[11] But behind this bait of falsehood lurks a series of truths. Firstly, the 'parasitic' declarations present truths in that their false nature merely reflects the lies which dominate the court world and thus shows, as Hamlet wished, 'the very age and body of the time his form and pressure' (III. ii. 23-4). In addition, their self-conscious artifice exposes all utterances as repetitions of an already-written script, however truthful they may be. By demonstrating the dramatic truth of each particular fictional moment, the actors anticipate Derrida's response to Austin, showing that all speech acts are performative (dependent on the context in which they are produced and received) and that all are performances, even though they may be authentic.[12]

Theatre therefore provides Hamlet with the ideal metaphor to expose the rhetoric of power which operates in Elsinore. He questions Polonius about his role as an actor (III. ii. 97-105) and welcomes Rosencrantz and Guildenstern, using imagery of performance (II. ii. 366-71). By contrasting the hypocritical welcome he gives them with that he will give the players, he suggests the equally rhetorical nature of all such 'fashion and ceremony' (II. ii. 368),

whether it be genuine or not. His quaint revenge on Rosencrantz and Guildenstern is to create new roles for them in England in a play of his own devis-
ing (V. ii. 30-2).[13]

The combination of truth and illusion in theatre is what Foucault identifies
as a 'tamed' madness: 'theatre develops its truth, which is illusion. Which is,
in the strict sense, madness.' Since this madness carries its illusion to the point
of truth, it provides the ideal expression of Hamlet's dilemma. After the success of his own performances, he asks 'Would not this ... get me a fellowship
in a cry of players?' (III. ii. 269-72). The scene highlights important ideas
about Hamlet's role as a madman. He adopts his 'antic disposition' quite
openly, telling Horatio, 'I must be idle' (III. ii. 90). Whether Hamlet is clinic-
ally mad or mad in craft is finally irrelevant since there is no difference between illusion and truth once the play of language is exposed as a 'crafty madness' (III. i. 8). For this reason, *Hamlet* contradicts Foucault's view of
madness in Shakespeare's work as 'beyond appeal', where 'Nothing ever re-
stores it either to truth or to reason'. In the case of Hamlet, it occupies a me-
dian rather than an extreme place, displaying both the breakdown of reason
and the control of insanity in language. Hamlet's 'tamed' madness is not considered as a 'tragic reality' but only in 'the irony of its illusions'. It already
exhibits elements of self-reflection which provide a prototype for classical
madness:

> Tamed, madness preserves all the appearances of its reign. It now takes part in the
> measures of reason and in the labour of truth. It plays on the surface of things and
> in the glitter of daylight, over all the workings of appearances, over the ambiguity
> of reality and illusion, over all that indeterminate web, ever rewoven and broken,
> which both unites and separates truth and appearance.

The balancing act which Hamlet is able to maintain throughout the play is
dependent on his ability to use a verbal and theatrical metalanguage with
which to construct and contain the experience of insanity. This is a language
which Ophelia does not have. Her experience seems much closer to Foucault's definition of madness in Shakespeare's work. He cites her as one
example of insanity which 'leads only to laceration and thence to death'.[14] It
is not that Ophelia's grief for her lost love or her father's death is more intense
than Hamlet's. She suffers differently because of her gender. To examine this
further, I want to use Irigaray's thesis that in madness 'there are specific
linguistic disturbances according to sexual differences'. Irigaray argues that,

in cases of schizophrenia, gender appears to dictate a patient's access to a language with which to articulate trauma, that a woman in a state of madness does not have the same means for elaborating a delirium as a man. Since female patients cannot transpose their suffering into language, they suffer schizophrenia as corporeal pain: 'instead of language being the medium of expression of the delirium the latter remains in the body itself'.[15] This theory is echoed very closely in Burton's discussion of 'Women's Melancholy' (indeed, the book itself shows a marked contrast in the documentation of male and female experience, since 'Women's Melancholy' occupies only five out of a total of over a thousand pages of analysis). Burton remarks:

> Many of them cannot tell how to express themselves in words, or how it holds them, what ails them; you cannot understand them, or well tell what to make of their sayings; so far gone sometimes, so stupefied and distracted, they think themselves bewitched, they are in despair, *aptæ ad fletum, desperationem* [prone to weeping, despondency]; *dolores mammis et hypochondriis*, Mercatus therefore adds, now their breasts, now their hypochondries, belly and sides, then their heart and head aches; now heat, then wind, now this, now that offends, they are weary of all; and yet will not, cannot again tell how, where, or what offends them, though they be in great pain ...[16]

The play shows clearly that Ophelia does not have the speech and writing which Hamlet uses to cope with mental crisis. While Hamlet is 'as good as a chorus' (III. ii. 240), Ophelia has only a tenth of the number of lines he speaks. She does not appear able to discuss her distraction in a rational way and turns her suffering inwards on her body. The gentleman who reports her madness to Gertrude says that Ophelia 'hems, and beats her heart' (IV. v. 5) and implies that she communicates through physical gestures (IV. v. 11). He tells Gertrude, 'Her speech is nothing' (IV. v. 7). Such details appear to endorse the links between silence and hysteria proposed by Cixous, who writes:

> Silence: silence is the mark of hysteria. The great hysterics have lost speech ... their tongues are cut off and what talks instead isn't heard because it's the body that talks and man doesn't hear the body.[17]

Using this idea to read the play produces a depressing picture of Ophelia as 'Deprived of thought, sexuality, language'; and concludes that her role becomes 'the Story of O - the zero, the empty circle or mystery of feminine difference', as Showalter remarks.[18] Attempts such as Ranjini Philip's to read Ophelia's suicide in positive terms as 'an existential act of partial self-aware-

ness' in order to tell her story as 'something' seem pessimistic.[19] In the hope
of finding a more positive image, I want to turn to the work of one of Shakespeare's female contemporaries. Far from remaining silent, this woman produced a written account to explain her mental breakdown to physicians, fellow sufferers and, more importantly, to herself. A brief examination of Dionys
Fitzherbert's manuscript, written in 1608, provides the opportunity to see
Ophelia's ravings in a new light.[20]

Dionys's text, *An Anatomie for the Poore in Spirrit* contradicts those who
would link female hysteria and silence. Her aim is to differentiate her breakdown from other types of madness by analyzing it as a spiritual test, a trial by
God. In a preface, she openly challenges those who would label her case as
madness and outlines in detail the differences between melancholy, as defined
by contemporary medical theory, and her own symptoms. She points out that
'the like passages doth more then distinguish their case from all others in the
judgement of any well seeing eyes'.

Dionys frequently makes reference to reading, writing and speech, suggesting their importance as means of rationalizing her experience. She points
out that at the height of her fits and torments she was 'for the most part speech-
les if not altogether' and suggests the physical dangers caused by this loss:

> they thought yt almost impossible many tymes for me to live an hower, but that my
> hart must needs splitt and rent in peeces with the unutterable groanes and sighes
> that were continually powred forth, being neither able by teares nor speech to ex-
> presse the unspeakeable dolour and torment of my sowle.

When she first recovers speech, her voice is split between declarations of
atheism and expressions of religious faith, a confusion which she calls 'the
discourse of the mynd'.[21] She is later able to converse more lucidly and uses
reading and writing to recover and prove her sanity. She stresses the importance of allowing a patient access to literature and the means to write and tells
how upsetting it was to have her books removed so that she could no longer
continue her study of Scripture. When she was recuperating in Oxford, her
greatest affliction was occasioned by visiting the libraries:

> the multitude of books which I saw in which I had taken such singuler delight, now
> strooke me to the hart to thinke I could have noe comfort of them.

Her recovery is helped by the gift of a book, *The Comforter*, and by the
writing of a religious meditation. Her restoration to complete mental health is

seen in the account itself. *An Anatomie for the Poore in Spirrit* is the means by which Dionys is able to explain what has happened to her and it stands as testimony to her sanity. In describing her case, she often confuses the identities of patient and analyst, the afflicted Dionys of the past and the recovered and diagnostic Dionys who writes, but for the most part the text reads lucidly. The preface in which she challenges those who would label her as mad is logically organized and forcefully argued. She points out how strong opposition can sometimes allow patients to 'find out the truth even in themselves, as my example ... doth evidently shew'.

In *Hamlet* we cannot read Ophelia's *Anatomie* of her condition, nor does the text indicate that she ever has the opportunity to write one. Without the language with which to discuss her case, she remains largely incoherent. This is not due to a failure in language itself or to an essential silence on the part of women hysterics. Whatever the limitations of words in expressing female experience, Dionys's case proves that they remain a valuable tool for the transposition of internal distress. More important than an inadequacy of language is Ophelia's very limited access to any verbal communication with which to unpack her heart. Polonius's advice to Laertes, 'Give every man thy ear, but few thy voice' (I. iii. 68), is taken to an extreme with Ophelia who is forbidden to 'give words or talk with the Lord Hamlet' (I. iii. 134) or with anyone else except under supervision. She becomes a private document where her father and brother imprint their words and control the articulation of ideas by means of lock and key. In the sense that Ophelia's mind is forced to accommodate voices inserted from outside, she is a schizophrenic from the beginning of the play. These imposed voices conflict with a repository of emotional and critical perceptions which she is rarely able to express. Only occasionally does Shakespeare give hints about the contents of Ophelia's thought book, as in her response to Laertes's advice which implicitly mocks the double standard (I. iii. 46-51). When she tells Hamlet, 'I think nothing, my lord' (III. ii. 116), she refers not to a lack of thought but to the censure placed on the expression of her own emotions and opinions. This lady cannot 'say her mind freely' (II. ii. 323-4) at moments of crisis. In her interview with Hamlet in III. i., she speaks what she ought to say rather than what she feels. Having suffered a torrent of abuse, she describes herself as the viewer / analyst of his mental collapse rather than giving full voice to her own feelings (III. i. 152-63). Since Polonius silences her completely with the words, 'You

need not tell us what Lord Hamlet said, / We heard it all' (III. i. 181-2), she
has no opportunity to communicate her distress.

The death of Polonius confronts Ophelia with an unprecedented access to
language which is both liberating and frightening. It unlocks her tongue from
the repetition of patriarchal meanings and allows her to speak as author of herself, a situation for which she and the court are totally unprepared. Even
though Polonius's censure is removed, other characters try to silence or ignore her. Gertrude says, 'I will not speak with her' (IV. v. 1), and she and
Claudius constantly interrupt Ophelia. Laertes attempts to impose meaning
on her language, reducing her from an active speaker to an object of interpretation, a document in madness. She is first of all a text of filial love, whose
wits are bound to her beloved father in the grave (IV. v. 159-63). She then
becomes a petition for revenge (IV. v. 167), and finally, an aesthetically pleas-
ing translation (IV. v. 185-6). Unlike Dionys Fitzherbert, Ophelia is only able
to express the confused 'discourse of the mynd' which is then documented by
others with explanatory footnotes. The gentleman who reports her madness
to Gertrude points out that Ophelia's 'unshaped' speech

> doth move
> The hearers to collection. They aim at it,
> And botch the words up fit to their own thoughts,
> Which, as her winks and nods and gestures yield them,
> Indeed would make one think there might be thought,
> Though nothing sure, yet much unhappily.
>
> (IV. v. 8-13)

Even in this role as a 'document in madness', Ophelia finds a way of
speaking. The gentleman may say 'Her speech is nothing' (IV. v. 7), but
David Leverenz is wrong to conclude that 'even in her madness she has
no voice of her own'.[22] Ophelia's songs and quotations give her a very
definite register, one which demonstrates the 'citationality' of all speech.
Her lines are confused but they have 'matter' (IV. v. 172). As Bridget Gellert Lyons points out, 'While her language is more oblique, pictorial, and
symbolic, she expresses the discords that Hamlet registers more consciously and with greater control in his language and behaviour.'[23] Although Ophelia cannot analyze her trauma, her language of madness is
appropriate to the expression of such ideas.

By distributing flowers in IV. v., Ophelia draws attention to the breakdown
of unique meaning in Elsinore, revealing the ambiguous signification of Flora

and flowers as symbols of both innocence and sexual prostitution.[24] She parodies Elsinore's attempts to structure its environment verbally in her own definitions of the flowers and their meanings. These are undercut when she points out the ambiguity of rue: 'You must wear your rue with a difference' (IV. v. 180-1). The plant may signify repentance, but the word 'grace' means nothing if applied to Claudius. Ophelia's songs, which give clues to the causes of her distraction, are in the same mode as Hamlet's adaptation, *The Mouse-trap*, and his use of ballad (III. ii. 265-78); but, unlike Hamlet, she will not act as a chorus. She tells her listeners, 'pray you mark' (IV. v. 28 and 35), obliging them to make a variety of subjective interpretations. Claudius's attempt to impose a single masculine meaning by saying the song is a 'Conceit upon her father' (IV. v. 45) is rejected out of hand by Ophelia. She tells him, 'Pray let's have no words of this, but when they ask you what it means, say you this' (IV. v. 46-7), and then sings another ballad which, rather than explaining the song, illustrates the 'deferral' of meaning. One ballad can only be interpreted in terms of its difference from another, and all are blatant repetitions of the 'already written'. It is therefore impossible to 'make an end' (IV. v. 57) in terms of meaning. Ophelia's determination to finish her song reveals a preoccupation with the performative nature of speech. She has just as much cause as Hamlet to mistrust vows, and the last verse about oaths (IV. v. 58-66) deconstructs the seriousness of all such declarations by demonstrating the equally rhetorical nature of false and true vows.

While Ophelia's thoughts lack the self-control and clear articulation found in many of Hamlet's speeches, the scenes do show that she is struggling to convey important ideas. Because of the rigid prohibition on her speech earlier in the play, it is not surprising that she 'speaks things in doubt / That carry but half sense' (IV. v. 6-7). In this she is surely typical of her period. Dionys Fitzherbert's text gives inspiring evidence of a woman's success in challenging the conventional view of the silent hysteric; the case of Margaret Muschamp, some forty years later, gives a more accurate impression of the difficulties encountered by such women. Margaret fell into fits and heard 'voices' between the years 1645-7. Believing she was bewitched, she tried to communicate the names of her tormenters by writing, after she had come out of the extremity of her fit. The account shows the degree of corporeal pain suffered by the female schizophrenic:

After a while she would make her hand goe on her brest, as if she would write, with
her eyes fixt on her object; they layd paper on her brest, and put a pen with inke in
her hand, and she not moving her eyes, writ, Jo. Hu. Do. Swo. have beene the death
of one deare friend, consume another, and torment mee; whilst she was writing
these words, she was blowne up ready to burst, shrinking with her head, as if she
feared blowes; then would she be drawne, as in convulsion fits, till she got that
writing from them that had it, and either burne it in the fire, or chew it in her mouth,
till it could not be discerned ...[25]

Like Ophelia's lines, Margaret's accusations against John Hutton and Do-
rothy Swinnow are a spontaneous outpouring, an incompletely articulated
discourse of madness. The impulse to write is combined with an equally
strong negative response to the document she produces. Unlike Burton or
Hamlet whose transcriptions ease the mind, Margaret's experience of writing
provokes fear which is expressed in bodily terms as painful convulsions and
swellings. Far from helping her condition, the literal expression of her ideas
causes guilt and stress. The only way of relieving her physical torment is to
destroy the illegitimate product of her labours: to burn it or to eat it, thus re-
incorporating her words. Even if the paper was taken from her and hidden,
Margaret Muschamp would continue to suffer, until she had sought out the
document and destroyed it. When 'none could discerne one word she had
wrote, then immediately she would have ease'.[26]

The discussion of writing here has important implications outside the immediate context of the extract, since the account was written by Margaret's
mother, Mary Moore. Does Margaret's experience provide Mary with a meta-
narrative to discuss her own problems in producing the text in a period where
female chastity was equated with silence? To transgress and articulate, —let
alone write, was to be regarded as deviant, abnormal. To write a document on
madness was to become a document in madness to a certain extent. The experience of Ophelia, trying to find a voice in the play, can therefore be read
as a model for the difficulties facing Renaissance women writers; not only
those like Dionys Fitzherbert and Mary Moore who were documenting madness, but also those who were endeavouring to express their ideas in poetry,
prose and plays. Like Ophelia, they may 'speak things in doubt' but they do
not remain silent.

Finally, it is sobering to note that the experiences of these women find a
further reflection in the work of female scholars trying to write themselves
into the bibliographical history of the play. *Hamlet* has never been edited by

a woman.[27] The text is notoriously challenging since the contradictions between the 'Good Quarto', the 'Bad Quarto' and the Folio make *Hamlet* itself a 'document in madness'. At I. iii. 21, the creation of 'sanity' has been, to date, the privilege of Theobald and subsequent male editors, from the starting points of 'safty' in the 'Good Quarto', the third Quarto's 'safety', and the Folio's 'sanctity'. The opportunity to rationalize the different voices of this schizophrenic text has been limited to men, the Hamlets rather than the Ophelias of the academic world, thus reproducing the gender imbalance in the play.

Notes

1. Robert Burton, *The Anatomy of Melancholy*, ed. Holbrook Jackson, 3 vols (London: Everyman, 1968), I, 408.

2. Michael MacDonald, *Mystical Bedlam: Madness, Anxiety and Healing in Seventeenth-Century England* (Cambridge: Cambridge University Press, 1981), pp. 72-3.

3. Andrew Gurr investigates in detail the double metaphor of Hamlet's 'distracted globe' in *Hamlet and the Distracted Globe* (Edinburgh: Sussex University Press, 1978).

4. Michel Foucault, *Madness and Civilization: A History of Insanity in the Age of Reason*, tr. Richard Howard (London: Tavistock Publications, 1967), p. 19.

5. Cited in Jenkins's edition of *Hamlet*, p. 241.

6. Foucault, *Madness and Civilization*, p. 37.

7. Burton, *Anatomy*, I, 21.

8. MacDonald, *Mystical Bedlam*, pp. 146-7.

9. Luce Irigaray, 'Women's Exile' in Deborah Cameron, ed., *The Feminist Critique of Language* (London: Routledge, 1990), pp. 83-4.

10. Discussed by Barbara Johnson, 'Writing' in Frank Lentricchia and Thomas McLaughlin, eds, *Critical Terms for Literary Study* (Chicago and London: University of Chicago Press, 1990), p. 46.

11. *How To Do Things With Words* (Cambridge, Mass: Harvard University Press, 1962), pp. 21-2.

12. In *How To Do Things With Words*, Austin asserts a difference between utterances of a constative nature (answerable to a requirement of truth in their relation to the world) and those of a performative nature (dependent on the context in which they are produced and received). He further distinguishes between 'serious' and 'non-serious' performative utterances: for the utterance to be 'serious', its speaker must take responsibility for what

s/he says to guarantee the meaning of the performative in its context. In 'Signature, Event, Context' in *Margins of Philosophy*, tr. Alan Bass (Chicago: University of Chicago Press, 1982), Derrida expands Austin's idea that actually all constative utterances are context-dependent and therefore performative; he further demonstrates that all speech acts are social constructions with an indirect rather than a direct relationship to the actions or objects they describe. This ultimately dissolves the boundaries between 'serious' and 'non-serious' utterances, revealing all speech acts to be produced in a more or less 'staged' setting.

13. For discussion of the complex nature of theatre as a form of metalanguage in the play, see Phyllis Gorfain, 'Towards a Theory of Play and the Carnivalesque in *Hamlet*', *Hamlet Studies*, 13 (1991), 25-49, and Robert Weimann, 'Mimesis in *Hamlet*' in Patricia Parker and Geoffrey Hartman, eds, *Shakespeare and the Question of Theory* (New York and London: Methuen, 1985), pp. 275-91.

14. Foucault, *Madness and Civilization*, pp. 35, 31, 32, 36, 31.

15. Irigaray, 'Women's Exile' in Cameron, ed., *Feminist*, p. 94.

16. Burton, *Anatomy of Melancholy*, I, 416.

17. Cited in Elaine Showalter, *The Female Malady: Women, Madness and English Culture 1830-1930* (London: Virago, 1987), pp. 160-1.

18. Elaine Showalter, 'Representing Ophelia: women, madness and the responsibilities of feminist criticism' in Parker and Hartman, eds, *Shakespeare*, p. 79.

19. Ranjini Philip, 'The Shattered Glass: The Story of (O)phelia', *Hamlet Studies*, 13 (1991), 75.

20. I am grateful to Kate Hodgkin for drawing my attention to Dionys Fitzherbert's writings. *An Anatomie for the Poore in Spirrit* exists in two versions: an original manuscript in Dionys's own hand (e Museo 169) and a fair copy in another hand with additional prefaces and letters attached (Bodley 154). Both are in the Bodleian library. Quotations are from the fair copy. My discussion of the texts is indebted to Kate Hodgkin's unpublished paper, 'Religion and madness in the writing of Dionys Fitzherbert', given at the conference, *Voicing Women: Gender / Sexuality / Writing 1500-1700*, at the University of Liverpool, 15 April 1992.

21. This phrase is taken from a letter by Dionys to M.H.

22. David Leverenz, 'The Woman in *Hamlet*: An Interpersonal View', *Signs*, 4 (1978), 301.

23. Bridget Gellert Lyons, 'The Iconography of Ophelia', *English Literary History*, 44 (1977), 73

24. Lyons, 'Iconography', 63-4.

25. Mary Moore, *Wonderfull news from the North* (London, 1650; Wing M2581), p. 5. In assigning the text to Mary Moore, I follow Maureen Bell, George Parfitt and Simon

Shepherd, eds, *A Biographical Dictionary of English Women Writers 1580-1720* (New York: Harvester Wheatsheaf, 1990).

26. Moore, *Wonderfull news*, p. 5.

27. In the New Penguin Shakespeare (1980), Anne Barton wrote the introduction, but the text was edited by T. J. B. Spencer.

Histories and Appropriations

HAMLET WITHIN THE PRINCE

MARTIN WIGGINS

One of the ways in which we are accustomed to talk about fictional characters is in terms of depth, or conversely of shallowness: we prize 'deep'
characters and disvalue 'shallow' ones. It is a metaphor that has become
so familiar as a piece of our critical rhetoric that we often use it unconscious of all that it implies. A way of revealing those implications is to
look at some of the other uses to which we put the same metaphor. For
example, our description of people as deep or shallow seems to be informed by the same values, albeit transferred from an aesthetic discourse
to a moral one: we blame an author for creating a 'shallow' character, and
a human being for possessing one. Yet the development of what has been
called 'depth psychology' has shown us that in fact there are no 'shallow'
human beings: we all have hidden, unconscious areas of our minds that
reveal themselves only in conditions of distress, and under psychoanalysis. So if we accept that all human beings are 'deep', then our praise for
'deep' fictional characters is based on the assumption that characterization involves mimesis — that an author seeks to create characters that are
lifelike representations of human beings.

Probably the character who is most often praised for these qualities of
depth and naturalism is Hamlet. From the eighteenth century onwards, it has
been a critical commonplace to call him the most true-to-life of Shakespeare's
creations. One of the earliest critics to make this claim was William Guthrie
in his *Essay upon English Tragedy* (1747), in which he made a comparison
between Shakespeare's play and one of the most admired works of contemporary tragedy, Joseph Addison's *Cato* (1713). What he found was that the two
leading characters spoke in very different linguistic registers: 'Cato talks the
language of the porch and academy. Hamlet, on the other hand, speaks that of
the human heart ... His is the real language of mankind, of its highest to its
lowest order ... The words of Cato are not like those of Hamlet, the emanations of the soul '.[1] Guthrie argues for the authenticity of Hamlet, then, because Shakespeare's characterization draws on areas of the human personality

that are neglected in the drily ratiocinating character of Cato. On this basis, he attributes to Hamlet a soul.

Today the doctrine of the soul has been largely supplanted by the theory of the Freudian Unconscious, and critics from Freud himself onwards have been ready to see depths of this nature in Hamlet. The result is a very different reading of the character. When Guthrie speaks of Hamlet's dialogue as 'the emanations of the soul', he assumes that the soul projects emotions which translate directly into language and so communicate with the reader or audience. Freud's Unconscious is rather less talkative. It is a concept imbued with nineteenth-century feelings of embarrassment and shame: for Freud, the unconscious mind tries to conceal itself as assiduously as a Victorian maiden did her ankles. In search of the evasive Unconscious, then, psychoanalysts must by indirections find directions out; and the depths which they discover will be very different from surface appearances.

Freud's diagnosis of Hamlet, made in *The Interpretation of Dreams* (1900), was that he had an Oedipus complex.[2] The argument was developed in detail by the psychoanalyst Ernest Jones, whose findings were first published in 1910 and reached their final state of revision in his book *Hamlet and Oedipus* (1949). Briefly summarized, the interpretation is as follows. Hamlet's love for his father is in fact a mechanism of repression which conceals unconscious feelings of hatred and jealousy. These feelings derive from the infant Hamlet's perception of his father as a rival for the love and attention of his mother – a desire which Freud associates with infantile sexuality. This means that the death of Hamlet Senior satisfies these unconscious desires by leaving his wife available to devote all her attention to her son: how could Hamlet wish the death undone, the issue of it being so fair? No wonder, then, that he resents Claudius, who has popped in between them; it is, says Jones, 'the jealous detestation of one evil-doer towards his successful fellow'. Claudius has committed the murder and incest that was only a dark phantasy for Hamlet, and so 'incorporates the deepest and most buried part of [Hamlet's] personality'; and this means that Hamlet cannot kill Claudius without also killing the image of himself.[3]

Clearly this approach depends on a naive development of the long-standing critical tradition of the lifelike Hamlet: the psychoanalysts assume that the character has as great an inner authenticity as that which is apparent in performance. The basis for this belief is another critical tradition, which both Freud and Jones appeal to, that Hamlet is Shakespeare's self-portrait. A. C.

Bradley, for example, concludes his lecture 'Shakespeare the Man' (1904) by observing, 'Hamlet is the most fascinating character, and the most inexhaustible, in all imaginative literature. What else should he be, if the world's greatest poet, who was able to give almost the reality of nature to creations totally unlike himself, put his own soul straight into this creation, and when he wrote Hamlet's speeches wrote down his own heart?'[4] So if Hamlet has an unconscious mind, it is incidental to the fact that Hamlet is Shakespeare; and analysis of Hamlet leads the psychiatrists directly back to the traumas of his creator.

Since Freud and Jones assume a peculiarly intense mimesis in Shakespeare's creation of Hamlet, their biographical arguments are fundamental to their case; and they are also its weakest part. Shakespeare did not write *Hamlet* as a controlled work of art, they assume, but as an outpouring of mental disturbance. Instead of a play, they see a psychiatric document: there is, says Jones, an 'inner connection between mental suffering (nowadays called "neurotic illness") and the need of relief through poetic creation'.[5] Freud believes that in Shakespeare this distress was occasioned by the death of his father in September, 1601, in which case the play could scarcely have been on the boards before 1602, rather later than most scholars now believe. Jones, however, holds that Shakespeare was upset by the double betrayal of the Dark Lady and the Young Man of the Sonnets. This is, of course, no more than to defend the autobiographical assumption about *Hamlet* by making it again about the Sonnets; and Jones duly spends much time on the theories advanced by antiquarians and *belle-lettristes* about the identity of the Dark Lady, theories which, he admits himself, are ultimately unprovable. These are indeed the *mythical* sorrows of Shakespeare.

The second premise on which Jones and Freud build their diagnosis is the notion that there is a compellingly unclear quality in Hamlet's behaviour: one of the commonest words in the vocabulary of these psychoanalyzing critics is 'mystery'. The mystery is, of course, the reason for Hamlet's hesitancy in taking the revenge enjoined on him by the Ghost: Jones calls it 'the Sphinx of modern literature', and prefaces his exposition with a survey showing how conventional methods of literary criticism have been unable to find a solution.[6]

Perhaps the most influential of these conventional critics whose arguments Jones rejects is Bradley. Hamlet's hesitancy is the problem around which Bradley constructs his account of the play in *Shakespearean Tragedy* (1904), and with which he begins. He imagines someone's reaction on hearing the plot of *Hamlet* for the first time. This hypothetical person begins by clicking his tongue with typical pre-First World War distaste for the violence and intrigue of much English Renaissance drama: 'What a sensational story!' he exclaims. (You must remember that the word 'sensational' had pejorative connotations at this time).[7] 'Why, here are some eight violent deaths, not to speak of adultery, a ghost, a mad woman, and a fight in a grave! If I did not know that the play was Shakespeare's, I should have thought it must have been one of those early tragedies of blood and horror from which he is said to have redeemed the stage.' And then he stops himself and asks that key question which has become such a chestnut in *Hamlet* criticism: 'But why in the world did not Hamlet obey the Ghost at once, and so save seven of those eight lives?'[8]

There are two points to note about Bradley's strategy here. First, there is the way he asks this question in the voice of Everyman. By doing so, he insinuates the problem upon us as an issue of common sense, rather than one that occurs only to Oxford Professors of Poetry. Secondly, Everyman asks this question not after seeing the play but after hearing a summary of its plot, a summary which, Bradley takes care to specify, has left out all information about the character of Hamlet himself. This allows Bradley to do two things: he can go on, as he does, to advance the character of Hamlet as the play's chief merit, the one thing that saves it from the charge of sensationalism; and, more insidiously, he can separate character from plot as a discrete object of study. In other words, he attributes to Hamlet an essence or identity that exists and can be analyzed independently of the character's dramatic context, just as we take real people to have the quality which some recent cultural historians have termed 'subjectivity' – to have, that is, integrated selves which function continuously in many different situations. So Bradley, like the psychoanalyzing critics after him, has fallen prey to the tradition that mistakes Hamlet for a real human being.

Like them, too, he believes that Hamlet's hesitancy is the product of an unconscious psychological inhibition from action, which he terms 'melancholic paralysis'.[9] He arrives at this quasi-medical diagnosis by drawing a distinction between the Hamlet we see in the play and a pre-existent, 'original' character which has been perverted by circumstances: Hamlet in good and ill health, so to speak. To the earlier Hamlet he attributes a 'moral sensibility' akin to the intensity of imaginative power which Burckhardt saw in Renaissance Man: for Bradley's Hamlet, a moral judgement, whether positive or negative, is a powerful intellectual and emotional experience. The danger of such a sensibility is that 'Any great shock that life might inflict on it would be felt with extreme intensity'.[10] That shock, coming at a moment when Hamlet is 'weakened by sorrow' for his father's death, is the discovery of his mother's immoral, incestuous sexuality which makes her remarry 'a man utterly contemptible and loathsome in his eyes'.[11] The object poisons sight: it interferes with Hamlet's perception of the world, which seems dominated by 'things rank and gross in nature' (I. ii. 136). The result is the mental aberration which the clinical psychology of Shakespeare's time called melancholy, and which was not significantly different in its immediate effects from the traits denoted in our own, post-humorous usage of the word (though Bradley rightly stresses that in 1600 it was seen as a medical condition). The result is a tendency to question, to pick over the idea of action rather than taking it — 'otiose thinking hardly deserving the name of thought, an unconscious weaving of pretexts for inaction, aimless tossings on a sick bed, symptoms of melancholy which only increased it by deepening self-contempt'.[12] And thus it follows that the man was hesitant: Bradley's Hamlet falls from a 'moral sensibility' into a disgust, thence to a melancholy, and by this declension into the paralysis seen in the main action.

This reading turns the entire play into a game of hunt-the-pretext: if the central character is psychologically incapable of fulfilling the Ghost's instructions, then the story is about his search for reasons not to get on with the job — for delay, read procrastination. So in Bradley's account, like that of the psychoanalyzing critics, the significant action of *Hamlet* takes place within the Prince.

This approach had its advantages for Bradley's time. If the essence of *Hamlet* is a conflict inside the mind of its hero, then Bradley and his audience can pass over as incidental those external aspects of the play which his version of Everyman found so vulgarly sensational: it is an interpretation which suits Victorian ideas of good taste. The problem is that it also locates the action beyond the limits of what can be represented on stage. Hamlet's behaviour is treated as a symptom generated by a mental condition that is at best only hinted at, and, in the case of the psychoanalytical reading, wholly unarticulated. In the theatre, it is hard to communicate something that is unarticulated.

This brings me back to the sample of our critical vocabulary with which I began: the depth or shallowness of characters. Fictional characters must by nature be shallow in the sense that their every facet, whether stated or implied, overt or latent, must at some point in the text be visible from the surface that is presented to the audience. This is not to say that a playwright cannot create a character who is, in A. D. Nuttall's phrase, 'described in such a way that we always feel there is more to be said'. Such characters, says Nuttall, have the air of authenticity because they reproduce our own experience of real people, about whom we always know less than everything.[13] But we should not suppose that the unseen parts of these characters are in themselves definable or significant, as they might be if we were trying to explain a real person's behaviour. For the purposes of critical interpretation, we must work with what we are given: parts of a character that are not visible, or not inferrable, are not there. So it is mistaken and misleading to talk of the depth of a character like Hamlet, when in fact we mean his complexity.

One reason why Bradley's account of Hamlet's complexity carried such authority for so long is that it secures the reader's consent through a subtle form of duress. Built into his account is an implicit threat: if we do not accept his views, then our alternative is to regard *Hamlet* as a bad play – bad not just by the standards of Victorian high culture but also on the grounds of sheer incomprehensibility. This is the import of his starting with the suggestion that the problem of Hamlet's procrastination is simple common sense. It is a standard lecturer's power-strategy: the audience's intelligent interest enables it to form a question, and the lecturer's specialist skills provide the answer. The occasion of Bradley's lecture thus becomes a kind of Messianic event in the critical history of the play which saves it from the charge of obscurity. Of course, such a strategy merely confirms the judgement which it seeks to challenge. The psychoanalytical approach involves an even more arcane methodology as the key to understanding the play's action: in his essay 'Psychopathic Characters on the Stage' (1905–6), Freud says, 'the conflict in *Hamlet* is so effectively concealed that it was left to me to unearth it'.[14] Faced with claims such as these, one may well wonder why *Hamlet* was so popular with a seventeenth-century audience which had never heard of psychoanalysis.

This is not to say that modern psychology is entirely irrelevant to our understanding of seventeenth-century stage characters. J. I. M. Stewart has defended his Freudian interpretation of Leontes in *The Winter's Tale* by suggesting 'that the dramatist in composition has access among other depths to that which such a psychology as Freud's explores; and ... that the audience in some obscure way are brought to share his awareness, and so are not disconcerted by matters of which a conventional psychology and an unkindled reader will make little'.[15] In other words, a sensitive playwright could represent aspects of human behaviour which were not then discursively understood, but which are now recognized by modern psychology. Even so, the applications of that discipline to literary understanding are very limited. For example, Shakespeare evidently recognized that a mother's sexuality, and in particular a widow's remarriage, can be irrationally resented by her son; and we may infer that his audience did too, since the trait reappears in a number of early Jacobean plays like Middleton's *The Phoenix* (1603-4) and Robert Armin's *The Two Maids of Mortlake* (1608). If these seventeenth-century dramatists could see this without having read Freud, then so could we today. A knowledge of the Oedipus complex might help to supply our deficiencies in human sensitivity, but it should not lead us to imagine truths about the characters that are undiscernible by common sense. In short, if there are mysterious depths to be sounded in Hamlet, the text itself must refer us to them.

In fact, *Hamlet* is a play that is much concerned with hidden aspects of human character – hidden, that is, from the other persons of the play. Hamlet directs the audience to his own interior in his first scene when, after seventy lines of sulky taciturnity, he takes issue with his mother for using the word 'seems':

> Seems, madam? Nay, it is. I know not 'seems'.
> 'Tis not alone my inky cloak, good mother,
> Nor customary suits of solemn black,
> Nor windy suspiration of forc'd breath,
> No, nor the fruitful river in the eye,
> Nor the dejected haviour of the visage,
> Together with all forms, moods, shapes of grief,
> That can denote me truly. These indeed seem,
> For they are actions that a man might play;
> But I have that within which passes show,
> These but the trappings and the suits of woe.

(I. ii. 76-86)

For about five minutes, we have watched this character, distinctive in his black clothes even if we do not guess his identity, wrapped up in himself; and then, at length, he draws attention to his interior, an interior that 'passes show'. It might seem that there is, after all, some textual warrant for the exploration of Hamlet's undramatizable inner self.

In suggesting this, however, I am not only misreading the passage, but also reading against the text. When Hamlet says that his feelings within 'pass show', he is not saying that they are inexpressible. Clearly they are all too expressible, for his melancholy moping is causing the new regime some political embarrassment. Rather, Hamlet is asserting the congruence of his outward forms of grief with his inward feelings, in contrast with the mourning habits which the rest of the court has so easily exchanged for wedding garments: he has something within that surpasses such empty show. Implicitly, he is making his first criticism of his mother's speedy remarriage; but for our purposes the overt moral orientation of his statement is more important. Like many of Shakespeare's young idealists, Hamlet attacks hypocrisy: to show an unfelt sorrow, to smile and smile and be a villain, to have that within which is not expressed in the outward man, is morally wrong.

It is true that we don't see Hamlet in the best of lights at this point: his refusal to compromise his integrity, to divide the seamless wholeness of his being into an inside and an outside, results in a kind of adolescent social awkwardness. But though in the course of the action he grows out of that awkwardness, and of the over-scrupulous concern for his personal honesty that lies behind it, his fundamental criticism of the court of Elsinore settles in the texture of his language, and that of his friends. Throughout the play, unseen things, insides, are associated with repellent images of putrefaction: 'rank corruption' (III. iv. 150) inside an ulcer that has skinned over, or an abscess that bursts inside the body, 'and shows no cause without / Why the man dies' (IV. iv. 28-9). In Marcellus's most famous line, the kingdom is like a room with a dead rat slowly decomposing behind the hangings: the smell of decay is there, but the nose cannot quite trace it back to source, so it is only an unspecific 'something' that is rotten in the state of Denmark.

Hamlet arranges the same olfactory experience for Claudius and his courtiers when he hides the body of Polonius: 'if indeed you find him not within this month, you shall nose him as you go up the stairs into the lobby' (IV. iii. 35-7). In saying this, of course, he pre-empts such an experience: he imagines the court troubled by the stench of a rotting corpse, but telling them what it is and where it is ensures that they will never have to sniff it out for themselves. That is often the case with the nasty secrets of the play. You either know them or you don't. Hamlet learns that Claudius is a murderer not by detective work, but because the victim's ghost returns from the grave to tell him so. Certainly he proceeds to test out the Ghost's word — and recent commentators have shown that this was a real issue for an audience in 1600 — but all he discovers is that it was what it seemed to be, his murdered father's spirit. The play's schema proves to be one of revelation, not detection: it is a play in which human beings are told secrets rather than finding them out for themselves.

Here is where we return to the question of the textual basis for the internalizing critics' account of Hamlet. For there is a character in the play who believes, like them, that Hamlet's behaviour may be attributed to some unexpected interior motivation, which investigation may reveal:

> I will find
> Where truth is hid, though it were hid indeed
> Within the centre.

> (II. ii. 157-9)

In short, the critics who believe in some unseen truth about Hamlet hidden deep in the centre of his being, are imitating Polonius. It scarcely needs saying that Polonius is not the best of role-models, an over-eager detective who makes an easy victim of revelation: his working hypothesis is that Hamlet is mad, and that is something that Hamlet has shown him; so even as he thinks he is sniffing out the secret springs of the Prince's behaviour, he is really being misled into delusion.

Like Polonius, Bradley and his psychoanalytic successors are handicapped by a false premise in their investigations of Hamlet's behaviour; for uninformed common sense would find the character's delay far less problematic than Bradley would like us to believe. There is one point in the play, and only one, when we see Hamlet actively decide to postpone the King's death: the scene where he finds Claudius praying, and passes up the chance to stab him in the back. He gives full reasons for this decision. Claudius's victim died without the opportunity to make his peace with God, so to kill the murderer at prayer, and thus ensure that he got to heaven first, would not truly be revenge. Since Claudius has acquired his brother's throne by the murder, he admits himself that 'the wicked prize itself / Buys out the law' (III. iii. 59-60): he is a man beyond the reach of earthly justice. In acting against such a man, it is apt that Hamlet should send him to the punishment he has escaped on Earth: he should send him to hell. And so he puts off the killing.

A common-sense reading of the play would take Hamlet at his word here, for the text offers us no reason to doubt him; but doubt him is exactly what we must do at this point if we are to believe in an irresolute, procrastinating

Hamlet whose behaviour requires arcane psychological explanation. The common-sense reading cuts no ice with the psychoanalyzing critics: like the anti-Stratfordian authorship theorists whose cases rest on hypothetical conspiracies that produced the surviving evidence that Shakespeare wrote Shakespeare, they are determined to mistrust appearances. For them, the very reasonableness and adequacy of Hamlet's explanation for his delay in the prayer scene gives cause to doubt it: 'no pretext would be of any use if it were not plausible', writes Ernest Jones.[16] Against persons so persuaded, reason can never prevail.

The tradition of disbelieving Hamlet at this point, which lies at the root of the internalizing urge in critical readings of the character, dates from the middle of the eighteenth century. The sceptical critics hold that Hamlet's reasoning is designed, unconsciously or otherwise, to excuse to himself his own irresolution. The idea was first advanced in print by William Dodd, in a note to his collection of *The Beauties of Shakespeare* (1752): presented with a prime opportunity to take vengeance, says Dodd, 'he shuffles it off with a paltry excuse and is afraid to do what he so ardently longs for'.[17] Hamlet puts off the moment of action, backs away from his revenge, not for the reasons he gives but because he has no stomach for the task. It would be truer to say that the sceptical critics have no stomach for a Hamlet who would cold-bloodedly engineer a person's damnation.

Broadly speaking, the writers of the 1750s and 1760s were well-disposed towards Hamlet: it is common to find them praising him for his filial piety and obedience. But his resolution to send Claudius to hell was something they could not forgive. '*Hamlet*'s speech upon seeing the King at Prayers has always given me great Offence', wrote George Stubbes in his essay, *Some Remarks on the Tragedy of Hamlet* (1736); 'There is something so very Bloody in it, so inhuman, so unworthy of a Hero that I wish our Poet had omitted it.'[18] In his book *The Dramatic Censor* (1770), Francis Gentleman said that Hamlet in this speech 'forms a design and utters sentiments more suitable to an assassin of the basest kind than a virtuous prince and a feeling man'.[19] Samuel Johnson's reaction was the strongest of all: his note to the passage in his edition of 1765 reads, 'This speech, in which Hamlet, represented as a virtuous character, is not content with taking blood for blood, but contrives damnation for the man that he would punish, is too horrible to be read or to be uttered.'[20] And indeed, the speech was not uttered in many eighteenth-century productions of the play.[21] This was an act of moral censorship on the part of Johnson and the actors: unable to make Shakespeare leave the passage unwritten, as Stubbes had wished, they sought that it might at least remain unread, much as modern copyright libraries collect pornography but restrict access to it. Like all censorship, this was an unsatisfactory compromise.

After all this talk of eighteenth-century reactions, let us take a sample of the forbidden fruit itself:

> Then trip him, that his heels may kick at heaven
> And that his soul may be as damn'd and black
> As hell, whereto it goes.

(III. iii. 93-5)

The underlying image here is of a man keeling over backwards on the balls of his heels, so that trying to keep his footing only propels him to the ground – or lower. What is terrible is the vision of kicking heels and the heaven beyond them, a vision Hamlet seems to imagine through the eyes of the inverted Claudius as he falls. It is terrible because of the gloating tones in which it is expressed: envisaging what his victim will see breeds no fellow-feeling in Hamlet, only sadism.

If what is horrible about these lines is their sincerity, we can begin to understand why some eighteenth-century commentators should have wished to disbelieve them. But the matter is more complex than this. Here is the case for a self-deceiving Hamlet, as it was put to Boswell over dinner in 1763 by the actor Thomas Sheridan, the father of the dramatist: 'this, if really from the heart, would make Hamlet the most black, revengeful man. But it coincides better with his character to suppose him here endeavouring to make an excuse to himself for his delay.'[22] What is notable is that, like Johnson, Sheridan reads the speech with an idea of Hamlet's character already in mind, rather than taking it as a piece of evidence that will go towards understanding that character. Both writers share a preconception that Hamlet is (as Sheridan puts it) 'a young man of a good heart and fine feelings', and this preconception determines the different ways in which they respond to his behaviour in the scene in question. To contrive a man's damnation would no doubt have shocked Johnson whoever proposed it; but what made the speech so peculiarly obscene was that Shakespeare put it in the mouth of his hero, an ostensibly good man. Sheridan's suggestion, which was amplified at length and in print by William Richardson twenty years later, served to mitigate the horror of the passage by subverting its express meaning. What had seemed a speech 'more reprehensible ... than any part of Shakespeare's works' was transformed into 'a most exquisite picture of amiable self-deceit'.[23] A *canard* was born.

It is easy today to patronize these eighteenth-century critics for their faulty logic, or to blame them for their wrong-headed ingenuity; but we do them an injustice if we take their mistakes out of the context of the drama and scholarship of the time. Johnson's belief that we are to take Hamlet as a wholly admirable and virtuous character reflects the same assumptions that made him say that 'every reader rejoices' at the fall of Macbeth.[24] Clear-cut heroes and villains were what the Augustans' prescriptive and moralistic 'Rules of Art' required, and got in the sentimental melodramas that contemporary dramatists produced for the stage. Hamlet is a hero, heroes are morally uncomplicated, therefore the prayer scene is a problem – so the unarticulated reasoning goes. To solve that problem by effectively changing the story may seem rather drastic, but it is little worse that what editors like Pope did to the actual words of the text when they were not to contemporary tastes; even Johnson, who did so much for editorial rigour, made Hamlet '*groan* and sweat under a weary life' (III. i. 77, his reading), because *grunt*, though 'undoubtedly the true reading', could 'scarcely be borne by modern ears'.[25] From this it is not far to changing meanings that offended contemporary sensibilities; and with Shakespeare's words left intact, it was the less obvious to subsequent ages that the resultant interpretation of the prayer scene was groundless and erroneous.

What I have argued, then, is that writers who internalize the action of *Hamlet* are not in fact discussing Shakespeare's play at all, but a palimpsest created through repression in the middle of the eighteenth century, a palimpsest that was subsequently digested and transmitted into the folklore of the play by A. C. Bradley. But in this I am over-simplifying. Error is rarely absolute: more often than not, it originates in the distortion of a perception that is fundamentally true. The other foundation of the internalizing approach (that is, the tradition of the lifelike Hamlet) does have a basis in Shakespeare: *Hamlet*, with its many soliloquies, is a play much concerned with the mental life and development of its hero.

I have already alluded to one such development by saying that during the action Hamlet grows out of his concern to express his inner feelings. This is not a development that comes of a straightforward maturing process, however; it happens to Hamlet perforce when he meets the Ghost. This is because what the Ghost commands, the killing of Claudius, is a criminal act. Whatever its moral status in view of the facts of the case, the deed's legal status is clear: it is High Treason. What this means is that Hamlet can no longer continue in the youthful egotism which imposes his inner thoughts and feelings upon others, unmediated by the social graces; when those inner thoughts are of regicide, such candour could cost him his head. Like all criminals, intending or actual, Hamlet must maintain an exterior persona that is wholly discontinuous with his inner self.

This means that the Ghost's command entails a double danger to Hamlet. On the one hand, if his intentions are found out, he will be executed as a traitor: in the Treason laws that Shakespeare's contemporaries knew, even to imagine the King's death would lead to the block. But the alternative is that, to avenge a king's murder, Hamlet must make himself like the murderer: he must create in himself one of those unseen interior spaces which, in his discourse, always contains corruption. In his case it will contain criminal intent; and the danger is that his nature will be subdued to what it works in. It is this, the less obvious of the two risks, that the Ghost warns him against with paternal solicitude: 'howsomever thou pursuest this act, / Taint not thy mind' (I. v. 84-5). But by the middle of the play, Hamlet's mind is tainted indeed.

William Richardson believed that Hamlet's sentiments in the prayer scene were congruent with his behaviour nowhere else in the play: 'There is nothing in the whole character of Hamlet that justifies such savage enormity.'[26] He had clearly overlooked the speech with which Hamlet was last seen leaving the stage:

> 'Tis now the very witching time of night,
> When churchyards yawn and hell itself breathes out
> Contagion to this world. Now could I drink hot blood,
> And do such bitter business as the day
> Would quake to look on.

(III. ii. 379-83)

This sorts well with the cruelty with which he imagines Claudius tumbling to perdition. If the latter is insincere, then so too must this be: not an expression of genuine feeling, but an effusion designed to disguise it. What follows, as Hamlet anxiously restrains himself from considering matricide, would make a lame ending to such a speech. Murderous feelings that are willed are also targeted. If Hamlet is trying to put himself into a passion (or persuade himself that he is in one), it is for a particular purpose, his uncle's murder: his mother is therefore in no danger, and so there is no need for the latter half of the speech. Not that there is any need for the first half either: he is going to see the Queen, so the King's death is not to hand. The speech can only make sense, then, if it expresses a real murderous passion: Claudius's reaction to *The Mousetrap* has just established for Hamlet that he is indeed guilty, and so a deserving object of vengeance; the first half of the speech indicates Hamlet's emergent psychological readiness to mete out that vengeance. But he must ensure that this lethal frenzy does not o'erflow the measure and, contrary to the Ghost's command, induce his mother's destruction.

That frenzy does not, in the prayer scene, sweep Hamlet to his revenge because for him (in contrast with Macbeth), part of the satisfaction of killing Claudius lies in anticipation of the deed. In saying, 'Now could I drink hot blood', he not only expresses a desire to do so, but also finds a sensuous pleasure in imagining it — hence the specification that it be *hot* blood. And so, again, he runs through the stabbing of Claudius before doing it:

> Now might I do it pat, now a is a-praying.
> And now I'll do it.
>   And so a goes to heaven;
> And so am I reveng'd.

>   (III. iii. 73-5)

He moves swiftly enough through the three 'now' clauses to a decision, but he cannot resist pausing to savour the result. In that dress rehearsal comes the realization that such a revenge would be imperfect. The two last clauses express logical consequentiality ('And so ... And so ...'), but the logic doesn't follow: if Claudius goes to heaven, then Hamlet will not be revenged.

Revenge in *Hamlet* entails a balancing of deed for deed. When Hamlet learns that the purpose of his trip to England is his immediate execution, 'no leisure bated' (V. ii. 23), he arranges the same nasty surprise for his escorts — with, be it noted, 'Not shriving-time allow'd' (V. ii. 47). So it is, too, that he not only stabs Claudius with Laertes's anointed rapier but also commends the ingredients of his poisoned chalice to his own lips – he is, after all, to blame for both. It is the same congruity of crime and talion punishment that Hamlet reasons out in the prayer scene. The speech illustrates the savagery of the intellect, determined to make action and reaction equal and opposite irrespective of humane considerations: revenge becomes an exercise in pure logic. No wonder Samuel Johnson, so thoroughly a product of the Age of Reason, found it horrible.

So far I have argued that Hamlet is reasoning, not rationalizing, in the prayer scene, and therefore that he means what he says. But we should not allow this conclusion to obscure the irrational elements in his discourse: on the one hand, he has a university-trained mind, but on the other he is in an extreme situation and an admitted state of passion. In this case, though, reason and unreason both offer the same conclusion, that he should await the chance to send the King to hell.

It is well-attested that victims of violent crimes (such as rape) can suffer from the irrational conviction that they are somehow to blame. There may be a hint of this phenomenon when Hamlet realizes the full implications of killing Claudius at prayer:

> A villain kills my father, and for that
> I, his sole son, do this same villain send
> To heaven.
> Why, this is hire and salary, not revenge.

(III. iii. 76-9)

It is not simply that the punishment does not exactly fit the crime: to consign the murderer to everlasting bliss is not a punishment at all. Paying Claudius his hire and salary will turn him into a hired assassin; and by entering such a relationship, Hamlet will himself take on moral responsibility for the murder.

What makes this plausible is Hamlet's aspiration to the crown that his father's death released: he later says that Claudius 'Popp'd in between th' election and my hopes' (V. ii. 65). What is more, when Claudius dies in turn, Hamlet has assurance that he will wear that crown: in the second scene of the play, the King named him as his successor, 'the most immediate to our throne' (I. ii. 109). This means that in the act of paying off the killer, Hamlet will effectively make himself the beneficiary of the murder. There could be no stronger inhibition to a loving son such as he.

It is delicate and subtle touches like this that humanize Hamlet, without making him any the more sympathetic, as he follows through the appalling logic of the situation. His acquiescence to his conclusion is not without an understandable hint of disappointment, too. He compares the postponement to a medicine that will only delay death, and so extend the pain of a mortal illness: 'This physic but prolongs thy sickly days' (III. iii. 96). Temporarily balked of his revenge, he is making the best of it: his anticipation may no longer have the thrill of immediacy, but he can still relish the thought of the condemned man's 'sickly days' waiting for his nephew to strike.

The experience that is dramatized at this point in the play, then, is that of the criminal mind in a state of premeditation. I have argued elsewhere that premeditation had a particular horror and significance for sixteenth-century thinkers, in that it betokened a settled evil intent.[27] The long-established philosophies of Man in the period, and their criminological derivatives, accepted the doctrine of free will to virtuous action, but denied the possibility that a man could knowingly intend evil; crime was understood as the result of a more powerful force, whether physiological, psychological, or metaphysical, controlling the will of the criminal. These concepts were threatened by the new humanist philosophy that developed in fifteenth-century Italy and was influential in England. In this system, human action was attributed to the autonomous prompting of the will; in other words, it created what is now called human subjectivity. But because it admitted no moral limitation on the will, merely a difference in moral effect, its implications endangered the more established systems of thought. Human minds protected themselves from philosophical anarchy by creating a taboo against evil intent, which early Tudor legislators enshrined in the law of homicide by taking premeditation as the factor distinguishing murder from manslaughter. The concept of crime fulfilled its usual function as the dustbin into which people dump those parts of human behaviour that they do not want to understand.

Early Jacobean drama broke through this taboo, this wilful ignorance about the autonomous evil will, in its treatment of villains: there is an interest in the causes of criminal action, and in the mental experience of premeditated criminal intent. In Shakespeare, the growth of this interest runs from *Julius Caesar* (1599) to *Macbeth* (1606), and it is still evident later in *Cymbeline* (1609) and *The Winter's Tale* (1610). In *Julius Caesar*, Brutus has a horrified sense of the mental phantasmagoria that the criminal undergoes 'Between the acting of a dreadful thing / And the first motion';[28] and in *Macbeth*, Shakespeare achieved his most subtle and sophisticated portrait of this area of human experience. Clearly the prayer scene in *Hamlet* reflects the same interest; only Hamlet, with less reason than Macbeth for moral qualms about his crime, displays a far more savage sensibility in his anticipation. In this sense, there is indeed a part of the action that takes place within the Prince.

The ultimate effect of these dramatic representations of the criminal mind was to contribute to the acceptance and understanding of human subjectivity that had developed by the middle of the seventeenth century. This is relevant to the subsequent critical fortunes of the character of Hamlet, in that the process involved creating an intense illusion of subjectivity in certain characters. Since the outcome of that process determined the concept of humanity that was current in subsequent ages, the literary critics of those ages naturally looked back on the characters involved as peculiarly lifelike figures; and Hamlet, whose development takes him through so many phases, was exalted as the most lifelike of all. The myth of the deep-brained Prince was not far behind.

Notes

1. Brian Vickers, ed., *Shakespeare: The Critical Heritage*, 6 vols (London: Routledge and Kegan Paul, 1974-81), III, 201-2. The comparison between these two plays became a cliché of eighteenth-century Shakespeare criticism.

2. Sigmund Freud, *The Interpretation of Dreams*, ed. Angela Richards (Harmondsworth: Penguin, 1976), pp. 366-8.

3. Ernest Jones, *Hamlet and Oedipus* (London: Victor Gollancz, 1949), p. 88.

4. A. C. Bradley, *Oxford Lectures on Poetry* (London: Macmillan, 1909), p. 357.

5. Jones, *Hamlet and Oedipus*, p. 103.

6. Jones, *Hamlet and Oedipus*, p. 22.

7. *OED* 3a, examples.

8. A. C. Bradley, *Shakespearean Tragedy*, 2nd edn (London: Macmillan, 1905), p. 89.

9. Bradley, *Tragedy*, p. 135.

10. Bradley, *Tragedy*, p. 113.

11. Bradley, *Tragedy*, p. 118.

12. Bradley, *Tragedy*, p. 123.

13. A. D. Nuttall, 'The Argument about Shakespeare's Characters' in C. B. Cox and D. J. Palmer, eds, *Shakespeare's Wide and Universal Stage* (Manchester: Manchester University Press, 1984), p. 28.

14. Sigmund Freud, *Art and Literature*, ed. Albert Dickson (Harmondsworth: Penguin, 1985), p. 126.

15. J. I. M. Stewart, *Character and Motive in Shakespeare* (London: Longmans, 1949), pp. 36-7.

16. Jones, *Hamlet and Oedipus*, p. 54.

17. Vickers, ed., *Heritage*, III, 474.

18. Vickers, ed., *Heritage*, III, 59.

19. Vickers, ed., *Heritage*, V, 379.

20. H. R. Woudhuysen, ed., *Samuel Johnson on Shakespeare* (Harmondsworth: Penguin, 1989), p. 242.

21. Thomas Davies said that Garrick was 'the first actor who rejected this horrid soliloquy' (Vickers, ed., *Heritage*, VI, 381), but George Steevens, advising Garrick on his adaptation, seems to imply otherwise when he says that the speech 'had better have been omitted, as it is in the Representation' (Vickers, ed., *Heritage*, V, 448).

22. F. A. Pottle, ed., *Boswell's London Journal, 1762-3* (Harmondsworth: Penguin, 1966), p. 258.

23. Vickers, ed., *Heritage*, VI, 381, 368.

24. Woudhuysen, ed., *Samuel Johnson on Shakespeare*, p. 229.

25. Woudhuysen, ed., *Samuel Johnson on Shakespeare*, p. 241.

26. Vickers, ed., *Heritage*, VI, 367.

27. Martin Wiggins, '*Macbeth* and Premeditation' in Arthur Marwick, ed., *The Arts, Literature, and Society* (London and New York: Routledge, 1990), pp. 23-47.

28. *Julius Caesar*, ed. T. S. Dorsch (London and New York: Routledge, 1989), II. i. 63-4.

SPEAKING DAGGERS: T. S. ELIOT, JAMES JOYCE AND *HAMLET*

CHRISTINA BRITZOLAKIS

> I will speak daggers to her, but use none.
>
> (III. ii. 387)

Hamlet is the theme of two of the founding texts of Anglo-American High Modernism, the 'Scylla and Charybdis' chapter of James Joyce's *Ulysses* (1921) and T.S. Eliot's essay, '*Hamlet*' (1919). Both Joyce and Eliot institute the play at the centre of their writing as an allegory of the aesthetic process, and as a stage for the exploration of creative authority. Eliot's reading of *Hamlet* forms the occasion for him to propound his notion of the 'objective correlative', and thereby furnishes the lens through which much poetry, including his own, has since been viewed. Similarly, Stephen Dedalus's disquisition in the Dublin National Library, which identifies Shakespeare with the ghost of Hamlet's father, has been adduced as one of the major organizational frameworks of the novel, second in importance only to the *Odyssey*.[1] In both cases, the boundaries between critical and creative fictions, between aesthetic theory and praxis, are undermined.

Both Eliot's '*Hamlet*' and Joyce's 'Scylla and Charybdis' are concerned to relocate Shakespeare the author within *Hamlet*. The play is seen less as an autonomous aesthetic creation than as a disguised autobiography, riddled with the obsessive residues of the authorial psyche. In Bloomian terms, this demystification of Shakespeare's 'precursor' text could be seen as clearing a space for the Modernist reappropriation of *Hamlet*. The objective, 'disinterested' stance of the critic is a fiction which enables Joyce and Eliot to engage, through the question of *Hamlet*'s relation to its author, the autobiographical investments of their own texts. Joyce, of course, never produced a critical doctrine of impersonality akin to Eliot's, and the centrality of Dublin in his work attests to the strength and persistence of affiliations of place, neighbourhood and locality. Only through the myth of voluntary exile, however, can these affiliations be transfigured into art. Stephen Dedalus's description in *A*

Portrait of the Artist as a Young Man of the artist as 'the god of creation, within or behind or beyond his handiwork, invisible, refined out of existence, indifferent, paring his fingernails', though not, of course, ascribable to Joyce, became, along with a handful of Eliot's essays, one of the major theoretical supports of the mythic ideology of Modernism expressed in Eliot's essay on *Ulysses*. Eliot writes that Joyce's use of the *Odyssey* 'is simply a way of controlling, of ordering, of giving a shape and significance to the immense panorama of futility and anarchy which is contemporary history'.[2] As I shall argue later, Joyce's use of *Hamlet* cannot be so smoothly assimilated to a mythic negation of history, for the operation of literary influence in *Ulysses* persistently invokes the shadow of imperial expropriation. For Stephen Dedalus in *Portrait*, authorship is constituted as a negativity, the *non serviam* pronounced against the institutional claims of Church, State and Family. In *Ulysses*, however, the writer's control over the meanings his texts produce has become part of a wider exploration of the self-contradictory nature of authority.[3] In this essay, I wish to use the readings of *Hamlet* by Eliot and Joyce as a starting-point for an exploration of the Modernist reassessment of the creative subject. Through their readings, Eliot and Joyce signal their insertion into a literary genealogy which they themselves help to constitute. For them, *Hamlet* is the Oedipal locus of an 'anxiety of influence', at once underwriting and dismantling paternity as the structure through which the Modernist author tries to name himself. If the orphan prince is, as has repeatedly been demonstrated, a privileged literary-historical trope for Continental and Anglo-American Modernism, from Baudelaire to Tom Stoppard, much criticism has shown a marked reluctance to inquire into the specific mediations between history and aesthetics which it performs.[4]

Hamlet and Modernism

where's that bleeding awfur?[5]

By the early twentieth century, Shakespeare was well on the way to his present canonical status as national poet and complete creative genius, the supreme author whose mastery forms the horizon of all subsequent literary efforts. Both T.S. Eliot and Joyce's Stephen Dedalus produce notably reductive readings of the play, which tend to dismantle the ideology of Shakespeare's infinite depth and sublime myriad-mindedness. Their iconoclasm in relation to Shakespeare, like their Modernist renovation of English literary history, is bound up with their status as foreigners and exiles. In English culture, the figure of Hamlet became, in the course of the nineteenth and twentieth centuries, a byword for high-flown and impractical metaphysical speculation. As the type of the intellectual, he is somehow surplus to Englishness, yet inhabits it like an enemy agent, forever asserting its lack of identity with itself and estranging it from within. The theological model of creativity invested in the idolization of Shakespeare is, of course, thrown into question by the radical 'textuality' of *Ulysses* and *The Waste Land*, which tends to sever language from the expressive activity of an authorial ego, ceding the initiative to words themselves. However, the spectre of the author cannot be wholly discarded, for it is the institution of authorship that inserts Joyce and Eliot into a historical process. Modernism, in the historical perspective afforded by its assumption of 'classical' status, is a contradictory formation, which banishes metaphysical affirmations at one level of the text only to reinstate them at another.

The progressive adoption of Hamlet as a prototype of the artist in the course of the nineteenth century is parallel to the evolution of the aesthetic as an 'autonomous' sphere, detached from the cognitive and moral spheres.[6] The post-Romantic artist becomes a displaced and dispossessed figure, forever unable or unwilling to adopt an active role on the social stage. The myth of alienation has its roots in the double-bind of the institution of art itself, at once resisting and introjecting the structure of the commodity. It was the task of the aestheticist and Decadent movements to transform the historic necessity of this process into a virtue, endowing art with an idealized negativity (the triumph of 'pure' form over content), bought at the cost of material exclusion and powerlessness. The affinity between *Hamlet* and Modernism inhabits a specific moment of this dialectic, in which the myth of the author comes under the strain of global imperialist crisis and the consequent dispersal and fragmentation of pre-war Europe. The *explication de texte* which treats *Hamlet* as one of the multifarious troves of Modernist intertexts, to be unearthed and enumerated within a purely synchronic perspective, tends to duplicate the Modernist ideology of mythic unity. The result is an absorption of disjunct historical moments into the empty simultaneity of a commodified cultural history, an imaginary museum.[7]

How does the negativity of Hamlet, which interferes with the sources of action and produces, in their place, a maddened discourse, become an exemplary model for the Modernist writer? The interpretation of the play's hero as a character clogged by a murky, unrepresentable inward lack, began with the Romantics and became one of the key texts of psychoanalysis. The first version of Ernest Jones's essay on *Hamlet* and the Oedipus complex was published in 1910. For Jones, Hamlet represented the omnipresence of neurosis in psychic life. As heir to the throne, Hamlet is mortgaged to, and representative of, paternal law. But revenge, or successful identification with the father, is hindered by his obsession with a cloying maternal sexuality. For Lacan, Hamlet's delay becomes an object-lesson in the tragic nature of desire as the subject's alienation in language. He points out the importance of 'maim'd rites' in *Hamlet*. Mourning, the ritual which heals the breach left in the symbolic order by death, has gone wrong, leaving a disorder of language which is also a crisis of the subject. Hamlet's desire, stuck in the moment of the dissolution of the Oedipus complex, unravels the symbolic structure of the patriarchal family, revealing its roots in the twin crime of incest and parricide. More precisely, Hamlet's crisis is provoked by the shattering revelation that the authority of the father relies on mystification: 'one cannot strike the phallus, because the phallus ... is a *ghost*'.[8] The discovery of the fragile basis of paternal law, its ghostly insubstantiality, is inseparable from the discovery that the primordial object of desire, the mother, is herself capable of desire. When the father absconds from the symbolic order founded in his name, his absence turns the world into a treacherous carnal snare.

In Hamlet, mourning has turned into melancholy, which, according to Freud, not only empties the world of meaning, but also impoverishes the ego itself. His melancholy produces a disgust with, but also a manic proliferation of language: 'Words, words, words' (II. ii. 192). Hamlet installs himself in the ambiguity of language; his 'crafty madness' demarcates a space of subversion within the court, where its codes and rituals are negated.[9] In this hermetic space, he can repudiate the 'rotten' state of Denmark with impunity, while suspending the act of revenge itself in the realm of the hypothetical. Irony, wit and wordplay become weapons against the corrupt machinations of Claudius, Polonius and the rest. But at the same time, of course, these stratagems implicate him in the disease of social reality and of representation which he longs to purge; he becomes an actor, corrupting language to his own purposes.

It has been pointed out that Hamlet is a transitional figure, poised between feudal and capitalist modes of production, foreshadowing the split between private and public spheres, yet looking backward to the lost unity of religious, monarchical and social orders.[10] His 'antic disposition' introduces into the pragmatic discourse of the court the wild card of a putative inwardness withdrawn from social transactions. He accuses Rosencrantz and Guildenstern of trying to 'pluck out the heart' of his 'mystery' (III. ii. 356-7). But that unique and unspeakable inwardness which is the proleptic sign of an emergent bourgeois subjectivity may itself be no more than a fiction. Hamlet's modernity therefore lies in his regressiveness, his inability to name himself.[11] He is at home neither in the old theocratic hierarchy nor in the new individualist ethos of self-authorship.

Like Hamlet, the Modernist author is faced with a crisis of patriarchal authority, amongst whose most obvious aspects may be counted the Great War which redrew the map of Europe, the Russian Revolution, the suffragette movement and the emergence of mass culture. In particular, Modernism articulates the challenge presented to European self-understanding by the disturbing appearance of its previously invisible colonial others. Paul Valéry, in his essay 'The Crisis of the Mind', first published in *The Athenaeum* in 1919, had figured pre-war imperial Europe as a hysterical body racked by the memories of its cultural past. 'As though in desperate defence of her own physiological being and resources,' he writes, 'all her memory confusedly returned. Her great men and her great books came back pell mell.'[12] To exorcize the threat of disorder, he unearths the figure of Hamlet, casting him as representative of the threatened authority of European high culture:

> Standing, now, on an immense sort of terrace of Elsinore that stretches from Basel to Cologne, bordered by the sands of Nieuport, the marshes of the Somme, the limestone of Champagne, the granites of Alsace … our Hamlet of Europe is watching millions of ghosts.
>
> But he is an intellectual Hamlet, meditating on the life and death of truths; for ghosts, he has all the subjects of our controversies; for remorse, all the titles of our fame. He is bowed under the weight of all the discoveries and varieties of knowledge, incapable of resuming this endless activity; he broods on the tedium of rehearsing the past and the folly of always trying to innovate. He staggers between two abysses — for two dangers never cease threatening the world: order and disorder.
>
> Every skull he picks up is an illustrious skull. **Whose was it?** This one was **Leonardo**. He invented the flying man, but the flying man has not exactly served his inventor's purposes...And that other skull was **Leibnitz**, who dreamed of universal

peace. And this one was **Kant ... and Kant begat Hegel, and Hegel begat Marx, and Marx begat ...**[13]

Hamlet, tottering on the brink between 'order and disorder', becomes a talisman of civilizing culture against the dreadful spectre of a continent plunged into revolutionary chaos. He represents the contemplative intellect, bewildered by the accelerated historical change which is causing an inert female 'mass' to outweigh the virile heroism of mind. The health and sanity of this spiritual centre — 'the elect portion of the terrestrial globe, the pearl of the sphere, the brain of a vast body' — undergoes a progressive degradation as it passes from Renaissance humanism through the Enlightenment, ultimately bringing disease and disorder (in the form of revolutionary struggle) upon Europe:

> Hamlet hardly knows what to make of so many skulls. But suppose he forgets them! Will he still be himself? ... His terribly lucid mind contemplates the passage from war to peace: darker, more dangerous than the passage from peace to war; all peoples are troubled by it ... 'What about Me,' he says, 'what is to become of Me, the European intellect?'[14]

For Valéry's Hamlet, the past becomes a vista of ruined cultural fragments in which the classical humanist subject can no longer see himself mirrored. Eliot's concept of 'the mind of Europe', as outlined in 'Tradition and the Individual Talent', is his response to Valéry's call to order; *The Waste Land* can be read either as poised on the brink of the abyss, or, according to post-structuralist readings, as lodged firmly within it. But the contrasted examples of Eliot and Joyce show that the European Hamlet's dilemma could be articulated in widely divergent ways, not only as a threat but also as a promise. Modernist irony is not, as Edward Said claims, simply a form of passive resistance to historical change, a set of 'paralyzed gestures of aestheticised powerlessness'.[15]

The privileging of abstract or subjective potentiality over concrete existence which Lukács long ago identified as characteristic of Modernism takes its cue from Hamlet the failed revenger, contemplative ironist and melancholy estranger of language.[16] Material struggle is converted into the travails of stylistic 'defamiliarization'; words acquire the status of substitute weapons, instruments of the poet's immaterial revenge against a rotten state. But if Hamlet amongst the Modernists becomes a poet *manqué*, by the same token, the Modernist poet is also always an avenger *manqué*. The mission imposed upon Hamlet, which he can neither fulfil nor ignore, is to 'set ... right' a 'time ...

out of joint' (I. v. 196-7). Hamlet is, as Lacan argues, in mourning for that impossible moment of desire which is interdicted by the threat of castration. His melancholy contains the seeds of a challenge to the constituted order of things. As Freud points out, the self-castigation of the melancholic conceals a 'mental constellation of revolt', an aggression against the other which has been turned inward. Hamlet, that is to say, foreshadows, more than any other Shakespearean hero, the thwarted protopolitical vocation of Modernism. The analogy of feudal Denmark with the age of imperial crisis culminating in the First World War may well be symptomatic of the mythic ideology of modernism, which collapses past and present through 'depth structures'. But for both Eliot and Joyce, Hamlet turns out to be in some sense an object lesson in the futility of a merely formal subversion as a response to the Old World's loss of legitimacy.

T. S. Eliot and the trials of personality

HAMLET: ... and yet, to me, what is this quintessence of dust? Man delights not me — nor woman neither, though by your smiling you seem to say so.
ROSENCRANTZ: My lord, there was no such stuff in my thoughts.

(II. ii. 308-11)

For Eliot, *Hamlet* is an 'artistic failure', because its author was unable to transcend the accidents of personality.[17] Shakespeare, like Prince Hamlet, could not find the 'objective correlative' or aesthetic formula for the emotions he wished to express. In Freudian terms, the repressed impulses which engendered the play have not been adequately sublimated. The principles on which Eliot's critique is based are closely linked to those set forth in 'Tradition and the Individual Talent' (1919). By approving the theory that *Hamlet* is a based on a lost earlier *Hamlet* by Kyd which conformed to the conventions of the revenge play, he is able simultaneously to downplay its claims to originality and to stigmatize it as a deviation from the norm. For Eliot, the play suffers from an interrupted lineage. 'Shakespeare's *Hamlet*, so far as it is Shakespeare's, is a play dealing with the effect of a mother's guilt upon her son ... Shakespeare was unable to impose this motive successfully upon the "intractable" material of the old play' (*SE*, p. 143). Shakespeare's concern with the psychological motive is seen as adulterating or obstructing the adaptation. The shadowy original of *Hamlet*, the ur-*Hamlet* in which content was fitted to form, is lost, but continues to haunt all future versions of the play.

For Eliot, then, Shakespeare was unable to objectify the emotion which he wished to express; the failure to find the objective correlative is a failure of self-mastery, a surrender to inarticulate feeling: '*Hamlet*, like the sonnets, is full of some stuff that the writer could not drag to light, contemplate, or manipulate into art' (*SE*, p. 144).[18] The *Hamlet* essay performs a curious feat of author-psychology which denies any substantive content to the author's psyche. An emotion that is not in adequation with its object, absorbed by it, is properly inconceivable; it is 'stuff' or detritus, in both the intellectual and the moral sense. Hamlet's 'antic disposition' is 'the buffoonery of an emotion which can find no outlet in action' (*SE*, p. 146). The literary innovation represented by Shakespeare's psychologizing of Kyd's revenge play is deeply ambivalent for Eliot, because it issues from a split subject, constituted (as Freud's researches suggested) by repression and unable to naturalize its authority.

Like many of the essays, '*Hamlet*' employs a distinctly Hamlet-like mode of reasoning: the idealized perfection of the remembered father (attested in the play by Hamlet's recurrent comparisons to mythical divinities such as Hyperion, Jove or Mars) is muddied by the son's unruly subjectivity. Eliot's 'dissociation of sensibility' is another covert and hostile reading of *Hamlet*. After the seventeenth century, poets no longer felt their thought as immediately as the odour of a rose; instead, they 'thought and felt by fits, unbalanced; they reflected' (*SE*, p. 288). This poetic dithering results from the dissolution of a hierarchical structure and the unleashing of Protestant individualism: the very moment, in fact, which produces Hamlet.

Eliot recasts the situation of Hamlet confronted by the ghost of his murdered father as the novice poet's awareness of the literary past; 'not only the best, but also the most individual parts of his work may be those in which the dead poets, his ancestors, assert their immortality most vigorously' (*SE*, p. 14). He starts from the position that the poet is always already disinherited; for tradition is not a matter of straightforward inheritance but must be earned. His 'great difficulties and responsibilities' (*SE*, p. 15) consist in learning that the mind of Europe is much more important than his own private mind (*SE*, p. 16). The 'ideal order' of literature is a paradoxical mixture of monumentality and organicism; it is 'a living whole' (*SE*, p. 17), dialectically open-ended, constantly modified by literary innovation, but 'the idea or form of European, of English literature' remains nonetheless providentially complete and unchanging. Hamlet was characterized by the dissipation of his will to act; the 'impersonal' poet, on the contrary, is characterized by a salutary 'concentration, of a very great number of experiences which to the practical and active person would not seem to be experiences at all' (*SE*, p. 21). Like Hamlet, he is cut off from the realm of praxis, but that disjunction, which Hamlet experienced as an onerous necessity, Eliot turns into a virtue.

The poet's task, then, is to find the 'objective correlative'. This will enable him to express not only a subjective mood but the collective sentiments of his culture, for the objective correlative, as students of Eliot's anthropological borrowings have pointed out, is to some degree a totem.[19] Eliot's own poetic practice constitutes a highly self-conscious and ironic attempt to doctor the malaise of what he might have called, with Max Jacob, Hamletism.[20] It has been seen as readjusting the balance between thought and feeling through the corrective principles of 'impersonality' and 'tradition', yet Eliot's pedagogical authority constantly undoes itself, sliding vertiginously between diagnosis and symptom.[21] In the early poems, the subject becomes an elusive phantom amidst the Protean alternation of voices, lost or endlessly deferred in the labyrinthine passages of literary history. An imperilled poetic self adopts linguistic masks as ironic weapons of defence against a rootless and treacherously shifting metropolitan culture. In Eliot's early poetry, the mingled fascination and threat of the city is one with the impure seductions of a commodified and fragmented femininity. The mother's body, with its insurgent desires, belongs to the degraded context of urban experience; the disenchanted urban wanderer is also unavoidably a voyeur. His melancholic discourse occupies a no-man's land between a shadowy, unknowable interiority and a social realm imaged insistently in terms of hollowness, banality and contamination. J. Alfred Prufrock's skilful deployment of literary masks enables him to delay or evade the necessity of posing an 'overwhelming question':

> No! I am not Prince Hamlet, nor was meant to be;
> Am an attendant lord, one that will do
> To swell a progress, start a scene or two,
> Advise the prince; no doubt, an easy tool,
> Deferential, glad to be of use,
> Politic, cautious and meticulous;
> Full of high sentence, but a bit obtuse;
> At times, indeed, almost ridiculous —
> Almost, at times, the Fool.

> I grow old ... I grow old ...
> I shall wear the bottoms of my trousers rolled.[22]

The figure of J. Alfred Prufrock sums up within himself the ambiguous movement of the text of *Hamlet* through literary history: on the one hand, enshrined in 'the mind of Europe' as a canonic text; on the other, increasingly transformed into commodified layers of pastiche. Prufrock is an Anglo-American version of French Symbolist adaptations of Hamlet by Mallarmé, Valéry and Laforgue. His refusal of the tragic role of Hamlet, couched in Shakespearean blank verse, epitomizes Eliot's treacherously double-edged use of the literary past. By casting himself as an attendant lord, the butt of Hamlet's wit, Prufrock seems to defer to the shadow of Shakespeare's greatness. But his denial of tragic status is a subtly self-aggrandizing gesture, a bid to out-Hamlet Hamlet. It might seem that his part undergoes a progressive degradation from the prince through the courtiers Rosencrantz and Guildenstern to the Fool. The Shakespearean Fool (who so often has all the best lines) is outside of the action altogether, commenting upon it in a privileged space of hermetic wordplay. Prufrock demonstrates the equivocal nature of Eliot's precepts in 'Tradition and the Individual Talent'; in the process of subordinating his voice to the voices of the dead, he is covertly locked in an Oedipal struggle with his predecessor's 'high sentence'.

Prufrock, then, is both a failed Hamlet, and a Hamlet to the second power: he is incapable not merely of action, but even of articulation: 'It is impossible to say just what I mean!' The urban labyrinth is populated by hostile others, by 'women who come and go / Talking of Michelangelo', and 'eyes that fix you in a formulated phrase' (*SP*, 16, 14, 15). The city is a place where damp, unhealthy souls fester in a haze of indecision; at the same time, it is filled with busy, meaningless external movement, a caricature of true action. Prufrock, whose volition is muffled in an anaesthetizing yellow fog, is the end-product of Hamlet's reduction of the cosmos to a 'foul and pestilent congregation of vapours' (II. ii. 302-3). In 'Portrait of a Lady', the speaker cries:

> And I must borrow every changing shape
> To find expression ... dance, dance
> Like a dancing bear,

Cry like a parrot, chatter like an ape.
Let us take the air, in a tobacco trance.

(SP, p. 22)

Eliot's early poems repeat Hamlet's circuit of misogynistic obsession, which locates woman as the source of all untruth. Duality, fragmentation, shifting appearance and instability seem to characterize both femininity and social performance. In the 'Fresca' passage deleted from the drafts of *The Waste Land*, Eliot writes, 'For varying forms, one definition's right: Unreal emotions, and real appetite'.[23] The monstrosity of female desire is seen as underlying the depradations of modernity. Indeed, the realm of history is itself figured as a carnal, or more specifically vaginal, snare in 'Gerontion':

> History has many cunning passages, contrived corridors
> And issues, deceives with whispering ambitions,
> Guides us by vanities. Think now
> She gives when our attention is distracted
> And what she gives, gives with such supple confusions
> That the giving famishes the craving.

(SP, p. 40)

The passage recalls Hamlet's response to Rosencrantz and Guildenstern's announcement that they are Fortune's 'privates': 'In the secret parts of Fortune? O most true, she is a strumpet' (II. ii. 235-6). The Hall of Mirrors at Versailles becomes the scene of the dismemberment of imperial Europe through an act of international diplomacy figured in terms of Jacobean courtly intrigue. A contagion of false mimesis displaces and distorts the syntax of the poem, 'adulterating' narrative and territorial unities alike.

Hamlet enables Eliot to legitimate, in terms of a certain reading of literary history, a reaction against the emotions, women and nature as a threat and a source of disgust. It is the recalcitrant problem of the body — at once social, sexual and historical, undergoing new forms of fragmentation in its passage across the denatured space of the metropolis — that the ghostly patrilineage of 'Tradition' is intended to correct. Hence the irresolvable duality of *The Waste Land* as both 'impersonal' rite of mourning and melancholic obsession. It is perfectly consistent with the spirit of *Hamlet* that Eliot should describe the poem as 'the relief of a personal and wholly insignificant grouse against life'.[24] The poem's original title, 'He do the police in different voices' (borrowed from Dickens, the novelist of the industrial metropolis), announces the

238 Christina Britzolakis

polyphonic mode, translating Hamlet's 'antic disposition' into a systematic fragmentation and dispersal of lyric subjectivity. For Eliot, at this moment of cultural crisis, the *polis* could be reconstituted only as an assemblage of disembodied social and literary voices. Thus the hysterical ventriloquy of Ophelia is intercut with Hamlet's contemplative, self-lacerating despair in 'A Game of Chess'.

The dizzying, recursive movement of irony within the text is both diagnostic and symptomatic of the fracturing and mutilation of tradition; the verbal echoes at once do homage to and deface their originals. The self-cancelling structure of Hamlet's wordplay and punning is writ large in the rhetoric of *The Waste Land*; his disgust at the usurper Claudius, 'A king of shreds and patches' (III. iv. 103), is re-enacted as a revenge on literary history, the weaving of a 'Shakespeherian rag' of quotations. That *tour de force* of Renaissance humanism, 'What a piece of work is a man', ends with the words, 'and yet, to me, what is this quintessence of dust?' (II. ii. 308). Eliot cuts even this dying fall down to size, in the line 'I will show you fear in a handful of dust'. At its close, in a volley of nested quotations, the poem delivers the last twist of the knife to its precursor text, echoing the revenge plot not of Shakespeare but of Kyd: 'Why then Ile fit you. Hieronymo's mad againe' (*SP*, pp. 64, 79). In *The Spanish Tragedy*, Hieronimo's staging of the play-within-the-play is strategic; but Hamlet's feigned madness, like that of *The Waste Land*, is also the madness of writing when it loses its anchorage in the name of the Father.[25]

Eliot's quest was to reinstate at the level of myth the uncorrupted body politic of a hierarchical, pre-individualist social order. The American expatriate who installed himself at the conservative heart of Englishness, declaring himself in 1927 for Anglo-Catholicism, royalism and classicism, was haunted by a double parricide. The very existence of the United States constituted a death-blow against 'tradition' in the Burkean sense; to deepen the wound, the Unitarianism of Eliot's family diluted the authority of religion to the point where it became almost inseparable from democratic civic-mindedness. The American father is not only a king-killer but a priest-killer. The Jamesian flight from the provincial shallowness of American culture to a Europe saturated with manners turned out to be a hollow mockery; the Great War had plunged imperial Europe into chaos and disintegration, leaving its metropolitan centres vulnerable to infiltration by newly resurgent and mobile Others from the colonized margins of Europe, to whom the 'cunning corridors' of history had given access. For Eliot, Europe was now a paralyzed, decentred waste land, haunted by the ghosts of a pre-war imperial order. The imaginary unity of high culture generated by 'the mind of Europe' was an antidote to the fragmentation of culture precipitated by the Western encounter with strangers whom it could not assimilate.

After 1927, Hamlet could no longer serve Eliot as a poetic *persona* because he could not provide a solution to the problem of order; his tortured and baffled doubleness belonged all too clearly to the fallen world of history. Eliot's loss of interest in Hamlet answers to his rejection of Protestant individualism, liberalism and humanism: the forces which Eliot saw as privileging the 'inner voice' against institutional authority. The psychological model of the creative subject broached in '*Hamlet*' was placed under interdiction; language had to be cleansed of the miasma of subjectivity and sexual desire, and become a transparent carrier of the Logos. Eliot saw Dante's 'allegorical' method as a model of aspiration for his later poetry, precisely because in his view it bypassed the Hamlet complex or 'dissociation of sensibility', restoring the primal relation of word to thing prevalent in medieval culture: 'in Dante's time, Europe, with all its dissensions and dirtiness, was mentally more united than we can now conceive. It is not particularly the Treaty of Versailles that has separated nation from nation; nationalism was born long before; and the process of disintegration which for our generation culminates in that treaty began soon after Dante's time' (*SE*, p. 240). Accordingly, Eliot places Dante above Shakespeare, because his language is 'the perfection of a common language' rather than his own, merely local language (*SE*, p. 252). Hamlet had become too stubbornly Protestant, English and secular a figure to serve the project of disembodying Europe, purging it of the accidents of history and uniting its scattered members in the image of God the Father. The misogynistic snarl, the horror of the mass, and the melancholy phantasmagoria of the city are all ritually evacuated from Eliot's language in the penitential rhythms of *Ash Wednesday*. It is true that the 'familiar compound ghost' appears in 'Little Gidding', urging the poet 'to purify the dialect of the tribe', and incarnating the tradition, from Virgil, through Dante to Shakespeare and Yeats. But the ghost of Hamlet's father is ultimately subsumed in the Holy Ghost, which promises 'a condition of complete simplicity' (*SP*, p. 222).

　　　　　　　　Christina Britzolakis

Joyce and the fictions of paternity

ROSENCRANTZ: My lord, you must tell us where the body is and go with us to the King.
HAMLET: The body is with the King, but the King is not with the body. The King is a thing —
GUILDENSTERN: A thing, my lord?
HAMLET: Of nothing.

(IV. ii. 24-9)

How did the the Olympian view of Paul Valéry's 'Hamlet of Europe', contemplating the ghosts of civilization from his continental terrace, strike James Joyce, himself a colonized subject of imperial Europe, and thus with even less claim than the American Eliot to be its legitimate heir? Stephen Dedalus is implicitly a Hamlet figure, hesitating on the brink of the symbolic order, rejecting the roles allotted to him by his class, nationality and religion. In the *Portrait*, Stephen's claims to an 'impersonal' art are caught within the metaphysical dualities of body and spirit. But it is not until *Ulysses* that the reading of *Hamlet* becomes part of a political as well as an aesthetic project. As Declan Kiberd has pointed out in his introduction to *Ulysses*, Irish writers rewrote the paternal texts of Shakespeare in the cause of inventing a revolutionary national consciousness (*U*, pp. lxix-lxxv). The period between the inception and completion of *Ulysses* — between 1904 and 1922 — was a period of massive historical transformation both at home and abroad, spanning the Irish Rebellion, the Great War, and revolutions in Russia and Germany.

Joyce's writing, like Eliot's, constitutes a critique of the idea of an author, moving as it does from the 'transparent' naturalism of *Dubliners* to the dissolution of narrative point of view and the explosion of styles in *Ulysses* and *Finnegans Wake*. But the critique of authorship is complicated by Joyce's ambivalent relation to an English literary history entangled with the history of imperialism. The Irish Hamlet's wit, eloquence and mimicry was mortgaged to an occupied Ireland deprived of its leaders. In Joyce's world, as Declan Kiberd points out, fathers and rulers exercise power without authority (*U*, pp. xlix-lxxx). If Eliot was in quest of an ideal civilization where the authorities of church and state would be seamlessly identified, Joyce had encountered this unity in its most vicious form in his native land, 'Where', he wrote, 'Christ and Caesar are hand and glove'.[26] The opening scene of *Ulysses* is the Martello Tower, fortified stronghold of the British; and the analogy between Martello and Elsinore is put into the mouth of Haines, the Englishman engaged in collecting specimens of Irish literary culture for British consumption. Haines's need to see Ireland refracted through *Hamlet* is fed by his admiration for the Wildean epigrams of Stephen and Joyce and aligns itself with the Arnoldian ideology of Celticism, which casts the Irish as sensitive, hyperimaginative souls doomed to failure in the actual world. In 'Aeolus', Professor MacHugh tells the assembled journalists that the Irish are subjects of 'the empire of the spirit, not an *imperium*, that went under with the Athenian fleets at Ægospotami' (*U*, p. 169). This romanticization of feudal and classical culture ends in colluding with that material empire in which, as Stephen wryly notes, 'Khaki Hamlets don't hesitate to shoot' (*U*, pp. 239-40).

Joyce's alertness to possible political readings of the Hamlet myth is not always shared by his critics. He was fascinated by the figure of Parnell, the 'dead king' betrayed by the Irish, whose ghost haunted national politics and inspired the Irish Revival.[27] The Irish nation itself, subjected to the British interloper, is traditionally figured as a woman, alternately betrayed and betrayer, obdurate victim and devourer. In 'Circe', it is this nightmarish image of the suffocating mother, 'Old Gummy Granny', that appears to Stephen in the place of the ghost of Hamlet's father. 'Aha! I know you, grammer! Hamlet, revenge! The old sow that eats her farrow!' (*U*, p. 692). The apparition is provoked by the harassment of the British soldiers, who become chauvinistic travesties of Hamlet: 'I'll wring the neck of any fucking bastard says a word against my bleeding fucking king' (*U*, p. 694). 'Personally, I detest action', Stephen announces to the British Privates, only to be beaten up (*U*, p. 687) ; Wildean wit is constituted as the feminized other of the British Empire's militarist chauvinism.

Like *The Waste Land*, *Ulysses* turns *Hamlet* into a Shakespeherian rag, obsessively unmaking, remaking and democratizing the language of this paternal text. For Joyce, to wreck the inherited structures of the oppressor's language was the only way of forging an authentically Irish literary Modernism that would not cut off the travails of an Irish state in the making from the larger global stage of imperial crisis. That is why his alternative Hamlet, Leopold Bloom, a Jew of Hungarian extraction, is the representative of another dispossessed and subject people, indeed the very Other whose newly visible presence in Europe occasioned such dismay in Eliot and Valéry. Bloom's meditations in the 'Hades' and 'Lestrygonians' sections, for example, expand

Hamlet's graveyard witticisms into a levelling populism based on the centrality of the body in human existence.

Joyce was wary of the literary nationalism of the Irish Revival, which he saw as duplicating the fantasies of racial purity and homogeneity that fuelled imperial oppression. Instead, he preferred to see art as a displaced, bloodless revenge against authoritarianism. The artist's 'cold steelpen' (U, p. 6) would act upon the rottenness of the state like a surgical instrument. Dublin was, for Joyce, 'the centre of paralysis'.[28] The metropolis under imperialism (as opposed to Eliot's landscape, the imperial metropolis) suffered from a stagnating inability to translate intention into action, resulting in the proliferation of symbolic practices as a substitute for political action.[29] Thus Hamlet's ironic and performative use of language becomes a generalized condition of inflated rhetoricity which is an index of powerlessness. In 'Aeolus', the ear of Ireland is seen to be abused by the journalistic hot air pouring from the printing presses.

Stephen's *bravura* performance in the library, an attempt to impress the literary world of Dublin from which he is excluded, 'nookshotten' and marginalized, participates in this condition. His disquisition on *Hamlet* is concerned, like Eliot's '*Hamlet*', with questions of creative authority and literary tradition. He, too, sees *Hamlet* as the product of obsession. But Stephen's author-psychology, unlike Eliot's, relies heavily on the construction of a biographical narrative as the origin of the text: Shakespeare's resentment and humiliation at his wife's betrayal. As *Hamlet* constitutes Shakespeare's aesthetic revenge against the wife who had betrayed him, so Stephen's speech constitutes his rhetorical seduction of, and revenge against, the literary world of Dublin which has disowned him. Through his 'dagger definitions' he attempts to expose the shallowness of the audience he is ostensibly trying to impress. Yet his own theory is explicitly for sale; its recreation of the past, using an *ersatz* Elizabethan idiom, turns history into a costume drama, and relies on the commodification of Shakespeare mocked by Mulligan: 'William Shakespeare and company, limited. The people's William' (U, p. 262).[30]

In the course of Stephen's performance, the biographical reading is overtaken by the conceit of the artist as the God of the Trinity, father, son and ghost in one. This is often taken as a metaphor for Joyce's authorship of *Ulysses*, in which Stephen Dedalus, a portrait of the artist as a young man, intersects with Bloom, a portrait of his future, complementary self (the artist at the time of the novel's composition). The estranged son in quest of a father meets the father in search of a son; and Joyce, as the encompassing authorial sensibility, contains, it is argued, both within himself. To adopt this myth as the framework of the novel leaves Joyce in that position of transcendent mastery which Stephen Dedalus described in the *Portrait*, and duplicates the Shakespeare myth. Yet the language of *Ulysses* refutes the theological model of authorship at least as much as it underwrites it. In 'Scylla and Charybdis', Stephen repudiates his own theory, announcing that he himself does not believe in it. His discourse on Shakespeare is destabilized by the interplay and contagion of different narrative voices. Other characters and incidents in the chapter lose their objectivity and are subsumed into a drama of style.

Unlike Eliot, Joyce is intent on exposing the fictional nature of paternity, and its dependence on the female body as the source of all life. Stephen claims that fatherhood is:

> a mystical estate, an apostolic succession, from only begetter to only begotten. On that mystery and not on the madonna which the cunning Italian intellect flung to the mob of Europe the church is founded and founded irremovably because founded, like the world, macro- and micro-cosm, upon the void. Upon incertitude, upon unlikelihood. *Amor matris*, subjective and objective genitive, may be the only true thing in life. Paternity may be a legal fiction. Who is the father of any son that any son should love him or he any son?

> (*U*, p. 266).

Ulysses refuses to efface or repress the materiality of writing, the intervention of the body in the creative process, and the rootedness of style in a particular history. Patriarchal authority, whether it manifests itself in empire, in the bourgeois nuclear family, or in literature is a mythical construct, a 'thing of nothing'. 'Nothing' is, of course, Ophelia's response to Hamlet's interrogation, and the pun on female genitals with which he taunts her at the play-within-the play. In 'Oxen of the Sun', Joyce links the rise and decline of literary traditions with the fate of European civilization, but his diagnosis departs from that of Eliot's *Waste Land* on the question of the body. Set in a maternity hospital, the prose is governed not by the metaphor of rape but by that of conception, the delayed and laborious birth of Mrs Purefoy's child, in which Bloom's imagination sympathetically participates. The central and generative role that woman plays in *Ulysses* is played out in the androgynous tendencies of Bloom, 'the new womanly man' (*U*, p. 614). Thinking of Mrs Bandman Palmer, the actress and male impersonator, he goes so far as to wonder if Shakespeare was a woman.

For Joyce, *Hamlet* is a text that reveals the political nature of the author's stylistic choices. The dream-play of 'Circe' corresponds to the play-within-the play in *Hamlet*, a representational trap for the usurper who disclaims responsibility for the rottenness of the state. Hamlet urges the players to hold the mirror up to nature, but his own object in arranging the play-within-the play is to hold up a glass wherein the King may see his face. Joyce, having had Stephen declare that Irish art is the cracked looking glass of a servant in 'Telemachus', proceeds to shatter and reform the mimetic level of narrative, using a dreamlike logic of displacement and condensation:

> LYNCH: (*Points*) The mirror up to nature. (*He laughs*). Hu hu hu hu hu hu.
> (*Stephen and Bloom gaze in the mirror. The face of William Shakespeare, beardless, appears there, rigid in facial paralysis, crowned by the reflection of the reindeer antlered hatrack in the hall.*)
>
> (*U*, p. 671)

Throughout the novel, hats have suggested the inessential and provisional nature of personal and authorial identity: Stephen's Hamlet hat, Bloom's 'high grade hat', Parnell's hat, knocked off and restored to him by Bloom, the prostitute's hat that finds its way into Molly's bedroom. Shakespeare, '*rigid in facial paralysis*', crowned by the reflection of the reindeer antlered hatrack, represents the author frozen into an icon by literary history. The 'crown' of reindeer antlers fixes him as a finite individual, circumscribed by class, gender and personal history: a cuckold, as in Stephen's psychobiography. But at the same time it is a travesty of the 'mastermind' model of the author as everybody and nobody, able to assume at will any and every identity. For Joyce, then, literary influence is, far more than in Eliot's 'Tradition and the Individual Talent', a reciprocal operation between past and present, between historicity and literary value, which destabilizes the identities of both the living and the dead.

In *Ulysses*, the horror of female sexuality that Eliot derives from *Hamlet* is largely absent. Hamlet visits his mother in her bedchamber, where he launches a climactic verbal assault on her. Joyce ends his novel with Molly Bloom's monologue in bed, a flood of unpunctuated 'oral' discourse which supplants the exhausted written or scholastic tradition, represented by 'Ithaca'. Molly's language rejects logical sequence for the unauthorized, illegitimate networks of meaning produced by puns, jokes and parapraxes. The slipperiness of words, which escapes the control of the Word, and testifies to a communal rather than a unitary creativity, is lamented by Eliot in 'Burnt Norton'; for Joyce, however, it points the way forward to *Finnegans Wake*.

The comic treatment of Molly Bloom's adultery, registered in Bloom's complex and changing response to it over the course of the day, rewrites Hamlet's hysterical disgust at Gertrude's transgression. It is not her violation which leads to the forces of paralysis, but rather, the genteel denial of the body that Joyce shows to be in collusion with the forces of state and church. Molly is not a doomed victim, the pawn of others' desires, as Ophelia is; she defiantly asserts her sexuality and remains unrepentantly, indeed triumphantly sane. Joyce's identification with Molly Bloom is diametrically opposite to Eliot's use of the Ophelia figure in *The Waste Land*; in *Ulysses*, woman has the status of 'sacred lifegiver' and 'the link between nations and generations' (*U*, p. 694); for Eliot, the female body can only signify blight and sterility, for it interferes with the transmission of the Word from father to son.

In adopting the mourning garb of Hamlet, then, the Modernism of Eliot and Joyce testifies to the breakdown of older, organic unities — of the subject, of narrative, and of community — into fragments. Patriarchy, filiation and inheritance are at the mercy of the transformative energies of modernization, whose destructive consequences have become glaringly obvious in a Europe crippled and devastated by the warring imperial powers. The preoccupation of Modernist literature with self-invention and the attempt to father oneself bears witness to an age of war and revolutionary transformation, which threatened to sweep away fixed, inherited meanings and create radically new values.

Notes

1. Richard Ellmann, *The Consciousness of Joyce* (London: Faber and Faber, 1977).

2. T. S. Eliot, '*Ulysses*, Order and Myth' (1923) rpt. in Frank Kermode, ed., *Selected Prose of T.S. Eliot* (London: Faber and Faber, 1975), p. 177.

3. See Vicki Mahaffey, *Reauthorizing Joyce* (Cambridge: Cambridge University Press, 1988).

4. See, for example, Martin Scofield, *The Ghosts of Hamlet* (Cambridge: Cambridge University Press, 1980).

5. James Joyce, *Ulysses*, ed. Declan Kiberd (Harmondsworth: Penguin, 1992), p. 556. This edition is referred to hereafter as *U*.

6. See Peter Burger, *The Theory of the Avant-Garde*, tr. Marion Shaw (Minneapolis: University of Minnesota Press, 1984).

7. See, for example, Scofield, *The Ghosts of Hamlet*.

8. Jacques Lacan, 'Desire and the Interpretation of Desire in *Hamlet*' in Shoshana Felman, ed., *Literature and Psychoanalysis* (Baltimore and London: The Johns Hopkins University Press, 1982), p. 50.

9. See James L. Calderwood, *To Be and Not to Be: Negation and Metadrama in 'Hamlet'* (New York: Columbia University Press, 1983).

10. See Francis Barker, *The Tremulous Private Body* (London and New York: Methuen, 1984).

11. See Terry Eagleton, *William Shakespeare* (Oxford: Blackwell, 1986), pp. 70-5.

12. Paul Valéry, 'The Crisis of the Mind' in James R. Lawler, ed., *Paul Valéry: An Anthology* (London and Henley: Routledge and Kegan Paul, 1977), p. 95.

13. Valéry, 'The Crisis of the Mind', pp. 99-100

14. Valéry, 'The Crisis of the Mind', pp. 102, 100.

15. Edward Said, 'Representing the Colonized: Anthropology's Interlocutors', *Critical Inquiry*, 15 (1989), 223.

16. Georg Lukács, *The Meaning of Contemporary Realism*, tr. E. Bone (London: Merlin Press, 1963), pp. 19-27.

17. T.S. Eliot, *Selected Essays* (London: Faber and Faber, 1951), p. 143. Referred to hereafter in the text as *SE*.

18. The model of artistic creation which is assumed here — the matching of 'emotions' and 'objects' — is informed by Eliot's reading of F. H. Bradley. Grappling with the problem of the split between subject and object attendant on the notion of Immediate Experience, Eliot came to the conclusion, in his doctoral dissertation on Bradley, that there is no such thing as consciousness independent of its object. See Richard Wollheim, 'Eliot and F. H. Bradley: an account' in Graham Martin, ed., *Eliot in Perspective* (London: Macmillan, 1970), pp. 169-93.

19. See Marc Manganaro, *Myth, Rhetoric and the Voice of Authority: A Critique of Frazer, Eliot, Frye and Campbell* (New Haven and London: Yale University Press, 1992).

20. See Max Jacob, 'L'Hamlétisme' in *Art Poétique* (Paris: Émile-Paul, 1922).

21. See Maud Ellmann, *The Poetics of Impersonality* (Brighton: Harvester, 1987).

22. T. S. Eliot, *Selected Poems* (London: Faber and Faber, 1974), p. 17. This edition is hereafter referred to in the text as *SP*.

23. See Valerie Eliot, ed., *The Waste Land: A Facsimile of the Original Drafts* (London: Faber and Faber, 1971), p. 27.

24. Quoted in B. C. Southam, *A Student's Guide to the Selected Poems of T. S. Eliot* (London: Faber and Faber, 1968), p. 33.

25. See Daniel Sibony, '*Hamlet*: A Writing-Effect' in Felman, ed., *Literature and Psychoanalysis*, pp. 53-93.

26. James Joyce, 'Gas from a Burner' in A. Norman Jeffares and Brendan Kennelly, eds, *Joycechoyce: The Poems in Verse and Prose of James Joyce* (Schull, West Cork: Roberts Rinehart, 1992), p. 45.

27. See Dominic Mangianello, *Joyce's Politics* (London: Routledge and Kegan Paul, 1980).

28. James Joyce, *Letters*, ed. Stuart Gilbert and Richard Ellmann, 3 vols (London: Faber and Faber, 1957-66), I, 55.

29. In *Joyce's Voices* (London: Faber and Faber, 1978), p. 53, Hugh Kenner defines the discourse of colonial Dublin as 'Pyrrhonism': 'a whole community agreed upon this one thing, that no one at bottom knows what he is talking about because there is nothing to know except the talk'.

30. Stephen borrows from popular 'reconstructions' of Shakespeare's biography, such as Maurice Clare's *A Day with William Shakespeare*. See Ellmann, *The Consciousness of Joyce*, pp. 59-61.

THE (PREGNANT) PRINCE AND THE SHOWGIRL: CULTURAL LEGITIMACY AND THE REPRODUCTION OF *HAMLET*

KATE CHEDGZOY

It's a wise child that knows its own father, but a wiser father that knows his own child.

This epigraph to Angela Carter's last novel, *Wise Children,*[1] is described as an 'old saw', and is thus located in a popular, collective, oral culture to which the notion of the name of the father as origin and guarantor of meaning is irrelevant. It foregrounds one of the themes of the novel: that paternity can never be more than a problematic hypothesis, or as *Ulysses* calls it, 'a legal fiction'.[2] The novel's deployment of textual and structural allusions to Shakespeare collapses together comedy and tragedy in a complex web which makes it impossible to ascribe originary authority to a single pre-text. *Hamlet* looms large, however, both at the level of allusion, and because for the late twentieth century, it constitutes — however anachronistically — the paradigmatic Shakespearean representation of the nuclear family which Carter's novel deconstructs. Moreover, the canonization of the Oedipal *Hamlet* embeds the play within modern Western culture's most powerful theory for thinking through familial relations: psychoanalysis. In this article, then, I will take the key themes of *Wise Children* as a starting point for a rereading of the historical vicissitudes of the Freudian and Shakespearean myths of the family which finally converge in Carter's text.

Wise Children is full of idealizations and misrecognitions of the relationship between father and child: misconceptions of authenticity and legitimacy which can offer a metaphor for Shakespeare's position as cultural father, source and guarantor of all that is finest in English literary history, which is both secure and ambivalent, unchallengeable yet grounded in the shakiest of foundations. The security of his pre-eminence is assured by the diffusion of his works and myth throughout the English-speaking world, supported by institutions as various as the Hollywood film industry and the National Curriculum in British schools. Yet this unparalleled cultural dominance has historically been accompanied by a certain unease as to whether Shakespeare is a sufficiently substantial figure to bear the great cultural burden placed on his shoulders. The contest over whether 'the man from Stratford' actually was the author of the plays ascribed to 'Shakespeare' is one version of this uncertainty about origins. Alternatively, Marianne Novy has recently argued that for the first century and a half or so of his *Nachleben*, Shakespeare was a curiously marginal, even feminized figure, stranded outside the patriarchal boundaries of high culture because he lacked a classical university education, worked in the relatively low-class form of drama, and broke many of the prescriptive rules favoured by neo-classicists.[3] How, then, did this shadowy and marginal figure come to occupy such a dominant position in English-speaking culture? Examining some of the various myths of cultural paternity which have accreted around 'Shakespeare' may make it possible to construct a symptomatic account of his protean and problematic centrality.

Harold Bloom's eccentric and influential book, *The Anxiety of Influence*,[4] constructs a father-son model of literary heritage from which Shakespeare is explicitly excluded. Bloom states that Shakespeare did not suffer from the anxiety of influence because he was the largest instance of 'the complete absorption of the precursor',[5] in that his chief precursor, Marlowe, was a lesser figure,[6] and because he was a dramatist, while Bloom's theory constructs lyric poetry as the central vehicle of poetic patrimony. Whether or not one agrees with these arguments, it is curious that Bloom only seems able to conceive of Shakespeare as a literary son, not a father. In this essay, I want to explore the possibility that Shakespeare has indeed been a crucial literary father figure, for artistic daughters as well as sons, but that nevertheless, Bloom is right to exclude him from his own agonistic schema, in that his paternal / poetic power has most often been experienced as benevolent and enabling.[7]

With or without Bloom's sanction, Shakespeare might have been seen as a disablingly powerful Oedipal precursor. Yet since the Restoration, his literary sons have demonstrated a remarkable ability to negotiate with his cultural power and appropriate it to their own ends. Restoration actor-manager and playwright Sir William Davenant did nothing to quash — and may have fostered — rumours that he was Shakespeare's illegitimate son, and used his dubious parentage to give his production of *Hamlet* an authority supposedly grounded in authenticity, converting illegitimate parentage into a sign of cultural legitimacy.[8] To quote the dazzling fantasia on Shakespeare in *Ulysses*, 'if the father who has not a son be not a father can the son who has not a father be a son?'[9] Davenant's career is paradigmatic of the empowering and troubling dimensions of male writers' figurations of Shakespeare as a literary father, locating *Hamlet* as a key symbol of the transmission from father to son of cultural authority.

William Davenant had succeeded Jonson as Poet Laureate in 1638, and remained loyal to the royalist cause throughout the Civil War period, occasionally staging private performances of plays for the exiled court. At the Restoration, his company, the Duke's Men, was one of the two recognized by Charles II. The rival company, the King's Men led by Thomas Killigrew, included many veterans of the pre-1642 stage, while Davenant's men were younger. He compensated for what might have been perceived as a disadvantage by deploying the trope of artistic sonship in order to capitalize on his company's belatedness. We cannot know how much credence was attached to it, but the rumour that Davenant was Shakespeare's illegitimate son was still in circulation as late as 1778, which suggests that even if untrue, it was felt to hold some significance or interest. The earliest written account is to be found in a manuscript note by John Aubrey dating from about 1681, which states that Davenant's father kept a tavern in Oxford, where Shakespeare supposedly stayed on his annual journey to Stratford, and 'was exceedingly respected' — particularly, it would seem, by the innkeeper's wife. According to Aubrey, Davenant would claim:

> that it seemed to him that he writt with the very spirit that Shakespeare, and was *seemed* contentented enough to be thought his Son: he would tell them the story as above. [In which way his mother had a very light report, whereby she was called a whore.][10]

Joseph Spence's *Anecdotes, Observations and Characters* cites a comment supposedly made by Pope, that the 'notion of Sir William Davenant being more than a poetical child only of Shakespeare, was common in town; and Sir William himself seemed fond of having it taken for truth'.[11] As well as allowing the rumour of his descent from Shakespeare to go unchecked, Davenant stressed the continuity of artistic succession, which contemporaries saw as an element in the Duke's men's success, as the account of their *Hamlet* given in *Roscius Anglicanus* indicates:

Sir *William* (having seen *Mr. Taylor* of the *Black-Fryars* Company Act it, who being
Instructed by the Author *Mr. Shakespeare* taught Mr. *Betterton* in every Particle of
it; which by his exact Performance of it, gain'd him Esteem and Reputation, Super-
lative to all other Plays. ... No succeeding Tragedy for several Years got more
Reputation, or Money to the Company than this.[12]

The virtue of Betterton's performance lies in the precision of his reproduction of the role as it was taught him by his artistic mentors, and as Gary Taylor points out, 'The questionable accuracy of such accounts matters less than
the evident importance of authenticity.' [13] The notion that an artistic son's
highest glory lies in memor(ial)izing his father echoes Hamlet's own repeatedly enjoined responsibility to remember his father, and to act on this
memory — a commitment which is itself imaged in literary terms:

> Remember thee?
> Ay, thou poor ghost, whiles memory holds a seat
> In this distracted globe. Remember thee?
> Yea, from the table of my memory
> I'll wipe away all trivial fond records,
> All saws of books, all forms, all pressures past
> That youth and observation copied there,
> And thy commandment all alone shall live
> Within the book and volume of my brain,
> Unmix'd with baser matter.

> (I. v. 95-104)

While Hamlet swears to make his mind a *tabula rasa*, inscribed only by
his father's desires, Davenant's Shakespearean sonship is constructed as
a palimpsest of mutually supportive genealogies. In a recent essay on
Hamlet and history, Francis Barker has warned that stressing the psychic
work of mourning and recuperation may serve to erase the historical difference and political valency involved in remembering the dead:

Hamlet must remember his father: this is recognisable from within more or less
modern liberal humanist perspectives where the emphasis on the authenticity of the
personal and the familial both masks and counters the social. It may be the *project*
of the text to remember the king, that major sign, still, in the play's world, of historical power. But the mourning of fathers ... becomes its dominant articulation.[14]

Barker's formulation seems to imply that the personal and familial are
somehow other than social, denying their imbrication in what he calls
historical power — as if history were the province only of kings, warriors,

lawmakers. But I would argue that one of the reasons so many later writers have felt obliged to negotiate with their Shakespearean patrimony by way of *Hamlet* is because the play reveals so precisely the interweavings of psychic and political structures by means of which our culture makes sense of the experience of being beholden to a father figure.

The extent to which Shakespeare could represent a distinctly anxiety-producing father figure is illustrated by the case of Dryden, who, *pace* Bloom, appears to have suffered from a classic version of the anxiety of influence, bizarrely triangulated via Davenant, with whom Dryden collaborated on an adaptation of *The Tempest*. In the preface to their version, published after Davenant's death, Dryden notes that the play *'was originally* Shakespear's: *a Poet for whom* [Davenant] *had particularly a high veneration, and whom he first taught me to admire'*.[15] In the verse prologue to the play, Dryden expresses how Shakespeare as artistic precursor entirely pre-empted and absorbed his followers:

> Shakespear, *who (taught by none) did first impart*
> *To* Fletcher Wit, *to labouring* Johnson Art.
> *He Monarch-like gave those his subjects law,*
> *And is that Nature which they paint and draw.*
>
> . . . .
>
> *If they have since out-writ all other men,*
> *'Tis with the drops which fell from* Shakespear's *Pen.*
>
> . . . .
>
> *But* Shakespear's *Magick could not copy'd be,*
> *Within that Circle none durst walk but he.*[16]

Davenant coped with this potentially disabling pre-eminence by appropriating it by means of the trope of reproduction: Dryden, seeking in *All for Love* to move beyond Shakespeare, is in a more imperilled position. This passage is curiously ambivalent about Shakespeare's poetic power, however, invoking the image of the untaught Shakespeare, a passive conduit for Nature's creative forces, at the same time as registering anxiety about his pre-emptive excellence. This neo-classical version of Shakespeare which stresses his 'native genius' while decrying his ignorance may be a way of dealing with the Oedipal threat. Perhaps this is what is at stake when Dryden, in the Preface to *All for Love*, says:

> I hope I need not to explain my self, that I have not Copy'd my Author servilely: Words and Phrases must of necessity receive a change in succeeding Ages: but 'tis

almost a Miracle that much of [Shakespeare's] Language remains so pure; and that
he who began Dramatique Poetry among us, untaught by any, and, as *Ben Johnson*
tells us, without Learning, should by the force of his own Genius perform so much,
that in a manner he has left no praise for any who come after him.[17]

Dryden as playwright constantly returns to Shakespeare, and in the context
of the repertoire of the Restoration theatre, there are good pragmatic reasons
for this. Nevertheless, the terms in which Dryden expresses his sense of cultural succession do seem to suggest that there is something more at stake; that,
like Hamlet, he is haunted by the ghost of his precursor. Shakespeare, according to Nicholas Rowe, gave 'the top of his Performance [as] the Ghost in his
own *Hamlet*'.[18] In the prologue to his adaptation of *Troilus and Cressida*,
Dryden has the ghost of Shakespeare — played by Betterton, the greatest
Hamlet of his age — say:

> *Now, where are the Successours to my name?*
> *What bring they to fill out a Poets fame?*
> *Weak, short-liv'd issues of a feeble Age;*
> *Scarce living to be Christen'd on the Stage!*[19]

A similar sense of paternal disappointment and filial frustration gives point
to a passage from the essay *Of Dramatick Poesie*:

> But it is to raise envy to the living, to compare them with the dead ... [Jonson,
> Fletcher and Shakespeare] are honour'd and almost ador'd by us, as they deserve
> ... Yet give me leave to say thus much, without injury to their Ashes, that not onely
> we shall never equal them, but they could never equal themselves, were they to rise
> and write again. We acknowledge them our Fathers in wit, but they have ruin'd
> their Estates themselves before they came to their childrens hands.[20]

There may be a general sense of cultural belatedness at work here, such as
afflicted many of Dryden's contemporaries, given that this statement is made
in the context of a dialogue which works through the competing claims of the
Ancients and Moderns. However, the image of the son dispossessed by the
father is surely significant.[21] It's interesting that Shakespeare, in this instance,
is one of a triumvirate of fathers, and it seems appropriate to invoke Marjorie
Garber's analysis of the multiplication of fathers in *Hamlet*:

> The more the father is idealized, the more problematic is the presence of doubt, the
> gap in certainty that instates paternal undecidability ... Hamlet finds both too many
> fathers and too few — he is too much in the son, but where is paternity, where is
> the law? ... [A]s in the case of the Medusa, where a multiplicity of penises is im-

agined to cover the unimaginable horror of no penis, of castration, so here the multiplicity of fathers covers the fact of lack.[22]

Restoration male playwrights' fantasies of Shakespearean artistic succession correspond to the Freudian concept of the family romance, in which the child casts into question the authenticity of its parentage, in order to be free to select parents which correspond more closely to its own idealized self-image.[23] The family romance is a function of the child's over-determined efforts to construct an identity in relation to its parents. The antagonistic nature of this enterprise generates feelings of ambivalence towards the parents, which in turn find expression in the form of day-dreams, in which the child replaces its parents with others of higher birth. When the child subsequently discovers the truth about sexual reproduction and realizes that, in Freud's words, '*pater semper incertus est*, while the mother is *certissima*',[24] the family romance is transformed. Henceforward, the child exalts the father, but no longer casts doubt on the maternal origin which is regarded as unalterable. If anything, the child's image of the mother is revised downwards, as s/he tries to picture situations which might have given her the opportunity for infidelity. The consequent over-valuation of the father and degradation of the mother, of which Shakespeare's supposed seduction of Davenant's mother is a particularly precise and vivid instance, is a formulation which crops up repeatedly in Freudian contexts. More than that, I would suggest that it is a precise diagnosis — if such a pathologizing term may be permitted — both of the structure of Hamlet's relations with his parents, and of the familial structure of Shakespearean artistic succession, from Davenant onwards. Marjorie Garber has suggested that the structure of cultural authority instantiated by the myth of Davenant's exalted parentage and Dryden's defensive invocation of Shakespeare's ghost remains the essential structure of the modern preoccupation with Shakespeare:

> The Ghost is Shakespeare. He is the one who comes as a revenant, belatedly instated, regarded as originally authoritative, rather than retrospectively and retroactively canonized, and deriving increased authority from this very instatement of authority backward, over time ... Shakespeare is for us the superego of literature, that which calls us back to ourselves, to an imposed, undecidable, but self-chosen attribution of paternity.[25]

Samuel Schoenbaum has suggested that Freud's own bizarre preference for the Oxfordian authorship of 'Shakespeare's' plays could be seen as a version of the family romance: given the crucial role played by Shakespearean texts, especially *Hamlet,* in the early formation of his theories, bourgeois Freud may have found it difficult to accept his intellectual father's humble origins.[26] By extension, it could be argued that Shakespeare has long embodied the idealized father of Western culture's collective family romance of its own past, which provides the structuring myth of the literary institution.[27]

*

I now want to skip forward a century or so, and consider the curious nineteenth-century phenomenon of the feminization of Hamlet, a product of the intersection of the post-Romantic revaluation of the tragic passions as being gendered feminine, with changes in the conditions of performance and the social and aesthetic role of the actress. The burgeoning discipline of Shakespearean literary criticism initiated the perception of Hamlet as somehow unmanly in the 1780s, while from 1776 to the beginning of the twentieth century more than fifty actresses played the role.[28] In this section, I shall explore the complex relationship between masculine cultural authority and the production of Hamlet as a liminal and feminized figure.

Sarah Siddons was the first actress recorded as playing Hamlet, in Birmingham in 1776; her career in the role lasted until 1802, and she was quickly joined by other actresses, among them Elizabeth Inchbald, who in her time was a noted Shakespearean critic as well as performer. Dozens of others followed during the nineteenth century and the early decades of the twentieth.[29] Reviewing the history of the phenomenon in 1911, William Winter speculated that actresses had been encouraged in their 'adventurous endeavour' by

> the critical assurance, which has been mistakenly urged, that the character is more feminine than masculine ... It was a bad day for 'the glass of fashion' when some misguided essayists began to call him 'feminine' and the ladies heard of it.[30]

Winter complains that many of the female Hamlets he had seen were 'affectedly and unpleasingly mannish'; it is predictable, given the rigidity of bourgeois gender roles in the nineteenth century, that while Hamlet's putative femininity may have been what made the role accessible to women, they were frequently charged with unbecoming masculinity. One of the more admired female Hamlets, the eminent American actress, Charlotte Cushman (a lesbian who enjoyed cross-dressing in real life), was somewhat euphemistically said to be 'endowed with a masculine port'.[31]

The most celebrated female Hamlet of the nineteenth century was undoubtedly Sarah Bernhardt. Unlike most of the other women who played the role, she made public play of the importance of gender ambivalence in her interpretation. When a *Daily Chronicle* reporter asked, 'Can any man quite grasp the inner nature of Hamlet?', she replied, 'Perhaps not. There is much that is feminine in it. It takes the brains of a man and the intuitive almost psychic power of a woman to give a true rendering of it.'[32] Scathingly witty accounts of the performance, by Winter and Max Beerbohm, attest to an artistic distaste on the part of critics which was strongly inflected by unease at the play made with gender, Beerbohm crushingly describing the performance as '*très grande dame*'.[33]

The motivation of the earliest female Hamlets must remain opaque, but what does seem clear is that women turned to the role at the moment when Romanticism began to construct an image of Hamlet as a man of exquisite — and therefore implicitly feminine — sensibility. The gendering of the experience and display of certain kinds of emotion is, of course, a culturally and historically specific phenomenon, and in Enlightenment Europe the equation of sensibility with femininity was canonical.[34] Henry Mackenzie's articles on Hamlet, published in the magazine *The Mirror* in 1780, constitute the *locus classicus* of this theme. In Mackenzie's account, Hamlet is characterized by 'an extreme sensibility of mind, apt to be strongly impressed by its situation ... a person endowed with feelings so delicate as to border on weakness, with sensibility too exquisite to allow of determined action'. It is precisely this feminine sensibility, says Mackenzie, which gives rise to 'that indefinable charm in Hamlet, which attracts every reader and every spectator'.[35] The same terms recur throughout the closing decades of the century, in essays by William Richardson, Thomas Robertson and, most famously, Goethe's evocation of a fragile soul unable to bear the responsibilities placed on it.[36] Coleridge, discussing the first scene of *Hamlet*, indirectly signals the power of this tradition in that he feels obliged to deny its relevance when he speaks of 'the language of sensation among men who feared no charge of effeminacy for feeling what they had no want of resolution to bear'.[37]

The feminine in Hamlet was most visible in the form of the actresses who played the role, but the notion had an influence on male actors' interpretations, too, as they sought to create a more intimate and expressive alternative to the declamatory acting style which prevailed, particularly in the American theatre. Edwin Booth (who later lent his costume to Charlotte Cushman) was said

by one commentator to be particularly suited to the role by virtue of the feminine qualities of his style: subtlety, tunefulness, gentleness and mobility.[38]
While Sarah Bernhardt's performance of Hamlet in 1899 was seen by many
to mark the end of an era in which the feminization of Hamlet had any hope
of being taken seriously, the emergence of psychoanalytic theory at the turn
of the century gave the concept a new valency. Whereas the Romantic and
Victorian eras had constructed Hamlet's putative femininity in terms of the
behaviour prescribed for bourgeois women — sensibility, gentleness, deli-
cacy, sweetness of temper — psychoanalysis locates its source in Hamlet's
unresolved pre-Oedipal attachment to his mother. In Freud's earliest accounts
of the Oedipus complex, in *The Interpretation of Dreams*, Hamlet is almost
as central to the concept as Oedipus himself. Initially, the main emphasis is
placed on Hamlet's rivalry with his father, but Freud's disciple Ernest Jones,
in 'A Psychoanalytic Study of Hamlet',[39] which draws heavily on the nineteenth-century construction of a feminized Hamlet, gives the first indication
of a shift of focus when he suggests that Hamlet's excessive devotion to his
mother 'impart[s] a strikingly tender feminine side' to his character.[40] Later,
Ella Freeman Sharpe, a colleague of Jones at the London Institute of Psychoanalysis, traced Hamlet's unconscious 'feminine identification' to textual
metaphors. In her 1929 essay, 'The Impatience of Hamlet', she points to Gertrude's description of the ostensibly melancholic Hamlet as being 'as patient
as the female dove', and notes that Hamlet himself dates the origins of his (in
this context suspiciously homoerotic) friendship with Horatio to the time
when 'my dear soul was mistress of her choice'.[41] A crucially symptomatic
text in this account is Hamlet's self-castigation for preferring effeminate
words to masculine action.[42]

> This is most brave,
> That I, the son of a dear father murder'd,
> Prompted to my revenge by heaven and hell,
> Must like a whore unpack my heart with words
> And fall a-cursing like a very drab,
> A scullion!

(II. ii. 578-83)

The Signet edition, which adopts the 'Good Quarto' reading, 'stallyon',
notes that 'stallion' means 'male prostitute', adding anxiously, 'perhaps
one should adopt the Folio reading, scullion = kitchen wench'.[43] Since
Hamlet has already likened himself to a whore and a drab, this is one

stable door which hardly seems worth shutting. Hamlet here represents himself as effeminized and degraded by his failure to fulfill his responsibilities to his father. Ella Freeman Sharpe connects this with another key text for the psychoanalytic account of *Hamlet* when she comments, somewhat cryptically:

> The 'prostitute', male and female, is rooted at the oral level, where mother and father are merged into one figure. 'My mother: father and mother is man and wife; man and wife is one flesh: and so, my mother.' [44]

The associations which these passages set up between negation of the Oedipal father's role and the degradation of female sexuality are key themes in recent psychoanalytic readings of the play. 'Man and wife is one flesh' is the title of the chapter on *Hamlet* in Janet Adelman's book, *Suffocating Mothers*. In Adelman's analysis,

> the character of Gertrude as we see it becomes for Hamlet — and for *Hamlet* — the ground for fantasies quite incongruent with it ... This [incongruence] is, I think, the key to her role in the play and hence to her psychic power: her frailty unleashes for Hamlet, and for Shakespeare, fantasies of maternal malevolence, of maternal spoiling, that are compelling exactly as they are out of proportion to the character.[45]

Adelman concurs with the argument advanced in Jacqueline Rose's influential essays on *Hamlet* in locating Gertrude at the heart of the dynamic which makes the play's representation of familial structures at once so compelling and so troubling.[46] The twentieth-century fascination with the Oedipal drama of *Hamlet* has become more preoccupied with the ambiguities of Hamlet's relationship with Gertrude than his presumed rivalry with his father, and thus has enabled feminist psychoanalytic criticism to interrupt the exclusively masculine model of cultural inheritance which I sketched earlier. For Adelman and Rose, *Hamlet* typifies a key trope of patriarchal culture: the construction of masculine subjectivity over and against the desired and feared maternal body. In their accounts, what gives the play its unique authority is its capacity to embody, while failing to diagnose or contain, this most powerful and troubling fantasy. *Hamlet* becomes a drama of liminality; of the inability to maintain boundaries between male and female, mother and son, self and not-self, life and death. These interventions have put the mother-son rather than father-son relationship centre stage. The danger is that in emphasizing the extent to which *Hamlet*'s representations of maternal sexuality are defensive fan-

tasies which reveal the discontents of Oedipal masculinity, they may serve
to reinscribe the mother as a troubling locus of cultural unease, and thus
reproduce the idealization of the father and disgusted repudiation of the
mother which has characterized the cultural history of *Hamlet.*

*

Finally, I return to *Wise Children*, where Hamlet's most celebrated soliloquy, one of the iconic moments of English culture, becomes a dance rou-
tine for identical twin sisters, dressed as bellhops and wondering whether
a parcel should be delivered to '2b or not 2b' (p. 90). Carter's novel is a
celebration of illegitimacy and low culture which at the same time exposes the damaging falsity of the categories and practices which make
such terms meaningful. 'Mother is as mother does' and 'a father is a mo-
veable feast' in this text where the politics of legitimacy are inseparable
from deconstructive play, and the cultural power of *Hamlet* is appropriated, made benign and lavished open-handedly on Shakespearean knight
and game-show hostess alike. *Wise Children* demonstrates the value of
creatively appropriating Shakespeare's most culturally powerful text in
order to show 'how thoroughly the legitimate and illegitmate worlds are
entangled ... in a country whose cultural life continues to be crippled by
a false distinction between "high" and "low".'[47]
    The subversive reinvention of Shakespearean families was a recurring
theme in Carter's fiction long before she wrote *Wise Children*. In *Nights at
the Circus*, the American journalist, Walser, loses his memory — and thus his
identity — as the result of a head injury when the circus train crashes in Si-
beria. Rescued by an escaped murderess and her lesbian lover, he is adopted
by a homosexual shaman and reborn into language when he drinks his father
/ mother / lover's hallucinogenic urine and is inspired to declaim, 'What a
piece of work is man!' (p. 238). Shakespearean allusions weave through the
novel, supporting the alternative family networks which the characters patch
together out of friendship, loyalty and need. As Lizzie, ex-prostitute, anarchist, and adoptive mother of navel-less trapeze artist Fevvers declares, 'We
dearly love the Bard, sir ... What spiritual sustenance he offers!' (p. 53). In
the collection *Black Venus*, two stories revolve around similar themes. The
role of Ophelia becomes a fatal reality for a struggling repertory actress in
'The Cabinet of Edgar Allan Poe', with the difference that this Ophelia is a

mother, rather than a daughter, and her death precipitates the Shakespearean dissolution of her family:

> Lovers of the theatre plied her hearse with bouquets: 'And from her pure and un-corrupted flesh May violets spring.' (Not a dry eye in the house.) The three or-phaned infants were dispersed into the bosoms of charitable protectors ... When shall these three meet again? The church bell tolled: never never never never never.

(p. 55)

More cheerfully, the story, 'Overture and Incidental Music for *A Midsummer Night's Dream*', is written from the point of view of the 'changeling boy' who becomes the cause of dissension between Oberon and Titania in that play, and whose lineage — 'it was all between my mother and my auntie wasn't it' (p. 66) — forces a reconsideration of what constitutes a family anyway. The juxtaposition within the collection of these two tales from Shakespeare both embodies the notion, commonplace in recent Shakespeare criticism, that the boundaries between comedy and tragedy are multiple and labile, and fore-shadows Dora's realization, in *Wise Children*, that 'comedy is tragedy that happens to *other* people' (p. 213).

Carter's revision of Shakespeare — in *Wise Children* and elsewhere — is frequently refracted through the work of other writers and artists who have engaged in the same enterprise: Brecht, Mendelssohn, Joyce, Marx, Freud. *Wise Children*'s flirtation with the hypothesis of paternity evokes Joyce's exploration of the same issue in the 'Scylla and Charybdis' episode of *Ulysses*, where Stephen Dedalus mediates his own encounter with Shakespeare via multiple literary fathers, and meditates on the possibility that '*Amor matris*, subjective and objective genitive, may be the only true thing in life. Paternity may be a legal fiction.'[48] Nevertheless, in Stephen's speculations on the 'apostolic succession, from only begetter to only begotten', it is the mother who is eliminated from the family, which is reconstructed as an exclusively masculine space where the capacity for procreation and literary creation are coextensive, as Buck Mulligan parodically notes:

> — Himself his own father, Sonmulligan told himself. Wait. I am big with child. I have an unborn child in my brain. Pallas Athena! A play! The play's the thing! Let

me parturiate!
He clasped his paunchbrow with both birthaiding hands.[49]

One of the epigraphs to *Wise Children* quotes Shakespearean actress Ellen
Terry's wistful comment, 'How many times Shakespeare draws fathers and
daughters, never mothers and daughters.' Carter transforms the patriarchal
family romance which provokes such an anxiety of origins in Stephen Dedalus by making the daughter's subjectivity central.

Wise Children is a self-consciously Freudian and Shakespearean family romance, the story of Dora Chance and, through her, of the four generations of
parents and children which compose the doubled — and doubly fictional,
doubly theatrical — Hazard and Chance families. Doubly theatrical: because
the families are split between the legitimate classical theatre, and the illegitimate, *declassé* world of music hall, song and dance, the movies — although
as the novel goes on it collapses the possibility of maintaining such a distinction between legitimate formal culture and illegitimate popular culture.
Doubly fictional: because within the fictional world of the novel, the history
of a family is represented as a fabulous romance which the participants tell
themselves as they go along. Carter twice invokes the notion of the family romance, in order to deconstruct the hegemony of the bourgeois nuclear family
which founds its legitimacy in biological succession and the name of the
father, replacing it with a carnivalesque family of elective affinities, a thing
of shreds and patches which has to be constantly and lovingly reinvented by
those who claim to be part of it. As Dora embarks on her tale, she celebrates
the memory of

> Our paternal grandmother, the one fixed point in our fathers' genealogy. Indeed,
> the one fixed point in our entire genealogy; our maternal side founders in a wilder-
> ness of unknowability and our other grandmother, Grandma, Grandma Chance, the
> grandma who fixed the grandfather clock, the grandma whose name we carry, she
> was no blood relation at all, to make confusion worse confounded. Grandma raised
> us, not out of duty, or due to history, but because of pure love, it was a genuine fam-
> ily romance, she fell in love with us the moment she clapped her eyes on us.

(p. 12)

The end of the novel brings the family Grandma Chance invented full
circle, as Dora and her identical twin sister Nora at the age of seventy-five
themselves become adoptive grandmas to twin foundlings, like them the
illegitimate offspring of the Hazard line. It's as well that Carter appends

a '*Dramatis Personae*' to her novel in five acts: this Shakespearean proliferation of twins, siblings, parents and children creates ample room for
confusion. As they push their newly acquired pramload home from their
father's hundredth birthday party — at which he has finally acknowledged them as his children — Nora ponders the fictions of paternity:

> 'D'you know, I sometimes wonder if we haven't been making him up all along',
> she said. 'If he isn't just a collection of our hopes and dreams and wishful think-
> ing in the afternoons. Something to set our lives by ... We can tell these little dar-
> lings here whatever we like about their mum and dad ... but whatever we tell them,
> they'll make up their own romance out of it.'

(p. 230)

The text records the pain of cultural exclusion and exile from the legitimate family; at the same time, it subverts the power structures which give rise
to family romances by revealing that the exceptional psychic power which the
father figure holds may be in an asymmetrical and unstable relation to both
familial and social structures. Melchior Hazard's symbolic power in Dora and
Nora's eyes, as the guarantor of their uncertain origins and the embodiment
of the legitimate culture from which they are excluded, is in excess of his representation as a largely absent and impotent figure. Until the final reconciliation at his hundredth birthday party, he refuses to support Nora and Dora
either financially or emotionally, while Saskia and Imogen, the twin daughters he acknowledges as his, were actually fathered by his own twin brother
Peregrine; the pregnancy which triggers his second marriage, to 'Hollywood
harlot' Daisy Duck, turns out to be 'a twinge of indigestion', and the end of
the honeymoon is the end of the marriage; his house burns down when a
Twelfth Night party is sabotaged by his daughter's insatiable sexual desire; his
attempt to make a Hollywood film of *A Midsummer Night's Dream* is a complete flop; and, as 'the twentieth century's greatest living Shakespearean', he
scores his biggest stage success in a musical burlesque called 'What You
Will'. Eventually, the reconciliation with their father enables Nora and Dora
to recognize to what extent he is the glorious but insubstantial creation of their
own family romance, and to understand that for the orphaned Melchior his
most cherished possession, the tattered cardboard crown which is the only
memento of his own parents' Shakespearean success, fulfilled much the same
purpose. In Dora's words, at the very moment when Melchior acknowledged

his paternity, the moment which seemed to offer the twins a guarantee of cultural and personal legitimacy, he

> looked two-dimensional ... too kind, too handsome, too repentant ... he had an imi-
> tation look, even when he was crying, especially when he was crying, like one of
> those great, big, papier-maché heads they have in the Notting Hill parade, larger
> than life, but not lifelike.

(p. 230)

Nora and Dora compensate for Melchior's inadequacies by doubling their
family romance, appropriating their uncle Perry as a father figure. The realization that, in Freud's words, *"pater semper incertus est "* — or as mother-
to-be Tiffany more succinctly puts it, 'there's more to fathering than fucking'
— is what triggers, in the classical Freudian family romance, the overvalu-
ation of the father and degradation of the mother. However, separating the assumption of the name of the father from biological paternity can cause more
problems than it solves. The Oedipal anxiety which the family romance seeks
to assuage is parodied by Melchior's reluctance to play Hamlet, for fear that
'the critics might think he wasn't half the man his mother had been' (p. 89)
— it was his birth that interrupted his mother Estella's dazzling career as a
Shakespearean hero on the nineteenth-century American stage, since 'a female Hamlet is one thing but a pregnant prince is quite another' (p. 16).

Wise Children, in a sense, is *Hamlet* without the prince, in that Carter takes
the structures of desire and loss which characterize that play's representations
of familial dynamics from the point of view of the son, and makes the
daughter's experience central to them. So Hamlet himself figures only as Melchior and Peregrine's dead mother, inheritor of the alternative female tradition of theatrical succession embodied by Sarah Siddons, Charlotte Cushman
and others. As in the short story, 'The Cabinet of Edgar Allan Poe', it is Ophelia who takes centre stage. Carter's Ophelia is Tiffany, 'the first Black in the
family', whose own father was 'here today and gone tomorrow' (p. 35), and
her mad scene is triggered by her own unplanned pregnancy and rejection by
her child's feckless father, Tristram Hazard (yes, one of *those* Hazards), host
of the game show in which she unpredictably co-stars:

There was a bit of wallflower stuck in her hair, over her ear, and her hands were full of flowers, daffs, bluebells, narcissi, she must have picked them out of the front gardens and the window boxes and the public parks.

(p. 43)

Like Ophelia, Tiffany sings distracted little songs which range from the meaningless to the indecent, distributes symbolic flowers, speaks in disjointed phrases which say more than she knows. Unlike Ophelia, though, Tiffany is a mother-to-be as well as a daughter, and when she strips off the T-shirt Tristram had given her, an epiphanic revelation of maternal presence is generated by her temporary madness:

It was a shock to see her breasts under the cruel lights — long, heavy breasts, with big dark nipples, real breasts, not like the ones she'd shown off like borrowed finery to the glamour lenses. This was flesh, you could see that it would bleed, you could see how it fed babies.

(p. 46)

In her representations of Tiffany and Estella, Carter inscribes the maternal subjectivity which Shakespeare's text occludes. Elaine Showalter has noted that Ophelia's 'visibility as a subject in literature, popular culture, and painting ... is in inverse relation to her invisibility in Shakespearean critical texts' — and indeed her relative marginality in Shakespeare's text.[50] Carter rewrites Ophelia to give her a way out of the madness caused by male rejection, representing her as a dungaree-clad, happily independent mother-to-be. Nora's question, 'if the child is father of the man ... then who is the mother of the woman?' (p. 224), is answered by the multiple voices of the novel's panoply of mothers who are also daughters, daughters who become — however belatedly or inappropriately — mothers. Leaving sons to fend for themselves, Carter puts the marginalized daughter's experiences and desires at the heart of the novel, and in the process subverts some of the more damaging myths of paternity and maternity. This gesture in itself cannot counter the patrilineal tradition of reproductions of *Hamlet*, which surely owes its pervasive influence precisely to its focus on sonship, which Freud calls one of the great myths of Western culture — Shakespeare's sons are, after all, the gatekeepers of cultural centrality. The very ambivalence of *Hamlet's* representations of sexual and familial relationships seems to have enhanced rather than diminished the myth's cultural power — as the existence of this essay testifies.

Nevertheless, Carter's challenge to the hegemonic accounts of cultural and familial legitimacy serves to clear a space for new voices, new visions of the family, which may offer the next generation of Chances a happier alternative to the tragi-comic histories of *Hamlet*'s family romances: "'We're both of us mothers and both of us fathers," [Nora] said. "They'll be wise children, all right'" (p. 230).

Notes

1. Angela Carter, *Wise Children* (London: Chatto and Windus, 1991). I shall also refer to *Nights at the Circus* (London: Chatto and Windus, 1984) and *Black Venus* (London: Chatto and Windus, 1985); further references to these works are in the text of the essay.

2. James Joyce, *Ulysses* (Harmondsworth: Penguin, 1969), p. 207.

3. Marianne Novy, ed., *Women's Revisions of Shakespeare* (Urbana: University of Illinois Press, 1990), p. 2.

4. (Oxford: Oxford University Press, 1973).

5. Bloom, *The Anxiety of Influence*, p. 11.

6. In contrast, Jonathan Bate has argued that the Bloomian schema *is* relevant to Shakespeare, but that Ovid was his key precursor. See Jonathan Bate, 'Ovid and the Sonnets: or, Did Shakespeare feel the Anxiety of Influence?', *Shakespeare Survey*, 42 (1989), 65-76.

7. Bate has explored one aspect of this process in his *Shakespeare and the English Romantic Imagination* (Oxford: Clarendon, 1986). Different perspectives are explored by contributors to *Women's Revisions of Shakespeare*, and in Peter Erickson's *Rewriting Shakespeare, Rewriting Ourselves* (Berkeley: University of California Press, 1991).

8. See Gary Taylor, *Reinventing Shakespeare* (London: Hogarth, 1990), pp. 13ff, to which my discussion of Davenant and Dryden's careers is indebted.

9. Joyce, *Ulysses*, p. 208.

10. This last sentence is scored through in MS. Quoted by E.K. Chambers, *William Shakespeare: A Study of Facts and Problems*, 2 vols (Oxford: Clarendon Press, 1930), II, 254.

11. Chambers, *Shakespeare*, II, 271-2. Chambers cites four other eighteenth-century references to the tale, the latest dating from 1749.

12. John Downes, *Roscius Anglicanus, Or an Historical Review of the Stage* (1708; New York: Garland, 1974), p. 21.

13. Taylor, *Reinventing Shakespeare*, p. 14.

14. Francis Barker, 'Which dead? *Hamlet* and the ends of history' in Francis Barker, Peter Hulme and Margaret Iversen, eds, *Uses of history: Marxism, postmodernism and the Renaissance* (Manchester and New York: Manchester University Press, 1991), p. 50.

15. John Dryden, *Works*, ed. Maximillian E. Novak, George R. Guffey and Alan Roper, 20 vols (Berkeley: University of California Press, 1956-89), X, 3.

16. Dryden, *Works*, X, 6.

17. Dryden, *Works*, XIII, 18.

18. Brian Vickers, ed., *Shakespeare: The Critical Heritage*, 6 vols (London: Routledge and Kegan Paul, 1974-81), II, 192.

19. Dryden, *Works*, XIII, 249.

20. Dryden, *Works*, XVII, 72-3.

21. In 'To the Right Honourable My Lord Ratcliffe', prefixed to *Examen Poeticum* in 1693, Dryden was still expressing his sense of his age's inferiority and belatedness *vis-à-vis* Shakespeare and Jonson. Similarly, in 1696, John Oldmixon called Shakespeare 'the Father of our Stage'. See Vickers, ed., *Shakespeare: The Critical Heritage*, II, 3, 62-3.

22. Marjorie Garber, *Shakespeare's Ghost Writers: Literature as uncanny causality* (New York and London: Methuen, 1987), pp. 133-4.

23. Sigmund Freud, 'Family Romances' (1909) rpt. in Angela Richards, ed., *On Sexuality* (Harmondsworth: Penguin, 1977), pp. 217-56. While the standard English translation calls the child 'he', I have preferred the somewhat inelegant 'its' or 's/he'. In German, the word for child — *das Kind* — is neuter, and the gender of the possessive pronoun is determined by the object of the phrase, not the subject. In Freud this unproblematic gender neutrality is disrupted, at the moment when the action that the family romance is motivated by produces a certain hostility towards the parents — a hostility which is differentiated according to the gender of the child.

24. Freud, 'Family Romances', p. 223.

25. Garber, *Shakespeare's Ghost Writers*, p. 176.

26. Samuel Schoenbaum, *Shakespeare's Lives* (Oxford: Clarendon, 1971), pp. 612-13.

27. A similar argument has been advanced by Terry Eagleton in 'The Crisis of Contemporary Culture', an unpublished paper given at the Glasgow University conference, 'Changing the Subject', 1 July 1992.

28. The definitive account to date of female Hamlets is given by Jill Edmonds, 'Princess Hamlet' in Viv Gardner and Susan Rutherford, eds, *The New Woman and Her Sisters* (Hemel Hempstead: Harvester, 1992), pp. 59-76. I am extremely grateful to Jill for her generous help with the present essay. Intriguingly, Charlotte Charke claims to have played the role of Hamlet in the late 1740s or early 50s — the precise date is not clear,

but the autobiographical narrative where she makes the claim was published in 1755. See Fidelis Morgan with Charlotte Charke, *The Well-Known Troublemaker* (London: Faber and Faber, 1988), p. 143.

29. J. C. Trewin, writing in the *Birmingham Post* in 1965, pointed out that the later performances tended to be in all woman/schoolgirl productions — or in one case, a one woman version of the entire play. Frances de la Tour gave an acclaimed performance in the 70s, and the spring of 1992 saw a London production with an all-female cast.

30. William Winter, *Shakespeare on the Stage* (New York: Benjamin Blom, 1911), pp. 427, 431.

31. *Illustrated London News*, 17 June 1899.

32. Cited by Edmonds, 'Princess Hamlet', p. 61.

33. Cited by Charles Shattuck, *Shakespeare on the American Stage*, 2 vols (Washington: Folger Shakespeare Library and Associated University Presses, 1976-87), II, 138.

34. On the cult of sensibility and its association with femininity, see Janet Todd, *Sensibility* (London: Methuen, 1986).

35. Henry Mackenzie, *Works*, 8 vols (Edinburgh: J. Ballantyne, 1808), IV, 375.

36. Cited in Horace Howard Furness, ed., *A New Variorum Edition of Shakespeare's 'Hamlet'*, 2 vols (London: J. B. Lippincott, 1877), II, 149, 272ff.

37. Cited in Furness, ed., *'Hamlet'*, II, 154.

38. E. C. Stedman, *Atlantic Monthly*, 1866, cited by Shattuck, *Shakespeare*, II, 136.

39. Ernest Jones, 'A Psychoanalytic Study of Hamlet'. Jones's study of *Hamlet* appeared in several versions between 1910 and 1949. I have drawn on the earliest version first published in the *American Journal of Psychology* (1910) rpt. in Jones's *Essays in Applied Psychoanalysis* (London: Hogarth Press and Institute of Psychoanalysis, 1923).

40. Jones, 'A Psychoanalytic Study of Hamlet', p. 48.

41. Ella Freeman Sharpe, *Collected Papers on Psychoanalysis* (London: Hogarth Press and the Institute of Psychoanalysis, 1950), p. 209.

42. On the historical association of loquacity with femininity, see Patricia Parker, 'On the Tongue: Cross-Gendering, Effeminacy, and the Art of Words', *Style*, 23 (1986), 445-65.

43. *Hamlet*, ed. Edward Hubler (New York: New American Library, 1963), p. 90.

44. Sharpe, *Collected Papers*, p. 212.

45. Janet Adelman, *Suffocating Mothers: Fantasies of Maternal Origin in Shakespeare's Plays, 'Hamlet' to 'The Tempest'* (New York and London: Routledge, 1992), p. 16.

46. Jacqueline Rose, '*Hamlet*, the Mona Lisa of Literature', *Critical Quarterly*, 28 (1986), 35-49; 'Sexuality in the reading of Shakespeare: *Hamlet* and *Measure for Measure*' in John Drakakis, ed., *Alternative Shakespeares* (London and New York: Methuen, 1985), pp. 95-118.

47. Unidentified reviewer from *The Guardian*, quoted in the 1992 Vintage paperback edn of *Wise Children*.

48. Joyce, *Ulysses*, p. 207.

49. Joyce, *Ulysses*, p. 208.

50. Elaine Showalter, 'Representing Ophelia: women, madness, and the responsibilities of feminist criticism' in Patricia Parker and Geoffrey Hartman, eds, *Shakespeare and the Question of Theory* (New York and London: Methuen, 1985), p. 78.

Nation and Culture

THE HAMLET PERPLEX: STANISLAW WYSPIAŃSKI'S 1904/5 ESSAY ON HAMLET

MICHAL KOBIALKA

Shakespeare's *Hamlet* opens with the question, 'Who's there?' Heiner Müller's *Hamletmachine* begins with the answer, 'I was Hamlet.'[1] This single line speaks and describes a complex network of both epistemological and ontological statements all of which refer to the concept of representation and the Self's desire / need to be represented. 'I was Hamlet', says the character from Shakespeare's play, who is now standing at the shore with his back to the ruins of Müller's Europe, talking with the serf BLABLA. Post-1968, the ruins of Europe are an appropriate setting for this drama about dreams that did not come true, about historic chances that have been lost and, finally, about the consequences of missed occasions painfully recorded in the 'Family Scrapbook'. 'I was Hamlet', says the actor who, after the show, puts Hamlet's face 'on the rack in the dressing room' before assuming her or his own identity. 'I was Hamlet', says the human being who will go home and 'kill the time, at one / with my undivided self'.

At the same time, 'I was Hamlet' draws attention to the multiple fragments of all Hamlets / actors / human beings who have played, play and will play this character in their particular spaces of representation defined by varying political, social, ideological and aesthetic parameters. *Hamlet* scholarship exposes the wealth and diversity of interpretations of the part — the Elizabethan Hamlet, the Romantic Hamlet, the Symbolist Hamlet, the Futurist Hamlet, the Existential Hamlet, the Our-Contemporary Hamlet. These various interpretations prevent us from constructing a composite picture of what and who Hamlet is. Indeed, every time the play has been staged since its first performance, the famous Shakespearean question, 'Who's there?' desperately reverberates in the air. In the dark corners of the stage and of our imagination, Hamlet assumes the shape of an ephemeral ghost that is constantly transforming in order to accommodate our desires, our questions, our order and our confusion. He is thus an image or a formless mass, containing in its borderless volume a limitless number of possibilities, that is forced into shape by interpreters desperately trying to delineate the contours of that which, I hope, will always remain unidentified and will refuse to answer Bernardo's question.

This essay will address some of the issues concerning the processes of forming ontological and epistemological boundaries around *Hamlet* and Hamlet that are positioned within a field of specifiable relationships rather than contexts. This field of specifiable relationships will be constructed here by Stanisław Wyspiański's 1905 essay on *Hamlet*. The essay will be discussed in terms of a discursive formation created by the author who attempted not only to displace the boundaries which defined *Hamlet* in turn-of-the-century Europe, but also to establish the new position and the new role of Hamlet with respect to the fine arts and society in general.

Polish stagings of *Hamlet* have a long tradition of imposing restrictive and restricting temporal and spatial boundaries upon Shakespeare's work, turning *Hamlet* into being a 'text' which is assigned both a location and a concrete shape. Notably, for more than two hundred years, Shakespeare and his plays have enjoyed an unrivalled significance in the Polish national repertory. His plays have been staged and restaged more often than those of any Polish playwright. One of the possible explanations of this prominence may be that, in post World War II Poland, for example, Shakespeare's plays were used as a medium through which theatre directors could freely express opinions otherwise challenged by censors. As Jan Kott indicates in *Shakespeare Our Contemporary*, Zawistowski's 1956 production of *Hamlet* in Kraków occurring a few weeks after the twentieth Congress of the Soviet Communist Party, was viewed by critics and audiences as a symbolic prediction of a new era in which order and freedom would prevail over the abuses of the Stalinist period.[2] Here, Hamlet stood alone against the system which, like floating lava, suffocated everything and everyone encountered in its way. The martyred Hamlet's place was taken by Fortinbras, whose arrival at the court was greeted with euphoria — a spotlight marked his movement to the throne, a 'strong-armed-man', who came to purge a rotten Denmark. Fortinbras thus became a model of the New Man who was not an intellectual, but a pragmatic force against the pressures, constraints and necessities of his new world. Such an interpretation of *Hamlet* not only made Shakespeare our contemporary, but reflected discussions concerning the future shape of Poland taking place outside the theatre.[3] Indeed, changes in the political climate in Poland, and especially the political changes of 1956, 1968, 1970 and 1989, altered the readings of *Hamlet*, the perception of its characters, and the words of forlorn heroes to mirror and contextualize the predicaments of *Realpolitik*.[4]

As Peter Brook suggests in the preface to *Shakespeare Our Contemporary*, Jan Kott's book and his salient analyses of select Polish productions of Shakespeare introduced both an entirely new dimension into Shakespearean criticism and the concept of 'Shakespeare-Our-Contemporary' to Europeans and Americans.[5] In eastern Europe, however, and especially in Poland, the very idea traces not to Kott but to Stanisław Wyspiański's 1904/5 essay on *Hamlet* where it emerged and acquired a very particular shape. In an important sense, this essay addresses ontological and epistemological dilemmas expressed in Müller's opening line by locating them within the space of the turn-of-the-century discourse about the political climate in Poland, the role and the function of the arts in general and theatre arts in particular, and about the actor-director creative relationship.

Stanisław Wyspiański (1869-1907) was a prominent Polish playwright, painter and stage designer whose creative work and theory of the 'monumental stage' granted him a permanent place in Polish theatre at the turn of the century.[6] Wyspiański's 1904/5 *Tragicall Historie of Hamlet Prince of Denmark by William Shakespeare, Read and Deliberated upon Anew by Stanisław Wyspiański* can be treated both as a statement about Polish theatre at the turn of the century and, as Leon Schiller suggests, as a guidebook to Wyspiański's own theory of theatre, acting and dramaturgy.[7] It was written as a response to Kazimierz Kamiński's request to provide him with some insights into the part of Hamlet that he was supposed to play.[8] The essay is dedicated to him and to Polish actors. Wyspiański's treatise envisions a world, like Hamlet's, of 'people living on the stage, who walk through the labyrinth called theatre, whose destiny both in the past and now is to serve as a mirror [held] up to nature, to show virtue her own feature, scorn her own image, and the very age and body of the time his form and pressure' (p. 3).

This dedication offers interesting clues about Wyspiański's attitude towards the theatre of his day. The essay is not directed to theatre historians or directors, but to the actors who lived at the turn of the century and who were also the most precise barometer of the tension between traditional and modern theatre aesthetics. It was they who had to find their way through a maze of co-existing and contradictory Naturalist and Symbolist theories of acting, performing and playwriting.[9] And this is why he chooses the actors as the sole recipients of his theory of theatre that shows affinities with, but ultimately cannot be incorporated into other theories of the period. Significantly, Shakespeare's *Hamlet* is selected as the medium through which this theory will be communicated.

Why does Wyspiański use Shakespeare and *Hamlet*? Wyspiański informs us that he did not read any critical commentaries, but used the text of the play to stimulate his own thinking processes.[10] He wants to deal with Shakespeare's *Hamlet*; that is, with those parts of *Hamlet* which were supposedly written by Shakespeare himself and with the Shakespeare who wrote *Hamlet*.[11] This idiosyncratic argument and the act of appropriation of the text merit further consideration. Wyspiański believed that Shakespeare altered, edited and completed plays which had been poorly constructed by other playwrights in order to salvage the world of thought and tragedy that was inadvertently blurred and obfuscated in Elizabethan revenge tragedy. *Hamlet* is read by Wyspiański as a record of this practice:

> [Shakespeare] starts to rewrite the play.
> His imagination flares up unblocked by the scene with the Ghost. He finishes the first act — writes more — the rest of the plot will follow the old one. Only the words will be changed.
> Suddenly, the idea comes to his mind.
> Should the Ghost triumph at the end of the play?
> Where does it come from?
>
> Shakespeare, the author-to-be of *Macbeth*, begins to doubt the nature of the Ghost; begins to question its words — his faith in it disappears — and a new faith wins over. He accepts that Satan and Wrong Doing are the Ghost's creators.
> And Shakespeare cannot follow the Ghost.
> He stops writing.
> But the part is too good to waste.
> So, why waste it? Shakespeare himself will play the part. It could be developed to present the actions of the Ghost. And because it appears throughout the play, the Ghost becomes important.

(p. 26)

As this quotation indicates, Wyspiański views Shakespeare's creative process as an act of a continuous negotiation between the text of the well-known legend, its inner logic and the space where all the events of the plot unfold. At the same time, this space is not simply a performance space, but an autonomous space whose topography is mapped out once it is in contact with history, the world of an artist's imagination and intellect. The characters in a play are, therefore, autonomous beings who manoeuvre through the labyrinth of their own reality located within and without the imaginations of a playwright or an actor.

Within the space of their representation, these beings are alive and are guided through its landscape by their free will. During a performance, the fate of these beings and their world move through a physical reality and leave their traces behind. Thus, a performance space is only a three-dimensional screen onto which their lives and world, which assume concrete contours in the mind of a playwright, are projected and deciphered with the help of the actors:

> Every time [Shakespeare] was writing, describing the events, he had a concrete reality in mind. And this is why such things as doors, windows, the shape and the division of rooms in a palace or a castle, were in agreement with architectural designs and the logic of actual buildings.

> (p. 11)

This does not mean that Shakespeare's plays performed four hundred years later should be staged without a set. Wyspiański's target here is the antiquarian or the turn-of-the-century tradition of ornamental theatre claiming to reconstruct in detail the place of the stage action. He expressly notes that it is impossible to reconstruct visually the text created by a playwright or to establish the relationship between the legend, the playwright's rendering of it and his physical reality. Consequently, while staging Shakespeare now, in order to stay faithful to the logic of Shakespeare's creative process, one ought not to raise on stage the façades of Elizabethan buildings; but to locate the play within the frames of the existing buildings, that is, buildings where the logic of an architectural design will correspond to the logic of Shakespeare's text:

> We know as much about Elsinore as Shakespeare did when he was writing *Hamlet*, that is, we have no idea what Hamlet's castle looked like. ... Did Shakespeare know anything about architectural styles? Maybe he did, but this is of no interest to us. Every time he accessed his imagination, however, Shakespeare found a real style and once he chose it, he kept its image. ...
> And so, for example, if this tragedy were to be staged in Kraków, one needs to find a castle where such a tragedy could take place.
> What castle? Where can one find a castle where the Ghost of a king lingers around a tower, where the stars appear on the horizon and the clock strikes the hour...?

> Where can one find a gallery measured for hours by the steps of Prince Hamlet, a
> melancholy boy carrying a book in his hand?
> Do you see him? He is there. He is walking through the upper gallery of the Jagiel-
> lonian Royal Castle.
>
> (p. 14)[12]

These statements concerning the process of writing a play and its location
bring to mind the Symbolists' desire to abandon the Positivist practice of imposing temporality upon human beings and objects, and, instead, to pass
through a threshold into the unknown world of the Other. How this passage
towards the Other could be accomplished is considered in, for example, Sté-
phane Mallarmé's aesthetic of drama as the expression and revelation of inner
life.[13] Similarly, Maeterlinckean devices used in his early dramas such as
Home and *The Intruder* seek to bring forth onto the stage images of inner consciousness,[14] while the experiments envisioned by Alexander Scriabin or Tadeusz Miciński, who were inspired by the example of 'total theatre', represented attempts to stage the Other by establishing playing areas for their
dramas outside traditional theatre buildings.[15] While discussing Shakespeare,
Wyspiański, as did the Symbolists, implies the existence of an ideal world of
drama that is populated by real human beings. An artistic creativity and a theatrical representation allow us to enter this world. Accordingly, both playwrights and actors do not conceive the characters, but are mediums through
which these characters can reveal their identity and their truths to a world beyond their own. The character's existence does not depend upon an interpretation within the confines of a literary / artistic trend or an acting style; these
can only appropriate the character, shape it with the help of the tools at the
disposal of playwrights or actors, silence it and produce a false image.

Wyspiański suggests that the way to avoid the conventional theatre's procedures of intervention is to probe the network of relationships established
among the characters and between them, and the action registered by the
playwright. To substantiate this claim, he focuses upon the analysis of the
structure of *Hamlet*, posing questions about the nature of the characters. First
there is Hamlet. Why, for example, does Hamlet want proof of the existence
of a ghost?

> Hamlet reads Montaigne.
> Shakespeare reads Montaigne and makes notes in the margin.
> Hamlet and Shakespeare add to Montaigne by incorporating their own thoughts

and ideas, because they are intellectually on a par with him.
This will explain why Hamlet and, by extension, the court and Horatio, needed to
be educated.
Consequently, the court leaves the boundaries into which it was squeezed [by tradi-
tion] and becomes Shakespeare's and Montaigne's contemporary.

(p. 16)

The 'squeezed' court is Wyspiański's metaphor for how the courtiers as
well as Ophelia and Horatio were presented in the ur-*Hamlets* of Saxo Grammaticus, Belleforest and Kyd. For example, Saxo Grammaticus' Ophelia-
courtesan becomes a naive and noble woman in Shakespeare's play, while
Horatio assumes the function of the pedagogue from Greek mythology. Only
Polonius, the character from the traditional theatre where he was called Cor-
ambis, is the same. While these characters are reduced to foils to Hamlet, re-
taining only traces of their past characteristics and identities, Hamlet is supposed to bridge the gap existing between the two worlds, between past and
present. This explains, asserts Wyspiański, why Hamlet is usually played
badly in the theatre:

Should Hamlet be a university student?
Should Hamlet be a prince driven by a desire for the crown?
Should Hamlet be a philosopher, who does not care for the crown with which he
would not know what to do or for the power bestowed upon him?
Should Hamlet be an artist, a philosopher, a doctor of souls, and a judge of human
nature?
Is Hamlet's duty to reform the world and the governments which are run by ignoble
people? ...
Is Hamlet bereft of will and a need for action? ...
Whoever interprets Hamlet, and s/he could not play the part without interpreting
it, plays Hamlet badly,
because neither of these Hamlets embraces the wholeness of Hamlet, a character
who has been evolving from the traditions of each century since Shakespeare.
Is this the actor's fault?

(pp. 24-5)

Wyspiański answers this question by saying that the reason that Hamlet is
played poorly is because nobody has ever considered the possibility that
Hamlet is two characters: one who believes in ghosts and who belongs to the
old tradition, and another who abandons the paradigms of old cosmology and

who, 'like Holbein, reads human souls and faces and shows these features in a painting' (p. 27).

Shakespeare's desire to maintain the old legend and the Ghost forces him, notes Wyspiański, to modify the legend:

> How to change that? Forget the Ghost? Destroy Beauty? Holy theatrical tradition? Destroy the legend?
> Why? But all can be discovered without the Ghost.
> How?
> Through the works of the mind.
>
> (p. 26)

Intellect will thus be the weapon of a new Hamlet who will rely upon logic to understand events rather than upon messages from the world beyond, the world of the legend. Shakespeare's tools are a travelling troupe of actors, a portrait in Gertrude's chamber, and a churchyard. The actors play *The Murder of Gonzago* in front of the 'actors' who committed a similar crime. Hamlet stares at an illusionary image of his father in Gertrude's bedroom, an image as illusionary as the Ghost who appears to him. In the churchyard, Hamlet is faced with a heap of broken images of the human body reminding him of death and, by negation, of the essence and the value of life. According to Wyspiański, these three scenes counterbalance the traditional theatres of Polonius and their 'tragedy, comedy, history, pastoral, pastoral-comical, historical-pastoral, tragical-historical, tragical-comical-historical-pastoral, scene individable, or poem unlimited' (II. ii. 392-6).

As a result, the play which emerges is, like its title character, dual:

> Hamlet believes in the Ghost and trusts him; this probability is established in Act I.
> Hamlet does not know anything about the Ghost, unconsciously hates his uncle, and the Actors are brought in by Providence; this different probability is also established in Act I. In this scenario, the Ghost would not appear at all.
> And now, a compromise.
> Let the world of the legend be THE NIGHT.
> THE DAY will disperse the thoughts and oaths of the night; they will lose their power.
>
> (p. 50)

The play of the night and the play of the day each has its own individual logic. Hamlet is the only character who is able to transgress the boundaries between the two worlds. He will follow the logic of the night which vanishes during the day. Conversely, he will follow the logic of the day which vanishes during the night. How can any actor play Hamlet well? How will the audience be able to follow the changes between the night and the day?

Like other Symbolists, Wyspiański wanted his actors and the audience to participate actively in the creation of the stage reality. Describing his own reaction to the actors he saw on stage, he demands that the audience be conscious of the power of truth of this 'other' world that transcends theatrical illusion:

> It happened often that I was backstage and visited the actors in their dressing rooms. I am on stage: in the courtyard of Macbeth's castle in Inverness. There are people scattered around. Bright lights.
> The curtain is down. I can hear the music played on the other side.
> Everyone is in a hurry. Soon, the play will begin.
> And suddenly, Lady Macbeth enters and walks towards me.
> Her walk is bold, stable, and energetic; — she must have reached a decision.
> She has just received a letter about Duncan's arrival.
> I have immediately removed my hat and kissed her hand.
> I kissed Lady Macbeth's hand. Nobody will convince me that this was not Lady Macbeth, but Modrzejewska.

(p. 31)[16]

Structurally, the double nature of the play is evident in both its division into different places of action as well as in its logical arrangement of scenes. Wyspiański reconstructs the events and places them in the following chronological sequence: (1) Horatio sees the Ghost; (2) Horatio informs Hamlet about the phantom; (3) Laertes's farewell to his father and sister; (4) Hamlet meets the Ghost; (5) Polonius spies on Hamlet; (6) Polonius informs the King about Hamlet's madness; the actors arrive at the court; (7) Claudius and the courtiers spy on Hamlet; (8) the Actors' performance; (9) Claudius's prayer; (10) Hamlet meets with Gertrude; (11) the courtiers look for Polonius's body; (12) Hamlet meets the courtiers; (13) Claudius sends Hamlet off to England; (14) Hamlet's journey; (15) Laertes returns to Elsinore; (16) Horatio receives a letter from Hamlet; (17) Claudius convinces Laertes to revenge his father's death; (18) Ophelia's funeral; (19) the epilogue. However, not all the episodes can be arranged according to this pattern. The probabilities established in I. i., in the dialogue between Horatio and Marcellus, for example, indicate that the play should finish with a duel between Hamlet and Fortinbras to parallel a similar duel between their fathers.[17] The ending of the play, however, does not conform to the original plan set up in the first act.[18] The closing minutes of the tragedy thus provide additional support for Wyspiański's assumption that Shakespeare's *Hamlet* is a compilation of two separate texts: a traditional revenge tragedy and a modern Elizabethan drama. Only such an interpretation can adequately explain the presence of Fortinbras at any point in the play, actions like V. i. (the churchyard scene), where Hamlet's existential speech concerning life and death answers questions asked by Horatio in a previous scene,[19] or IV. v., where the return of Laertes is celebrated by the crowd pronouncing that "'Laertes shall be king'" (IV. v. 106), words which should be directed to Hamlet, the legitimate heir to the crown.[20]

Wyspiański's juxtaposition of Shakespeare and *Hamlet* with other playwrights of the Elizabethan period and with older texts allows Wyspiański, creator of a new type of drama, to conceive of the Elizabethan playwright as someone who also lived and worked in a transitional period. That is to say, both Shakespeare and Wyspiański wrote at the time of the shift between the old and new traditions, and their plays expressly reflected this change in the perception of the artists' role in their societies.[21] Wyspiański used Shakespeare to express his own doubts concerning the turn-of-the-century old theatrical tradition and to present a new model of ideal theatre arts.

This model cannot, however, adequately function without actors. It should be remembered that the essay is dedicated to them and that it was inspired by conversations about the creation of Hamlet with a Polish actor, Kazimierz Kamiński. Actors, for Wyspiański, are the leading force behind the theatre reforms; new concepts, new styles and new ideas are introduced not by directors or designers, but by actors. They are the most immediate factor that will decide whether theatre and art in general will play a significant role in the life of a nation. Therefore, if *Hamlet* were to be an epitome of an ideal theatre art and Hamlet a medium through which the ideals were to materialize on stage, both the text and the character would require actors who could incorporate all these new elements into their craft.

This brings Wyspiański to the analysis of the relationship between a playwright, a character that he creates and an actor. He perceives Shakespeare as a man who was not only familiar with the drama of his day, but, more importantly, with the actors who lived backstage and acted on stage. He wanted to breathe into them the life they led outside the theatre walls, to give them gestures and words that existed in everyday situations and to bring into focus the fundamental questions about existing and acting as exemplified by Iago's curious words, 'I am not what I am.'[22] Wyspiański develops this thought in his analysis of Shakespeare's theatre-within-theatre. The famous classification of dramatic styles enumerated by Polonius is contrasted with art:

> whose end, both at the first and now, was and is to hold as 'twere the mirror up to nature; to show virtue her own feature, scorn her own image, and the very age and body of the time his form and pressure.

> (III. ii. 21-4)

By so doing, Shakespeare, says Wyspiański, wanted the actors to be a living chronicle of the time and, as the play shows, an instrument of torture that would make the murderers reveal their crimes. Similarly, contemporary actors playing *Hamlet* are engaged in a double process. On the one hand, they enter the world of characters and bring them forth onto the stage. They do not become the characters they play, however. Rather, they are engaged in a dialectical relationship by struggling with the problems facing both the actors and the characters. As the above quoted passage indicates, Modrzejewska, who enters the stage, does not become Lady Macbeth by ceasing to be herself. She is simultaneously Lady Macbeth and Modrzejewska. On the other hand, the image of Lady Macbeth will have to be transformed by the actor who sees the character through the prism of the character's problems, brought to light through the actor's commentary about her / his life here and now. This dialectical relationship is established in a performance space where the world of the legend / characters overlaps with the world of the actors. This is why Wyspiański devotes much of his essay to the description of Hamlet's part and his role in the play.

Wyspiański is interested neither in Hamlet's psychology nor the ideology of the play, but in exploring possible positions and functions of the character. They can only be derived from the play itself; that is, from the plot, the arrangement of the episodes, and the relationships between the *dramatis personae*. This method of analysis breaks away from traditional turn-of-the-century historical-literary analysis of a dramatic text which was frequently subordinated to the personality of the actor creating the part. Instead, Wyspiański focuses upon particular scenes and tries to place them in context. This analysis of Shakespeare's *Hamlet*, read as the combination of an old tradition of legends / ghosts with a new Hamlet who follows the rules of intellect,

strives to help actors to construct a dialectical model of character behaviour
for any role. In the essay, he presents concrete analyses of particular scenes
followed by a meticulous study of the inner actions of an actor as perceived
by a spectator. 'Suit the action to the word, the word to the action' (III. ii. 17-
18) becomes the ruling principle in Wyspiański's method for indicating the
relationships between words and action, and for generating actions from
words, as this example from the text reveals:

> Ophelia
> (ashamed)
> (covers her eyes with hands)
> (lowers her hands and folds them to say a prayer before Hamlet)
> Hamlet
> (with a stern voice)
>> Be all my sins remembered
> (aside)
>> so you can mention them to the king.
> Ophelia
> (after a long pause)
> (she does not know what to say)
>> How does your honour for this many a day?
> Hamlet
> (with a stern voice)
>> Well, well, well,
> (with pride so his words can counteract his actions)
>> I humbly thank you.
> (turns his head, looks in the opposite direction).

> (pp. 164-5)

Another aspect of Wyspiański's analysis of *Hamlet* is the attitude of an
actor towards his character. It is not enough, however, to understand the logical arrangement of the episodes in a play and to generate actions suiting the
words. The most important element in role creation to Wyspiański is the emotional / mental attitude of the actor. The interpretation of a text should correspond to an actor's ability to create, to express truth, since truths expressed by
characters are the same as the ones expressed by the actors / people of the
theatre in everyday situations. In his text, Wyspiański defines the correspondence between lines / gestures and mental interpretation. The scene between Hamlet and Osric, for example, reads:

Hamlet

Sir, his definement suffers no perdition in you;	Laertes's virtues enumerated by you are only his virtues in your eyes; thus you are his equal

though, I know, to divide him inventorially would dizzy the arithmetic of memory

(points to his head to indicate an abnormal behaviour)

and yet by yaw neither, in respect of his quick sail ...	and only would show his low standing.

(lowers his hand)

Osric

(perceiving Hamlet's hesitation, Osric realizes that Hamlet mocks him; however, does not dare to interrupt the Prince)

Hamlet

(raises his hand)

But in the verity of extollment, I take him to be a soul of great article	describing Laertes, I see him as a person not worth my attention.

(pp. 146-7)

Such an analysis of character and attention to building a scene closely parallels what Stanislawski would later express as the core of his philosophy in *Building a Character*: that emotional involvement with and a psychological link between an actor and a character could be achieved through a transformative magic 'if'. Wyspiański, however, goes further than Stanislawski in his speculation. For him, the psychological link between actor and character is not merely a technique which will yield a realistic image of the world and reflect a Positivist organic link between body and mind, or to establish a link between actor and character. The naturalistic magic 'if' transformation is, therefore, an attempt to establish a correspondence between the life of an actor and that of a character;

hence, it would always be false and artificial. Rather, he argues, an actor can only present herself or himself, and thus present her or his own life in the process of intersecting with the life of a character. The consequences of an act on stage will be felt in the actor's life outside the theatre. In an important sense, Iago's words lose their ambiguity here, because Wyspiański equates the truth in *life* with the truth in *theatre*:

> Truth inside a man enables him to perceive truth on other people's faces. Hamlet is truth, and, thus, can perceive lies and judge. Shakespeare could see that and, therefore, makes the actors be the judges.

(p. 20).

Both theatre and life are, for Wyspiański, grounded in honesty and truth rather than in conventions and exaggeration, in holding the 'mirror up to nature; to show virtue her feature, scorn her own image, and the very age and body of the time his form and pressure' (III. ii. 22-4). This parallel drawn between art and life, and the visionary perception of art as the only authentic form of life, bestow upon the actors an entirely new function: to destroy Polonius's theatre of false pretence and to bring to the fore what Wyspiański calls:

> the Fate of Human Beings, those people who became the subject of tragedy. They were born in legend or in the minds of the creator. They came alive and had their own will. Their will was everything. The stage was used to show them. This was the function of the stage. 'Speak the speech, I pray you, as I pronounced it to you.' Shakespeare was an artist … When he was writing … he had certain reality in mind and his characters lived in his mind; were placed on the map of reality so well known to Shakespeare. He wanted to give [his characters] true gestures — those gestures which did not exist on stage but in real life … meaningful words — those words which did not exist on stage but in real life.

(pp. 9-11)

This equation of art with life, as Wyspiański demonstrates in his essay, has far-reaching repercussions. An actor in a performance, as a character in a play, becomes the carrier of a certain fundamental truth concerning human existence. Consequently, the tragedy of a triad, Hamlet / actor / human being, stems from the fact that Hamlet, the actor, and people generally live under certain conditions which are fully determined by history and historical momentum. All one can do, therefore, is to maintain one's dignity and try to understand the influences moulding one's fate. This is why the play does not end with the inevitable duel between Hamlet and Fortinbras, but with a different kind of a duel, one which led to the 'casual slaughters' that were not at all an act of vengeance instigated by the Ghost, but rather the direct outcome of the clash between Claudius and Hamlet. Wyspiański uses Shakespeare's text to point out that: (1) Hamlet / actor / human being can only defend, and has the right to defend, his own wrongs, not those of his father (thus there will be no fight between the two Princes); (2) Hamlet / actor / human being punishes only those crimes which he sees happen; and (3) sons are not responsible for the deeds of their fathers, since their own actions are 'now — and at no other time / now and here — and nowhere else' (p. 157).

Hamlet's actions interpreted according to such a model become the actions of an actor/human being who is destined to free a 'Denmark' from injustice and crime. The history of the Prince of Denmark described by Wyspiański becomes, in short, the history of Poland. And if this tragedy were to be staged in Poland, one needs to find a castle where such a tragedy could take place — the Jagiellonian Royal Castle. Indubitably, this is Hamlet who lives at the Wawel, the castle of the Polish kings in Kraków. This is Hamlet who thinks about history in terms of the wheel of Fortune. The *action* of the father forces the son, in turn, to take action, a pattern which corresponds to the lives of Poles under the tutelage of slavery. In order to be free, however, both he and they must perform the actions which are demanded by their own histories:

> Play Hamlet anywhere you want to in Poland. Everywhere your words of wrong-doing, falseness, and injustice will mean wrongdoing, falseness, and injustice, and will demand and cry for vengeance. Unless . . . unless you cannot see who this villain, scoundrel, and murderer is.
>
> (p. 98)

Wyspiański argues that 'what there is in Poland to think about, is the problem of the production of Shakespeare and of that Shakespeare who wrote *Hamlet*' (p. 97). The Polish playwright can draw such a conclusion because his ideal theatre, built upon his analysis of both the acting and the meaning of *Hamlet*, corresponds to his concept of theatre as the sanctuary of the soul, 'a temple in which people pronounce judgements on themselves, in which they seek their own Truth, in which they behold in the magic mirror of the poet the countenance of their souls' (p. xxxii). Similar statements notwithstanding, Jan Kott implies that Wyspiański's analysis of *Hamlet* cannot be perceived as universal, because it only makes one aware of 'deadly issues' in turn-of-the-century Poland, because Wyspiański's perception of Shakespeare, makes Shakespeare Wyspiański's contemporary, but not ours.[23] Paradoxically, from the perspective of nearly thirty years since Kott's publication, the same argument can be made about both Kott's perception of Shakespeare and Peter Brook's analysis of Kott.

Historically, Wyspiański's essay on *Hamlet* has had a notable impact on both acting and the productions of Shakespeare. The essay inspired, for example, 1908 and 1912 productions of *Hamlet* in Łódź, a translation and staging of IV. iv. by Miciński at a Shakespearean conference in Lwow (this scene, in translation, directs attention to the importance of Fortinbras who, prior to Wyspiański's essay, was traditionally omitted in Polish productions), a 1946 production in Opole, a 1960 production in Gdańsk and a 1971 production in Szczecin (staged at the castle of the Pomeranian Princess). The essay, and especially Shakespeare's / Wyspiański's perception of the actor and of theatre, are reflected in the Reduta Theatre's manifesto of 1919, while parts of Wyspiański's essay were performed in Grodno in 1940, in Kraków (Teatr Rapsodyczny) in 1942, in Siedlce (Szkoła Krawiecko-Gospodarcza) in an underground performance in 1943, in Warszawa (Teatr Polski) in 1947 and (Klub Krzywe Koło) in 1957, in Opole (Grotowski's Teatr Laboratorium) in 1964, in Bydgoszcz (Teatr Polski) in 1969, in Kraków (Klub Pod Jaszczurami) in 1970 and in Łódź (Teatr Nowy) in 1975.

More importantly, however, Wyspiański's essay on *Hamlet* displaced the traditional boundaries which had defined the scope and the nature of Shakespearean studies in turn-of-the-century Poland. His analysis of the scene arrangement, of the probabilities established in Act I and of the characters established the new position and the new function of Hamlet / actor / human being in the space where they are being represented. At the same time, it indicates that *Hamlet*, as written by Shakespeare and analyzed by Wyspiański, can simultaneously be read as an abstract and a brief chronicle of any time and a particular time, of any space and a specific space, where our lives and the shadows we cast into the past founder together.

'Who is there?' 'I was Hamlet', says the character who is to bridge the gap between the world of the night and the world of the day. 'I was Hamlet', says the actor who has joined the ranks of all the actors who have played, play and will play the part. 'I was Hamlet', says the human being who lives here and now. As Shakespeare, Wyspiański, Kott and Müller indicate, 'I was Hamlet' is thus both an answer and non-answer to the original question, since 'Hamlet' will always escape the closure of representation and remain a perplex to accommodate our field of specifiable relationships where the Ghost of the human being acquires political, social, ideological and aesthetic contours.

Notes

1. Heiner Müller, *Hamletmachine and Other Texts for the Stage*, ed. Carl Weber (New York: Performing Arts Journal Publication, 1984), p. 53.

2. See Jan Kott, *Shakespeare Our Contemporary* (London: Methuen, 1967), p. 54.

3. For a detailed discussion of this production, see Kott, *Shakespeare*, pp. 47-60.

4. Having broken away from Marxist interpretations and having moved away from the post-1956 euphoric readings of the play, Polish directors used *Hamlet* to record the changes happening in the country. The return of a pro-Russian policy in the late 1950s led Babel, Aleksandrowicz and Holoubek to believe that Poland's post-war history followed the stringent rules and dogmas of *Realpolitik*. A new regime was therefore seen as incapable of introducing anything truly new and meaningful. The old system simply perpetuated itself. Rather than allowing themselves to be placated with illusions about the creation of national heroes, these directors returned to the analysis of Hamlet as an individual and as a representative of their generation. Hanuszkiewicz's 1970 production of *Hamlet* exemplified a shift in the Polish tradition of thinking through Shakespeare and the history of the Prince of Denmark. Hanuszkiewicz focused his attention on the questions about Hamlet's identity rather than about his political dilemmas. The actors did not wear make-up or period costumes. They moved around in a hermetically sealed box whose walls could move forward or backward, giving an impression of a loop loosened or tightened by a hangman. The productions staged in the 1980s reflected the existing chaos in the world of Elsinore (Warmiński's post-martial law *Hamlet*) or the self-reflexive nature of Hamlet's world (as demonstrated in Wajda's 1989 *Hamlet, IV*). For a more detailed account see Andrzej Żurowski, *Myślenie Szekspirem* (Warszawa: Instytut Wydawniczy PAX, 1983).

5. Peter Brook effuses that 'Shakespeare is a contemporary of Kott, Kott is a contemporary of Shakespeare — he talks about him simply, first-hand, and his book has the freshness of the writing by an eyewitness at the Globe or the immediacy of a page of criticism of a current film. To the world of scholarship this is a valuable contribution — to the work of the theatre an invaluable one.' See Kott, *Shakespeare*, p. x.

6. See, for example, Tymon Terlecki, *Stanisław Wyspiański* (Boston: Twayne Publishers, 1983); Julian Krzyżanowski, *History of Polish Literature* (Warszawa: Państwowe Wydawnictwo Naukowe, 1978), pp. 501-12; and Alicja Okońska, *Stanisław Wyspiański* (Warszawa: Państwowe Wydawnictwo 'Wiedza Powszechna', 1991), for biographical information and critical analysis of Wyspiański's works.

7. Stanisław Wyspiański, *Hamlet* (Wrocław: Zakład Narodowy im. Ossolińskich, 1976), p. xv. All page numbers in this essay refer to page numbers in the volume. All the translations are mine.

8. Kazimierz Kamiński (1865-1928), one of the best actors of his times, was highly praised by his contemporaries for his realistic style of acting in Wyspiański's *The Wedding*, Zapolska's *This Other* and Gogol's *The Inspector General*. In his autobiography, written in 1927 and published in 1951, Kamiński states that his analyses of *Hamlet* were questioned and proved inadequate by Wyspiański who, during a few meetings, made Kamiński abandon his interpretation of the part. It is worth noting that Kamiński never played Hamlet. See Leon Płoszewski, ed., *Stanisław Wyspiański: Dzieła Zebrane*, 18 vols (Kraków: Wydawnictwo Literackie, 1958-68), XIII, 248-9.

9. Polish theatre at the turn of the century was the forum for an ongoing debate concerning the relationship between traditional bourgeois theatre experience and the new theatre aesthetics, as put forth in the works of Appia, Craig and the Symbolists. The artists of 'Young Poland' (Brzozowski, Ortwin and later, Leśmian, Wrończyński and Drabik) fought for the acceptance of the new concepts of modern theatre; the concepts which had already been incorporated in and moulded theatre practices in Paris (Théâtre Libre) and London (The Independent Theatre). Their reforms called for changes in the perception of theatre's function in society as well as in the stagings of plays. They opposed the realistic/naturalistic desire for theatre to be an ideal 'slice of life' transferred to the stage, and stressed in its stead the ideas presented by Wagner in his *Das Kunstwerk der Zukunft* or Craig in his *The Art of the Theatre*. The theoretical assumptions of 'Young Poland' are best summarized by Leśmian, who asserted that theatre was a collaborative process between an actor, a painter and a musician under the guidance of a director. Even though theatre drew on other art forms, it was an autonomous art which used its own and unique means of expression: a human body, a performance space and the audience actively participating in the creative process.

10. Płoszewski asserts in his notes to Wyspiański's essay that Wyspiański probably read *Hamlet* in 1885. Wyspiański made references to the play in notes written during his train journey from Loan to Reims in 1890 and used *Hamlet* to describe his emotional states in a letter to Lucjan Rydel dated 3 July 1890. It is quite possible that Wyspiański saw *Hamlet* produced in Kraków in 1887 and 1889, and there is clear evidence that he saw *Hamlet* in Dresden in August 1890 and in Kraków in September, 1903. See Płoszewski, ed., *Dzieła Zebrane*, XIII, 201-2.

11. Wyspiański knew *Hamlet* in Józef Paszkowski's translation. While talking about scholarship referring to the play, Wyspiański indicates that he knew about J. I. Kraszewski's introduction to Paszkowski's volume and Leon Kellner's *Shakespeare*. Płoszewski suggests that Wyspiański must have also been familiar with a four-hundred page introduction to Władysław Matlakowski's critical study of *Hamlet*. See Płoszewski, ed., *Dzieła Zebrane*, XIII, 204-5. In the context of these remarks, it is interesting to note that, even though Wyspiański did not speak English, he provided new translations of Hamlet's soliloquies in his study. These new translations were based on Paszkowski's text. While working on the monologues, Wyspiański was not interested in providing a 'correct' literary rendering of the original text, but in a poetic depiction of the images

contained in it. In this sense, his 'translations', an amalgam of Shakespeare's and his own artistic aesthetics, were provided to explain the metaphors, rather than the words or plot development, to the actors working on the part.

12. Even though Wyspiański sees Hamlet walking through the galleries of the Jagiello-nian Royal Castle, at the end of the essay, he describes a very specific architectural or stage design for the play. The stage was a three-storied building divided into seven rooms where the plot could be developed simultaneously. Okońska suggests that Wyspiański's design was connected with his plans to reform Teatr Stary in Kraków if chosen for its director. (Wyspiański submitted his candidacy to the town's council on 19 February 1905. He lost, however, to Ludwik Solski who was elected as new director of the theatre on 11 May 1905). See, Okońska, *Stanisław Wyspiański*, pp. 418-36 for details concerning the election.

13. Mallarmé's symbolist aesthetic emerges from his essays, theatre reviews and his series of articles about Wagner. He believed that drama was the expression of an *état d'âme* and the revelation of hidden wonders of the universe. The language of drama was poetry, rather than prose, evocative, rather than descriptive. The stage was detheatric-alized; that is, reduced to the barest and simplest elements of histrionic performance. The theatre was to bring into play all of the arts which were interrelated within a poetic structure. See, for example, Haskell Block, *Mallarmé and the Symbolist Drama* (Detroit: Wayne State University, 1963) and A. G. Lehman, *The Symbolist Aesthetic in France* (Oxford: Blackwell, 1968).

14. See Maurice Maeterlinck, 'The Tragical in Daily Life' in Bernard F. Dukore, ed., *Dramatic Theory and Criticism* (New York: Holt, Rinehart and Winston, 1974), pp. 726-30.

15. Daniel C. Gerould and Jadwiga Kosicka, 'The Drama of the Unseen: Turn-of-the-Century Paradigms for Occult Drama', *New York Literary Forum*, 4 (1980), 3-42.

16. Helena Modrzejewska (1840-1909), a famous Polish actress, played Lady Macbeth in Kraków on 10 January 1903.

17. See Horatio's description of the conflict between Old Hamlet and Old Fortinbras (I. i. 82-110).

18. It is interesting to note that, in his analysis, Wyspiański suggests that Hamlet was sent to Norway by Claudius. On the way, the ship is captured by Fortinbras's army, and Hamlet with Rosencrantz and Guildenstern are brought to Fortinbras's camp, where they meet for the first time. Wyspiański explains this meeting provides Hamlet with the opportunity to reveal to Fortinbras his desire to revenge his father's death. If Fortinbras would support the plan, Hamlet would return the land that had been conquered by his father, thus punishing Claudius and regaining the crown.

19. This delay, according to Wyspiański, is yet another trace of the traditional drama that was altered by Shakespeare. Thus, the function of this scene was not to provide information that would advance the plot, but to emphasize the change in Hamlet that

was first made visible in the 'How all occasions do inform against me' soliloquy in IV. iv. 32-66.

20. According to Wyspiański, this is the third example of Shakespeare's attempt to combine two texts: whereas in the traditional revenge tragedy, the words of the crowd were directed to Hamlet, in the new tragedy, they refer to Laertes, a character transformed by the playwright to function as a satirical double, or a crooked image, of the Prince of Denmark. An interesting interpretation of this line is given by Witold Chwistek in his *Polska w Hamlecie* (Wrocław: Zakład Narodowy im. Ossolisńkich, 1956). Chwistek quotes Botero's *A Briefe Description of the Whole World* (London, 1601) to indicate that 'Laertes shall be king' refers to the notion of free election. Chwistek argues that Shakespeare was aware that Poland was the only electoral monarchy in Europe at the time *Hamlet* was written, hence the many references to Poland throughout the play.

21. Wyspiański's dramas were his attempt to clarify the function of an artist in society. His plays about the November Uprising (*Lelewel, Warszawianka, Noc listopadowa*) present a poignant critique of national myths of heroism and patriotism. *Legion* and *Wyzwolenie* are a critique of Polish romanticism and its ideological legacy.

22. *Othello*, ed. M. R. Ridley (London and New York: Methuen, 1985), I. i. 65.

23. Kott, *Shakespeare*, p. 56.

IS HAMLET GERMANY? ON THE POLITICAL
RECEPTION OF *HAMLET*

HEINER O. ZIMMERMANN

Whenever Shakespeare's unequalled greatness is extolled and his increasing importance for an endlessly growing audience rehearsed, the old
cliché of eternal human values, truths and emotions rears its head. That
essential human nature which we supposedly share with him is alleged to
bridge the gap of the centuries which separates us from him and to permit
us to identify with his characters across the borders of national cultures.
Closer investigations of the history of Shakespeare's reception, however,
have made evident the fundamentally historical relativity of these values,
truths and emotions.[1]

The appropriation or, rather, the national German 'expropriation'[2] of *Hamlet* is to be examined here as an example to show how thoroughly the recipient's historical position and interests can predetermine the meaning distilled
from a text, and how far the history of the reception of a text in another culture can acquire an autonomous momentum.

The shaping of a myth

Let us start with some milestones of the early German reception of *Hamlet*, which established the myth, and ensured that 'this tragedy had a more
profound impact on German cultural life, than any other poem except
Faust'.[3]

If, as Friedrich Gundolf thought, the history of the German assimilation of
Shakespeare in the eighteenth and nineteenth centuries determined the process of the self-discovery and fashioning of the German mind, *Hamlet* forms
the core of this process.[4] The early actualizations of this tragedy's meaning
are based on identification with the protagonist. By finding ever new ways of
recognizing themselves in Hamlet, the Germans made their understanding of
him a pattern of their national comprehension of themselves in crucial historical situations over the last two centuries. Hence, what interests us is not only

the different meanings of *Hamlet* generated by these identifications, but also the different interpretations of the German intellectual's attitude to politics, society and the process of history implied in them, their preconditions and consequences as well as their dialectical relationship with one another. These actualizations use Hamlet as a mirror in which they decipher the meaning of their own reality. The portrait it shows can, of course, be construed either as a model which personifies the ideals or justifies the weaknesses of its admirers, or as an alarming satirical caricature. The tragedy thus gains topicality and political importance. To put it pointedly, we could say that a new view of it is frequently engendered not so much by the effort to get closer to Shakespeare's meaning as by the political resolve to discredit a traditional self-assessment perceived as outmoded and which needed to be replaced. A change in the evaluation of German political reality in the nineteenth century was thus repeatedly underpinned by the revision of a traditional reading of *Hamlet*. The nationalist myth of *Hamlet* soon formed a tradition which, whether it is regarded as a model or as a burden, cannot be ignored. Its emergence was favoured by the fact that Hamlet's fame started in the newly flourishing German theatre and was enhanced by the admiration of major poets such as Lessing, Herder, Goethe and Schiller, who were highly respected as critics. Their praise of Shakespeare and their enthusiasm for *Hamlet* monopolized public literary discussion and not only initiated the national appropriation of the English dramatist, but also guaranteed great authority and wide popularity for their Hamletisms.

Authors as well as the theatre usually make their own standpoints fairly clear in their interpretations and adaptations of Shakespeare, which are never limited to the aesthetic sphere, but form part of their search for meaning in present reality. An outline of the political reception of *Hamlet* will therefore focus above all on its metamorphoses on the stage and in literature. Both are conscious of national tradition in the understanding of the tragedy. In its early days in the nineteenth century, academic criticism, too, quite openly promoted the political myth of Hamlet, but later it tended to conceal its contemporary point of view behind strivings for historical objectivity.

Identification with Hamlet

The encounter with *Hamlet* in the 1790s broke the ground for Shakespeare's fame in Germany. To this day the history of the reception of this tragedy serves as the paradigm of the appropriation of his work,[5] and has therefore been intensively studied.[6] Wieland's prose and Schlegel's verse translation of Shakespeare, the influence of Goethe's admiration and the lack of historical models in the vernacular literature quickly elevated the English poet to the status of a national classic and model for young German writers. The German mind felt closer to Shakespeare than did the English according to Tieck, who thought that the latter did not understand Shakespeare correctly.[7] In an era of growing enthusiasm for the theatre, *Hamlet* became a legendary success on the stage, and this prepared the way for Shakespeare's breakthrough on a broader scale. A '*Hamlet*-fever' is reported to have spread amongst the bourgeois intellectuals of the seventies and eighties which was based on an idealization of the prince. The adaptations staged in 1773 at Vienna and in 1776 at Hamburg by Franz Heufeld and Ludwig Schröder assimilate the tragedy to the conventions of the fashionable domestic sentimental drama.[8] Heufeld changes Hamlet into a relatively uncomplicated, active hero whose melancholic soliloquies stand in strange contradiction to his heroic triumph at the end. His version omits the search for Polonius's dead body, Ophelia's madness, Laertes's return, the major part of the grave-digger's scene, the duel and Fortinbras's arrival at the end. Gertrude poisons herself; Claudius is killed by Hamlet, who then seizes power. The actor Brockmann's conception of the role, however, anticipates Goethe's opinion as expressed in *Wilhelm Meister*: 'A noble young man, too sensitive to respond to the situation he finds himself in.'[9]

This dreamer, who wavers between world-weariness and aimless energy, and who triumphs at the end of the play, became the idol of Germany's youth. His contradictory combination of sentiment and victorious rebellion against a corrupt feudal court gratified the young German intellectuals' melancholic irresolution and fulfilled their dream of overcoming absolutism. As Goethe recalls in *Dichtung und Wahrheit* (1806): 'Everybody believed that he could be just as melancholy as the prince of Denmark.'[10] Egged on by Herder, Goethe became the most influential pioneer for Shakespeare in Germany. In *Wilhelm Meister* (1795), he erected a monument to the German identification with Hamlet as the personification of the spirit and the feelings of the time. This view remained as a landmark long after the era of Romanticism was over.

Wilhelm Meister's analysis of *Hamlet* or, more precisely, of its prose translation by Wieland, forms the core of the novel.[11] It is seldom realized that Goethe's interpretation is itself based on a version of the play which had been revised according to the literary taste and moral convictions of the time. Wieland's omissions and transformations of the original in translating it purge Hamlet of all cruelty, madness and frivolous or vulgar speech. They transform him into a pure, noble, sentimental and rather weak melancholic.[12] In his commentary at the end of the translation, Wieland adumbrates a Hamlet who lacks a plan of action and is at the mercy of an overwhelming fate. Unlike the stage version, Wilhelm Meister does not alter the prince's tragic end. But he lays the responsibility for Hamlet's hesitation on his fate, which makes him suffer innocently and sink into melancholy. It does not require 'the impossible in itself, but the impossible for him'.[13] It is not a blindly raging exterior power, but a transcendental necessity which colludes with the individual's incapacity to respond by purposeful action. In the conflict between thought and action, the protagonist proves unequal to his task. He lacks the will to accomplish the duty which the overall purpose imposes on him. His insight paralyzes his vigour. This disparity between thought and action, soul and reality, forms the foundation of the emerging myth of *Hamlet*.

Wilhelm Meister places Hamlet's character in the foreground. The actor speculates about the prince's original nature as if he were a real person. In his view, Hamlet was only corrupted by his tragic experience and driven to irresolute brooding: 'A beautiful, pure, noble, and most moral nature, without strength of nerve, which makes the hero sink beneath a burden which it can neither bear nor throw off.'[14] The same problem haunts several of Goethe's protagonists, such as Goetz von Berlichingen, Werther and Faust. His admiration of the noble prince implicitly justifies the political torpor of an idealistic intelligentsia. It fosters the idea that the evasion of political action is the precondition of the poetic and philosophical achievements of German classicism and idealism.

The two Schlegel brothers internalize Goethe's idealized image of Hamlet and reinforce its impact. Friedrich Schlegel enthusiastically exclaims: 'His explanation is truly divine.'[15] He declares *Hamlet* the paradigm of modern philosophical tragedy.[16] He, too, recognizes the heart of the tragedy as located in the protagonist's character, in the discrepancy between his force of thought and action. But his deliberations discover a new motivation for Hamlet's behaviour: 'The cause for his inner death lies in the greatness of his mind; if it were less great, he would be a hero. For him it is not worth the trouble to be a hero. If only he wanted it, it would be an easy game for him.'[17] Unlike Goethe, Friedrich Schlegel discovers in Hamlet no incapacity to perform his great task, no inability to act. Due to his deeper insight, his philosophical hero no longer *wants* to act like the classical model, for he realizes the futility of the heroic deed. It cannot change the world. Hamlet's tragedy reveals the insoluble dissonance between man and fate. It is not an individual imperfection but a universal condition of human existence. This moral rehabilitation makes the prince the model of the romantic antihero.

August Wilhelm Schlegel's image of Hamlet is closer to Goethe's, to whose authority he pays tribute in his essay of 1796.[18] His verse translation set the standard for one and a half centuries and prompted him to translate the whole canon. As in *Wilhelm Meister*, his Hamlet is motivated by high moral principles and appears more sentimental, more inward-looking than Shakespeare's.[19]

The melancholic prince who studied philosophy at Wittenberg with a genius so close to madness, with his inability to act and his innocent suffering, becomes a personification of the Romantic mind. Everybody sympathizes with him as much as with Werther. The German Romantic in the period after the French Revolution finds in Hamlet his own distress at his fate, his own rejection of the world and his inward-looking nostalgia, and emulates him as model. Thus the tragedy is annexed as one of the most influential works of art of German Romanticism.

The political allegory

The subsequent step to a reading of the tragedy as a political allegory carries its Germanization to extremes, but reverses sympathy and identification with Hamlet into dissociation and criticism as a result of the intellectuals' shift from self-apology to self-criticism.

Ludwig Tieck, August Wilhelm Schlegel's friend and adviser on the verse translation of Shakespeare, sounds the first note of discord in the chorus of those who, like Goethe and the Schlegel brothers, idealize Hamlet. As early as the turn of the century, he argues critically that the new image of the hero is to blame for the general political inertia, for the general escape into inwardness, and finally for subjugation: 'With the loss of freedom the power to act and all magnificent will power have been extinguished: men that history declares to be heroes appear like pale shadows, at most they are only a remembrance of the lost age of heroes.'[20] His angry criticism of the misery of recent German history culminates in a reading of *Hamlet* as a political allegory equating the course of events in the tragedy with that of recent German history and reversing the pernicious image of Hamlet created by his contemporaries: 'Hamlet, who can never be saved, must of course perish with the others. May heaven permit that the magnificent figure of Fortinbras, who then must enter the stage, will bear out his name by his deeds and start a new realm with youthful strength.'[21]

Adam Müller was among the first university critics to discuss the newly established national classic, Shakespeare. In his *Fragmente über William Shakespear* (1808), he draws an analogy between the Danish state, falling into ruins because of Hamlet's irresolute brooding, and Prussia 'under the system of nullity' after the decay of feudal order and in the situation following the dissolution of the Holy Roman Empire in 1803:

> All efficiency is being increasingly reduced to an intricate game of powers of thought which must soon collapse as it is not assisted by deeds. We do not need any miracles or resurrections of the dead from their graves in order to prove that the state is actually perishing. — I am not talking about our times, as it might seem, but about Hamlet.[22]

The prince's death appears to him, as to Tieck, a just punishment for his political ineptitude. He, too, welcomes Fortinbras as a figure of hope in the face of subjugation by Napoleon.

Even August Wilhelm Schlegel, in his Vienna *Vorlesungen über dramatische Kunst und Literatur* (1809-11), finally revised his view of Hamlet, and thus set himself up against Goethe. He emphasizes that he does not share the latter's high opinion of the prince's character and reveals its dark side: 'It is not only necessity which compels him to guile and deception, he has a natural inclination to pursue crooked ways; he dissembles to himself'.[23] Schlegel deprecates his weakness of will, his callousness towards Ophelia, his perfidious maliciousness, sly treachery and his sudden fits of anger, accuses Hamlet of believing neither in himself nor in anything else, and calls him an irresolute weakling.[24]

The Hegelians also denounce Hamlet's refusal to act as a moral weakness. Heinrich Theodor Rötscher, for example,[25] believed that Hamlet's desire to remain absolutely innocent whilst performing the deed cannot be fulfilled. He is, moreover, convinced that action is a moral necessity. In Hamlet, therefore, the general guilt of the theoretical consciousness is individualized in its refusal to proceed from the vast expanses of thought to the narrowness of the deed.

His thought intervenes between his will and action. It finds pretexts for inaction. According to Rötscher, Shakespeare has thus provided the key to a profound understanding of the strength and the weakness of the German people. What was first realized by Tieck now gradually dawned on everybody. The Romantic renunciation of political action during the period after the French Revolution entailed a high price. The German middle classes had shirked the political revolution by retreating into inwardness; what they achieved instead was the philosophical revolution of idealism. Thus liberation from the Napoleonic yoke was an equally impossible requirement of fate. In the light of historical insight, the melancholic hero who embodied the spirit of the age becomes an irritant. He is turned into a target for the younger generation's devastating criticism. After the appropriation of Hamlet as an incarnation of the German spirit, after the reverence he inspired as a paragon, his tragedy is transmuted into a mirror of the calamity of German political history.[26] The audience's altered political conception of themselves demands a new reading of Shakespeare's drama and its revaluation. The reception of *Hamlet* becomes a locus for the political controversy surrounding the social obligations of the intellectual. With the reading of the tragedy as a political allegory, its purported meaning develops a dynamic of its own.

The key role which the cult of Hamlet occupied in the preceding generation's spiritual life provokes the politically committed poets of the 'Vormärz' to take possession of this symbolic figure and to transform it to suit their own ends. The angry young generation once more expresses its disappointment at the political failure of the German middle class in the guise of criticism of its paragon, Hamlet. In the era of restoration and reaction which followed liberation from the Napoleonic yoke and the Congress of Vienna, with the Carlsbad resolutions and the persecution of the 'demagogues', the 'Young Germans' thus castigate their country's inability to enforce political reforms and national unity.

In an essay on *Hamlet* written two years before the July revolution of 1830 in Paris, Ludwig Börne maintains that the Danish prince is an idle dreamer who lacks courage, a philosopher of death, a scholar of the night. His real target, however, is the romantic idealists: 'Like one of Fichte's disciples, he does not think anything but, "I am I", and achieves nothing but an affirmation of his own self.'[27] Börne recognizes in Hamlet the Germany which can neither think nor act politically nor make up its mind to perform the deed of liberation. He recognizes in him the German who is always active but achieves nothing, who is constantly moving but makes no progress: 'Had a German written *Hamlet*, I should not have wondered at the work. He makes a copy of himself and Hamlet is done.'[28] Heine, too, believes, 'We know this Hamlet as we know ourselves.'[29] In his eyes he is not a hero but a 'weakling'.[30]

The disappointed patriot, Freiligrath, explicitly equates Hamlet with Germany in trying to rouse his compatriots who, after failing to achieve national unity, shunned the fight for liberty. The political allegory of his poem, 'Germany is Hamlet' (1844), makes the prince a deterring example to the irresolute German bourgeoisie that shuns the revolutionary deed. Their 'buried freedom' haunts them as the reproachful ghost haunted Hamlet. Like him, they have studied philosophy for too long. They are infirm of purpose and incapable of fighting. But it is not too late for Germany to bestir herself. The poem culminates in the call to strike out in order to anticipate a French or Prussian attack. The speaker, however, confesses that he, too, is one of those dreamers and ever-hesitant schemers whom he attacks. The pithy, self-critical words of the 'Young Germans' remain, indeed, mere symbolic gestures.

The historian, Gervinus, one of the committed liberal Göttinger Seven, who had protested against the absolutist rejection of democratic reform in 1837, combines in his monograph on Shakespeare (1849/50) an analysis of *Hamlet* with a scrutiny of the failure of the revolution in March 1848 as well as of the Frankfurt National Diet's incapacity to unify the particularist powers in a national state. He vents his indignation at the slackness of the German fight for freedom which, 'like thousands of others', he finds prefigured in the image of Hamlet drawn by Goethe and the Schlegel brothers. The German people's view of themselves, which was influenced by this model, could only result in misunderstanding even the simplest tasks of reform in everyday political life as impossible demands to set right a world out of joint:

> We feel and see our own selves in him, and, in love with our own deficiencies, we have long seen only the bright side of this character; only of late have we also had a glimpse of its shadows. We look upon the mirror of our present state as if this work had been written in our own day.[31]

This insight entails his harsh judgement of the character of the German people: 'When the heroes in words were finally called upon to take action and prove themselves effective, for which they had for such a long time gauged themselves, the poison within them broke out in loathsome pus, and cruelty, bloodthirsty vindictiveness and treacherous murder disgracing the German name.'[32]

Germany is not Hamlet

In the subsequent era of the new German Empire under Prussian dominance, the patriotic literary scholar Friedrich Theodor Vischer rejects this allegorical identification which presents such a negative image of Germany. The earlier self-portrait is no longer in accord with Prussia's growing self-importance. He adopts the *Vormärz* poets' equation, only to relate it to Franco-German rivalry and to reject it as history which will be superseded. For him, Hamlet's inaction symbolizes Germany's passivity in the strife between the two peoples, while Laertes's poisoned rapier becomes, as in Freiligrath's poem, the image of the enemy's treachery. But Hamlet's final victory over him gives him hope of devastating German retaliation, which will finally disprove the topos of the Germans as a race of irresolute thinkers and poets. In a revised edition of his *Shakespeare Vorträge*, he triumphantly celebrates the victory of Sedan as this historical rebuttal.[33]

Horace Howard Furness included Vischer's earlier comment (as well as a translation of Freiligrath's poem) in his selection of German criticism on *Hamlet* in the second volume of his 1877 edition, underlining its prophetic quality.[34] This honorary member of the German Shakespeare Society, with a doctorate from Halle University, not only devoted a great deal of space to German scholarship but also dedicated his variorum edition to 'The "German Shakespeare Society" of Weimar representative of a people whose recent history has proved once and for all that "Germany is *not* Hamlet",' and thus intervened from the 'outside' in the national political discourse in which *Hamlet* had become involved. It seems as if Furness was fascinated by the German political appropriation of Hamlet. He inserted, however, a conciliatory essay by Karl Elze to form a transition between the selections from German and French criticism. But the latter occupies only a few pages. The proud affirmation of Germany's triumph over history, 'Hamlet *was* Germany', was repeated from now on time and again in essays and reviews up to the turn of the century.

In this spirit, the first editor of the yearbook of the *Deutsche Shakespeare Gesellschaft*, Friedrich v. Bodenstedt, writes a critique in 1870 of *Hamlet* which is animated by the ethos of the Wilhelmian era.[35] His depreciation of the Danish prince defines the difference beween him and the then current German ideal of manliness. Hamlet can no longer serve as a model in the Second Empire. The newly unified nation finds its mood and martial values better personified by Fortinbras. But soon scholars such as Kuno Fischer developed a new construction of Hamlet as a bold and strong hero, who once again embodied the spirit of the age.[36]

The Teutonizing of Hamlet not only draws him into the depths of German patriotism but also into the slough of racism. The 'Young German' Heinrich Laube's criticism of the actor Bohumil Dawison's performance of Hamlet in his history of the Vienna Burgtheater, compiled in the second half of the nineteenth century, is an appalling adumbration of fascist writing half a century later: 'The original Germanic nature of Hamlet's character was and is beyond the reach of Dawison's Polish-Jewish nature. He lacks the searching soul. He tries to replace it by a searching mind ... but of course that means much less than the representation of a full human being with a rich inner life.'[37]

In scholarly criticism, the rise of an analytical historical approach at the turn of the century relegated the national identification with Hamlet or its rejection to a minor role. Reception of the play diversifies. But the German people's special relationship with *Hamlet* remains as a reminiscence and forms part of the mythical aura which continues to distinguish this tragedy in the general consciousness. Its former historical meanings survive detached from their historical context and thus remain available. The name of Hamlet becomes the metaphor of the tragedy's historical meanings which can thus be referred to in literary shorthand. In this form, the tragedy lives on in modern literature and theatre, where its historical meanings are nostalgically retrieved or rejected as a burden and parodied. We shall, however, continue to single out the political strand in the multifarious reception process.

Whereas Friedrich Gundolf in his influential study, *Shakespeare und der deutsche Geist* (1914), fathoms the importance of the English bard for the development of German thought far beyond any topical reference, the socialist anarchist writer, Gustav Landauer, cannot completely ignore the political confusion of 1917/18 in his lectures on Shakespeare.[38] He recalls the pre-revolutionary critical identification of Hamlet with Germany by the *Vormärz* poets in order to extend it suggestively to humanity as a whole.

The question of whether Shakespeare should be read and performed in spite of the war with England is readily answered in the affirmative. The dramatist Gerhart Hauptmann expresses the prevailing conviction that the poet's work transcended war issues.[39] But the ardent nationalist goes on to say: 'There is no people, not even the English, who have a better justified claim to own Shakespeare ... and even if he was born in England and died there, Germany is the country where he really lives.' This provocative jingoism, which also set the tone for the Shakespeare festival of 1916 in Weimar, incited the English dramatist Henry Arthur Jones to retaliate.[40] He finds a resemblance between Germany and Macbeth rather than Hamlet. War-time reviewers such as Walter Friedemann praise *Hamlet* for its 'purity and self-less patriotism, which make it the most German of all poems'.[41] He explains that 'because a unified Germany discarded Hamlet's guise and developed a sense of commerce and technology it provoked the envy of the whole world'. The republican writer's final threatening gesture, however, is aimed at the Kaiser, for he identifies the German people with Fortinbras battering his iron fist against the throne and exclaiming: 'I have a right to claim this throne.'

The republican Hamlet

Leopold Jessner was the first to introduce the analogy between Hamlet and Germany in the theatre. His Berlin production of December 1926 superimposed on Shakespeare's Danish court the satiric stage image of the militarism and imperialism of the decaying Wilhelmian empire. The courtiers wear gaudy uniforms with huge epaulets and dangling medals. They bow, click their heels, stand to attention and speak in commanding tones. State scenes are acted out as imperial rituals of power which transform the characters into puppets. After the play scene, Claudius's right arm has gone stiff as the result of a stroke. This, as well as the fact that he reads his opening speech, recalled the former Kaiser. At the end of the tragedy, Fortinbras also reads his speech in the snarling tone of a Prussian officer, and thus annihilates any hope of a new and better order. He, the soldier incarnate, is the real antagonist of a Hamlet who carries no rapier and embodies the intellectual's hopeless revolt against power. Indeed, the Jewish actor Fritz Kortner was criticized for impersonating Hamlet more like a Hebrew scribe than a Danish prince.[42] Laertes's revolt was presented as a rebellion of officers, which reminds one of the end of the Wilhelmian reign.

Jessner's stab at the conservative monarchists of the *Deutschnationale Volkspartei*, who rejected the Weimar Republic and wanted to restore an authoritarian state, provoked their intervention in the Prussian Diet with a demand for his dismissal as he 'endangered art, culture and morality'.[43] His defence was taken up in an article which revealed the political motives of those who accused him of annihilating the tragedy's aesthetic beauty and timeless meaning by 'debasing the greatest poet of virility and combat and making him a bragging pacifist', and by forcing 'the bard of royalty to lead the way to world revolution'.[44]

Gerhart Hauptmann, one of the republican figureheads, was fascinated for over a decade by the problem of Hamlet. He grappled with it in a play, *Hamlet in Wittenberg* (1935), as well as in the novel, *Im Wirbel der Berufung* (1936). In an adaptation of Shakespeare's tragedy which he directed in Dresden in 1927, he attempted to reconstruct Shakspeare's real *Hamlet*, which he thought buried in a corrupt textual tradition.[45]

The National Socialists' Dilemma over Hamlet

Shakespeare was, in general, annexed by National Socialist cultural ideologists as a German classical author in the Schlegel and Tieck translation.[46] They praised him as 'the great creator of Nordic character drama' and 'the great liberator of the German spirit'.[47] But there were also official voices that rejected him as 'typically un-German' and called his great influence on German dramaturgy a disaster.[48] The images of *Hamlet* which were created at that time were in no way uniform. Some scholars, such as Schücking and Glunz, remained imperturbable and wrote well-balanced historical analyses which disregarded or contradicted the ruling ideas.[49] Articles in literary journals as well as in the press, however, propagated constructions of *Hamlet* which were impregnated with the official racist and fascist ideology. A new reading of the equation of Hamlet with Germany was hammered out, relating him to the new departure of politics after Hitler's seizure of power: just as the Danish prince suffered from the insuperable obstacles preventing him from revenging his father and setting the time right, so the German people suffered from the injustice of the Treaty of Versailles and a powerlessness to change its political condition.[50] This led the German soul, like Hamlet, into a slump of depression from which it then recovered and gained the strength to take resolute, courageous action. Later, during the war, Huch decided: 'Hamlet is neither English nor a Dane, he is the Germanic, we may say the German, thinker, poet, dreamer and fighter in every sense of the word.'[51] Other, more discriminating, philosophical interpretations are critically thoughtful. Hans Rochocz, a grammar school teacher, takes Hamlet's part against the *condottiere*'s contemptuous smile at his irresolution and weakness.[52] He identifies the prince with no less a figure than the Nietzschean superman who rules out any contradiction between his ethical insight and his action. In an era setting out to establish a new order, Hamlet's uncompromising moral nobility should, therefore, become a model for German youth.

Hamlet, 'the most Nordic' of Shakespeare's tragedies, was the most frequently staged Shakespearean play during the Third Reich. It was performed throughout the war, when the history plays had been banned.[53] In accordance with fascist aesthetics, monumental open-air performances were arranged which, as in Frankfurt (1938) and Augsburg (1939), used historical architecture as a backdrop. The theatre was ordered to honour the integrity of the great classical texts by remaining strictly faithful to the original (*'werkgetreu'*) and avoiding any modernization. Thus, critical reflection on reality was suppressed, even in coded form.[54]

The complexity of Shakespeare's tragedy, as well as its open form, however, made it difficult to contain audience reactions. There existed, moreover, differences of opinion between the rival camps of the chief ideologists. Thus Lothar Müthel's and Gustav Gründgens's production of *Hamlet* at the state theatre in Berlin in 1936, one of the highlights of the theatre under Hitler's regime, was first enthusiastically praised,[55] and then condemned by an ally of Rosenberg as 'degenerate, un-German and decadent'.[56] Göring intervened in favour of his protégé, Gründgens, and stifled the incipient controversy by commissioning laudatory reviews.

A massive, angular stage design and costumes recalling the silhouettes of Vikings located this *Hamlet* in the sphere of Nordic saga. William Robson-Scott criticized this importation from abroad as arising from a 'lack of imagination'.[57] The performance focused on the affairs of state which were inflated to present a monumental spectacle.[58] The comic aspects were muted. Gründgens's Hamlet was neither sentimental nor irresolute but a very active, blond Germanic hero who resembled the 'unfathomable Nordic man'.[59] He overcame his individual tragedy by proceeding from domestic drama to political action.[60] His fight against the King is not only revenge, but a struggle for a people. This 'heroically struggling man' became the norm for the productions of *Hamlet* during the Third Reich.[61] One reviewer, Ortrud Stumpfe, insists, however, that he cannot yet be a radiant hero as the present era still marks only the dawn of a golden future.[62] So she sees Hamlet more as a warning against too rash an attempt to overcome fate. The hint that Gründgens sometimes offered mere rhetorical fireworks rather than meaningful acting is reinforced by Robson-Scott, who denounces 'an inconsistency in the interpretation'.[63]

Although Klaus Mann's Hendrik Höfgen in *Mephisto* cannot be simply identified with Gründgens, the novel provides the complementary perspective of the exile on the Berlin production of *Hamlet*. Höfgen is conscious of the hollowness of his acting which transforms Hamlet into 'a Prussian lieutenant with neurasthenic features', mirroring the audience's state of mind.[64] In a detailed critique of the performance, the novel also trenchantly sums up the fascist party's dilemma over the play: a functionary admits *Hamlet* to be *the* representative Germanic drama and its protagonist a great symbol of German man. But he also emphasizes that Hamlet is a dangerous model for the man Hölderlin described as 'inactive and thoughtful': 'For we all have him within us and must overcome him.'

The two Hamlets

The political division of Germany after the Second World War also led to a parting of the ways in the appropriation of Shakespeare, a phenomenon that was formally sanctioned by the German Shakespeare Society's split in 1964.

Official Marxist criticism as well as the theatre in the GDR made out of the prince a classical hero with whom the audience had to sympathize. He is a revolutionary who fights against a corrupt feudal system for a sublime humanist ideal, a struggle which anticipated their own.[65] At the same time, however, his negative double appears on stage as he does in the Adolf Dresen / Maik Hamburger production in Greifswald in 1964, which was officially condemned as scandalous.[66] This Hamlet was conceived, in accordance with Brecht's dramaturgical principles, as an ironical, reckless character with whom audiences cannot identify. He reveals the danger of imposing ideals regardless of actual historical circumstances. Later productions of the classics increasingly subverted officially prescribed interpretation and obliquely treated topical political problems. Thus, Benno Besson's *Hamlet* in East Berlin (1977) or the 1983 production in Potsdam presented the state of Denmark as a nest of informers and gave prominence to the struggle of the individual against surveillance by a totalitarian state.[67]

The images of Hamlet created in West Germany since the war are diverse. Manfred Pfister, however, discerns some features characteristic of portrayals of the Prince both in scholarly discourse and in the theatre.[68] This Hamlet, just like the contemporary intellectual, has no firm ground on which to base word and deed. He has a Pirandellean awareness of the theatrical character of his existence and sees reality as a construct established by society and its media. He can therefore no longer simply draw a line between fiction and reality.

But there are also readings which discover in Hamlet reflections of social and political developments. Günter Grass, in a poem 'Gesamtdeutscher März', once more refers to the *Vormärz* poets and attacks political inaction at the time of the cold war by identifying Germany with an irresolute Hamlet.[69] Alfred Döblin in his late novel, *Hamlet oder die lange Nacht nimmt kein Ende* (1946), was the first to link Hamlet's task with the postwar obligation to lay bare the roots of the guilt which led to disaster. Twenty years later, Martin Walser called Hamlet the ally of the postwar generation of sons haunted by the idea of their fathers' guilt.[70] Like Hamlet, they become dramatists who stage the recent past in order to make their fathers speak.

The simultaneous desire to probe the possibility of identification as well as to reject it as no longer possible are the driving forces behind two productions of the play in West and East Germany, a description of which may bring to an end this tour of German versions of *Hamlet*. In both cases the allegorical reading is replaced by a more open and complex metaphorical interpretation in which several texts are related to one another. An understanding of *Hamlet* based on its historical national meanings is paralleled to a concept of present reality indebted to sociological, psychological, philosophical or journalistic texts.

George Tabori's production of *Hamlet* in Bremen in the seventies focuses on the relationship between father and son, i.e., on the son's inability to mourn his father.[71] The Hamletism at the core of this interpretation is the protagonist's Oedipus complex. It not only prevents him from punishing his uncle for the deed which he secretly desired to do himself, it also prevents him from genuine mourning: he only acts grief which he does not feel. He is haunted by the idea that he might have caused the loss of his father by wishing it. So

Hamlet exaggerates the expression of an emotion of which he is not sure. He suffers because he cannot suffer. He turns his aggression against himself and becomes a melancholic. In contrast to mourning, this is not a normal state of mind but an illness. Tabori's new attempt to identify a fundamental German social problem with Hamlet relies on the parallelism between Freud's analysis of the tragedy and Alexander and Margarete Mitscherlich's psychoanalytic explanation of German society's behaviour after the Second World War in *On the Inability to Mourn*. While Hitler was the German people's hero, he had personified their collective dream of grandeur. But the idol's monstrosity had been revealed, and the beloved *Führer*-father was killed by others, just as Hamlet's father was. Like the prince, the German people fail to accomplish a genuine 'grief-work' (*Trauerarbeit*) which would enable them to come to terms with their loss and their past. They practise self-control, ritualize self-castigation and humility instead of admitting their feelings of loss and 'wallowing' in the past. Like Hamlet, they sink into melancholy.

The new reading takes up the history of *Hamlet*'s reception in order to reject it. The world-weariness which the Romantics revered so much in Hamlet is here exposed as an incapacity to experience genuine feeling, as autoaggressive, sick and dangerous. Like Hamlet, who had been educated in Protestant rationalism at Wittenberg, the German people generalized their inability to mourn into an inability to feel. They repressed their feelings as Hamlet censured his rage at Claudius's court, and with tense rationalism invested their energy in the frenetic activity of rebuilding the country. Only those who come to terms with their feelings concerning the past can hope not to have to repeat it all over again. What is only repressed will return, like the ghost in *Hamlet*.

At a moment of heated discussion of German postwar terrorism, Tabori thus also recalls the connection between the emotional asceticism of the German left and the irrationality of terrorist actions.

His theatre is therapeutic in intent. It is a theatre of cruelty, as defined by Artaud, whose shocks are designed to liberate the emotions from the control of the superego in order to achieve a cathartic effect. The German Hamlet in the audience is to be taught to grieve and to feel.

Tabori's production was the first to test Heiner Müller's translation of *Hamlet* on stage.[72] In the same year, the latter dramatist also published his *Hamletmachine*.

Müller's choice of *Hamlet* as his last theatre production under the socialist regime was, of course, made with an eye to the history of the play's political reception. He ironically adopts the official reading when he defines it as: 'A play which is about state crises, with two epochs and a gap between them. In the gap an individual who does not really know what to do does the splits.'[73] When rehearsals started in November, 1989, Honecker's Stalinist government was still in power. The first night, in March, 1990, took place after the first free elections. The staging of the tragedy as a state funeral is initially only a mirage.

For a short while a close connection developed between the work in the theatre and the revolutionary movement. Ulrich Mühe, who played the lead, and some other actors were among the main organizers of the historic demonstration on the Alexanderplatz in Berlin on 4 November 1989. Müller also put in an appearance. The actors' and intellectuals' illusion of making history together with the people only lasts for a brief instant. It was never shared by Müller. Soon the revolution took a new turn, excluded them and transformed them into helpless spectators — a development in line with the historical pessimism which Müller expresses in the *Hamletmachine*.

His production of the tragedy sets up a dialogic relationship between his translation of Shakespeare's text and his 'destruction' of it, the *Hamletmachine*, as well as the autonomous stage scenery designed by Erich Wonder.[74] To this gigantic collage he adds passages from other Shakespearean plays, a text by Zbigniew Herbert and music by Mozart, Chopin, Schönberg and the Stranglers. Wonder's stage sets suggest the interior of a bunker, and he 'quotes' masterworks from Italian Renaissance painting as well as leading contemporary stage designers. This kind of multiple intertextuality does not admit any hierarchy of statements which could be condensed into an allegorical meaning. It signalizes, rather, a plurality of meanings which range from the level of family drama to that of tragedy of state, from psychoanalytical insight to political philosophy and the philosophy of history. In this maze of meanings, the production repeatedly brings into view topical political developments. The Hamletism of the failed German revolution cynically comments on the events of November, 1989.

As long as Shakespeare writes our plays for us we will not have found
ourselves.[75]

The *Hamletmachine* defies any attempt to reduce it to one meaning. It dramatizes general aspects of a postmodernist view of history and the human condition in highly ambiguous metaphorical images. In the context of the political reality in which it is staged, i.e., the events of November, 1989, its universality, however, is charged with topical significance.

The historical location of the text is only sparingly alluded to. The goose step of the councillors who, at the beginning of the play, follow a state funeral procession, the reference to the rising against the Stalinist regime in Hungary in 1956 or the author's ironical description of himself as a privileged person who is 'protected by a wall, barbed wire, prison' suggest a standpoint in the communist camp (p. 96).[76] The title of the first of its five scenes, 'Family Album', recalls programmatically the history of *Hamlet*'s reception: the Hamletisms of the intellectual's relationship with power or the relation between knowledge and action. 'I was Hamlet' (p. 89) and later 'I am not Hamlet' (p. 93) express a refusal to make the usual entry in the family album. Instead, this text marks out the distance which separates it from Shakespeare's *Hamlet*. Identification with the prince has become impossible. The encounter with Hamlet, however, leads directly to the Marxist intellectual's reflections on his condition.[77] 'I was Hamlet' recalls the time when grief and hope still existed and tragedy could still take place. Now the loss of belief in a socialist utopia has to be coped with: 'SOMETHING IS ROTTEN IN THIS AGE OF HOPE' (p. 89). Within the utopia of the communist state, self-realization for the individual has proved impossible. Any hope that the machinery of power which extinguishes the individual as subject can be smashed by a revolutionary act, or that the course of history can be controlled, is lost. The intellectual is conscious of the history of failure suffered by all bourgeois as well as by all proletarian revolutions. He knows that a murder does not eliminate the system but only its representative.

The subject which determines the meaning of history has abdicated. With the father (Stalin), the utopia of the communist state is buried. The gigantic monument of the man who made history is razed to the ground. The myth of progress has died. The fourth scene shows the history of Marxism between humanism and terror, merging references to the revolts in Hungary, Berlin, and Prague with one another.[78] Like the father who, contrary to his declared intention, only continued the repression of the individual, the son (Hamlet, the Marxist intellectual) has turned into a bloodhound. He splits the heads of the stylites of the revolution, Marx, Lenin and Mao, and thus in turn perpetuates the cycle of history, in which power falls into decline and is renewed by resistance, in which hope is followed by disillusion: 'The overthrow of the monument is followed, after an adequate period, by revolt. If my drama took place again, it would happen in a time of revolt' (p. 93). In the context of the production of November, 1989, this sounds clearly prophetic. Even in the improbable case of another revolution, however, belief in its healing effect has gone. The actor who played Hamlet once leaves no doubt about his position in the *theatrum mundi* : 'If my drama took place again, my place would be on both sides of the front, between the opposing fronts, above them' (p. 94).

As he can no longer make sense of history and as the disciplinary forces of society have transformed the subject into a machine, the intellectual in the old sense, Hamlet, no longer exists. Hamlet's self, like the author's, dissolves into mere intertextuality.[79] Hamlet is no longer recuperable. The tragedy of Hamlet no longer occurs. The symbols of affluence, such as a refrigerator and a television set, appear instead as the new driving forces of history.

Müller begins his production of Shakespeare's tragedy, like his own *Hamletmachine*, with a state burial accompanied by the sound of Chopin's funeral march. The ghost of Hamlet's father appears while loudspeakers broadcast the original Russian report of Stalin's interment. Hamlet's father was a hero in the old style, a man of power who made history. This super-father and his totalitarian concept of the state weigh heavily on the son. The intellectual sees through the mechanisms of power, which disgust him. The end of the Stalinist era announces itself. Wonder encloses the stage events in a gigantic ice cube suggested by strips of transparent, milky gauze. The ice age, the Stalinist winter of frozen relationships and political stagnation, draws to its end in the state of Denmark, which is the German Democratic Republic. It begins to thaw and drip everywhere in this slushy weather. Hamlet shouts his soliloquy 'To be or not to be' lying in a puddle, venting his desperate impotent anger about a state where nothing works any longer. The increasing decay of the state is accompanied by a heating up of the atmosphere. The tragedy ends under a scorching sun, in a drought, in ochre-coloured sand. Ophelia goes up in flames. The allusions to the manic, overheating process of the development of capitalism as well as to the threatening ecological catastrophe are merged with references to Beckett. The blueprint for this is again to be found in the

Hamletmachine, where in the fifth scene Ophelia / Electra, referring to Artaud, speaks 'under the sun of torture' (p. 97).

A 'hellmachine' moves with a metallic rattle on a rail above the heads of the audience. It unites emblems of the surveillance state, the sword, loudspeaker and searchlight. When, during the performance, the monitor screens on both sides of the stage show the audience in the stalls and the gallery, the meaning of this device becomes inescapable.

In this production, Fortinbras, who appears on the stage twice, is a caricature of imperialism. Like a Mannerist portrait, he consists of war emblems. He carries a gilded briefcase. In the last scene, he holds a gilded mask before Hamlet's face, obstructing the latter's vision. At the same time, the flicker on the television monitors turns gold.

As expected, the citizens' action groups, the intellectuals and artists who instigated the revolution lose control of it. Their aims are perverted, and the revolution's benefits are appropriated by the power of capitalism, which has long since occupied the people's consciousness. Fortinbras's golden visor resembles the one worn by the ghost of Hamlet's father who is identified with both Stalin and the Deutsche Bank. The visible power and repression of communism is followed by the invisible counterpart of the capitalist mode of production and consumption. 'Fortinbras's Complaint' by Zbigniew Herbert is quoted: 'I must also elaborate a better system of prisons since as you justly said, Denmark is a prison.'

The last words are also the last words of the *Hamletmachine*. They are spoken by Ophelia who has risen from the dead. According to the author, they echo the words of Susan Atkins, a member of the Manson community, which committed collective suicide in 1977: 'You will know the truth only when it enters your bedroom with a carving knife' (p. 97).

Like his *Hamletmachine*, Müller's production of *Hamlet* once more marks a turning point in the history of the play's reception in the German theatre. It denies the possibility of identifying with Shakespeare's hero and his tragedy. As Hamlet, the historical subject, no longer exists, the equation 'Hamlet is Germany' can no longer be drawn. The myth can only be coupled with another 'machine'.[80] Its difference, however, continues to provide self-knowledge for the present, which after the loss of the belief in enlightenment can be only an end in itself. The play's postmodernist scepticism and aesthetics bridge the gap between the play's reception in the Eastern and Western part of the country.

Notes

1. John Drakakis, ed., *Alternative Shakespeares* (London and New York: Methuen, 1985); Graham Holderness, ed., *The Shakespeare Myth* (Manchester: Manchester University Press, 1988); Gary Taylor, *Reinventing Shakespeare* (London: Hogarth, 1990).

2. Klaus Peter Steiger, *Die Geschichte der Shakespeare-Rezeption* (Stuttgart: Kohlhammer, 1987).

3. Georg Gottfried Gervinus, *Shakespeare*, 3 vols (Leipzig: Engelmann, 1849), II, 96.

4. Friedrich Gundolf, *Shakespeare und der deutsche Geist* (Berlin: Bondi, 1914).

5. Steiger, *Die Geschichte der Shakespeare-Rezeption*, chapter three: '*Hamlet* or *What You Will*'; Wilhelm Hortmann, 'Spielorte und Bühnenräume: zur Szenographie von Shakespeare-Inszenierungen der jüngsten Vergangenheit', *Shakespeare Jahrbuch West*, 124 (1989), 13-42; Willi Schrader, 'Shakespeare-Rezeption in der DDR im Lichte der Shakespeare-Tage in Weimar', *Shakespeare Jahrbuch West*, 124 (1989), 68-87.

6. The following observations are based on Claude C. H. Williamson, *Readings on the Character of Hamlet, 1661-1947* (London: Allen and Unwin, 1950); Hans Jürg Lüthi, *Das deutsche Hamletbild seit Goethe* (Bern: Haupt, 1951); Walter Muschg, 'Deutschland ist Hamlet', *Shakespeare Jahrbuch West*, 101 (1965), 32-57; Maximilian Schell, 'Deutschland ist nicht Hamlet', *Shakespeare Jahrbuch West*, 117 (1982), 9-26; Manfred Pfister, 'Germany is Hamlet: The History of a Political Interpretation', *New Comparison*, 2 (1986), 106-26 and 'Hamlet und der deutsche Geist', *Shakespeare Jahrbuch West*, 127 (1992), 13-38.

7. Johann Ludwig Tieck, 'Briefe über Shakespeare' (1800) in *Kritische Schriften*, 4 vols (Leipzig: Brockhaus, 1848-52), I, 159. See also Johann Wolfgang von Goethe, *Dichtung und Wahrheit* in Erich Trunz, ed., *Werke*, 14 vols (Hamburg: Christian Wegner, 1949-60), IX, 492, ll. 19-21: 'Shakespeare has been appreciated by the Germans more than by all other nations, indeed, perhaps even more than by his own people.'

8. Simon Williams, 'Shakespeare introduced: Schröder's *Hamlet* and other adaptations' in *Shakespeare on the German Stage*, 2 vols (Cambridge: Cambridge University Press, 1990), I, 67-87.

9. Williams, *Shakespeare on the German Stage*, I, 78.

10. Goethe, *Dichtung und Wahrheit*, 582, ll. 25-30.

11. In *Shakespeare und der deutsche Geist*, Gundolf, like A. W. Schlegel before him, warns that Wilhelm Meister's opinion must not be confused with that of his author. The character of Goethe's figures and their situation necessarily influence their view of Hamlet. It is precisely on this confusion, however, that the history of the reception of Wilhelm Meister's analysis depends.

12. Denis M. Müller, 'Wieland's *Hamlet* Translation and *Wilhelm Meister*', *Shakespeare Jahrbuch West*, 105 (1969), 198-213.

13. Goethe, *Wilhelm Meisters Lehrjahre* in Trunz, ed., *Werke*, VII, 246.

14. Goethe, *Wilhelm Meisters Lehrjahre*, 246.

15. Friedrich Schlegel, *Kritische Schriften*, ed. Wolfdietrich Rasch (Munich: Hanser, 1956) from letters to A. W. Schlegel, June, 1793, p. 110n.

16. F. Schlegel, 'Über das Studium der griechischen Poesie' in Rasch, ed., *Kritische Schriften*, pp. 144f.

17. F. Schlegel, *Kritische Schriften*, p. 109.

18. August Wilhelm Schlegel, 'Etwas über William Shakespeare: Bei Gelegenheit Wilhelm Meisters' in Emil Staiger, ed., *Kritische Schriften* (Zürich: Artemis, 1962), pp. 51-91.

19. Peter Gebhardt, *A. W. Schlegels Shakespeare Übersetzung* (Göttingen: Vandenhoek and Rupprecht, 1970), 'Zur *Hamlet*-Deutung der Übersetzung', pp. 239-54.

20. Tieck, 'Briefe über Shakespeare' (1800) from *Poetisches Journal etc.* in *Kritische Schriften*, I, 153.

21. Tieck, 'Briefe über Shakespeare', 156.

22. In Adam H. Müller, 'Fragmente über William Shakespeare' from *Vorlesungen über die dramatische Kunst*, *Phöbus*, 1, September/October issue (Dresden: Walther, 1808), 78.

23. August Wilhelm Schlegel, *Vorlesungen über dramatische Kunst und Literatur 2* in Eduard Böcking, ed., *Sämtliche Werke*, 12 vols (Leipzig: Weidmann, 1846), VI, 249.

24. A. W. Schlegel, *Vorlesungen*, 249f.

25. Heinrich Theodor Rötscher, *Die Kunst der dramatischen Darstellung zweiter Teil. Zyklus dramatischer Charaktere* (Berlin: Duncker and Humbolt, 1844), p. 99.

26. Samuel Taylor Coleridge, 'Lectures 1808-1819 on Literature' in Kathleen Coburn and Bart Winer, eds, *The Collected Works*, 14 vols (London: Routledge and Kegan Paul, 1971-90), V. ii., 515f. introduces this pattern of explaining recent German history in England: 'The Germans, unable to distinguish themselves in action, have been driven to speculation: all their feelings have been forced back into the thinking and reasoning mind.'

27. Ludwig Börne, '*Hamlet* von Shakespeare' in *Gesammelte Schriften*, 6 vols (Leipzig: Hesse, 1908), II, 436.

28. Börne, '*Hamlet*', 442.

29. Heinrich Heine, 'Shakespears Mädchen und Frauen' in Oskar Walzel, ed., *Sämtliche Werke*, 11 vols (Leipzig: Insel, 1911-20), VIII, 240.

30. Heinrich Heine, '*Hamlet, Faust* und *Don Quixote*' in Manfred Windfuhr, ed., *Historisch kritische Gesamtausgabe*, 15 vols (Düsseldorf: Hoffmann and Campe, 1981), VIII. i., 468.

31. Georg Gottfried Gervinus, *Shakespeare*, 4th improved edn (Leipzig: Engelmann, 1872), p. 129.

32. Gervinus, *Shakespeare*, p. 131.

33. Friedrich Theodor Vischer, *Shakspeare-Vorträge*, 6 vols, 2nd improved edn (Stuttgart: Cotta, 1905), II, 467 and 473f. In his panegyric on Field-Marshall Graf Moltke, Hoffmann v. Fallersleben hails the victor over the French as the hero who finally redeemed Germany from Hamlet's infirmity, transforming a people who only thought into a people capable of deeds. H. von Fallersleben, 'General Feldmarschall Graf Moltke zum 26. Oktober 1873' in Hans Benzman, ed., *Ausgewählte Werke*, 2 vols (Leipzig: Engelmann, 1905) II, 246f. Cf. also Werner Habicht, 'Shakespeare in Nineteenth-Century Germany: The Making of a Myth' in Modris Ecksteins and Hildegard Hammerschmidt, *Nineteenth-Century Germany* (Tübingen: Gunter Narr, 1983), pp. 141-57.

34. Furness read Vischer's interpretation in a version of 1861.

35. Klaus Reichert draws attention to this in 'Deutschland ist nicht Hamlet' in *Der deutsche Shakespeare*, Theater unserer Zeit VII (Basel: Basilius, 1965), 98f. Cf. Friedrich von Bodenstedt, 'Einleitung' in *William Shakespeare's Dramatische Werke*, 38 vols (Leipzig: Brockhaus, 1870), XV: *Hamlet*

36. Kuno Fischer, *Shakespeare's 'Hamlet'* (Heidelberg: Winter, 1896).

37. Heinrich Laube, *Das Burgtheater* in Heinrich Hubert Houben, ed., *Ausgewählte Werke*, 10 vols (Leipzig: Hesse, n. d.), V, 4.

38. Gustav Landauer, *Shakespeare*, ed. Martin Buber, 2 vols (Frankfurt: Rütten and Löning, 1922), I, 254f.

39. Gerhart Hauptmann, 'Deutschland und Shakespeare', *Shakespeare Jahrbuch*, 51 (1915), VII-XII.

40. Henry Arthur Jones, *Shakespeare and Germany* (London: Whittingham, 1916), p. 4, quoted from Werner Habicht, 'Shakespeare and Theatre Politics in the Third Reich' in Hanna Scolnicov and Peter Holland, eds, *The Play out of Context* (Cambridge: Cambridge University Press, 1989), p. 42.

41. Walter Friedemann, 'Als Hamlet starb ...', *Tägliche Rundschau*, Berlin, 24 September 1915.

42. Felix Hollaender, 'Der moderne Hamlet', 4 December 1926, review archive, Theatermuseum Köln, hereinafter referred to as r.a.

43. 'Die Jessnersche "Hamlet"-Inszenierung als Politikum', unsigned article of 14 December 1926 in *KFP*, r.a.

44. J. M., 'Hamlet der Republikaner", *Vossische Zeitung*, r.a.

45. Gerhart Hauptmann, '*Hamlet*. Einige Worte zu meinem Ergänzungsversuch', *Neue Freie Presse*, Vienna, 25 December 1927 and 1 January 1928.

46. Cf. Werner Habicht, 'Shakespeare in the Third Reich' in Manfred Pfister, ed., *Anglistentag 1984 Passau* (Giessen: Hoffmann, 1985), pp. 194-204 and 'Shakespeare and theatre politics in the Third Reich'. I am also indebted to G. Zähringer, Shakespeare im Dritten Reich, unpubl. M. A. diss., Munich, 1988.

47. T. v. Trotha, *National-Sozialistische Monatshefte* (1934) p. 1147.

48. E. W. Möller, a collaborator of Reichsdramaturg, R. Schlösser, quoted in Günther Rühle, *Zeit und Theater 1933-1945*, 3 vols (Berlin: Propyläen, 1973), III, 49. Cf. also Boguslaw Drewniak, *Das Theater im NS Staat* (Düsseldorf: Droste, 1983), pp. 245f.

49. Levin L. Schücking, *Der Sinn des Hamlet* (Leipzig: Quelle and Meyer, 1935); Hans H. Glunz, *Der 'Hamlet' Shakespeares* (Frankfurt: Klostermann, 1940).

50. See C. Nebel, 'Das Hamlet-Problem als Problem unserer Zeit', *Der Türmer*, 36 (1933), 57-9.

51. Rudolf Huch, *Die Bühne*, 20 February 1944, 25.

52. Hans Rochocz, 'Hamlet für die deutsche Jugend', *Die Neueren Sprachen*, 41 (1933), 211-20.

53. Drewniak, *Das Theater im NS-Staat*, p. 253, and I. Pitsch, Das Theater als politisch-publizistisches Führungsmittel im Dritten Reich, diss. Münster, 1952, p. 230.

54. In 1936, Goebbels issued a decree prohibiting theatre criticism, which had to be replaced by report and appreciation. 'Kunstbericht anstelle der Kunstkritik', *Zeitungsverlag*, 49, 5 December 1936.

55. Karl Heinz Ruppel, 'Hamlet. Von Garrick bis Gründgens. Wandlungen einer Bühnengestalt', *Koralle*, 9 (29 February 1936), 259-61.

56. W. Hartmann, 'Gedanken zum *Hamlet*, als der Tragödie nordischen Verantwortungsgefühls', *Völkischer Beobachter*, Berlin (9 May 1936) as well as 'Was ist uns Hamlet?' in April. Cf. also Habicht, 'Shakespeare and Theatre Politics in the Third Reich', p. 116.

57. William Robson-Scott, 'The Berlin Stage 1935-6', *German Life and Letters*, 1 (1936), 69.

58. W. K., 'Hamlet als Staatsaktion' (21 January 1936), r.a.

59. Rudolf Huch, 'Hamlet und wir', *Monatsschrift für das Deutsche Geistesleben*, 1 (1939), 100-3.

60. Heinz Pauck, 'Hamlet im Staatlichen Schauspielhaus', r. a.

61. Paul Fechter, 'Deutsche Shakespeare-Darsteller', *Shakespeare Jahrbuch*, 77 (1941), 123-30, with Gründgens's letter explaining his conception of the role.

62. Ortrud Stumpfe, 'Der Protagonist der Gegenwart', *Die Literatur*, 40 (1937), 328.

63. Stumpfe, 'Der Protagonist', and Robson-Scott, 'The Berlin Stage 1935-6', 69.

64. Klaus Mann, *Mephisto* (Reinbek: Rowohlt, 1981), pp. 333ff.

65. Pfister, 'Hamlet und der deutsche Geist', 28ff.; Hans Dieter Mäde, 'Hamlet und das Problem des Ideals', *Shakespeare Jahrbuch Ost*, 102 (1964), 7-22.

66. Thomas Sorge, 'The Sixties: Hamlet's Utopia Come True?', *Litteraria Pragensia*, 1 (1991), 33-42, discusses the cultural politics which oppose the Greifswald *Hamlet* to Mäde's production in Karl-Marx-Stadt.

67. Willi Schrader, 'Shakespeare-Rezeption in der DDR im Lichte der Shakespeare-Tage in Weimar', *Shakespeare Jahrbuch West*, 124 (1989), 68-87.

68. Pfister, 'Hamlet und der deutsche Geist', 33ff.

69. Günther Grass, 'Gesamtdeutscher März' in *Deutscher Lastenausgleich* (Frankfurt: Luchterhand, 1990), 72f.

70. Manfred Walser, 'Hamlet als Autor' in Joachim Kaiser, ed., *Hamlet heute* (Frankfurt: Insel, 1965), 153-62.

71. Not all his ideas on the 'Germanism of Hamlet as well as the Hamletism of the Germans' in his essay, 'Hamlet in Blue', *Theatre Quarterly*, 5 (1975-6), 116-32, were included in his performance.

72. Heiner Müller is the contemporary dramatist who studied Shakespeare most intensively by translating and adapting his works: *Wie es euch gefällt* (1967); *Waldstück* (1969); *Macbeth* (1971); with Kurt Langhoff, *Die tragische Geschichte von Hamlet: Prinz von Dänemark* (1977); *Die Hamletmaschine* (1977); *Anatomie Titus Fall of Rome: Ein Shakespeare Kommentar* (1985); collected in *Shakespeare Factory*, 2 vols (Berlin: Rotbuch, 1985-8).

73. Müller quoted in *Badische Zeitung* (24/25 March 1990).

74. Cf. Maik Hamburger's detailed review in his 'Theaterschau', *Shakespeare Jahrbuch Ost*, 127 (1991), 161-8. In view of the sheer multitude of allusions in this production, I cannot share Hamburger's impression of closure.

75. Heiner Müller, 'Shakespeare eine Differenz' in *Material* (Leipzig: Reclam, 1990), p. 106.

76. Page references in brackets refer to the edition of *Hamletmaschine* in *Mauser*, Texte 6 (Berlin: Rotbuch, 1978).

77. Genia Schulz and Hans Thies Lehmann, 'Es ist ein eigentümlicher Apparat', *Theater heute*, 10 (1979), 11; cf. also Theo Girshausen, *'Hamletmaschine': Heiner Müllers*

Endspiel (Cologne: Prometh, 1978) and interviews with the author in Heiner Müller, *Rotwelsch* (Berlin: Merve, 1982) as well as in Heiner Müller, *Gesammelte Irrtümer* (Frankfurt: Verlag der Autoren, 1990).

78. Schulz and Lehmann, 'Apparat', 13.

79. Bernhard Greiner, 'Explosion einer Erinnerung in einer abgestorbenen dramatischen Struktur: Heiner Müllers *Shakespeare Factory*', *Shakespeare Jahrbuch West*, 124 (1989), 88-113; Klaus Peter Steiger, *Moderne Shakespeare-Bearbeitungen*, 'Ein Fetzen Shakespeare: *Die Hamletmaschine*' (Stuttgart: Kohlhammer, 1990).

80. Müller, 'Shakespeare eine Differenz', 108.

NOTES ON CONTRIBUTORS

ROBERT BARRIE is Chair of the Department of English at Austin College in Sherman, Texas, where he teaches creative writing and medieval and Renaissance literature.

CHRISTINA BRITZOLAKIS was formerly a Research Fellow at St Hilda's College, Oxford, and is currently a Lecturer in English at the University of York. She has published articles on twentieth-century drama, poetry and fiction, and is completing a book-length study of Sylvia Plath.

MARK THORNTON BURNETT teaches in the English Department at The Queen's University of Belfast. His articles on English Renaissance drama and culture have appeared in *Criticism, English Literary Renaissance, Studies in Philology* and *The Yearbook of English Studies*. He is the author of *Authority and Obedience: Masters and Servants in English Literature and Society, 1580-1642*, to be published by Cambridge University Press.

JOANNA MONTGOMERY BYLES is Associate Professor in the Department of Foreign Languages and Literature at the University of Cyprus, Nicosia. She has published many articles on Shakespeare and psychoanalysis, and is currently working on a book on Shakespeare's tragedies. She has just completed a book on women and war, 1916-1980, from an international perspective.

KATE CHEDGZOY is a Postgraduate in the Department of English at Liverpool University, where she is writing a doctoral thesis on appropriations and reinscriptions of Shakespearean cultural authority. She has taught at Liverpool University, Liverpool Polytechnic and Chester College. Research interests include literature and culture in early modern England, and lesbian and gay theory.

ALISON FINDLAY is a Lecturer in English at Bretton Hall College, the University of Leeds. Her teaching of Shakespeare and Renaissance literature involves the use of practical drama, and she has worked professionally on theatre productions of *As You Like It* and *A Midsummer Night's Dream*. She has written several pieces for journals and is currently completing a book on bastardy in Renaissance drama.

ALASTAIR FOWLER is Regius Professor Emeritus of Rhetoric and English Literature at the University of Edinburgh, and Visiting Professor at the University of Virginia. He has edited *Paradise Lost* (Longman, 1968), and is the author of *Kinds of Literature: An Introduction to the Theory of Genres and Modes* (Clarendon, 1982) and *A History of English Literature: Forms and Kinds from the Middle Ages to the Present* (Blackwell, 1987). He is also editor of *The New Oxford Book of Seventeenth-Century Verse* (Oxford University Press, 1991).

LISA HOPKINS teaches English at Sheffield Hallam University. Her previous publications include *Elizabeth I and Her Court* (Vision Press, 1990) and *Women Who Would Be Kings: Female Rulers of the Sixteenth Century* (Vision Press, 1991). She is currently completing a book entitled *John Ford's Political Theatre* for Manchester University Press.

MICHAL KOBIALKA is a McKnight-Land Professor of Theatre at the University of Minnesota. His articles and reviews have been published in a variety of scholarly journals, including *Journal of Dramatic Theory and Criticism* and *Theatre Journal*, and his book, *Tadeusz Kantor's Theatre: A Journey Through Other Spaces*, is to be published by the University of California Press.

JOHN MANNING is Reader in English at the The Queen's University of Belfast. He is General Editor of the series, The Hamlet Collection.

ANDREW MOUSLEY is a Lecturer in Literature at the Bolton Institute of Higher Education. He has published articles on autobiography, news and national identity in the Renaissance, and is currently writing a book, *Renaissance Subjectivities*.

ELIZABETH OAKES teaches Shakespeare at Western Kentucky University and is working on a book entitled *Heiress, Beggar, or Strumpet: The Widow in the Society and on the Stage in Early Modern England*.

BILL READINGS teaches comparative literature at the Université de Montréal. He is the author of *Introducing Lyotard: Art and Politics* (Routledge, 1991) and of numerous essays on literary theory and Renaissance studies. He is currently working on a study of Milton.

KAY STANTON is an Associate Professor at California State University at Fullerton. She has published articles on Shakespeare, Marlowe, Milton and Arthur Miller, and is completing two books, one on Shakespeare's use of Petrarch, Boccaccio and Machiavelli in the construction of female characters, and the other on sex and sex roles in Shakespeare.

VALERIA WAGNER teaches English literature at the Université de Genève. She is currently working on her doctoral thesis, which is about the question of the relationship between subject and action in literature.

MARTIN WIGGINS is a Fellow of the Shakespeare Institute, University of Birmingham, and the author of *Journeymen in Murder: The Assassin in English Renaissance Drama* (Clarendon, 1991) and of articles on Shakespeare and Dennis Potter. He is one of the General Editors of the forthcoming Oxford World's Classics Drama Library series.

HEINER. O. ZIMMERMANN is an *Akademischer Oberrat* (Senior Lecturer) in the Department of English at Heidelberg University, where he teaches English literature, mainly drama. He has published on Fielding, Pinter, Shakespeare, Stoppard, Synge and Wesker.

Index

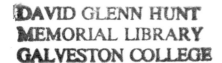

DAVID GLENN HUNT
MEMORIAL LIBRARY
GALVESTON COLLEGE